CANADIAN
PUBLIC
POLICY

Ideas, Structure, Process

SECOND EDITION

CANADIAN PUBLIC POLICY

Ideas, Structure, Process

SECOND EDITION

G. BRUCE DOERN
CARLETON UNIVERSITY

AND

RICHARD W. PHIDD
UNIVERSITY OF GUELPH

Nelson Canada

© Nelson Canada,
A Division of Thomson Canada Limited, 1992
1120 Birchmount Road
Scarborough, Ontario
M1K 5G4

To show your appreciation for the time and effort that the authors
and publisher have invested in this book, please choose **not** to
photocopy it. Choose instead to add it to your own personal
library. The investment will be well worth it.

Canadian Cataloguing in Publication Data

Doern, G. Bruce, 1942-
    Canadian public policy

2nd ed.
Includes bibliographical references and index.
ISBN 0-17-603530-3

1. Policy sciences.   2. Canada – Politics and
government.   3. Political planning – Canada.
I. Phidd, Richard W.   II. Title.

JL108.D64 1992   354.7107'2   C91-095525-5

Acquisitions Editor Dave Ward
Supervisory Editor Wayne Herrington
Art Director Bruce Bond
Cover Design Tad Aronowicz
Text Design Brian Lehen

Printed and bound in Canada

1 2 3 4   WC   95 94 93 92

TO JOAN, KRISTIN, AND SHANNON

AND

TO ISKAH, KARENA, RICHARD,
EASTON, AND NADIA-ELENA

Contents

Preface

Writing the second edition of a book often strikes its authors as a form of low-grade torture. One is torn on alternate days between starting with a clean slate and the certain knowledge that neither time nor the publisher will tolerate anything but judicious improvement interspersed with some second sober thoughts. When first published in 1983, this book was the first to provide a reasonably integrated look at the Canadian policy world. It can still make this claim, but happily it has been joined by other excellent texts that provide complementary perspectives.

More dauntingly, however, the purveyors of second editions also have to confront, and adequately incorporate, an extensive increase in the scope and sophistication of both Canadian and comparative research on public policy. This research in turn is trying to keep up with a world that is, as always, rapidly changing and increasingly refusing to cooperate with the jottings of mere academic mortals. The consequences of the 1982 recession, the impact of the Reagan–Thatcherite neoconservative revolution, the blindingly swift communication and computer revolution that allows capital to move internationally at breakneck speed are all events that have occurred in the intervening years. So has the breakup of the Soviet Eastern European empire, the 1992 integration of Western Europe, and renewed demands for environmental progress under the banner of sustainable development. Domestically, the Mulroney regime has brought Canada–U.S. free trade, massive tax reform, and a divisive constitutional debate. It has also brought an effort to restrain, reform, and reduce the role of the state.

In addition to updating the book to reflect these changes, we have sought to improve and clarify the framework that we introduced in the first edition. We advocated the need to view Canadian public policy as an interplay among ideas, structure, and process, and this has been made even more explicit in the second edition. The book has also been shortened considerably, in part by a complete rewriting of Chapters 14, 15, 16, and 17 and by the elimination of some policy fields given separate chapter status in the first edition.

Special thanks are owed to Michael Prince, Jim Rice, Allan Maslove, and Glen Toner for helpful comments on earlier drafts. And once again we are indebted to all our colleagues and the support staff at the School of Public Administration at Carleton University and the Department of Political Science at the University of Guelph for continuing intellectual encouragement and personal support.

G. BRUCE DOERN
and
RICHARD W. PHIDD
September 1991

Introduction

This book examines the evolution and current state of Canadian public policy-making, with a focus on the federal government. To set the scene for this overall undertaking, the two chapters in Part I of the book locate the analysis, first in relation to the major contending approaches used in the study and practice of policy formation, and second in the context of the overall Canadian political economy. Chapter 1 sets out five overall approaches—the rational, incremental-pluralist, public choice, class-corporatist, and comparative approaches—both to show their strengths and weaknesses and their overall intellectual importance in policy studies, but also to show how the approach used in this book parts company with these approaches. The book utilizes an interplay approach in which policy is seen as the outcome of interactions among ideas, structure, and process.

Policy-making also occurs within the larger setting of the Canadian and international political economy, and the main overarching institutions of the Canadian political system. This larger setting is briefly surveyed in Chapter 2. For the most part, however, our analysis is written with the assumption that the reader has a working knowledge of such institutions as cabinet-parliamentary government, Canadian federalism, the political party system, and the Charter of Rights and Freedoms. Our focus is on the policy system that both is driven by, and significantly influences, these larger political-economic and social forces.

While the policy system is a central part of the larger political system, the two are not fully co-terminus. The larger political system is primarily concerned with vital democratic issues and tasks that go beyond policy-making per se, such as preventing tyranny and ensuring orderly and legitimate changes of leadership, holding elections, selecting and recruiting political participants of many kinds within political parties, unions, and interest groups. It is also involved in inculcating, educating, and socializing citizens, voters, and leaders with views and ideas about Canada's achievements, prospects, and problems and with interpretations of how the larger world is being transformed.

The interplay framework—ideas, structure, and process—is constructed, inductively, so to speak. In short, it arises from careful observation and research on how policy is made and how it has evolved in several different policy fields.[1] This conceptual approach is introduced briefly at the outset and then is developed in more detail in Part II of the book. The approach owes a considerable debt to the main contending approaches set out in Chapter 1, but is different in that most of the other approaches are more deductive in nature and do not purport to be based on an examination of any single country's policy dynamics. Moreover, they do not spell out the presence of particular ideas, structures, or processes.

The third and fourth parts of the book then utilize these building blocks of analysis to examine policy dynamics in two more detailed ways. Part III examines the dynamics of resource allocation, with such allocations understood to include both political and bureaucratic power as well as values allocated through spending, taxation, and regulation. Part IV probes the dynamics as seen through the worlds of three overarching pairings of policy fields: foreign versus domestic policy tensions, economic and industrial policy, and social and labour market policy. Throughout the book our purpose is to understand both current practice and historical evolution, in short, the efficacy of what is presently being done and how and why Canada has got to where it is as the century ends and as a new millennium fast approaches.

The Approach: The Interplay of Ideas, Structure, and Process

The constituent elements of the framework we use for understanding Canadian public policy can be seen at a glance in Figure 1. *Ideas* refer to the desired end states, the sense of public purposefulness, that individuals and groups seek to obtain through state action, or often through preventing the state from acting. *Structure* refers to the main organizations through which and by which policy is influenced and made. Structure encompasses both the organizations of the state and the organizations of many private and cooperative institutions. It is not merely a synonym for dry bureaucracies. Rather, structure is also composed of an array of statutes, programs, headquarters and field entities, and people and employees with diverse views of how their organization is behaving and ought to behave. *Process* refers to the regularized rhythms of relationships and behaviour flowing from the inherent nature of policy- and decision-making activity in any modern government, especially those flowing from the basic instruments of governing (spending, taxation, and regulation).

FIGURE 1   The Components of the Interplay Approach

IDEAS	STRUCTURE	PROCESS
• Ideologies • Dominant Ideas • Paradigms • Specific Objectives	• Prime Minister • Cabinet • Executive Bureaucracy • Interest Groups • Provincial Structures • Policy Communities	• Priority-Setting • Expenditure • Taxation • Regulatory • Public Enterprise

The notion of there being a complex interplay among these three variables suggests that the direction of cause and effect is not simple and certainly not unidirectional. For example, the 1980s saw the strengthening of concerns about the idea of efficiency in virtually every realm of policy-making. As a result, policy structures and processes changed. Prime ministers became the heads of new budget-cutting Cabinet committees whereas before they were not directly involved in such matters. But structure and process have also generated ideas and produced outcomes that were not easily predictable just one or two short years before a given policy event. For example, energy interest structures, outraged by the interventionist Liberal National Energy Program of 1980, devised new energy policy ideas and orchestrated a policy process that produced new regional market-based energy accords less than a year after the Mulroney government came to power in 1984.

Policy processes and their cumulative outcomes also generate pressures for reform. Traditional tax breaks accumulate through the years, based on regular interest group lobbying of the finance minister, but in the process they yield a drain on federal revenues. Demands accumulate to eliminate such breaks in the name of making the tax system both more equitable and more efficient. Environmentalists, in alliance with environment departments, gradually devise elaborate new "stakeholder" processes for policy consultation, and gradually environmental policy begins to change, though often imperceptibly.

A second look at the three columns in Figure 1 suggests some of the particular elements of the ideas, structure, and process framework that the student of public policy must examine. The purposefulness of public policy finds expression in many shades of meaning and at different levels of generality. These range from broad and familiar ideologies such as liberalism, conservatism, and socialism to specific objectives such as reducing the inflation rate by two percentage points in the coming year. These kinds of expression help shape the nature of debate and discourse, at various times ruling some policy options and choices in and out of the band of power and feasibility. In between, though with the boundaries never totally clear, are what we label "dominant ideas" and "paradigms." Dominant ideas refer to constantly reoccurring demands that policies promote efficiency, equity, stability, regional sensitivity, or nationalism. These ideas must be understood at both their practical and rhetorical levels. That is, policies may or may not actually result in greater efficiency or equality, but the public advocacy of such ideas is important because such ideas are often vehicles for expressing hope about the future and for rallying interests to a common cause.

Paradigms refer to coherent conceptions of policy thought and action that become entrenched in particular policy fields, such as the Keynesian and monetarist paradigms in macroeconomic policy. Some policy fields have them; some do not—or at least, in some policy fields they are not as well developed. In other situations new paradigms emerge to challenge previously dominant ones. Environmental policy, for example, became increasingly influenced in the latter part of the 1980s by the paradigm of "sustainable development."

Under the structure column, the policy analyst's automatic checklist must include the prime minister and Cabinet, the executive bureaucracy (often viewed as a combination of the government departments and the powerful central agencies of government), interest groups, provincial departments and agencies, and policy communities.[2] Policy communities refer to an array of organizations in a particular policy field that include departments and interest groups, but also private sector research organizations, consultancy firms, and universities and think tanks.

When looking at these basic structures or at structures in particular policy fields, it is essential to appreciate the true and usually quite complex nature of such structures. The term structure is used in part to convey that this policy variable goes beyond bureaucratic organization per se. In short, structure is an amalgam of component organizational features. Structure consists of statutes, programs, headquarters and field entities, and employees with varying views about, and commitments to, the policy issues being examined.

Finally, the process column reveals several processes that, though linked, often have a capacity to live lives of their own within the political executive and hence must be understood on their own terms. These include the overall priority-setting and mandate-setting process revealed through occasions such as throne speeches and budget speeches, as well as the dynamics of the tax decision process, the expenditure process, the regulatory process, and the public enterprise process. As we will see in Part II, the relationships of power, the number of players involved, and the inherent problems of quantification and analysis vary enormously across these various processes. While such processes are intended broadly to facilitate the making of policy, they are also, partly by design, intended to prevent policy from being made. Most of these processes involve the basic instruments available to governments to achieve policy purposes, but such instruments are themselves the object of political dispute. In short, they are valued in part because they define how much and what kinds and degrees of legitimate coercion are being applied to secure support and compliance for any given policy initiative.

The interplay approach accordingly suggests that whenever a policy field, policy controversy, or change in the policy process is being studied and examined, several questions inherently ought to be asked. The following questions are illustrative only, but flow from the three elements of the approach:

- What ideologies and dominant ideas are involved in the policy controversy or field? How have they changed historically? What ideas are ranked highest by the prime minister, the minister, or the Cabinet? By the opposition parties? By the interests affected, including foreign and provincial governments? What rhetorical language is used to express or repackage these ideas or to cloud them over?
- What policy paradigms exist in the policy problem? Which paradigm is dominant and which, if any, is a contending one? Which policy communities are identified with these paradigms?
- What structures are involved in the policy field or issue, directly or indirectly? With which clientele interests do they define themselves to be most associated? By which competing policy structures do they most feel threatened? Which interest structures and policy communities must they consult or neutralize? Which policy instruments are under the control of which structures?
- Where does the policy field or question rank in the government's and opposition's priority list? (High? Low? Medium?) To what extent is current policy characterized by a strong Cabinet concensus? Or by a temporary, vulnerable concensus?
- What policy instruments are used in the policy field or problem? In what sequence were instruments used as the policy field evolved historically? What preferred instruments are being advocated as the primary basis of reform or change

by the government? By the interest groups affected? What instrument-based policy processes are involved and have to be traversed to achieve policy success or legitimacy?

Many other questions can also be posed just by keeping the main elements of the interplay approach in mind. This will be shown throughout the book.

Public Policy: Definition and Characteristics

We agree with William Jenkins that public policy is best defined as "a set of interrelated decisions taken by a political actor or group of actors concerning the selection of goals and the means of achieving them"[3] and that in principle these decisions "should be within the power of these actors to achieve."[4] But accordingly, public policy involves certain other inherent characteristics. It involves:

- the need to deal with uncertainty;
- the need to change or sustain human behaviour in desired ways; and
- a series of decisions and "nondecisions," that is, decisions not to act.

All public policies confront uncertainty in that to some extent each one is a hypothesis waiting to be tested—often only once. Uncertainty exists also because information is always in some sense limited and policy success usually depends on cooperation from private interests or at least their refrain from opposition.

Public policy also involves the need to change or sustain real human behaviour. Those who advocate a policy change do so presumably because they wish to see a desired change in human behaviour occur over a sustained period of time, in a reliable, predictable way. Alternatively, they wish to see the status quo preserved. Because of this, the study and practice of public policy cannot avoid grappling with models of human behaviour, with beliefs about what makes human behaviour change, and hence with human incentives and social causality.

Finally, the study of public policy involves the need to understand a series of decisions, including so-called nondecisions.[5] The serial nature of most policy-making is such that policy is usually revealed by many decisions rather than just one. It could appear in a statute, in a government statement, in a speech to a constituency meeting, in a ruling on an individual case, or in a combination of all of the above. Decisions not to act, whether announced as such, or whether only discoverable after the event, are also vital. While we will undoubtedly sometimes succumb to the literary fatigue of using the words decision and policy interchangeably, in general it is best to use decision as the smaller unit of analysis.

The Study and Practice of Canadian Public Policy

Anyone contemplating the study of public policy for the first time has a right to feel somewhat bewildered. In addition to being familiar with the environment of Canadian politics, the Canadian political system itself, and the public policy system outlined above, it is also necessary to sort out the different perspectives on the study and practice of public policy supplied by academics, applied policy-makers, advisers and analysts, and policy advocates.

The academic perspective of public policy can perhaps best be viewed as one that focuses on the attempt to *explain* the evolution of public policy or a particular policy field *over a significant period of time*.[6] The search for such explanations is an elusive but necessary one. The overriding purpose of this book is academic in this sense. For example, the analysis in Part II of policy fields seeks to present a longitudinal look at policy since World War II. It seeks to examine public policy in general and in selected policy fields in the broadest sense possible by focusing on the evolution and persistence of dominant ideas and by showing how these often transcend, but at the same time are always represented and articulated by, structures and personalities. We examine causes, but we show also how difficult it is usually to "prove" causality. This is not to suggest that academics are not also often applied analysts as well. Rather, we are at this stage merely distinguishing this broader academic perspective.

It is useful to contrast the academic perspective from the more applied perspective. A public policy decision-maker, analyst, or adviser, whether located in a government department, interest group, or corporation, is usually more preoccupied with the applied task of deciding what to do or not to do or what to advise in particular circumstances *at a particular point in time*. The policy analyst is severely constrained by role, position, power, information, time, and resources and may or may not be aware of broader causal forces in the policy field concerned.[7] The applied perspective puts a higher premium on techniques of analysis. Sometimes this may include so-called "hard" techniques such as cost-benefit analysis or even econometrics. More often, it includes softer "techniques," including talking and consulting with the right people. To do justice to the study of public policy one must appreciate both of these perspectives—the academic and the applied—and relate one to the other.

In this regard it is important to note another feature of the link between theory and practice. One often thinks of the academic perspective as being "theoretical" and the decision-makers' perspective as "applied." Often the former perspective is mistakenly equated with "abstract" thinking while the latter is supposedly concrete and practical. But policy "theory" and policy formulation and implementation are not the separate worlds that we are often led to believe they are. This is because both theory and practice are ultimately concerned with causality and its limits. The academic perspective wants to know if policy X is caused by factors, a, b, and c. The policy adviser and practitioner want to achieve policy result X by changing behaviour a, b, and c. The academic and applied perspectives are not identical, but they are linked by their vital common concern with causality. Several chapters show that many public policy-makers and analysts lack both theory and knowledge in this important sense. Hence, they necessarily "muddle through," much like the rest of us, making small marginal changes that help them avoid making large errors.

A third important perspective is that of the policy advocate. A policy advocate could be a politician, a bureaucrat, an editorial writer, an environmentalist, or anyone advocating his or her preferred solution to a problem or preferred policy result. Such a person may be only partly interested in, or informed by, the analysis of public policy per se or of the intricate interdependencies among policy fields. The focus of the policy advocate, especially those for single-issue advocates (for example, abortion or nuclear power), is on the normative condition to be rectified, changed, or re-established. In one sense all policy change starts with some kind of aggressive policy advocacy, sometimes informed by analysis, sometimes in opposition to "objective facts," and sometimes propelled by an affinity for both current facts and a preferred idea or future state.

Because of the main elements of public policy and the contending perspectives outlined above, it follows that within the academic setting public policy is not the preserve of any single academic discipline. The study of public policy is influenced by several academic fields, including public administration, political science, economics, management, sociology, and law.[8] This presents further problems for students since the primary literature is a minefield of both intra- and interdisciplinary quarrels and controversies, some important and substantive, but others trivial and frustrating for both the novice and the seasoned reader alike. Each academic discipline, however, makes important contributions to the study of public policy. The biases and value assumptions of political science, economics, and public administration and of the mixed "political economy" combinations will be more evident when we examine the formal models of policy- and decision-making in Chapter 1.

In general, we believe the approach taken in this book is valuable in comparison with other accounts of Canadian public policy for four overall reasons. First, by focusing on the interplay between ideas, structures, and processes, one is forced to deal more rigorously with the historical continuity, persistence, and drift of public policy over recent decades. In several chapters we view priority-setting and individual policy fields in this way. One therefore sees public policy as constituting both choice *and* governing relationships more clearly. Within the context of political science, the book also allows the reader to see how different parts of the public policy system in Ottawa interact and relate to the broader political system.

Second, we examine policies in several different fields: social, labour market, economic, industrial, and foreign policy. It is obvious that there are dozens of different policy fields, from agriculture to the environment, and from policies on the status of women to policies for youth and the aged, to name only a few. People have different interests in different policy fields. Does this mean the student of competition policy or medicare should not use the book? We believe our approach offers one way of coming to grips with these and other policy fields as well. It does so first by requiring the reader to look at policy in relation to the existence in Canadian political life of a small number of dominant ideas. These ideas as enumerated earlier are present in virtually all policy fields, especially when one seriously searches beyond the rhetoric that often accompanies policy debate and analysis. Because of this focus on ideas, our approach requires the reader to look for the social, economic, and foreign policy content of *all* policy fields. We also discuss several other particular policy fields in illustrative ways.

Third, the approach used provides a closer look at actual resource allocation, not only within the economic and social policy fields, but also in relation to the role of governing instruments such as taxation, spending, regulation, public enterprise, and symbolic acts or exhortation, as well as an understanding of the role of knowledge and analysis.

Finally, we believe our approach provides a useful antidote for those who see all or most policies only in terms of personalities and individuals or as remorseless pragmatism. Not surprisingly, journalists and even senior bureaucrats and business people often ascribe much to the personality or leadership variable. Even economists who advocate a public choice approach often attempt to reduce the behaviour of whole organizations to the self-interested dictates of their leaders. We do not wish to argue that individual leaders and their power do not matter. Quite the contrary. Leaders and ideas, structures, and processes are inextricably linked. But a focus on ideas, structures, and processes viewed in a historical time period requires us to confront the existence and persistence of ideas and policies that sometimes do not change or that drift along slowly despite many changes of leadership. Our approach also requires the reader to deal with organizational structures, whose behaviour and role cannot be reduced to, or summed up by, their leaders only.

Notes

1. For other excellent books employing either different approaches or focusing on selected aspects of Canadian public policy-making, see Leslie A. Pal, *Public Policy Analysis*, 2nd ed. (Toronto: Nelson, 1992), and Stephen Brooks, *Public Policy in Canada: An Introduction* (Toronto: McClelland and Stewart, 1989). See also James A. Brander, *Government Policy Toward Business* (Toronto: Butterworths, 1988).
2. See G. Bruce Doern and Peter Aucoin, eds., *Public Policy in Canada: Structure, Organization and Process* (Toronto: Macmillan, 1979).
3. See William I. Jenkins, *Policy Analysis* (London: Martin Robertson, 1978), 15. See also C. Ham and M. Hill, *The Policy Process in the Modern Capitalist State* (London: Wheatsheaf, 1986), and Brian W. Hogwood and L. A. Gunn, *Policy Analysis for the Real World* (London: Macmillan, 1984).
4. Jenkins, *Policy Analysis*, 15.
5. See Ham and Hill, *Policy Process in the Modern Capitalist State*, ch. 4.
6. See Richard Simeon, "Studying Public Policy," *Canadian Journal of Political Science* 9 (December 1976), 547–80.
7. See Pal, *Public Policy Analysis*, chs. 2 and 3.
8. See V. Seymour Wilson, *Canadian Public Policy: Theory and Environment* (Toronto: McGraw-Hill Ryerson, 1981).

PART

THE CONTEXT FOR POLICY STUDY AND PRACTICE

- Contending Approaches in the Study of Public Policy
- The Canadian Political Economy and Core Institutions

CHAPTER 1

Contending Approaches in the Study of Public Policy

In the Introduction we set out broadly how and why we believe it is necessary to understand Canadian public policy-making as an interplay among ideas, structure, and process. As explained, our approach is largely an inductive one based upon an assembled empirical understanding of how the Canadian policy system functions and how it has evolved. It seeks to show how one country's policy system works.

However, an understanding of Canadian policy-making must also be set in the context of the main contending approaches used in the study of public policy. The first four approaches profiled in this chapter—the rational, incremental-pluralist, public choice, and class-corporatist approaches—are more general and deductive in that they usually do not directly purport to be studying any particular country as such. Instead, certain features and tendencies of policy-making and related political features are deduced from the structure of the framework used and the assumptions on which it is based. The fifth approach, called simply the comparative approach, does seek to examine and compare specific countries, either on their policy dynamics as a whole, or in selected policy fields such as social or industrial policy or policy instruments such as spending or regulation.

3

The contending approaches are the product of many streams of thought, rooted in different values and analytical concerns and produced and synthesized by scholars from disciplines and areas of study including economics, political science, public administration, and business management and the study of organizations.[1] Our discussion of them is fairly straightforward. We describe the main features of the approaches showing the main analytical insights of each one, how the major approaches directly and indirectly provide an intellectual underpinning for most of the ideas about public policy, for several aspects of our own approach, and for how Canadians judge and evaluate the adequacy of public policies.

It is essential, however, to keep in mind the ultimate purposes of these approaches and to be aware of the limitations inherent in social science. At a minimum, analytical approaches exist to classify a phenomenon into manageable chunks of reality and to generate or suggest hypothesized relationships we might not otherwise see. At a more rarefied level, they help generate theories that will both explain behaviour and allow us to predict. It is doubtful that any of the approaches to public policy allow us to do the latter. Certainly, there is nothing even approaching unanimity among scholars nor among practitioners and policy advocates that any one approach is fully satisfying or accepted.

The Rational Approach

There are two streams of thought that influence the content of the rational model. One stream emanates from the hypothesized ideal behaviour of the economic person as consumer and decision-maker and hence is closely related to the public choice approach discussed below. The second stream is broader and embraces a belief in science, the scientific method, and as applied to both public and private decisions, in systematic planning. The first stream of thought is fairly straightforward and is perhaps the best known version of the rational model. Reflected in the numerous standard descriptions of consumer and investor behaviour in economics, the model depicts a decision-maker who decides on a course of action to maximize the achievement of an objective (or utility function) or to solve a problem by:

- identifying the problem or objective;
- examining the alternative means, costs, and benefits involved in solving the problem;

- selecting and choosing the best way;
- implementing the decision; and
- evaluating the degree of success and then changing one's behaviour to correct errors.

Such a model has been used to describe the ideal and sometimes real behaviour of individual officials making decisions in an organization (the micro level) and to whole organizations and entire governments (the macro level).[2]

The second closely related stream of thought in the rational approach is a belief in the scientific method.[3] This stream goes well beyond the search for alternatives and the specification of objectives. It embraces a faith in the need to identify causality, to establish "the facts," and to distinguish facts from values. Part of its intellectual baggage is a faith in quantification and scientific management. It should be remembered that the birth of science was hailed as the age of reason and the end of utopias, be they religious or ideological.

In recent years it has become fashionable and, in part, valid to reject the rational model. The other approaches examined below all, in part, reject it. After all, it is argued, most decisions and policies are not made that way. It does not explain behaviour. We agree that the rational model does not explain most government policies, but the model remains important since it supplies for many policy actors and organizations a general, albeit often vague, standard against which many decisions and policies and the policy process as a whole are tested in a rough-and-ready way, particularly in the rhetoric of debate. It frequently provides a code of language around which political and policy debate is engaged.

At a macro level the rational model can be said to influence the frequently held view that governments must set and stick to longer-term priorities. This may be accompanied by the view that government must plan and do "first things first." Business people often believe, in this sense, that they are more "rational" than politicians. Indeed, for them politics is often viewed as the very opposite of rationality. This does not mean that they support a "planned economy," but that they wish that governments would make decisions more like they think they do. In this regard rationality is also linked to the dominant idea of efficiency discussed in Chapter 3. The various Trudeau governments were often held to be influenced by a fascination with rationality, planning, and technocratic approaches. This does not mean that this is how policies and decisions were made by successive Trudeau governments, but concepts of rationality are certainly part of the standard against which the Trudeau regimes were assessed, favourably or unfavourably.

A second manifestation of the lingering value of the rational approach is reflected in the continuous concern expressed by some regarding the adequacy of the search for alternatives for given policies.[4] This shows up in several ways. In the ideal policy process it is expected that Cabinet documents and the verbal advice of officials will produce real alternatives for ministers, and not just "strawmen" options that one can triumphantly dismiss. Even though, as the incremental model teaches us, alternatives are not widely sought or perhaps even wanted by ministers, one of the tests of a good or rational decision process is nonetheless a system that does produce them.

A third example that can be cited as a reflection of the ongoing normative importance of the rational approach is public policies that involve scientific and technological controversy.[5] Most public decisions and policy fields obviously involve technical and scientific knowledge. Indeed, many policy fields are held to be dominated by experts and technocrats. But some policy areas are of more concern in this regard than others. Controversies arise over policies in such fields as toxic and hazardous substances in the workplace and environment, communications and space policy, and defence policy, where the quality, openness, and type of scientific and technological information is in dispute. In this growing realm of public policy, the rational model exercises an explicit and implicit influence in the way many persons, including scientists and technologists, think about such policy problems.

The Incremental-Pluralist Approach

The incremental-pluralist approach flows from the study of decision-making in organizations and from the examination of broader political behaviour. The incremental part of the approach refers to decisions made through discrete, small-risk-averse steps where consensus is valued highly. The pluralist variation is usually linked to broader interest group behaviour and to visualizing politics as a competitive, peaceful struggle among interests.[6] Another variant usually included in this overall approach is that which sees internal decision-making within governments as a competitive "bureaucratic politics" model.[7] The common feature of all these variants is that there are many players whose positions must be accommodated through compromise. The incremental-pluralist approach is accordingly the opposite of the rational approach to policy-making.

In its original form the concept of incrementalism is the joint product of Dahl and Lindblom, who identified it as but one of society's comprehensive processes or "aids to calculation."[8] The others identified by Dahl and Lindblom were science, calculated risk, and utopianism. Though later adapted by Braybrooke and Lindblom and by Lindblom on his own, the essence of the approach has not changed.[9] It purports to describe how decisions are made and should be made. The incremental model suggests that the best predictor of future policy is the recent past. Incrementalism consists of:

- small marginal adjustments to the status quo;
- a restricted consideration of alternatives and of consequences;
- the adjustment of objectives to policies; and
- the reconstructive and serial treatment of data and analysis.

Incrementalism places a high normative value on the need for agreement and consensus. The test of a good policy or decision is not just whether it produces good results, but also whether it can command a consensus. The model also appeals to the normal human desire to avoid making large errors. A series of small marginal adjustments helps to avoid large errors and ensures greater control.

The main attributes of incrementalism are derived from a logical and empirical criticism of the rational model. The rational model is weak because it is not adapted to people's limited problem-solving capabilities, the inadequacies of information and costliness of analysis, and to the diverse ways in which policy problems emerge. The rational model takes grossly insufficient account of the close relationships between facts and values and means and ends.

The pluralist aspect of the incremental-pluralist approach is derived from broader efforts to explain political behaviour rather than just policy- and decision-making in organizations. Pluralism implies that choice occurs at the level of individuals and groups operating through a more or less open and competitive process. Competition may not always be equal, but a premium is placed on constructive consensus and gradual change. A balance of power is sought among the players, and the state's role is to ensure that such a democratic balance is fostered and maintained. It is a fairly small step from this view of the way decisions are, and ought to be, made to the more particular conception of decision-making within government as a process of pluralistic "bureaucratic politics." Here the interests are the many departments and agencies of which the state is composed.

The incremental-pluralist approach is intuitively persuasive at a common-sense level. Its critics, however, are legion.[10] While many agree that it accurately describes how most decisions are taken most of the time, its critics argue that it does not *explain* much and that it is not the way decisions *should be* made. It is a conservative model. It is the *bête noire* of all those who covet either rational change or radical change.

As shown below, both the public choice and the class-corporatist approaches are dubious about the capacity of incremental-pluralist approaches to explain policy. Some of the criticism is valid, although it is doubtful that the former approaches have any greater claim to credibility. The essential conservatism of the model cannot, however, be denied. Improvement in small doses and broadly pluralistic adjustment seem to be the best that it can offer. And yet there is evidence that this is, indeed, the way that many societies learn and change, in part because political leaders cannot be too far ahead of the political system and society they lead.

The approach is sometimes difficult to apply. It begs the question, "When is a change fundamental as opposed to incremental?" How does one tell? The "evidence" of incrementalism is presumably found in the gradual increases or decreases in expenditure, regulation, taxes, or tax breaks, and in the changing array of agencies, bureaucrats, and officials. But was the decision to establish medicare in 1966 or the passage of the Canada–U.S. Free Trade Agreement in 1988 an incremental choice? Were the decisions to build the St. Lawrence Seaway in the 1950s or the Hibernia project in the 1990s marginal adjustments? How does one explain or deal with these apparent quantum jumps in policy or activity? In essence such judgments can only be reached by an examination of the normative content of policy, which in turn is tested by different groups in society against quite different ideological standards and dominant ideas. For example, the class-corporatist approach may well lead to a judgment that medicare is not a fundamental change since it does not fundamentally address the inequalities induced by capitalism. Others may judge the policy as being fundamental in the sense of promoting a broader view of equity among groups and regions.

The inability of the incremental model to handle these "exceptions," and the acknowledged weaknesses of the rational model, prompted Etzioni to suggest his "mixed-scanning" model.[11] In simple terms this approach suggests that societies do have a capacity to be fairly rational about a very small handful of decisions that they scan and identify, but that they leave the great majority of decisions to the inexorable drift of incrementalism.

The Public Choice Approach

The application of the public choice approach to the study of Canadian public policy essentially reflects the growing role of economists in the study of government in areas other than their traditional role in examining macroeconomic policy. Like the other models, it is not a fully coherent body of theory, but has received impetus from its vigorous attack in the 1970s and 1980s on the "public interest" assumptions and failures of liberalism, especially the social programs of the 1960s. It is associated with the emergence of neoconservatism, especially of the Reaganite and Thatcherite variety, but also among Canadian Conservatives as well. The approach basically involves the application of the assumptions of the self-interest-calculating behaviour of individuals to the study of public choice. Individual decision-makers are viewed as utility maximizers whose behaviour is best explained, not in terms of their pursuit of the public interest, but rather in terms of their self-interest.

The roots of the public choice approach can be traced to Adam Smith and classical liberal economics. Its more recent lineage begins with Milton Friedman, George Stigler, and others in the so-called "Chicago School" and Gordon Tullock, James Buchanan, and others in the so-called "Virginia School."[12] The approach has been used to study decision processes and institutions as varied as constitutions (society's basic decision rules), political parties and electoral behaviour, bureaucracies, interest groups, public expenditure, and regulation.

In Canada the approach has been used by Acheson and Chant to study the behaviour of the Bank of Canada; Edward West on education policy and minimum wage laws; Allan Maslove and Gene Swimmer on the behaviour of the Anti-Inflation Board; Bailey and Hull on revenue dependency and charging for government services; and in a more limited way by Stanbury on competition policy.[13] The most comprehensive use of a public choice approach in Canada has been by Albert Breton, who attempted to devise a macro theory of representative government based on it, and by Douglas Hartle writing on his own and with Trebilcock, Prichard, and Dewees.[14]

The basic framework views the policy process in cabinet-parliamentary government as a series of interlocking games: the special-interest group game, the political game, the bureaucratic game, and the media game, with each player's behaviour essentially best understood in relation to the self-interest maximizing behaviour of each sector's leaders.[15] Certain elements of the games played by these actors are obviously an important part of the policy process, and thus reflect the utility of the public choice approach in a general way. It is important to highlight and appreciate many of these essential behavioural attributes. However, we have much greater difficulty in agreeing with what the approach produces in a broader understanding of the Canadian policy process. The approach lacks a sufficient breadth of appreciation about the broader relations among institutions and among ideas, structures, and processes. The fact that the concept of a "public interest" is dismissed by public choice theory is not in itself a fatal flaw in that there is a genuine debate as to what the public interest is. However, it is certainly plausible to argue that self-interest is not necessarily its antithesis. In throwing out the public interest, however, the approach seems to throw out the existence of ideas as well.

The Class-Corporatist Approach

The class-corporatist approach is rooted first in the Marxist conception that capitalist societies and political economies are best understood as being composed of unequal economic classes whose positions are derived from their basic roles as the owners of capital and suppliers of labour.[16] The corporatist connection derives from later efforts in some, mainly social democratic, states to devise decision-making institutions through which tripartite concensus could be arrived at among business, labour, and the state, especially on key economic and social policy matters.[17]

The use of class concepts in the study and interpretation of Canadian public policy began to flourish noticeably in the 1970s, though this view was present much earlier in the work of C. B. Macpherson and in Lipset's study of agrarian socialism in Saskatchewan.[18] It was also a key feature of John Porter's classic book *The Vertical Mosaic* (1965), one of the first analyses to challenge fundamentally the then dominant pluralist or brokerage model of Canadian politics.[19]

Exponents of class analysis such as Leo Panitch have taken the approach well beyond the simpler versions of Marxist class conflict between workers and capitalists with the conspiratorial overtones of the capture of the state by the capitalist class.[20] Modern class analysis recognizes the existence of numerous sectors or "fractions" of capital and of dynamic relations between an autonomous state and the different classes that emerge from the fundamental conditions of social and economic production. Despite this increased sophistication, the approach retains two central tenets as they relate to public policy.

The primary tenet is that the relationships of power that exist in liberal capitalist societies are best explained by an understanding of a person's relationship to the means of production or, in short, to "one's ability or inability to dispose of labour—one's own and other's."[21] The second tenet is the characterization of the three main functions of the state. The approach asserts that the state in liberal capitalist economies exists to perform three functions: to foster capital accumulation by capitalists; to foster social harmony through "legitimating" activities; and to coerce or otherwise maintain or impose social order.[22] While it is not always clear which activities of the state are to be lodged in each function, it would appear that examples of capital accumulation activity would be such things as tax breaks for corporations and public investment in infrastructure (roads, railways, etc.). The legitimating functions would be represented by what non-class analysts would call social policy, that is, the whole apparatus of welfare, health, and unemployment insurance programs. While liberals would refer to these as major elements of social "reform," a class analysis regards them as legitimating activities, produced out of constant social struggle, but needed to placate the dependent classes in such a way as to ensure the dominance of the capitalist class, which owns the basic means of production. The third function of the state, coercion, would be illustrated by the activities of the military, the police, and other agents of the state.

Class analysis recognizes the relative autonomy of the state because it appreciates that there is often conflict among the different "fractions" of capital (finance, industrial, foreign-owned versus domestic) as well as between capital and labour. This is not, however, a back-door rediscovery of interest group pluralism, because the assertion is that the capitalist state, on balance, is not a neutral referee but rather succeeds over time in sustaining the essential dominance of the capitalist class and the inequalities of power inherent in capitalism. Thus, autonomy exists for the state, but when one probes the approach more closely and asks "how much" autonomy, the answer seems to be "some, but not much." Its essential verdict on all or most public policy made by liberal democratic regimes is that the latter maintains the status quo, albeit a marginally changing status quo. Thus, despite recent acknowledgments of autonomy, the class analysis approach still overwhelmingly sees the direction of causality in public policy flowing from economy to polity.

It is not difficult to see why the corporatist element of this approach emerged. While corporatism had a particularly negative image in its pre–World War II fascist versions, it has since been seen in social democratic political circles as a way of ensuring that economic classes—business and labour—are fully involved with the state in making the key overarching decisions needed by a modern political economy. Thus, corporatism involves tripartite macro policy-making through the so-called "peak associations" of business and labour interacting with the state to, in essence, divide up the economic pie.[23]

While forms of corporatist structure have been credited with generating and preserving the prosperity of countries such as Germany and Sweden, the critics of this system are legion. Critics argue that it is undemocratic precisely because it shuts out many other legitimate interests. Furthermore, its success depends on whether a particular country possesses the basic peak associations through which consensus can be forged. Corporatist structures, moreover, inherently are based on the assumption that political struggle is essentially between large political and social forces rather than being a process involving individuals and smaller groups or regions.

A class-corporatist approach is useful in several important respects. First, because of its central tenet, it is an approach that more than any of the others is informed by questions about the inequality of power and income in society. It inherently raises questions about the idea of redistribution both of income and power. At the level of Canada's political parties this is ultimately reflected in the critical role played by left of centre parties such as the Progressives in the 1920s and 1930s, and later the Co-operative Commonwealth Federation (CCF) and the New Democratic Party. While the NDP does not often engage in the rhetoric of class analysis, its ideas are certainly influenced by the redistributive idea inherent in the approach.

A second useful attribute of the approach is the view it brings to post–World War II social welfare programs. A class-corporatist perspective provides a different interpretation of these reforms, as well as of elements of the tax and expenditure reform movements. At the same time it shows some of the pitfalls of the approach. The use of terms such as the legitimating "function" of the state (the category into which all social programs seem to be put) raises important issues about the "purpose" as opposed to function of the state. The postwar reforms seem to be, in the class analysis view, "purposeless" or, at best, a mercilessly calculating set of adjustments conceded by the economic interests of capital. It is portrayed as normatively unredeeming behaviour, and seems to be driven by economic determinism in as mechanistic a way as the public choice approach.

A third feature of class-based conceptions has been to extend the approach into an analysis of federalism[24] and the structure of government and the bureaucracy. For example, Rianne Mahon's work on the theory of unequal representation raises important questions about how different segments of capital seek and gain representation in different portfolios and departments of government, while labour has difficulty securing such access even in "labour" departments.[25]

Finally, because the approach has a broad view of capitalism, it is sometimes more inclined than other approaches to raise policy questions about the international dimensions of capitalism and of the division of labour. This has contributed to alternative ideas about Canadian foreign policy, industrial policy, and social policy. In general, then, while it cannot be said that the approach is the dominant one in Canadian political, bureaucratic, or academic life, it has nonetheless emerged to raise important questions about policy ideas, structures, and processes.

The Comparative Public Policy Approach

The final approach reviewed is the comparative analysis of policy outputs and outcomes. This approach seeks to discover the nature and direction of causal relationships between various independent variables or environmental factors and the policy field or instrument being studied. This was part of an empirical quantitative and statistical effort to be more scientific about studying policy, an effort that required comparison among countries, or other units (states or provinces). The environmental factors were usually grouped into socioeconomic phenomena (industrialization, wealth, education, urbanization, etc.) and political variables (party competition, voter turnout, representation patterns).

While these approaches have reached a degree of statistical elegance, they also led to various interpretations that often bordered on the absurd. The early simple input-output studies often purported to show that socioeconomic factors were the key determinants in such cross-country comparisons and that "politics" (as measured by the specific variables selected) did not seem to matter much. Paradoxically, a 1970 Canadian study of public expenditure growth by economist Richard Bird seemed to argue the opposite, namely that broader socioeconomic interpretations did not seem to supply satisfactory explanations and that, therefore, one ought to look at political variables, what he called the "missing link," including the behaviour of bureaucrats.[26]

These broad, quantitative approaches illustrate further the ongoing debate and assumptions about "economic" versus other "political or social" models of human behaviour that underpin the study of public policy. What they gain in macro comparison they often lose, if they are too mechanical, in subtlety and genuine understanding. The comparative approach requires empirical care in specifying what the dependent variable (the policy field or instrument being explained) is and, as well, how the independent explanatory variables (the factors determining outcomes) are being defined and operationalized.[27] For example, if the dependent variable is social policy, then it matters whether social policy is defined to include the core areas of the social welfare state, such as health and welfare expenditures, or whether it is wider and encompasses education and training as well.[28] The independent variables also can vary widely, each with different problems in finding operational indicators of their presence. For example, the independent variables seeking to explain the variables in social policy spending could include: election systems, Cabinet representation, degrees of union versus business leverage, administrative systems, and the array of values present in each country's political culture.

There are also difficult problems of obtaining adequate data and different degrees to which policy fields or instruments have been subject to comparative study. For example, comparative regulatory outputs in environmental or occupational health suffer from greater problems in obtaining an appropriate or agreed measure of outputs, let alone outcomes, that can be used to compare even two or three countries.[29] Regulation has also been studied comparatively for a much shorter time period than has public spending or social welfare policy.

As we will see in Part IV, while broad multicountry comparative policy studies are an essential part of understanding Canadian policy performance, it is also important to see other modes of both internal comparison (among provinces) and more subtle studies where perhaps only two countries are compared and contrasted. Two examples of these latter types of study should be cited.

The first example is found in the work of Dale Poel who analyzed on a quantitative basis the degree to which legislative changes are diffused and emulated among provinces in Canada.[30] His work demonstrates in a practical way the degree to which federal systems facilitate collective learning and experimentation when one province initiates change and other provinces then adopt and adapt it later. It is a tidy study that reached plausible conclusions.

A second example is Hugh Heclo's comparative study of the introduction and evolution of social policies in Britain and Sweden.[31] Because only two countries are compared and because the *timing* of the introduction of key social measures differed greatly in two otherwise not dissimilar economies, Heclo was forced to seek out political explanations for why these countries seemed to learn differently and respond differently, at least in the timing of the response.

Conclusions

All the approaches surveyed in this chapter force us to simplify reality. But our own common sense constantly reminds us that policy reality is complex and refuses to cooperate with artificial analytical frameworks. We remind the reader that we have touched only briefly on the five major approaches and that other sources should be consulted for a more detailed use and criticism. We have attempted to highlight the main features and to analyze their empirical and value-based assumptions in a general way. We think, however, that the usefulness and the limitation of these approaches can only be fully appreciated in the Canadian context by a larger focus on the interplay among ideas, structures, and processes.

Notes

1. For other general reviews of approaches to the study of public policy, see A. J. Heidenheimer, Hugh Heclo, and Carolyn Teich Adams, *Comparative Public Policy*, 3rd ed. (New York: St. Martin's Press, 1990), ch. 1; W. I. Jenkins, *Policy Analysis* (London: Martin Robertson, 1978); Peter Aucoin, "Public Policy Theory and Analysis," in G. Bruce Doern and Peter Aucoin, eds., *Public Policy in Canada* (Toronto: Macmillan, 1979), ch. 1; Richard Simeon, "Studying Public Policy," *Canadian Journal of Political Science* 9 (December 1976), 547–80; and Claus Offe, "The Capitalist State and Policy Formation," in L. Lindberg et al., eds., *Stress and Contradiction in Modern Capitalism* (New York: Wiley, 1975).
2. Herbert A. Simon, *Administrative Behavior*, 2nd ed. (New York: Free Press, 1965); and Robert A. Dahl and Charles E. Lindblom, *Politics, Economics and Welfare* (New York: Harper Torch Books, 1953).
3. See Sanford A. Lakoff, "The Third Culture: Science in Social Thought," in Sanford A. Lakoff, ed., *Knowledge and Power* (New York: Free Press, 1966), ch. 1.
4. See Aaron Wildavsky, *Speaking Truth to Power: The Art and Craft of Policy Analysis* (Boston: Little, Brown, 1979), chs. 1, 2, and 6.
5. G. Bruce Doern, *The Peripheral Nature of Scientific and Technological Controversy in Federal Policy Formation* (Ottawa: Science Council of Canada, 1981).

6. See R. E. Goodin, *Political Theory and Public Policy* (Chicago: University of Chicago Press, 1982).
7. See Graham Allison, *Essence of Decision* (Boston: Little, Brown, 1971).
8. Dahl and Lindblom, *Politics, Economics and Welfare*, ch. 3.
9. See David Braybrooke and C. E. Lindblom, *A Strategy of Decision* (New York: Free Press, 1963); C. E. Lindblom, *The Policy Making Process* (New York: Prentice-Hall, 1968); and C. E. Lindblom, *Politics and Markets* (New York: Basic Books, 1978).
10. See A. Etzioni, *The Active Society* (New York: Free Press, 1968), chs. 11 and 12; and Y. Dror, *Design for Policy Sciences* (New York: Elsevier, 1971).
11. Etzioni, *The Active Society*, ch. 12.
12. See Patrick Dunleavy, *Democracy, Bureaucracy and Public Choice* (London: Harvester Wheatsheaf, 1991).
13. See K. Acheson and J. F. Chant, "The Choice of Monetary Instruments and the Theory of Bureaucracy," in J. P. Cairns, H. H. Binhammer, and R. W. Boadway, eds., *Canadian Banking and Monetary Policy*, 2nd ed. (Toronto: McGraw-Hill Ryerson, 1972), 233–52; E. G. West, "The Political Economy of American Public School Legislation," *Journal of Law and Economics* 10 (October 1967), 101–28; Allan M. Maslove and E. Swimmer, *Wage Controls in Canada 1975–78* (Montreal: Institute for Research on Public Policy, 1980); A. R. Bailey and D. G. Hull, *The Way Out: A More Revenue Dependent Public Sector and How It Might Revitalize the Process of Governing* (Montreal: Institute for Research on Public Policy, 1980); and W. T. Stanbury, *Business Interests and the Reform of Canadian Competition Policy, 1971–1975* (Toronto: Methuen, 1977).
14. See Albert Breton, *The Economic Theory of Representative Government* (Chicago: University of Chicago Press, 1974); Douglas Hartle, *Public Policy, Decision Making and Regulation* (Montreal: Institute for Research on Public Policy, 1979); and M. Trebilcock, R. S. Prichard, D. Hartle, and D. Dewees, *The Choice of Governing Instruments* (Ottawa: Minister of Supply and Services, 1982).
15. Hartle, *Public Policy, Decision Making and Regulation*, ch. 3.
16. See Leo Panitch, ed., *The Canadian State* (Toronto: University of Toronto Press, 1977).
17. See Leo Panitch, "Trade Unions and the Capitalist State: Corporatism and Its Contradictions," *New Left Review* 125 (January–February 1981), 21–44.
18. C. B. Macpherson, *Democracy in Alberta* (Toronto: University of Toronto Press, 1953), and S. M. Lipset, *Agrarian Socialism* (New York: Anchor Books, Doubleday, 1968).
19. John Porter, *The Vertical Mosaic* (Toronto: University of Toronto Press, 1965), ch. 12.
20. Panitch, *The Canadian State*.
21. Leo V. Panitch, "Elites, Classes and Power in Canada," in Michael S. Whittington and Glen Williams, eds., *Canadian Politics in the 1980s* (Toronto: Methuen, 1981), 176–77.

22. Panitch, *The Canadian State*, ch. 1.
23. See Keith Banting, ed., *The State and Economic Interests* (Toronto University of Toronto Press, 1986).
24. See Garth Stevenson, *Unfulfilled Union* (Toronto: Macmillan, 1979).
25. Rianne Mahon, "Canadian Public Policy: The Unequal Structure of Representation," in Leo Panitch, ed., *The Canadian State*, ch. 6.
26. Richard Bird, *The Growth of Government Spending in Canada* (Toronto: Canadian Tax Foundation, 1970).
27. See Heidenheimer, Heclo, and Teich Adams, *Comparative Public Policy*, ch. 1, and David Cameron, "The Growth of Government Spending: The Canadian Experience in Comparative Perspective," in Keith Banting, ed., *State and Society: Canada in Comparative Perspective* (Toronto: University of Toronto Press, 1986), 21–52.
28. See Catherine Jones, *Patterns of Social Policy* (London: Tavistock, 1985).
29. See David Vogel, *National Styles of Regulation* (Ithaca, N.Y.: Cornell University Press, 1986).
30. Dale Poel, "A Diffusion of Legislation Among the Canadian Provinces," paper presented to Canadian Political Science Association, Edmonton, June 1975.
31. See Hugh Heclo, *Modern Social Politics in Britain and Sweden* (New Haven: Yale University Press, 1974).

CHAPTER 2

The Canadian Political Economy and Core Institutions

Canadian public policy is made in the context of an evolving and changing political economy as well as social composition. It also occurs within an explicit set of liberal democratic political institutions that have been adapted and changed to meet new challenges. This chapter profiles the key features of the Canadian political economy and then takes stock of the main political institutions within which public policy formulation occurs. Our purpose here is not to offer a detailed account of the larger nonpolicy features of the main political institutions. Rather, we concentrate on highlighting features that are of relevance to public policy formulation.

The essential map of this terrain is different in the 1990s from that which might have been drawn in previous decades. Four developments make it different in degree as well as in kind: the rapid globalization of the economy; the launching of the Canada–U.S. Free Trade Agreement; the failure of the Meech Lake Accord; and the continuing experience with the policy consequences of the Canadian Charter of Rights and Freedoms. Each of these will be commented on briefly below, but some of their combined effects and contradictions deserve emphasis from the very outset of our policy journey.[1]

First, globalization—the rapid worldwide shifting and specialization of production and the movement of capital—has made Canadians more conscious of their interdependence with the rest of the world and with the inevitability of rapid change. Canadians have also developed a greater sense of vulnerability and of being a smaller player on the world stage. The free trade agreement both reflects and reinforces this in that there are fewer protections for the Canadian economy and a greater need for inherent competitive skills, while at the same time important areas of Canada–U.S. decision-making and consultation have been significantly institutionalized.

Second, both the failure to secure the Meech Lake Accord and the uncertainty surrounding future constitutional arrangements, in combination with the pattern of Charter cases and decisions, have served to weaken federal governmental authority. On balance, the Meech Lake Accord would have reduced federal powers, as probably will any post-Meech arrangements. The Charter, which was intended to strengthen the rights of individuals and groups against the state, undoubtedly has and will continue to do so.

The net effect of globalization from without and challenges from within has been that the "publicness" and certainty of Canadian public policy initiatives is made more difficult. The federal government has of course always been influenced by international pressures and domestic struggle, but what is important for a 1990s view of public policy is that these constraints are now more embedded through institutional and constitutional means. It is in the context of this difference that a review of the Canadian political economy and of the core political institutions must begin.

The Canadian Political Economy

Canada consists of an evolving amalgam of political, economic, and social characteristics. These features are clearly of critical importance in understanding how and why policies and decisions are made. They include: Canada's historical origins in relation to the United States and the United Kingdom; French–English relations and Canada's evolving ethnic composition; the role of geographical and spatial/physical realities; the uneasy co-existence of capitalism, economic classes, and recently challenged traditions of statism; Canada's dependence on foreign trade and the extensive foreign ownership of major sectors of the economy.[2]

Canada's political origins demonstrate an explicit rejection of the American Revolution and an acceptance of the "peace, order, and good government" offered by British traditions and institutions reflected especially in parliamentary government. At a basic constitutional level this also led to the adoption of a system of responsible cabinet-parliamentary government as opposed to the American system, which constructed an elaborate array of "checks and balances" between the three branches of government: the executive, the legislature, and the judiciary.[3] Canadian political leaders rejected the excesses of the American belief in individual liberty and distrust of government and authority. Even in the 1981 debate that led to an entrenched Charter of Rights, the Canadian system balanced its adherence to basic rights by providing for the right of legislative bodies to override these rights for a limited period of time. While Canada evolved into a liberal democratic state, it did so with a strong adherence to collectivist norms, whether of the Tory organic community-oriented variety or of a later social democratic kind.

The magnetic pull of the American giant has always been important—economically, politically, and culturally. The earliest definition of Canada's national and industrial policies after Confederation was an act of political will to counter American expansionism. It involved the deliberate creation of an east–west continental axis, physically and politically, to counter the efficiency of the north–south continental axis. In the last decades of the 20th century the American influence, aided by mass communication, has exerted an even larger cultural pressure, which Canadians have simultaneously welcomed and resisted.

The strong collectivist traditions in Canada are also a reflection of the central role of the relationships between French Canadians and English Canadians. In particular, the deeply rooted desire by French Canadians since "the Conquest" to preserve and enhance their collective cultural, religious, and linguistic independence, and even nationhood, is a central fact of Canadian political life.[4] The constant need to seek a new, delicate accommodation between French and English Canada affects many policy fields in ways that are not always obvious. Consequently, not only are policies on language and education so affected, but also policies tied to broader social issues (family allowances, for example), industrial location, and foreign policy.

Tensions in French–English relations have coincided as well with the growth and changing ethnic composition of Canada's population, and an increased focus on the rights and status of its native peoples. As a nation of immigrants, where immigration and settlement policy was once the centrepiece of economic development policy, the emergence of German, Italian, Ukrainian, and Polish Canadians, to name only a few of the ethnic groups, challenged the very definition of Canada, especially as viewed in western Canada where a large proportion of these peoples were located and whose work and sacrifice opened the western frontier. Similar changes have occurred in large urban centres where the immigration of visible minorities has transformed urban cultures and economies.

The enormous continental size and geographical composition of Canada, especially when contrasted with the thin ribbon of humanity that hugs the 49th parallel, imposes a spatial and physical reality to Canadian political life and public policy that even modern communications and the mass media cannot fully alter. Canada's most innovative contribution to social science, the work of Innis and others, was founded on an appreciation of this fundamental reality.[5] It focused on the importance of communication relationships between the centre and the periphery. As well, Innis showed the importance to Canadian economic development of basic staple resources from furs and fish, to grain and mineral resources. He also pointed out the limits and dependence created by reliance on a staples approach to economic development. In practical day-to-day public policy terms, the spatial and geographical realities cannot be underestimated. They affect the importance of staple resources as a central element of economic and industrial policy and of Canada's economic wealth and dependence; the importance of transportation and communication policy as a vehicle of national integration (with the infrastructure usually supplied by the state); the changing definition and response to demands for sensitive regional policy; the emotional and normative attachment, especially in western Canada but also in Atlantic Canada, to the question of resource ownership and the management of nonrenewable resources; and the perception by Canada's trading partners, especially the United States, of Canada as a stable supplier of basic resources.

Canada's economy is essentially a capitalist one and thus is rooted in a belief in the value and efficiency of the market and in the individual freedom and defence of property rights that capitalism helps sustain. The right to own property was a particularly important value to the immigrant settlers. Though linked to the values of liberalism and individualism, there has always existed in Canada an ambivalence about the idea of efficiency inherent in capitalism. The numerous rough edges of Canadian capitalism have always been moderated by an inclination to use the state. Statism was reflected not only in the frequent use of public enterprise or crown corporations, but even earlier in the extensive public subsidization and financing of major transportation networks.[6]

It must also be stressed that Canada's economy, like that of any continental country, is a regionally varied one. This reality arises from the physical and geographical attributes noted above. The geographic dispersal of natural resources such as fish, forests, grain, and minerals, the existence of different energy dependencies in each region, the proximity of different regions to population concentrations and therefore markets, and the widely varying modes and costs of transportation generate a need for regional policies and responses. They also result in distinctly different and often contradictory views about the soundness and appropriateness of national economic policy. These economic features are not ones that can be simplistically attributed to capitalism. They are influenced by capitalism, but they also predate and affect what capitalists and government entrepreneurs can do in the marketplace and in the exercise of political power.

Capitalism, however, does produce relations of dependence and economic subordination between those who own capital and those who supply their labour.[7] It also increasingly produces other "classes" such as government workers whose class orientations are at best vague and subject to other regional, ethnic, and individual cross pressures. The presence of capitalism raises fundamental questions about the role of class politics in the policy process. Several recent studies in Canada make it evident that the class aspects of Canadian politics cannot be viewed at the simplistic level of capitalists and workers in perpetual conflict, with the state operating as the agent of the owners of capital. It is increasingly acknowledged that the state has considerable autonomy. Nor can it be argued, on the basis of voting data and the failure of left-wing political parties such as the NDP to gain power at the national level, that class politics is irrelevant in electoral and party politics and hence in public policy. The truth lies somewhere in between.

The presence of capitalism and the ideas and beliefs associated with it and in opposition to it raises the age-old debate about efficiency versus equality. Since capitalism helps generate political parties of the left or socialist variety, it brings into organized political life a concern for the redistribution of income and power between rich and poor, between capital and labour, and among interests and regions.

A final but critical dual feature of Canadian capitalism and the Canadian economy is the considerable dependence on foreign trade and the extensive foreign ownership of the Canadian industrial and resource sectors, especially by American business interests.[8] About 25 to 30 percent of the income of Canadians is dependent upon foreign trade, much of it with the United States. These percentages are even higher in certain regions and subregions of Canada. The trade and foreign ownership imperatives affect and constrain Canada's conduct of policy both in foreign policy terms vis-à-vis the United States, and in domestic policy in fields such as energy, industrial, and regional policy. The presence of large blocks of concentrated foreign capital also affects the internal deliberations of major business interest groups, which must take positions that accommodate both indigenous capital and foreign-owned capital. Thus, foreign ownership and trade dependence are political and policy issues, not just because of the implied possible control by foreign enterprises operating through active support of their own foreign government, but also because they are a strong influence in the domestic counsels of Canadian federal and provincial governments and within major Canadian economic interest groups. These imperatives are reinforced by close relations among Canadian and American unions and by conflicts within the Canadian labour movement, relationships we examine in greater detail in Chapter 3.[9]

The Core Political Institutions

In the 1990s the core political institutions of Canadian politics include: the Canada–U.S. Free Trade Agreement; federalism; the Charter of Rights and Freedoms; cabinet-parliamentary government; interest groups; the electoral system and political parties; and the mass media. The institutions interact with each other. Once cannot understand their role in policy formulation by viewing each of them in isolation. Federalism and cabinet-parliamentary government interact with each other, partly through electoral competition and political party alliances and personalities. The media interact with all of the institutions since they are both an essential part of democratic life and a necessary forum for modern political communication and leadership. Interest groups seek to influence all the major institutions since they play a crucial intermediary role between the citizen and the state.

The Canada–U.S. Free Trade Agreement

The free trade agreement (FTA) between Canada and the United States was passed in 1988 and took effect in 1989.[10] Instituted by the Mulroney government, but with the support of seven provinces, the FTA creates by 1999 a tariff-free border as well as improving market access in areas such as services, agriculture, and resource trade. The most important aspects of the FTA for public policy purposes are threefold in nature. First, it entrenches in chapters 18 and 19 of the agreement two mechanisms that together significantly institutionalize the overall Canada–U.S. decision-making relationship. Chapter 18 sets up an overall trade dispute resolution commission and also requires new forms of formal advance consultation on pending policy initiatives in many policy fields. Chapter 19 has a specific dispute panel to review procedurally decisions regarding the application of trade remedies such as countervail duties against alleged subsidy activities that confer advantage on either country's exporters.

These and other provisions ensure that the FTA now stands as a new quasi-constitutional pillar in the Canadian institutional pantheon. It is effectively a North American economic constitution that partly constrains the state from acting in ways to which it had become historically accustomed. Moreover, because of the political divisiveness that accompanied its debate and introduction, the FTA also has become a potent symbol for the ongoing debate between those interests that favour a strong role for the state and those that place greater faith in markets and capitalism.

Federalism

Federalism is based on a belief in the need to balance national integration and unity with regional and cultural differences. It incorporates ideas of centralization and decentralization. It imposes a dominant reality on the Canadian policy process, namely the need to practise some form of cooperative federalism regardless of the short-term rhetoric of day-to-day politics.

Federalism is first an article of belief, not just a document containing the deathless prose of the British North America Act or the more inspiring ideals of the Constitution Act, 1982, and the Charter of Rights and Freedoms.[11] It legitimizes the existence of separate, but interdependent, realms of political power. In particular, sections 91, 92, and 95 of the Constitution Act, 1867 (formerly the BNA Act) enumerate federal and provincial legislative powers and thus, in part, constrain what each level of government can do. Federalism sanctifies the right of constituent governments to pursue different policy priorities at different times. It also makes possible public policy experimentation and "learning" where one province or the federal government adopts an approach tried elsewhere and adapts it to its own situation. But policy and program interdependence between the two levels of government is also an evident feature of federalism. Public policy is profoundly affected by joint statutory agreements on taxation, equalization payments, and major social programs such as medicare, education, welfare, and employment training. Interdependence is a reality in environmental regulation, agricultural policy, labour relations, and in the industrial, resource, and energy policy fields, to mention only a few.

The growing dominance since the 1960s of "executive federalism" where policy is made in a series of "behind-the-scenes" multilateral bargains struck among ministers and senior officials has led to concern about the process itself, about the policies it produces, and about the demoralizing inaction or mere tinkering it often produces. Indeed, in the immediate wake of the 1990 Meech Lake failure, many feared for the very existence of Canada as a viable political entity.

The Meech Lake Accord was an initiative of Prime Minister Brian Mulroney to bring Quebec back into the constitutional fold after Quebec's isolation from the 1982 Trudeau initiative that resulted in the patriation of the Canadian constitution from Britain and the entrenchment of a Charter of Rights and Freedoms. Had it been approved, the Meech Lake Accord would have done three main things of political and policy importance. First, it would have given some recognition to the existence of Quebec as a distinct society within Canada. Second, it would have recognized the right of the federal government to use its spending powers in areas of provincial jurisdiction provided it was approved by an appropriate number of provinces. Third, provinces would have the right to opt out of such joint initiatives with appropriate fiscal compensation, provided that their alternative programs were compatible with national objectives.

The Meech Lake Accord failed narrowly to win approval, in part because of outright disagreement over its substance, in part because of the "take it or leave it" process adopted, and in part because of its failure to address issues such as the rights of native peoples. In any event, its failure created a severe constitutional crisis and propelled angry demands by Quebeckers for independence or for an even more decentralized form of federalism than the Meech Lake formula had contained.[12] English Canadians were also increasingly less tolerant of the essential nature of their national political institutions. Western Canadians, in particular, had coupled their opposition to the accord with calls for an even more far-reaching establishment of a "triple E" Senate, "elected, equal, and effective," that would enhance regional representation in federal decision-making.

The Charter of Rights and Freedoms

The Charter of Rights and Freedoms became a central part of the Canadian constitution in 1982.[13] It sets out to protect several basic freedoms (of conscience and religion, association, and peaceful assembly) as well as basic legal rights (such as unreasonable search and seizure, and rights to life, liberty, and security of person). The Charter also protects certain equality rights, including equal protection and equal benefit of the law without discrimination based on race, national or ethnic origin, colour, religion, sex, age, or mental or physical disability. These freedoms and rights can only be subject to such reasonable limits by law as can be demonstrably justified in a free and democratic society.

The intent of the Trudeau government in pressing for the Charter was that such protections would establish freedoms for all Canadians against the powers of both levels of government and would accordingly become a unifying symbol and reality for Canadians. Since 1982 hundreds of Charter cases have proceeded through the courts to test the exact meaning of these protections. Our interest in the Charter is primarily with its possible effects on the content and processes of policy formulation. While few consistent patterns of effect can be discerned, there is little doubt that public policy-making has been influenced in several ways.

First, the role of the courts in supervising the executive and administrative arms of government has undoubtedly increased. This will over time bring different styles of policy reasoning since the judicial mind will bring to bear different factors than the administrative or political mind. Second, the equality provisions, in particular, have influenced the content of some social policy in areas such as maternity benefits and other eligibility provisions. Third, as policy is developed, proposals are being assessed within the executive even more carefully to ensure that they do not offend the Charter and that they do not involve the government in litigation.

A further effect of the Charter is on the policy strategies of interest groups. Groups have to consider more carefully whether to lobby in their accustomed ways or occasionally take issues to court either in fact or as a threat. The government too may use the Charter or its fear of threatened litigation as a way of leveraging excessive demands by interests groups seeking discriminatory action in their favour. All of these effects in combination cannot help but alter the actual policy agenda, throwing up surprises and unexpected strategies and court decisions that send the government's planned agenda into some disarray.

Cabinet-Parliamentary Government

Cabinet-parliamentary government exists at both the federal and provincial levels of Canadian government. It is a system of government that has significant implications for the relations between the executive, the legislature, and the judiciary. The executive, comprising the Crown, the prime minister, the Cabinet, and the bureaucracy, has the main powers of initiation in matters of policy, finance, and legislation. Parliament and provincial legislatures represent public opinion, legislate, oppose, and criticize, but legally, and by convention, they do not initiate policy per se.

In recent years there has been a strong tendency to attribute a declining, low, or even nonexistent policy role to Parliament or the legislature itself.[14] Nonetheless, it is patently evident that the *existence* of an assembly, democratically elected by voters in geographically based constituencies and charged with holding the majority party (expressed in votes in the assembly) accountable, has important implications for policy formulation. Under a parliamentary system, governed by rigid rules of confidence and party discipline, the government majority party has the main power to initiate policy, especially through taxation and spending. This fact, coupled with the growing complexity and technical nature of public policy, has contributed further to the view that Parliament has virtually no policy role—only the power to oppose, criticize, and scrutinize. The policy role of Parliament is held to be that of a mere "refinery" or, somewhat more grandly, the ultimate source of legitimacy through its exercise of legislative procedures in the passage of bills. While it is difficult to argue that Parliament has much power—almost by definition this is so—the refinery concept and other similar labels nonetheless seriously underplay the role of Parliament, particularly the role it plays when governments have to "anticipate" the opposition political parties' views and strategies expressed and forged in the House of Commons. Moreover, in the Mulroney period, reforms gave some increased leverage to parliamentary committees.

There is, of course, little dispute that the executive branch of cabinet-parliamentary government is the fulcrum of policy-making. This applies to the role of the prime minister and other cabinet ministers, but also to the role of the senior bureaucracy and the central agency apparatus that supports the Cabinet.[15] Policy is influenced by the central personal preferences and beliefs of the prime minister and of other ministers; by the inevitable and unavoidable need to delegate tasks to over forty ministers and hundreds of agencies; by the need to rank or balance ideas and to allocate resources of time, money, personnel, and political energy; by the size and representative composition of the Cabinet; by the advice, expertise, and longevity in office of senior officials, and by the presence, or lack, of resources, information, and knowledge.

Interest Groups

As a country with a strong belief in the right of persons to associate freely in groups, it is axiomatic that interest groups are important elements of Canadian politics and hence of public policy formulation.[16] While interest groups serve many important purposes for their members, our concern in this book is with their role in influencing policy development, by advocating change or marshalling political action to prevent changes unfavourable to them, by providing information to and withholding it from government, and by acting as a source of support for government. Interest groups are active in lobbying ministers and senior officials of the key departments and agencies that concern them. In Chapter 5 we highlight particular attributes of the evolving structure of interest groups, including questions about the changing composition of business and worker interests, the unequal power among such groups, and the role of the government in using groups to its own advantage. We will also refer to the role of policy communities.

Political Parties

The role of the electoral and party system in the development and formulation of public policy presents some puzzling paradoxes for the student of public policy, especially regarding the contrasting perspectives supplied by economists and political scientists. The latter have tended to downplay the formal policy role of parties by asserting that political parties are primarily agents for the recruitment of political leaders and the aggregation and mobilization of interests and voters for electoral purposes.[17] The two major Canadian parties, the Liberals and the Progressive Conservatives, are often viewed as cadre parties lacking even the British party traditions of the serious party "mandate" or platform and with only periodic policy meetings whose resolutions are not binding on the party leaders. The New Democratic Party, it is acknowledged, is more of a mass-based party and takes policy more seriously, but only, it is said by some, because it has no serious chance of gaining national office.

However, parties as electoral vehicles are the key link between voters and officer-holders. Both the governing and opposition parties cater to the views and perceptions of the *marginal* swing voter, especially in the swing constituency (electoral seats that were won or lost by a small plurality of votes). Political leaders, including central party advisers, often through the use of extensive public opinion polls, are particularly sensitive to the potential marginal vote changes in the fifty or so swing constituencies that make or break an election. Political parties help define what is to be viewed as "political" and how certain conceptions of politics, and therefore policies, can be successfully screened out of policy debates, out of the list of national priorities, and out of the very definition of the national interest.

The Mass Media

As with the other main institutions, the issue of the role of the mass media is important and complex.[18] Television and mass communications influence politics and public policy in several ways. An ability to communicate through the media is a prime factor in the selection and evaluation of leaders. It is said that a prime minister's dominance over policy and over the setting of the agenda is enhanced by an ability to command the media's attention. It is also evident that the media's short attention span makes it all the more difficult for government to hold any set of policy priorities constant for any extended period of time. Policies and decisions are often strategically timed either to minimize unfavourable coverage or to maximize coverage. The alleged bias of the media is held to be the major reason why governments and interest groups alike feel the need to spend increasing millions on policy advocacy advertising and on the marketing of their policies and leaders. Some assert glibly that question period in the House of Commons could not function without *The Globe and Mail.*

Judgments about the political rise and fall of ministers and their strengths and weaknesses are formed partly by a tight network of gossip and information exchanged among journalists, ministers, ministerial aids, and senior bureaucrats. The media's role is held by many policy practitioners to be a central reason why, in public policy-making, *perception* may be more important than reality. It contributes to the pressure that both politicians and officials feel constantly and that propels them to try at least to "be seen" doing "something" about a problem. This in turn contributes to excessive tinkering with policy and, it is suggested, to a growing disillusionment with government. Too many policies are "for show" and not "for real."

Conclusions

Canadian public policy is made within the larger national political economy and in the context of an important set of core institutions. These institutions now include the Canada–U.S. Free Trade Agreement and the Charter of Rights and Freedoms, as well as the more familiar institutions surveyed above. In the wake of the post–Meech Lake search for constitutional renewal, and in light of the rapid globalization of the economy, Canada's institutional setting for policy-making has never been subject to more challenges. While our profile of the core political institutions has been brief, each of their potential policy effects needs to be kept fully in mind as the policy journey proceeds.

Notes

1. See Thomas J. Courchene, "Global Competitiveness and the Canadian Federation," paper prepared for Conference on Global Competition and Canadian Federalism, University of Toronto, September 15, 1990; Richard Simeon, "Thinking About Constitutional Futures: A Framework," paper prepared for C. D. Howe Institute Conference, November 17, 1990; and G. Bruce Doern and Bryne Purchase, eds., *Canada at Risk: Canadian Public Policy in the 1990s* (Toronto: C. D. Howe Institute, 1990).
2. See R. Van Loon and M. Whittington, *The Canadian Political System*, 4th ed. (Toronto: McGraw-Hill Ryerson, 1986), chs. 1 to 13.
3. T. A. Hockin, *Government in Canada* (Toronto: McGraw-Hill Ryerson, 1976), and R. M. Dawson, *The Government of Canada*, revised by N. Ward (Toronto: University of Toronto Press, 1970). See also Reg Whitaker, "Images of the State in Canada," in Leo Panitch, ed., *The Canadian State* (Toronto: University of Toronto Press, 1977), ch. 2.
4. See Léon Dion, *Quebec: the Unfinished Revolution* (Montreal: McGill-Queen's University Press, 1976); Hubert Guindon, "The Modernization of Quebec and the Legitimacy of the Canadian State," *Canadian Review of Sociology and Anthropology* 15, no. 2 (1978), 227–45; Ramsay Cook, *Canada and the French Canadian Question* (Toronto: Macmillan, 1976); and Denis Monière, *Ideologies in Quebec* (Toronto: University of Toronto Press, 1981).
5. See Donald Creighton, *Harold Adams Innis: Portrait of a Scholar* (Toronto: University of Toronto Press, 1978), and Harold Innis, *Essays in Canadian Economic History* (Toronto: University of Toronto Press, 1956).
6. See Herschel Hardin, *A Nation Unaware: The Canadian Economic Culture* (Vancouver: J. J. Douglas, 1974); W. L. Morton, *The Canadian Identity*, 2nd ed. (Toronto: University of Toronto Press, 1972); and H. G. Aitken, "Defensive Expansionism: The State and Economic Growth in Canada," in W. T. Easterbrook and M. H. Watkins, eds., *Approaches to Canadian Economic History* (Toronto: McClelland and Stewart, 1967).
7. See Panitch, *The Canadian State*, and John Porter, *The Vertical Mosaic* (Toronto: University of Toronto Press, 1965), ch. 12.
8. See Robert Bothwell, Ian Drummond, and John English, *Canada Since 1945: Power, Politics and Provincialism* (Toronto: University of Toronto Press, 1981), ch. 5; and J. Fayerweather, *Foreign Investment in Canada* (Toronto: Oxford University Press, 1973).

9. See Gad Horowitz, *Canadian Labour in Politics* (Toronto: University of Toronto Press, 1968); John Anderson and Morley Gunderson, eds., *Union Management Relations in Canada* (Toronto: Addison-Wesley, 1982); and G. Swimmer and M. Thompson, eds., *Public Sector Industrial Relations in Canada* (Montreal: Institute for Research on Public Policy, 1983).

10. See G. Bruce Doern and Brian W. Tomlin, *Faith and Fear: The Free Trade Story* (Toronto: Stoddart, 1991).

11. See D. V. Smiley, *Canada in Question*, 3rd ed. (Toronto: McGraw-Hill Ryerson, 1980), ch. 1, and Garth Stevenson, *Unfulfilled Union* (Toronto: Macmillan, 1979).

12. See Simeon, "Thinking About Constitutional Futures."

13. See Peter H. Russell, "The Political Purposes of the Canadian Charter of Rights and Freedoms," *Canadian Bar Review* 61 (1983), 30–54; F. L. Morton and Leslie Pal, "The Impact of the Charter of Rights on Public Administration," *Canadian Public Administration* 28, no. 2 (1985), 221–43; and Michael Mandel, *The Charter of Rights and the Legalization of Politics in Canada* (Toronto: Thompson, 1991).

14. See Van Loon and Whittington, *The Canadian Political System*, ch. 19; Robert J. Jackson and M. Atkinson, *The Canadian Legislative System*, 2nd ed. (Toronto: Macmillan, 1980); and T. d'Aquino, G. Bruce Doern, and C. Blair, *Parliamentary Government in Canada: A Critical Assessment and Suggestions for Change* (Ottawa: Intercounsel Ltd., 1979).

15. G. Bruce Doern and Peter Aucoin, eds., *Public Policy in Canada* (Toronto: Macmillan, 1979), and T. Hockin, ed., *Apex of Power*, 2nd ed. (Toronto: Prentice-Hall, 1980).

16. A. Paul Pross, *Pressure Group Behaviour in Canadian Politics* (Toronto: McGraw-Hill Ryerson, 1975), and A. Paul Pross, *Group Politics and Public Policy* (Toronto: University of Toronto Press, 1986).

17. See, for example, H. Thorburn, ed., *Party Politics in Canada*, 4th ed. (Toronto: Prentice-Hall, 1979). For a broader view see M. J. Brodie and Jane Jenson, *Crisis, Challenge and Change: Party and Class in Canada* (Toronto: Methuen, 1980), and Conrad Winn and J. McMenemy, *Political Parties in Canada* (Toronto: McGraw-Hill Ryerson, 1976).

18. See Edwin R. Black, *Politics and the News* (Toronto: Butterworths, 1982); Douglas Hartle, *Public Policy, Decision Making and Regulation* (Montreal: Institute for Research on Public Policy, 1979).

PART **II**

THE INTERPLAY APPROACH: IDEAS, STRUCTURE, PROCESS

- Ideas and Canadian Public Policy
- Structure I: Prime Minister and Cabinet
- Structure II: Interest Structures and Policy Communities
- Process I: The General Policy Process
- Process II: The Expenditure, Tax, and Regulatory Processes

C H A P T E R *3*

Ideas and Canadian Public Policy

To study Canadian public policy is to inquire into the purposeful nature of democratic political activity or, in other words, its ideas. These ideas both influence and are embedded in the structures and processes of public policy. The student of public policy must grapple therefore with both the "ends" and "means" of political life, recognizing, however, that there is no tidy basis on which to separate ends and means since both are valued and are themselves the object of political dispute.

The central tenet of democratic politics, especially in a cabinet-parliamentary system, is that political parties offer a program of policies to the electorate and that the victor at the polls, expressed in parliamentary seats, possesses a majoritarian mandate to carry out its policies. The assumption is that democratic life is purposeful, a peaceful contest over contending ideas, preferences, and objectives. The assumption is that political power or the gaining of political office is a means to carry out policies, not that policies are a means to gain office.

In this chapter we examine the role of ideas in two ways. In the first part we begin by differentiating ideologies from other dominant ideas and from narrower objectives. In the second part we look at how the core ideas of major institutions directly affect policy formulation, especially the processes of policy-making.

In examining any public policy field or public policy in general it is essential to differentiate four different levels of purposeful activity and thought: ideologies, dominant ideas, paradigms, and objectives. This typology begins at the most general level with ideologies and ends with more specific objectives. It is evident that the boundaries between the levels can be only approximate. The purpose of the typology is to show why each is important to look for when analyzing any policy field in order to understand the evolution or drift of a policy field over a long period of time. What are the central ideas in the policy field in question? Where do they conflict and how have these ideas changed, if at all? In respect of all policy fields, how and why do some ideas and proposals gain acceptance and stay on the public priority list of governments while others do not get there at all, or emerge only for a brief period of time?

Ideologies

Ideologies encompass the broadest level of the typology. An ideology is an umbrella of belief and action that helps provide political and social identity to its adherents and that serves to integrate and coordinate their views and actions on a wide range of political issues. Given the inherent breadth and nature of ideologies and their role in determining views about the role of the state, it should not be surprising that they evoke contentious debate about power and control in society. Critics on the political left, for example, often regard liberal ideology as an instrument of class control designed to mystify and distort reality. The political right often regards socialism in a similar vein.[1] We equate ideologies with the broad "isms" of Canadian political life: liberalism, conservatism, and socialism. We reserve our discussion of nationalism to later parts of the chapter where we treat it as a dominant territorial and spatial idea that cuts across all the left–right political ideologies in the same way that regionalism does.

Liberalism encompasses a belief in the central role of the individual in a free society. Rooted in a defence of private property and a free market capitalist economy, 20th-century liberalism has also sought to smooth over the rough edges of capitalism through moderate amounts of government intervention, including measures to ensure the sharing and redistribution of wealth to the disadvantaged. In addition, liberalism encompasses a belief in scientific and technological progress. In relation to the role of the state, liberalism has often implied that the state plays a benevolent reformist referee-like role, balancing the ideas and power of contending interests in an even-handed way.

Conservatism, as the name implies, encompasses a belief in the need to preserve valued and proven traditions and hence places the burden of proof on those who advocate change. Despite a strong contemporary belief in the market (which is, in reality, a 19th-century liberal view) and an adherence to minimum government intervention, progressive conservatism also suggests a belief in an organic paternal view of society, of the need for the state and the community to care for those who cannot care for themselves.

Socialism rests on a class analysis of society and posits a collective view of society and a de-emphasis of individualism. It favours much more government intervention, particularly to achieve a significant amount of redistribution of both wealth and power to disadvantaged classes and groups. Accordingly, it sees less to defend in the status quo and is more disposed to see rapid change. While seeing the need for a socialist state that will redistribute income, the socialist view is ambivalent about centralized power. Power must be concentrated to achieve redistribution in a capitalist society, but at the same time there is a fear among social democrats about the possible bureaucratization of that power.

A capsule summary of the ideologies obviously does not capture all of the beliefs, partial contradictions, and nuances present in them. Moreover, as reflected historically in the positions of Canadian political parties, there has been a cumulative adoption or at least acceptance of major parts of one ideology by another. For example, the New Democratic Party supported an entrenched Charter of Rights in the Canadian constitution. The Liberals' dominance in power at the federal level for most of this century has been partly the product of their willingness to borrow and use as their own items ostensibly more at home in a competing ideology (for example, compulsory medical care).

Equally evident has been the presence of ideological mixtures *within* each of the major political parties. The nomenclature is both familiar and seemingly endless. The mixtures include red Tories, right-wing Socialists, social democrats, left-wing Liberals, the "radical centre," prairie populists, etc. These mixtures are even more difficult to interpret when they are combined with, or opposed by, regional variations within a political party and in the country as a whole. Prairie populism, for example, combined both a regional grievance and an agrarian class-based criticism of eastern capitalism. It has arisen both in the form of so-called third parties such as the Progressives, the Social Credit Party, and the Reform Party and as a movement within the Progressive Conservative Party.

It has often been argued that the crazy-quilt ideological mixtures of Canada's political parties, coupled with regionalism and the technological complexity of modern decisions, has brought with it the end of ideology. It is even argued that "middle of the road" liberalism is nonideological and pragmatic. The "ideologues," it is often suggested, are only on the extreme left or right of the political spectrum. Both of these strands of the "end of ideology" argument are highly questionable.

Ideologies remain an important element of political life not because ideologies "cause" or automatically lead to policy preferences and action by governments in power, but because ideologies can help foreclose certain policy options or reduce levels of commitment to particular courses of action and to particular ideas. They can help screen out ideas that are unacceptable or that will only be used as a last resort. Canada's political parties do coalesce roughly around different portions of the ideological spectrum. Because of this, they frequently advocate different policies, and they judge the policies of others according to different criteria. The presence of these ideologies in varying minority or majority concentrations *within* the major political parties is also of critical importance since, as beliefs, they represent a test against which policies to act, or not to act, are evaluated. They also affect party leadership strategies and coalitions both within and among parties since leaders must often appeal to, or react against, the presence of these basic ideologies both among their own supporters and among voters or interests whose support they would like to attract.

Perhaps the worst aspect of the view that ideologies no longer matter is that it quickly leads to the bland and blanket assertion that policies are made on pragmatic grounds. Pragmatism implies an idealess political world. Nothing could be further from the truth nor do more to dull one's analytical senses.

Dominant Ideas

We refer to the second level of purposeful activity as dominant ideas. While obviously related to the larger ideologies, these ideas often have a separate force of their own in that, rather than being always grouped or combined into a larger ideological view, the ideas may be combined or used to embody a particular preference in a given policy field. Several ideas of this magnitude exist. These include:

- efficiency;
- individual liberty;
- stability (of income and of other desired conditions);
- redistribution and equality;
- equity;
- national identity, unity, and integration; and
- regional diversity and sensitivity.

Their importance arises from the fact that any one or all of them can be part of the agenda of a particular policy field regardless of how they are defined by governments or even in the statutes that create them. They are also one of the main ways in which some common ground can be provided among diverse policy fields, from tariff policy to police and corrections policy.

Efficiency is an enduring market-based idea that places a high value on the realization of a goal at the least cost, with costs measured both absolutely and in terms of opportunity costs (alternatives foregone).[2] It is an idea rooted in the very notion of a free market where capitalists maximize wealth by mobilizing the factors of production, capital, land, knowledge, and labour to produce optimum returns. It is an idea that places a premium on change, particularly for those whose lives are "mobilized" to produce the desired goal.

Individual liberty is rooted in more than just economic freedom in that it embraces religious and other freedoms as well. Individualism implies a belief in the social value of self-interest and self-development. An entrenched Charter of Rights suggests in formal terms a belief that the purpose of the state is to serve the individual and not vice versa. While efficiency and individualism are important ideas, we have stressed in Chapter 2 that Canadians have not embraced them as enthusiastically as have Americans.

Stability of income (and of other desired conditions) over time is an idea that places a high value on predictability and reliability, the opposite of change. As an idea, it takes many forms. It can take the form of a general appeal for order and continuity in social relations such as in the call for law and order, energy security, strong defence forces, or the right to live and work in one's home region, near family and friends. It can show up in demands to protect income, as many agricultural commodity producers have achieved, to smooth out the uncertainties of income caused by the vagaries of climate and foreign markets.

Redistribution and equality is an idea that places the highest preference on the need to redistribute income and power from the rich and powerful to the poor and politically weak. It may imply a concept of absolute equality and a sharing of property, but at the very least it endorses the need for a significant reduction in the gap between rich and poor. One may be tempted to think that this is what social policy should be about. We see in later chapters that social policy embraces far more than the idea of redistribution and equality.

The concept of equity, reinforced by ideas about the rule of law and equality before the law, simultaneously enjoins policy-makers to treat people in equivalent situations equally, *and* to treat people who are not in equivalent situations unequally (that is, be fair and reasonable). Equity, in a broad sense, forms a consistent philosophical and democratic concept. In practice, however, its component injunctions often conflict. When formulating policy, decision-makers frequently have to "treat people equally" and "treat people unequally" within the framework of the same policy or program. This is because the practical physical situations of the object of the policy (a business, a person, a province, or a region) are rarely uniform or homogeneous. These ideas are present in issues of pay and employment equity; devising environmental, drug, and health and safety policies and regulations; developing and implementing welfare policies; devising tax policies; and allocating industrial subsidies and grants.

National unity and nationalism is an idea that flows from the territorial imperatives of politics, including foreign policy needs, sovereignty, and international relations. It places the highest value on decisions that enhance the identity of individuals and groups within Canada as a whole, its traditions, symbols, institutions, and collective memory. Nationalism may also be the dominant concern of territorially concentrated religious, cultural, and linguistic minorities such as French Canadians in the province of Quebec and therefore easily embraces the possibility or the threat of separatism. Many, of course, would place nationalism alongside the ideologies discussed above. National unity as an idea is thus linked to national independence and hence to foreign policy, but it may also be based on policies against domestic threats such as provincial governments or other narrower interpretations of the collective political will.

The converse of national unity is the idea of regional diversity and sensitivity. It is an idea rooted in a spatial or territorial view of policy, whether the region is defined as a province, the North, or the Gaspé. The idea of regionalism pervades Canadian politics and affects the very definition, as well as the administrative delivery, of many public policies.[3]

One could think of the foregoing ideas in many ways. For example, one could visualize them separately corresponding to single voters, each with one of these preferences. Alternatively, one could imagine a government comprising separate departments headed by ministers in charge of these ideas (a Minister of Efficiency, a Minister of Redistribution, etc.). Or one could envision separate political parties formed to appeal to voters who have each of these preferences. One could go on to construct an even more complex and realistic model of the public policy system. The points we wish to stress would be the same. To understand public policy one has to appreciate the enduring existence of several dominant ideas. These ideas influence political debate and the "evaluation" of public policy *regardless* of the particular preferences stated in the legislation or the ministerial speech accompanying the particular policy or decision. These ideas are each desirable. They also often totally or partially contradict each other (efficiency versus regional sensitivity, or redistribution versus stability of income).

The constant need to rank, balance, or otherwise deal with the relations and contradictions among dominant ideas is a central aspect of public policy. It is indeed the feature that puts the "politics" in public policy. The public policy system must not only continuously rank them, but actually allocate scarce resources among them in a manner that gives meaning to these ideas.

Ideas and Paradigms

In addition to the above, the student of public policy should be aware of the existence of another level of policy ideas. Manzer has referred to these as paradigms.[4] Policy paradigms tend to be somewhat more associated with a particular policy field. In some policy fields there may be one obvious dominant paradigm, while in others the field may be occupied by a dominant and a contending paradigm.

A well-developed paradigm provides a series of principles or assumptions that guide action and suggest solutions within a given policy field. Paradigms can become entrenched and thus change very slowly because they become tied to the education and socialization of professionals or experts and perhaps of the larger public as well. Thus, Keynesian economics was the dominant paradigm for macroeconomic policy-makers from the 1940s to the early 1970s. Since then, monetarism has emerged to challenge it. Similarly, health-care policy is said to be dominated by a "curative" approach (helping those who are already sick) and is doctor-dominated. Some advocate a more "preventative" approach that would prevent illness before it occurs. Since this would relate to broader lifestyles and environmental concerns, it would be less doctor-oriented.

Somewhat like the broader ideologies, policy paradigms often screen out policy options. They may help to explain why some policies do not change or change very slowly. They also alert us to the role of professional experts who have power partly because they are the successful purveyors of the dominant paradigm. Within the confines of a policy field the student of policy formulation should look for, and be aware of, the existence of such paradigms. For example, industrial policy formulation has always been influenced by contending paradigms, albeit not all as congealed or well formulated as the Keynesian macroeconomic policy paradigm was. Thus, industrial policy has been influenced by concerns about a "resources first" approach as opposed to an approach that focused on manufacturing and industry. In the field of labour market policies, "manpower" needs can be and have been viewed through either an "education" paradigm or a "training" paradigm.

It will be obvious that by defining a policy paradigm primarily in terms of it being confined to a single policy field we are being somewhat arbitrary, especially because the boundaries between policy fields are themselves not watertight. Paradigms can also be linked to ideologies and to the dominant ideas discussed above. For example, Keynesianism is viewed by many to be a policy prescription necessary to justify state intervention to help maintain a capitalist market economy, as well as to stabilize economic activity.

Specific Objectives

The fourth level of purposeful activity is, in a sense, a residual category, but not an unimportant one. We refer to it simply as "specific objectives." It includes the more specific purposes that may be debated or be in dispute within a policy field. The periodic enunciation of objectives also reflects the existence of specific structures and organizations in the public policy system. Thus, economic policy may be concerned with holding inflation to a particular rate of increase, or achieving a specific decrease in the level of unemployment. In energy policy the specific objectives may be over how much conversion from oil to gas or electricity is desirable and possible in different regions of the country.

We have set out the above four-part typology precisely to disabuse the reader of the simplistic assumption that one can understand public policy and can even later evaluate policies if one can only find out what the "objectives" are.[5] We suggest that the study of public policy must begin with an appreciation of the broader levels of democratic political life. It does not begin with a search for "objectives" only. The four levels we have identified in this section should be the first four items in one's mental checklist as the study of public policy formulation is carried out.

Institutions, Ideas, and the Policy Process

Public policy both shapes and is influenced by institutions and the ideas that give these institutions life. Because of this central fact, our four-level typology is not in itself a sufficient inventory of ideas. A focus on the connection between ideas and institutions deserves emphasis because it sensitizes us to a further array of ideas that deal with the policy process. This section therefore highlights selected *process* implications of the ideas that emanate from some of the major institutions introduced in Chapter 2. We exclude here only the role of interest groups in policy-making, which is examined in Chapter 5, and the Cabinet and bureaucracy, which are the subjects of Chapters 4 and 10. Our treatment of these major institutions is illustrative and is intended only to highlight some selected attributes of each institutional idea that are particularly important in understanding the policy process.

Capitalism, Debate, and Intervention

Two attributes of capitalism as an idea and as a system of economic production are especially important in relation to policy formulation. The first is the influence capitalism has in blurring and de-emphasizing the issue of redistribution and inequality in Canadian political life and public debate. The second attribute is the selective views held by business interests about what constitutes government intervention.

It is argued by many that business interests have succeeded in having Canadian political issues viewed through the dominant idea of regional conflict and national integration, and/or French–English relations. Thus, redistribution as a dominant political idea has had to take a secondary role in the definition and evolution of economic and social policy. A number of writers since the mid-1960s in particular have pointed out the capacity of capitalist interests to "distort" political debate in this way. They argue that business interests have succeeded by securing the support of both the major political parties through financing elections and leadership expenses and also through media ownership.[6] John Porter bemoaned the dominance of "brokerage" politics, the name he gave to regional politics and piecemeal accommodation.[7] Brodie and Jenson stress the historical capacity of the major parties to define what is political and to exclude a class interpretation of policy issues.[8]

We have already stressed above that redistribution is one of a handful of dominant ideas that pervade Canadian political debate. The question is whether the blurring of redistributive issues is a "distortion" of how Canada's politics does and *should* occur. There is clearly no "technical" answer to this question. Answers are rooted in the ideas various segments of the political system have and how they use them to interpret evidence or history. Defenders of liberal capitalism avowedly place a higher value on individual freedom and on efficiency than they do on equality, especially equality as expressed in income levels. The approach used in this book suggests that several dominant ideas do govern political life in Canada. Accordingly, it is evident that capitalism helps explain why redistribution is only one of these dominant concerns. We are therefore less inclined to argue that this distorts political life, since it is clear that the other dominant ideas have real as opposed to "distorted" roots in Canada's political history and political institutions.

A second attribute of capitalism and its core ideas is the issue of government intervention. We discuss this issue in Chapters 7, 11, and 12 when we review the growth of government and the role of governing instruments. It is important to stress at the outset, however, the degree of selectivity that exists when the business community engages in political debate as opposed to actual political behaviour. Therefore, the general "ideology" of business is to oppose intervention and to urge that the free market be allowed to flourish. There can be little doubt that this is a genuine article of belief for the business community in general. This does not prevent particular segments of business, because of their particular stake in the competitive struggle at particular points in time, from wanting to secure favours or protection from the state to stabilize or augment their incomes. When capital is mobilized, some segments of capital often lose and seek protection. Businesses covet stability of income over time as much as anyone else. If governments respond favourably, these actions will rarely be called "interventions" by business interests or by the individual business corporations involved. Rather, they will be referred to as "incentives" or, even more generally, as action that will create a stable "climate for investment."

The business community rarely wants untrammelled free enterprise. It prefers a controlled form of entrepreneurial climate—in short, the provision of a high degree of certainty by the state so that "risks" can be taken. The relations between business and government are thus at one and the same time both simple and complex, monolithic and heterogeneous, consistent and contradictory. They flow from the contradictory relations between capitalism, its modern business interest groups, and liberal democracy.

Capitalism also raises important issues about the labour movement and trade unions and about how they are visualized in the policy process. The majority of workers in Canada are not members of unions. In Chapter 5 we focus on labour unions, including their major federation, the Canadian Labour Congress (CLC), seemingly as if they were an ordinary interest group. Is labour then a class? The class-corporatist approach and a socialist view of politics would invite such a conclusion. But how then does one deal with divisions within the labour movement, with the CLC's own ambivalence about government intervention, and with the fact that most union members do not vote for the New Democratic Party? Can all or most of the evident lack of class cohesion be due to "distortion" propagated by liberal capitalist ideologies? These are questions to which we will return.

Federalism: Bilateral versus Multilateral Processes

Federalism institutionalizes the idea of regional diversity within the confines of a larger political union. Federal–provincial relations have evolved through several phases, the most recent of which have combined elements of executive and "province-building" federalism.[9] Executive federalism is characterized by the bargaining of ministers and officials behind closed doors in numerous conferences of the eleven governments. There can be little doubt that post–World War II federalism of the bureaucratic executive kind is different than federalism of earlier eras when governments functioned somewhat more independently and less interdependently. Federal–provincial relations are a dominant element of Ottawa's policy process both because of the interdependent effect of each level of government's decisions and because of the competition, partisan and otherwise, for citizen loyalty and the acquisition of political credit.

"Province-building" refers to the pronounced expansionist tendencies by major provincial governments since the mid-1960s to construct an elaborate state apparatus, including sophisticated bureaucracies, state enterprises, and legislative controls to protect and manage regional and provincial economies and to guard themselves against Ottawa's incursions. Despite the "province-building" realities, however, there has been a tendency in the general model of executive federalism to characterize the intergovernmental policy process as a general diplomacy and/or bargaining process between the federal government and "the provinces." The more one relates province-building to what is now known about particular policy fields, the less useful is the general bargaining notion of executive federalism. This is not to suggest that general bargaining aspects (such as the funding of established social programs) are not crucial in understanding public policy. Rather, we are suggesting that this view does not adequately allow us to understand either the *bilateral* (for example, Alberta–federal or Quebec–Ottawa) and multilateral (for example, federal–Maritime provinces) bargains that are struck or the particular effects of federal policies on particular provincial settings.

Provinces have to be treated equally, but yet everyone knows that each is different and that policy circumstances are different in different policy fields. But the need for bilateral bargaining and sometimes stalemating activity arises from more than just the dichotomy inherent in the idea of justice and equity. It is also a product of the different economies, market dependencies, and interests in each province, and the different partisan relations and political party configurations in each province vis-à-vis Ottawa. At times it is also a product of overt and deliberate strategy on the part of the federal government to "divide and conquer," so to speak—to play one province off against another. An even broader version of this strategy emerged in the early 1980s when the Trudeau government, bemoaning its lack of political credit and identity and attacking the Clark government's view of Canada as a decentralized "community of communities," sought to redirect some of its policies so as to increase the *direct* contact of Canadians with the federal government, rather than *through* the provinces.

All of the above also suggests that ongoing ideas of centralization and decentralization are inherent in federalism, but that they cannot be interpreted merely as aggregate swings of the federal–provincial pendulum. What centralization and decentralization mean can be truly understood only in the context of bilateral relations between Ottawa and particular provinces in specific policy fields.

Parliament and Alternative Priority Agendas

In Chapter 2 we stressed the tendency of many commentators to regard Parliament's policy role as marginal, even though the idea of majoritarian responsible government is the central idea of this institution. This view is understandable in a certain context since the constitutional powers of the executive are dominant. Moreover, numerous studies have shown the litany of weaknesses in the role of Parliament as a crucial link in the accountability of government, especially financial accountability.[10] These general views seriously underestimate other attributes of Parliament's role in policy formulation that arise less out of the things Parliament *does* than out of the fact that Parliament is simply *there*. Two attributes deserve emphasis: the government's tactical and political need to consider in advance the substantive views, priorities, and tactics of the opposition political parties in Parliament—a form of policy evaluation "by anticipation"; and the relationship between tough political partisan criticism and more formal policy and program evaluation.

The art of anticipating the opposition political parties in Parliament is a central feature of the policy process for any government. At a general level, priorities are forged in the context of what other contenders are proposing. We see this in Chapter 9 when we review past priorities expressed through throne speeches and budget speeches. The priority-setting process undoubtedly involves a constant search for the broad centre of political life, for the consensus that will hold a majority or win one at the next election. Parliament (and the coverage of it by the media) is the main stage on which this ultimate political theatre is presented. Its importance in policy formulation cannot be underestimated.

A practical example of Parliament's role in this anticipatory sense is found in the relationship between legislative priorities and general priorities. There are often fewer obstacles to a policy decision if it does not require new legislation, but can be carried out under an existing statute. Where new legislation is required even for an item that is a high priority for the government, it may receive a lower priority ranking *in legislative terms* because of the issues of timing and the expected parliamentary tactics and priorities of the opposition parties. In this sense priorities are influenced by the mood of the country as reflected in, and judged by, the House of Commons.

Parliament is first and foremost a place of aggressive adversarial partisanship and party discipline. The rigid rules regarding "want of confidence" ensure that partisanship is rampant. This is both a strength and a weakness. It allows more or less stable governments to be formed and criticized, but it also produces a frequently stultifying debate, where political truth is often the first victim. The partisanship of the House of Commons makes it particularly difficult for the government and opposition parties alike to acknowledge errors or to change when change is probably desirable.

The twin issues, anticipating the opposition and the partisan nature of debate, raise important questions about how policies and programs are and should be evaluated. The partisan cut and thrust of debate is viewed by rationalists as a messy and unsophisticated form of evaluation. Indeed, professional program evaluators would not regard it as "evaluation" at all. In their view it lacks the controlled cerebral quality of objective thought. While there is no doubt that the parliamentary struggle is often not ideal, it is by far the best democratic forum we possess for reflecting the broad ideas and preferences of Canadians. This is the ultimate form of rough-and-ready evaluation for which we have found no adequate substitutes.

The Mass Media: Perceptions and Reality

It has been glibly asserted that Ottawa practises "government by *Globe and Mail*"! While this is happily yet another example of Ottawa hyperbole, the media's role is very important in politics and policy-making. In Chapter 2 we focused on the core idea of a "free press" and on several features of the media's influence. Here we highlight two elements of the media's role in the policy process, both of which flow from this idea. These elements are its influence in causing politicians to respond to *perceptions* as opposed to reality, and its influence in communicating policy information, the weaknesses of which have led governments, political parties, and interests into the use of advocacy advertising to market or sell their policies.

The media help fuel the increased pace of demands on government and contribute through persistent criticism to a climate where it is often next to impossible for a politician "to be seen" doing nothing. Given the inevitability of scarce resources (money, time, expertise, etc.), this has helped lead to an increasing tendency to devise policies "for show" rather than "for real." Thus, governments have had to devise an elaborate array of ways in which they can express symbolic concern (studies, announcements, royal commissions, inquiries, conferences, reorganizations). The choice the politician often faces, at a minimum, is to "do something" or "do nothing." The latter choice is less and less viable in an era of intensive media scrutiny, since the politician is expected to at least show concern even though he or she cannot always respond in other more concrete ways through actual expenditure or regulatory programs.

There has been, of course, a reaction to this important policy phenomenon. It has resulted in a growing cynicism about government's capacity to solve real problems. It is one among many factors that has led small "c" conservatives to advocate less government and to assert that governments cannot solve all or even most of society's problems. It has also shortened the time frame of decision-making, forcing private decision-makers to play the same game as they postpone decisions to wait for a more favourable "priority" change from government, six or twelve months in the future.

Of particular importance to the policy formulation process is the impact of the media-induced "perception versus reality" issue on the communication of policy. In Chapter 13 we show how information, knowledge, and analysis interact in the policy process, but it is essential in this review of major institutions to link the marketing of public policy to the perception versus reality issue. Increasingly, government, opposition parties, and interests groups have become more and more distrustful of the media to impart "objective" information about leaders, programs, and positions. They are spending vastly increased sums on advocacy advertising to reach "the people" in a direct way.

It is evident that there are no easy answers to the above issues. There has always been and will always be a difficult tension between "freedom of the press" and the right and duty of a government to inform the public and carry out its policies, in short, between "information" and "propaganda," and there is clearly a fine and debatable line between what is reality and what is perception as viewed by different interests, regions, and classes.

Conclusions

Our two-step survey of the role of ideas in public policy, one focusing on four levels of policy content and the other on institutional ideas that influence the policy process, has been presented to help develop an appreciation of the complexity and the persuasiveness of the purposeful nature of Canadian public policy. This need to rigorously appreciate and dissect ideas is important because of the tendency to describe all policy as being remorselessly pragmatic. The policy process does involve the need for pragmatic balance, but it is not done without ideas. The evaluation of policy cannot proceed by blissfully focusing on one or two "objectives" without reference to the interdependence of ideas and the historical drift or evolution of these ideas.

Notes

1. See W. Christian and C. Campbell, *Political Parties and Ideologies in Canada*, 2nd ed. (Toronto: McGraw-Hill Ryerson, 1983); Denis Monière, *Ideologies in Quebec* (Toronto: University of Toronto Press, 1981). See also M. J. Brodie and Jane Jenson, *Crisis, Challenge and Change: Party and Class in Canada* (Toronto: Methuen, 1980); and Conrad Winn and J. McMenemy, *Political Parties in Canada* (Toronto: McGraw-Hill Ryerson, 1976).

2. See, for example, Richard B. McKenzie and Gordon Tullock, *Modern Political Economy: An Introduction to Economics* (New York: McGraw-Hill, 1978), chs. 1 and 2.

3. See Richard Simeon, "Regionalism and Canadian Political Institutions," *Queen's Quarterly* 82 (Winter 1975); Donald V. Smiley, *Canada in Question*, 3rd ed. (Toronto: McGraw-Hill Ryerson, 1980); Canada West Foundation, *Regional Representation* (Calgary: Canada West Foundation, 1981); David J. Elkins and Richard Simeon, *Small Worlds* (Toronto: Methuen, 1980).

4. Ronald Manzer, "Public Policies in Canada: A Development Perspective," paper presented to the Canadian Political Science Association, Edmonton, June 1975. See also Ronald Manzer, "Social Policy and Political Paradigms," *Canadian Public Administration* 24, no. 4 (Winter 1981), 641–48.

5. See Royal Commission on Financial Management and Accountability, *Final Report* (Ottawa: Minister of Supply and Services, 1979), ch. 9. For a critique of the management by objectives concept, see Aaron Wildavsky, *Speaking Truth to Power* (Boston: Little, Brown, 1979), ch. 9.

6. Brodie and Jenson, *Crisis, Challenge and Change*, ch. 1.

7. John Porter, *The Vertical Mosaic* (Toronto: University of Toronto Press, 1965), ch. 12.

8. Brodie and Jenson, *Crisis, Challenge and Change*.

9. See Smiley, *Canada in Question*, ch. 4; Edwin R. Black, *Divided Loyalties* (Montreal: McGill-Queen's University Press, 1975); John Richards and Larry Pratt, *Prairie Capitalism* (Toronto: McClelland and Stewart, 1979); Richard Simeon and David J. Elkin, "Regional Political Cultures in Canada," *Canadian Journal of Political Science* 3 (September 1974), 397–437; and Alan Cairns, "The Governments and Societies of Canadian Federalism," *Canadian Journal of Political Science* 10, 695–725.

10. See Royal Commission on Financial Management and Accountability, chs. 1, 2, and 3; and T. d'Aquino, G. Bruce Doern, and C. Blair, *Parliamentary Government in Canada: A Critical Assessment and Suggestions for Change* (Ottawa: Intercounsel Ltd., 1979).

CHAPTER 4

Structure I: Prime Minister and Cabinet

The second element of the Canadian policy system is structure. Structure refers to an array of organizations by which and through which policy is made and influenced. In this chapter the focus is on the prime minister and Cabinet and on the central agencies that support the political executive. We also look briefly at the role of government departments. In Chapter 5, we explore further structural elements in the form of interest group organizations, provincial government interests, and the policy communities that link them to the political executive.

To enter the executive arena of political life is to enter a world where the men and women involved, as often as not, view themselves as being "caught in the middle" rather than as persons sitting confidently "on top" with a clear, focused eye on the future. They are powerful in a hierarchical sense in that they occupy the highest rungs of the political and bureaucratic ladder. But they are often less than powerful in the sense of their individual or collective capacity to persuade, cajole, or even require Canadians to change their behaviour in response to the policy cues given. Ministers and senior bureaucrats are at the receiving end of much data and information, written and verbal, numerate and judgmental, but they frequently lack knowledge

not only about what to do in the future, but also on how they have
fared in the past. They must try to pursue a consistent course of action
into a future that often refuses to cooperate and in the context of a
series of policy contradictions, interdependent ideas, and scarce resources, including time.

The executive structures have also been the object of growing
political dispute about their growth and power. There has been a
visible and increased concern about the aggrandizement of prime
ministerial power, about the unwieldiness of a large Cabinet, and
about the degree to which central agencies, their bureaucrats, and
other senior mandarins in general are held accountable both to ministers and to the broader array of political institutions, especially
Parliament.[1]

The Prime Minister and the Cabinet

The prime minister and the Cabinet are the critical centre of the policy
process.[2] They are, in constitutional theory, collectively responsible
to an elected Parliament for new policy and for ongoing policies and
programs as well. The cabinet-parliamentary system requires ministers to be both individually and collectively responsible for policy.
Although the collective nature of the Cabinet is important, there are
obviously inequalities of power among ministers and the organizations they head. This fact is always recognized with respect to the pre-
eminent role of the prime minister, but it is less often recognized when
considering other characteristics of cabinet government.

A prime minister's dominant policy role flows from political
power, which in turn is derived from his or her position as the elected
head of a political party that has majority support in the House of
Commons. From this the prime minister derives power over Cabinet
colleagues, namely the power to seek dissolution of Parliament at any
time of his or her choosing and the power to hire and fire ministers.
The prime minister also has the power to appoint officials by order-in-
council at the deputy ministerial level, as well as their equivalents in
the many other agencies and boards. The analysis of prime ministerial
policy preferences in Chapter 8 shows how these and other power
"assets" must be invested and wielded with great care. Prime ministers, in dealing with both Cabinet colleagues and policy issues, cannot
recklessly "spend" their assets. Hence, they rarely win every battle or
have their way on every issue, preferring to concentrate their investments on strategically important items.

The Collective Role of the Cabinet

The Canadian Cabinet is a collective decision-making body in which ministers are both collectively responsible to Parliament for general government policy and individually responsible for their own Cabinet portfolios and departmental programs. While the position of prime minister is obviously pre-eminent, there are strong norms of collective responsibility and hence of the importance of some rough, formal equality of all ministers in the Cabinet. In the Canadian context the imperatives of collectivity are reinforced not only by the growing complexity of government decision-making, but also by the fact that the Canadian Cabinet is more than just a decision-making body.

The Canadian Cabinet is also a representative or legitimating institution, notwithstanding the existence of Parliament, in that it is judged not only on what it does, but on what it appears to do.[3] The Cabinet has always had not only to represent, but to appear to represent, the diverse regional and ethnic components of the Canadian population. Successive governments have not always been able to actually achieve the optimum representation, but most have been required to make a serious attempt.[4] While it is clear in our later analysis that the prime minister and some ministers and portfolios are obviously more influential than others, it is important to stress at the outset the continuing strength of collective norms in Canadian Cabinet organization and behaviour. These norms are visibly tested and reasserted precisely when, as in recent years, attempts are made to create an inner Cabinet or structure "inner" groups of decision-makers such as in the Cabinet Committee on Priorities and Planning, or "inner" groups of advisers such as those in the Prime Minister's Office.

The norms and traditions of collective Cabinet responsibility and solidarity also influence policy-making through the strong strictures regarding secrecy and confidentiality in intra-Cabinet and intra-bureaucratic decision-making processes. Ministers vigorously debate policy in confidence in Cabinet, but are expected to defend all policies in a united way. The dispersal of influence and responsibility among ministers is also a function of the related constitutional practice in parliamentary systems of assigning responsibility for legislation and programs to individual ministers and departments in order to facilitate parliamentary accountability. The assignment of individual responsibility is also a function of the sheer complexity of government and of the need to delegate functions to ministers and departments on administrative and technical grounds. The constitutional principles and administrative necessities that generate individual ministerial authority and delegation reinforce the collective nature of the Cabinet in the broad sense of dispersing influence. At the same time they create the need for some inner group to coordinate the leviathan. Thus, the ideas of decentralization and centralization are in constant tension because both are necessary to manage the government. Ministers (and their deputies) are pulled in two directions at once by their constitutional role—vertically in their line departmental roles where they are individually responsible for policy and decisions, and horizontally in their duties and obligations to all ministers to support government policy on a collective basis.

In recent years many changes have been made to formal Cabinet organization and policy processes.[5] These are examined in detail in Chapter 11. In particular, we focus on the Cabinet committees and their role in resource allocation. While the structure of committees is presented in Figure 4.1, it is essential to stress at this stage of our analysis the practical difficulty of putting policy into watertight compartments. Spillovers abound in the committee process as, for example, when social and economic programs interact or when energy and foreign policies partly conflict. Once again it must be emphasized that this is because the dominant ideas of political life enter the deliberations of all policy committees.

Three others features of Cabinet committees are essential to note at the outset. First, ministers are members of more than one committee, and thus some policy coordination occurs through this fact alone. But the degree of policy integration that occurs through multiple membership on committees must be qualified by recognizing the time demands that committee work places on ministers and by recognizing the widely varying degrees of interest and preparation by individual ministers. Second, there is always tension between Cabinet committees and similar committees at the deputy ministerial or senior bureaucratic level. For example, in the late 1960s and early 1970s the Cabinet committees were intended to help give more control to ministers and less to senior officials and, indeed, were explicitly intended to replace some senior official-level interdepartmental committees. Gradually, however, many ministers complained of burdensome committee duties and of their need to get out of Ottawa and into their constituencies across the country. Consequently, by the late 1970s official-level committees began to be created more frequently, and it was not uncommon for senior officials to participate in Cabinet committee meetings in ways that were virtually indistinguishable from their ministerial superiors. When the Mulroney government came to power in 1984, concern increased again about control by the senior bureaucrats.[6] The Conservatives also experimented with a chiefs of staff system. This enabled ministers to hire experienced

FIGURE 4.1 Decision-Making System

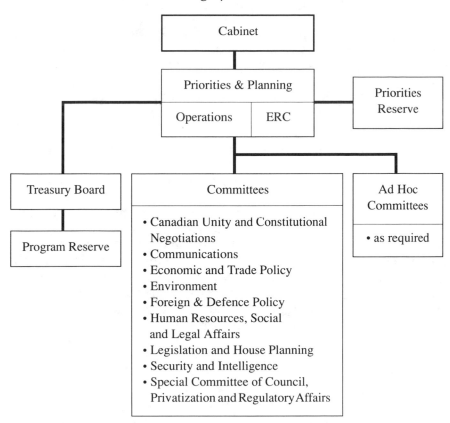

Source: Privy Council Office.

senior advisers of their own to partially counteract the advice of senior bureaucrats.

Finally, it is important to stress that the committee process has resulted in a considerable amount of decentralization of decision-making in that the committees have taken on de facto decision-making roles in areas that in early periods of Canadian cabinet government would have been decided by the full Cabinet. Degrees of centralization and decentralization are, however, difficult to gauge and may also differ among different prime ministers.

Ministerial Skills and Relationships

Central public policy processes ultimately rest on day-to-day, month-to-month relationships between and among individual cabinet ministers (and senior public servants). These include relationships between those who head the major line spending departments, between the Minister of Finance, and the prime minister. They include relationships between various ideological and loyalty groupings within the Cabinet. It is important to explore the general relationships between line ministers and the Finance and Treasury Board ministers in the general expenditure process. During the Mulroney years, the role of Deputy Prime Minister Don Mazankowski also assumed special importance through his chairmanship of the Operations Committee of Cabinet.

Though ministerial influence is affected by the broader sources of aggregate *organizational* and departmental influence, a minister is ultimately judged by what he or she gets done. A minister's reputation as a fighter for his or her department and region, intellectual prowess and popularity among voters, skills as an expenditure combatant and defender of the government in the House of Commons, and the degree to which he or she is informed and prepared in defending proposals in Cabinet are the ultimate determinants of real standing in the Cabinet. While there are many Cabinet and minister watchers in the media and in the bureaucracy, it is ultimately the judgment of his or her Cabinet colleagues that determines the current value of a minister's most precious political currency—his or her reputation. In recent years political credit has more easily accrued through spending (though this has not always been the case and may not be so in periods of expenditure restraint) in that it is the most visible instrument and indicator of political action. This is not to suggest that spending for the sake of spending is the only basic drive. Obviously, spending in the pursuit of certain public policy ideas and objectives is central, but the important value of spending as a governing instrument is that it is an essential grease for the Cabinet wheel.

One should not equate the above point with the notion that reputations as strong ministers are built only by an indiscriminate use of mutual backscratching. The decision process is sufficiently structured and the norms of Cabinet behaviour are sufficiently well ingrained that the successful minister must ultimately demonstrate some qualities of moderation as a team player as well. The size of the Canadian Cabinet alone makes formal alliance-building a difficult process. Many ministers do not know each other well in the sense of strong social or personal friendship. The minister must be constantly conscious of the fact that he or she can only infrequently appeal to the court of final ministerial appeal—the prime minister or to the full Cabinet. Frequent appeals in these forums will be indicative of one's inability to carry the day in other arenas such as before the Treasury Board or before other Cabinet committees.

The dynamics of public policy must also be understood in the relationship between the Minister of Finance and the prime minister. The Minister of Finance and, in the Mulroney years, the deputy prime minister are dependent on the fairly constant backing of the prime minister. Numerous appeals over the heads of both to the prime minister would be intolerable for all ministers. On a reciprocal basis, the prime minister needs the support of strong Finance and Treasury Board ministers to manage the overall fiscal and budgetary policy processes. Thus, there is a considerable political need to leave room in the budgetary and overall resource allocation process for negotiation and trade-offs to occur among several key ministers.

The relationship between the Minister of Finance and the prime minister is obviously one of the most critical in cabinet government. The difficulty of the finance minister's position must be particularly acknowledged by the prime minister.[7] In recent years the special character of this relationship has been formalized by the holding of weekly meetings on the state of the economy. The prime minister and Minister of Finance must also ultimately agree on the critical annual determination and shape of the fiscal framework. Once the basic figures on revenue and on the aggregate sum available for new expenditure—figures largely set by Finance—are determined, there can be only a marginal juggling around them. While relying on the latent and sometimes manifest support of the prime minister, the Minister of Finance's other major weapon is taxation. The outer parameters of the politics of the budgetary and fiscal policy process are set by the argument, frequently advanced by Finance, that either spending must be held down or taxes will have to be increased. This, of course, has always been an important political club. The importance of this political club was especially important in the Mulroney years when there was an unusually long tenure by one minister, Michael Wilson.

Ministers who otherwise may be inclined to challenge fiscal policy, even in the face of the above weapons, are likely to be ultimately dissuaded by the fact that they often possess inadequate information to make a successful challenge. This is not to suggest that they do not offer advice, as politicians, to the Minister of Finance at budget time, but they are fully aware that they cannot ordinarily challenge the minister in the core areas of fiscal and stabilization policy. The specific information gap is reinforced by the broader practice in cabinet government in which ministers are briefed by their political staffs and by their senior bureaucrats, primarily to "defend" their own portfolios rather than to be aggressive critics of other portfolios. This is true despite the fact that individual ministers may know something about other portfolios because of their previous Cabinet assignments or because of their work on Cabinet committees.

Thus, ministers are in part captured and constrained by the same nature of their portfolios and by other political constraints. But within these constraints there is considerable room for individual competence, drive, and ability to be the basis of political power.

It is thus essential to understand these special aspects of the key relations among ministers. It should be stressed, however, that these relations are not the only aspects of Cabinet behaviour that have important consequences. They are merely the ones that emerge when one looks at the central policy organizations. Regional and ethnic representational factors are also vital. Whether it is Don Mazankowski in the Mulroney Cabinet or Allan MacEachen in the Trudeau era, some ministers become virtual regional czars and the main conduit for demands from their region or province.[8] Both historical and journalistic accounts stress, in addition, the importance of personal loyalty by cabinet ministers, both in and out of the previously labelled inner group of ministers, to the prime minister.

Closely related, and often reinforcing such regional and loyalty structures, are ideological structures. Cabinets usually or eventually divide into "liberals" and "conservatives," at least insofar as it becomes possible to discern attitudes toward change. Often these ideological patterns become apparent to Cabinet participants only after a government has been in power for a while and these patterns begin to be clarified and, in part, stereotyped.

Hence, while "functional," "regional," "loyalty," and "ideological" patterns can be abstracted analytically, it is obvious that in general terms, and on any given policy issue (particularly involving a new policy issue), these patterns may be mutually reinforcing or they may be conflicting, or they be a mixture of both. The particular patterns of forces, events, and personalities that affect a particular Cabinet decision on an issue are further complicated by the involvement of the cabinet minister whose departmental "mission" is most directly affected by Cabinet decisions on his or her policy area. The involvement of ministers in policy issues (related to Agriculture, Health and Welfare, and so on) is obviously important in such cases, but these ministers will have a more intermittent policy role in the total scheme of things in comparison with the functional ministers who more often have an opportunity to be involved in all issues by virtue of the functional importance of their roles.

None of the earlier suggestions about the dynamics and subsystems of Cabinet behaviour should be taken to imply that no coordination exists. There are obviously centres of power and regular cycles of behaviour that contribute to the coordination of public policy. We see this in the more detailed look at the priority-setting and resource allocation processes analyzed in Part III.

Central Agencies

The expansion and bureaucratization of the central support agencies of the Cabinet have been influenced by a concern that particularly began to emerge in the mid-1960s about the adequacy of the prime minister's and the Cabinet's ability to plan and to manage the government.[9] By the 1980s the central agency structures had evolved to produce four recognizable central agencies with perhaps one or two others in the "latent" or contending central agency category. The four major central agencies are the:

- Prime Minister's Office (PMO)
- Privy Council Office (PCO)
- Treasury Board Secretariat (TBS)
- Department of Finance

In addition, the Federal–Provincial Relations Office, the Department of the Secretary of State for External Affairs, and the Department of Justice have some reasonable claim to central agency status, arising out of their roles as federal–provincial, foreign policy, and legal advisers, respectively. The mandates of some other ostensible line departments extend horizontally across the entire government, and thus the notion of what constitutes a central agency is not always clear-cut. For example, the Department of the Environment may become a more visible central presence if it is involved in assessing federal policies for their environmental consequences. This should not be surprising in that when one asks what is central one is asking questions about power and about key ideas at the same time. Mercifully, however, we will confine this initial look at central agencies to the four agencies enumerated above.

The roles of the main central-support organizations are important in three respects. First, they have considerable influence as organizations because of their custody over central crosscutting activities of government. Second, they must cooperate with each other because their roles continually overlap. For example, the TBS has responsibility for personnel management, but the PCO has a major role in advising the prime minister on the appointment of senior officials. Finally, the organizations afford great personal influence in the policy process to their bureaucratic heads, the Secretary to the Cabinet, the Principal Secretary to the Prime Minister, the Secretary to the Treasury Board, and the Deputy Minister of Finance.

In a general sense the roles of the PCO, PMO, TBS, and the Department of Finance have always existed. The roles of strategic governmental coordinator, partisan political adviser, general manager, and fiscal-policy adviser are present in government in one form or another. In the 1960s these central agency roles in the government of Canada underwent a transformation in that the roles became more organizationally differentiated, less personalized, more bureaucratic, and more active.[10]

It was precisely because of the differentiation and bureaucratization that the key roles were given more time and capacity and, hence, could be carried out in a more active and aggressive manner. This activeness has undoubtedly made it possible for more aggressive initiatives to emerge from the central agencies. With regard to the PCO and the PMO in particular, there arose renewed concern about both the degree and the legitimacy of the influence of these agencies and their key personalities such as Michael Pitfield in the Trudeau years and Derek Burney in the Mulroney period. They create and foster concern about "super groups" of unelected advisers usurping the legitimate roles of the elected politicians.[11]

Evidence about the exact nature of central agency influence is mixed. An empirical survey of the attitudes and characteristics of central agency officials by Campbell and Szablowski shows that, on the one hand, these officials tend to come from a broader socioeconomic strata of Canadian society than regular line departmental officials.[12] On the other hand, it indicates that they were attracted to the central agencies by an explicitly expressed desire to have and to exercise influence. But this kind of analysis does not necessarily tell us very much about actual decisions since the studies deal only with the perceptions of officials.

What may be just as important as hard "case" study evidence or more general studies about central agency influence are the beliefs or perceptions of such influence. In short, the central agencies are *believed* to have a growing and perhaps disproportionate influence. There is evidence that the governing Liberal Party caucus believed this, especially in relation to the role of the PMO in the 1970–72 period and in the early 1980s.[13] A paper by A.W. Johnson, a senior public servant with both line department and central agency experience, expresses a similar belief. Johnson disguises his verdict under a general veiled discussion of various ways to enhance "creativity" in policy-making, but it is clearly a critique of how Ottawa's coordinators were stalemating the "doers."[14]

The above concerns and beliefs about central agency power are normal and important, but their real import can be easily exaggerated, especially in the long run when one considers the other interplay of forces and ideas reflected in the Cabinet committees and in the regular departments of government. The essence of the central roles is still complementary in nature. The provisions of strategic political advice, including the ideas and priorities of the political system, are fed to the prime minister and Cabinet by the PMO and in part by the PCO (as well as, of course, by a host of other channels of political communication including the minister's staff, the caucus, Parliament, and the press). The PCO tends to be the main source of overall governmental and strategic organizational advice. The PCO provides the basic record-keeping support to the Cabinet and to all the Cabinet committees except the Treasury Board. The PCO ensures that adequate analysis and coordination of policies and policy proposals are carried out. The main source of advice regarding the broad economic and fiscal impact of government activity is the Department of Finance, and the main source of advice on the general expenditure, administrative, and managerial implications of both new and existing programs (and of the relationships between the two) is the Treasury Board and its staff.

Government Departments

Last but not least in this initial survey of executive structures are the main government departments. While a more detailed discussion of departments and other agencies occurs in Chapter 10, they warrant an initial look for several important reasons. The first is to appreciate that the thirty to forty departments (their numbers vary as reorganizations occur) headed directly by cabinet ministers exert a continuous "bottom-up" and horizontal pressure on the policy process. This comes in the form of both demands for new policy, legislation, and resources and also pressures to prevent other departments from obtaining scarce resources or from invading their areas of jurisdiction.

A second reason for the importance of departments is that they are legal entities having assigned custody over various statutes, some with responsibilities for a bare handful of laws and some with as many as eighty statutes. It is of no small import that policy initiatives must usually emanate from the legally responsible minister or that policy discretion within the meaning of a particular statute is assigned to a particular minister and not to others.

A third feature of the underlying departmentalization of government is that departments are also bundles of programs and possessors of their own organizational cultures and traditions in the making and implementation of public policy. Program structures will often overlap many statutory components, thus affecting the ease with which they can be changed or abolished. The professional composition of departmental personnel along with past histories produces the varied cultural traits and attitudes to policy-making. Finance as a department is dominated by economists. The Department of the Environment has been heavily influenced by scientific and technical personnel. The Department of Justice is dominated by lawyers.

Finally, it is essential to stress that departments as bundles of statutes, programs, and traditions have strong obligations and tendencies to preserve the status quo. They are legally bound to uphold and implement current laws and programs until they are changed. They are also bureaucratic entities with all the usual instincts for undesirable self-preservation as well.

Conclusions

An analysis of the basic roles played by the prime minister, the Cabinet, and the central agencies alerts us to the importance and continuing presence of inner centres of Cabinet power. Along with the prime minister's pre-eminent role, there are other cabinet ministers whose influence varies over time. The Canadian Cabinet and the concept of responsible cabinet-parliamentary government pulls ministers in two directions at once, as persons who are both collectively and individually responsible. Cabinet life is reinforced by the need to delegate, to specialize, and to deal with the diverse reality of public policy. The presence of government departments exerts continuous "bottom-up" and horizontal pressure on the policy process.

Notes

1. See G. Bruce Doern and Peter Aucoin, eds., *Public Policy in Canada* (Toronto: Macmillan, 1979), chs. 2 and 3; Richard French, *How Ottawa Decides* (Toronto: James Lorimer, 1980); and A. D. Doerr, *The Machinery of Government in Canada* (Toronto: Methuen, 1981).
2. See Thomas Hockin, ed., *Apex of Power*, 2nd ed. (Toronto: Prentice-Hall, 1977), and W. A. Matheson, *The Prime Minister and the Cabinet* (Toronto: Methuen, 1976).
3. R. Van Loon and M. Wittington, *The Canadian Political System*, 3rd ed. (Toronto: McGraw-Hill Ryerson, 1981), ch. 14.
4. Ibid., ch. 14.
5. See Doern and Aucoin, *Public Policy in Canada*, chs. 2 and 3; Andrew Johnson, "The Structure of the Canadian Cabinet," unpublished Doctoral Thesis, Oxford University, 1980; and Ian Clark, *Recent Changes*

in the Cabinet Decision Making System (Ottawa: Privy Council Office, 1987).

6. See Peter Aucoin, "Organizational Change in the Machinery of Canadian Government: From Rational Management to Brokerage Politics," *Canadian Journal of Political Science* 10, no. 1 (1986), 3–27.

7. See David Good, *The Politics of Anticipation: Making Canadian Federal Tax Policy* (Ottawa: School of Public Administration, 1980); and Douglas Hartle, *The Revenue Budget Process of the Government of Canada* (Toronto: Canadian Tax Foundation, 1982).

8. See Herman Bakvis, "Regional Ministers, National Policy and the Administrative State in Canada," *Canadian Journal of Political Science* 21 (1988), 539–67.

9. See Colin Campbell and George Szablowski, *The Superbureaucrats* (Toronto: Macmillan, 1979); French, *How Ottawa Decides*; Doern and Aucoin, *Public Policy in Canada*, chs. 2 and 3.

10. See Doern and Aucoin, *Public Policy in Canada*, ch. 2.

11. See Campbell and Szablowski, *The Superbureaucrats*, ch. 7.

12. Ibid., chs. 4 and 5.

13. See Christina McCall-Newman, *Grits* (Toronto: Macmillan, 1982), ch. 3; and Richard Gwyn, *The Northern Magus* (Markham, Ont.: Paperjacks, 1980), ch. 5.

14. A. W. Johnson, "Public Policy: Creativity and Bureaucracy," *Canadian Public Administration* 21, no. 1 (Spring 1978), 1–15.

C H A P T E R **5**

Structure II: Interest Structures and Policy Communities

The second part of the structure of Canadian public policy-making consists of interest structures and policy communities. This aspect begins outside the formal contours of the federal state in the literally hundreds of interest structures. These consist mainly of interest groups, but for our purposes we also include provincial governments and their departments in the category of interest structures. Both share the important feature of being organized bureaucracies themselves. Ordinarily the provinces would deserve separate treatment as a part of the federal–provincial policy process. Our inclusion of them here is intended to convey the fact that provincial interests may vary according to the provincial entities actively involved. Moreover, one should not assume that a province, any more than the federal government, arrives at the policy table as a unified entity.

Policy communities are also a structural feature of policy-making, albeit a more diffuse one organizationally. Such communities are a network of public and private entities that have a continuing stake in, and knowledge of, any given policy field or issue. These communities usually consist of the interest structures defined above as well as organizations and experts located in universities, research institutes, international agencies, and private firms. Whether or not governments are actively engaged in a new policy development exercise or process, such policy communities are alert, alive, and attentive.

In the chapter as a whole, we pay particular attention to interest groups. This is the largest element of the system of interest structures. Accordingly, we look in turn at the differences between producer versus public interest or collective rights associations and at the evolution of the macro umbrella associations for business and labour. This is followed by a much briefer look at the provinces as interest structures and finally at the role of policy communities, especially in relation to the ongoing demands for consultation and participation in the policy process.

Interest Groups

Interest groups are an integral part of the democratic policy process reflecting the fundamental idea of the right to associate freely. They range in their spectrum of interests from the Civil Liberties Association to the Canadian Manufacturers Association. Every department of government must deal with a number of such groups. Interest groups compete with political parties, the media, and others "for the privilege of interpreting the public will to key decision makers."[1] They also exist to provide goods and services to their members, as well as to represent the interests of their members to various levels of government. They act as a buffer between the individual and the state. In this chapter we are primarily interested in their role in policy formulation rather than in their internal service roles.

Paul Pross's analysis shows that Canadian interest groups perform two major politically relevant functions—communication and legitimation.[2] In addition, they act to regulate their members and to supplement governmental administration. The communications function includes everything from furnishing technical data to government to the communication of the intensity of the views of its members, which may range from apathy to concern or even anger. Groups also communicate the concerns of policy-makers and officials to their members. The legitimating function relates to the role interest groups play in broadening the base of information and the number of people involved in discussing policy problems. Interest groups are used also by government to test policy ideas, to obtain visible support, and to neutralize extreme opposition. The role of interest groups as formal or informal agents of government is also important. Numerous voluntary organizations provide services that are an essential complement to those supplied by public social service agencies. Some interest groups are given public funding to help them intervene in the policy process. The recognized leading professions such as medicine and law are in a very formal way conferred powers to regulate their members and to make policy decisions.[3]

While there is a mutual dependence in the relationships that develop between interest groups and public policy-makers, there are also a number of practical tensions and concerns. The first rests on the danger perceived by interest groups that they will be co-opted by governments, contrary to their own interests. Labour federations have been especially concerned about both the substance and the appearance of co-optation in wage control programs by government and business.[4] Unions are pulled in two directions by the pressure to cooperate and to maintain social peace, and by a knowledge that they will become an instrument of the state to enforce wage restraint. Labour federations have been somewhat ambivalent because of the normal desire of any group and its leaders to have influence on, and to be consulted by, other power centres in Canadian society. At the same time they must deal with these power centres from a position of strength, and hence a premium is placed on the appearance of solidarity and the need for a common front.

Interest groups, moreover, do not necessarily see the ideas that concern them as being properly handled even though they may have regular or even cordial relations with "their" department. They are cognizant of the complexity of government and of the fact that they must interact at both the federal and provincial levels with several ministers and officials, including the burgeoning central agencies. Relations between the interest group and the department are rarely of a simple one-to-one kind. They change as policy fields change and are redefined. For example, for several decades agricultural policy was essentially synonymous with farm policy. In the 1990s it is aligned with a broader concept of food policy. The latter embraces a larger number of interest groups, including food retailers and distributors as well as farm producers.[5]

Producer versus Collective Rights Associations

An essential first task is to distinguish between producer interest groups and broader collective rights associations. The former include business, agricultural producers, and professions such as law and medicine. The latter are often referred to as public interest groups and include groups that coalesce around broader nonproducer definitions of a group. These include labour unions, consumer and environmental groups, as well as groups such as women, students, tenants, or youth. In some respects the former are viewed to be involved in "economic" policy, while the latter are engaged in "social" policy.

This is in many ways a false and arbitrary distinction, but such a dual view of interest groups does reflect one reality of political organization, the "free rider" problem.

As economists have pointed out, all interest groups must grapple in varying degrees with the "free rider" problem or the "logic of collective action."[6] To organize politically is to incur significant costs. These usually have to be recovered through membership fees. But, as Hartle puts it, "if others are going to pay to advance your interests in pursuit of their own, why pay the fee?"[7] In short, why not be a "free rider"? This is the nub of the problem for sustaining groups, especially for broadly based groups. The narrower the group with the common producer interest, the easier it is to exclude "free riders." Otherwise, if belief in common ideals is not enough to secure paying adherents, then the group must often offer other remunerative services or, alternatively, have the capacity to coerce their members, such as through the compulsory check-off of dues.

The "free rider" problem is a major reason why some groups are weaker and less cohesive than others. There are, however, other explanations offered for this weakness. Those who use a class analysis approach would attribute the weakness of nonproducer groups to their dependent place in a capitalist system of production and to the role of the state that supports that system. Both the "free rider" and the class analysis diagnosis stress economic determinants. The "free rider" notion basically suggests that producer groups in industry and agriculture have far greater incentives and capability in organizing to exert pressure about a government policy essential to their livelihood than do broader labour, consumer, health, safety, and environmental groups. By analogy, one could use the "free rider" insights to see why other large social groupings such as political parties or the working "class" would also be less cohesive in sustaining both action and membership.

The literature on Canadian interest groups appears to agree that while interest groups exert some countervailing influence on each other, there has never been in Canada the extent of interest group pluralism that exists in the United States. The "separation of powers" system of government and politics in the United States provides many more points of influence and power for such groups. A significant inequality of power among groups in Canada is readily acknowledged to exist, as we show in greater detail below. But it is the institutional realities engendered by, and inherent in, the relations between Canadian federalism and cabinet-parliamentary government that also help explain the different roles of interest groups in the Canadian setting.

There is no satisfactory way to gauge the relative influence of interest groups in all policy fields relative to other institutions and centres of power such as the media, individual large businesses, political parties, or Parliament. How would one aggregate such evidence even if one had it? One cannot simply add up the few case studies of interest groups because, even when well done, they relate to a mere handful of policy case studies at specific points in time. Moreover, many such studies do not deal well with the problem of analyzing "nonevents" such as those inactions designed to maintain the status quo.

While interest groups undoubtedly initiate many demands for changes in policy, they also play a significant role in persistently "massaging" ministers and officials to preserve the status quo, or to prevent unfavourable acts from occurring. Many business groups, for example, spend considerable time trying to ensure that a favourable overall policy climate is maintained. Often this is a function of their own internal political needs. Public positions must be taken at a sufficient level of generality so as to paper over the inevitable cracks in the internal consensus of the interest group. The broader based the group, the more general the rhetoric must become. The generality of the rhetoric is also a function of the breadth of the policy occasion. For example, the ritual of pre–budget speech consultations between the Minister of Finance and business interests induces a high level of predictable rhetoric spiced with a few specifics, depending on the state of the economy and the industry in question. On the other hand, a discussion of foreign investment policy or competition policy may bring out more specifics. The existence of rhetorical generalities does not make the process any less real, especially when it is seen as part of a broader process of persistently asserting values and dominant ideas so as to *prevent* change that offends them.

There should be no doubt that interest groups, particularly cohesive producer groups, exert a significant influence both in preserving the status quo and in promoting manageable change favourable to their interests. Several examples can be easily cited. Canada's banks, through the Canadian Banking Association, have been instrumental in shaping the evolution of the Bank Act, reviewed approximately every ten years through a formal White Paper process and its accompanying consultative mechanisms.[8] They have, of course, not been the only group in the process; trust companies, the co-operatives, foreign banks, and consumers seek to influence the content of the Bank Act and other banking legislation.

In the energy policy field major oil and gas associations, such as the Canadian Petroleum Association, dominated by the large multinational companies, and the Independent Petroleum Association of Canada composed of smaller Canadian firms, successfully influenced energy policy in the 1960s and 1970s. They found themselves in strident opposition to the main features of the interventionist National Energy Program initiated in 1980, a policy that caused them, in part, to eschew their quiet behind-the-scenes lobbying and to adopt aggressive public advocacy advertising. In the mid and late 1980s they adopted the quiet lobbying tactic again and secured major reductions in federal intervention from a sympathetic Mulroney government.[9]

In the food and agricultural policy field, interest groups such as the Canadian Federation of Agriculture, the National Farmer's Union, and the prairie co-operatives, often operating in concert with provincial governments, succeeded until the early 1980s in preserving the subsidies to grain transportation first entrenched in the historic Crow's Nest Pass agreement.[10] It was not until the early 1980s that a new and broader coalition of "interests" centred in resource companies, and actively fostered by the federal Liberals, succeeded in making changes to the Crow system of subsidies. These changes were ultimately needed to give the railways, the CNR and CPR, more revenue so that they would invest in the new track and infrastructure needed to meet the high-volume demands of the booming resource trade in grain, coal, potash, and sulphur. Farm groups have also succeeded in persuading governments to create numerous marketing boards to protect and stabilize their incomes.[11]

Perhaps the most dominant producer group interests in their respective policy fields are the professions of medicine and law, in the health care and justice policy fields, respectively. They are overtly conferred a state monopoly over many aspects of decision-making. As with other groups, the professions seek to cultivate a certain mystique and set of ideas. These are both the product of genuine belief and conviction by their adherents and by many in the general public, but at the same time are intended to foster a sense of indispensability as to the social need of the producer group in question. For doctors and lawyers, part of the mystique centres on the need to protect the sanctity of the doctor–patient and lawyer–client relationships, respectively, and on the need to produce properly qualified people embued with proper professional ethics.

Doctors and lawyers are not the only groups to engage in this practice. In a slightly less explicit way, farmers have cultivated the notion that food producers, as custodians of the vital Canadian bread basket, are subject to the vagaries of both climate and international market fluctuations and are therefore especially deserving of measures to stabilize their incomes and to make their lives more predictable. Similarly, airline pilots and air traffic controllers seek to create an elevated rhetoric about the importance of public safety and their crucial role in preserving it.

The collective rights associations have not been without their moments of political success. The emergence in the 1970s of a significant amount of health, safety, and fairness regulations—so-called "social" regulation—can be attributed to their political influence. On the other hand, their political weakness can be seen in the effort to roll back, or at least "correct," some of these social regulation measures in the late 1970s and in the 1980s. Women's groups have pushed women's issues onto the political agenda. This success includes their remarkable lobbying of first ministers in the hectic constitutional debate of 1981 and their role in counteracting the strong anti-abortionist lobby in the late 1980s and early 1990s. However, women's issues are still in many ways vulnerable. This vulnerability was shown during the free trade debate of 1987–88 where women's groups that joined the anti–free trade coalition were threatened with a loss of federal funding.

Public interest associations have also managed to persuade governments to introduce some new structures in the decision process, some temporary and some permanent. These include: special inquiries such as the famous Berger Commission on the Mackenzie Valley pipeline and several provincial inquiries into uranium mining and nuclear power; statutorily based and nonstatutorily based environmental assessment processes for reviewing major projects; the establishment of consumer and environmental departments; and selected public funding of public interest interveners involved in different regulatory tribunals. Thus, the nonproducer associations have managed to secure a place for themselves in the policy process and in the departments of government. However, their organized political base is, on the whole, much weaker, less stable, and less coherent than producer associations.

It is important to stress the different levels of aggregation and differentiation inherent among producer groups. Business and producer groups are obviously not a homogeneous mass. Moreover, they interact with different departments and agencies of government. There are indeed different segments or fragments of capital that find it necessary to organize in different ways and that find themselves in opposition with each other as they seek to invest, introduce new technologies, protect themselves from intolerable uncertainty, and seek favours from government. Conflicts arise between foreign-owned and Canadian firms, between private firms and crown enterprises in the same industry, among firms in different regions, and between large firms and small firms. This is why regulators and policy-makers, while dutifully reading industry association briefs, and listening to the positions taken in numerous meetings, must ultimately develop policies that deal with these divisions, many of which will be papered over in the industry association's communications. The policy-maker must devise, as we stressed in Chapter 3, a policy that both treats people and firms equally (even when they are patently different) and that treats them fairly (even though some firms are clearly more powerful and better endowed economically than others).

The Evolution of Macro Business Interest Groups

The privileged power of business in the Canadian policy system is dual in nature.[12] In part it arises out of the functional requisites of a capitalist economy. Business has power because governments are extraordinarily dependent upon private firms to produce the jobs, the goods, and the services of a modern economy. But in part it is also directly political in that power is derived from the lobbying resources that business can employ, ranging from the financing of the Liberal and Progressive Conservative parties, to the lobbying of its macro and sectoral interest groups and extending to its financing of policy institutes and think tanks.

But the multiple levels of business and producer associations must also be appreciated. At the macro level there are general associations such as the Canadian Manufacturers Association, the Canadian Chamber of Commerce, the Business Council on National Issues, and the Canadian Federation of Independent Business. At the middle level there are dozens of specific associations such as for banking, oil and gas, and mining, to name only three. At the micro level there are thousands of more localized associations for even smaller industrial or producer units (for instance, tobacco growers in Ontario) or as chapters of the larger organizations. We cannot possibly deal with all of these levels in our brief treatment here, but it is essential to highlight trends in the development of the four macro associations as the umbrella organizations of the "business community."

None of the four macro business interest groups can individually claim to speak for the business community. The Canadian Chamber of Commerce (CCC) is probably the most broadly based. The CCC is a federation of six hundred Chambers of Commerce and Boards of Trade, which in turn embrace 170 000 businesses across Canada. The breadth of its membership forces the CCC to shift its lobbying strategy from narrow issues of concern to specific segments of its membership to broad brush positions (for example, general criticisms of greedy unions and aggressive bureaucrats) that will not offend any of its members. In the early 1980s, especially in western Canada, the CCC began a Legislative Action Program to improve lobbying efforts by its local members with Members of Parliament.

The Canadian Manufacturers Association (CMA) comprises 2500 member firms covering a wide range of industries. It is not, however, as disposed as the CCC to establishing a network at the grass-roots level. As its name implies, it is focused much more on the manufacturing sector per se. Because of this, it faces the normal problems of accommodating the views of foreign-owned and Canadian-owned firms. It has consistently argued that economic policy, whether at the level of macro fiscal policy or at the level of an industrial strategy, must be oriented to encouraging an incentive-oriented market system.

The Business Council on National Issues (BCNI) comprises about 150 chief executive officers of major Canadian-based corporations. Established in 1976 in the midst of the 1975–77 wage and price controls program, the BCNI has attempted to differentiate itself from the other business associations by taking a more "statesman-like" approach to national policy by operating quietly behind the scenes and with well-prepared positions and papers. Its role was pivotal in getting free trade on the agenda in 1985–86. Its work on competition policy extended to the point of actually preparing a draft bill incorporating its views. The BCNI directly involves the chief executive officers of its member firms and hence has a flexibility and an authoritative aura about it that other associations cannot match. It also saw itself as eventually being the fulcrum for the elusive but long sought consultative forum with government and labour. Thus, it has gone out of its way to foster more sympathetic relationships with labour through the Canadian Labour Congress. This highly tentative cooperation was most in evidence in a joint BCNI-CLC proposal that led to the establishment of an independent Labour Market Institute. Its wooing of labour, however, has not prevented the BCNI from being a strong advocate of public sector wage controls. The BCNI has not been immune to its own internal divisions, particularly between Canadian-owned and foreign-owned firms. It also lacks adequate representation among western Canadian and French-Canadian chief executive officers.

If the BCNI represents an elite behind-the-scenes business lobby, then it is the opposite of the second business association to emerge in the 1970s, the Canadian Federation of Independent Business (CFIB). It comprises over 88 000 small, primarily Canadian businesses, especially in the rapidly growing service and small manufacturing sectors. It evolved into an aggressive public lobby for the concerns of small business. Openly suspicious and often critical of the other business associations, the CFIB has used the media as well as numerous briefs and meetings to criticize policies harmful to small businesses. The establishment of the Ministry of State for Small Business can be directly attributed to the CFIB lobby. As well, the CFIB has spearheaded concern about the 1990 Goods and Services Tax (GST), excessive regulation, the governmental paper burden on small business, and the effects of taxation, interest rates, postal strikes, and increased postal rates. It continuously reminds the government that small businesses have created the largest number of new jobs in the Canadian economy.

It is evident from the above survey of macro business associations that the business community is not monolithic. Business interests, moreover, are not represented only through business interest groups. Major corporations and individual chief executive officers have their own network of access points and personal friends and contacts. Foreign and provincial governments serve as vigorous behind-the-scenes defenders of individual companies and industries as the political circumstances require. The several economic and resource departments of government play similar roles in Ottawa.

Despite the numerous tensions and disputes among industries and between segments of industry and government, the business community does share a broad official series of values and ideas, including a belief in efficiency and profit and in the freedom of the market, in individual freedom and the work ethic, and in a suspicion of organized labour and of bureaucratic government. During the Mulroney years, it enjoyed an especially influential period, buoyed by the international Reagan–Thatcher ethos that gave strong ideological support for capitalism.

The Evolution of Labour Unions and Macro Collective Rights Associations

As noted above, the nonproducer or nonbusiness interest groups have been variously labelled as public interest groups or collective rights associations. They include groups such as labour unions, environmental, health, and safety interests, consumer associations, women's and native interests, and social, community, and welfare voluntary associations. All of these groups are likely to suffer more than producer groups from the vagaries of the "free rider" problem enunciated earlier and are financially weaker. Some are funded by the state. All of them, more often than not, are likely to be instinctively associated by the public with social policy issues, including social regulation. All of them are suspicious of the established producer groups as well as the other centres of legitimacy—federal–provincial relations, Parliament, and executive government. They are far more inclined to use the media to attract political attention to their causes.

As a result, this grouping of interests has a much greater problem in creating and sustaining its macro associations. There is still no supra public interest group coalition. The labour movement has come closest to constructing one, but even its major association, the Canadian Labour Congress (CLC), is a fragile federation of labour unions only. Despite some congealment of the CLC in the wake of wage and price controls in the late 1970s, it remains an organization beset by internal division between industrial and craft unions, between international unions and Canadian unions, between rapidly growing public sector unions and private sector unions, and between English- and French-Canadian labour groups and federations. In 1982 construction unions left the CLC to form a new smaller macro body, the Canadian Federation of Labour (CFL).

The free trade debate of 1987–88 did produce a significant coalition of public interest groups opposed to free trade in particular and to the Mulroney government's pro-market policies in general. The formation of the Pro-Canada Network (PCN) was unprecedented in Canada's post–World War II history.[13] Its founders saw it as forming a popular counterweight to the BCNI, which they saw as having an extraordinary influence on the Mulroney agenda. The PCN was influential in helping to change public opinion about free trade with the United States, but it was not strong enough to prevent a second Mulroney Conservative majority government in 1988 and the passage of the free trade agreement into law in 1989. The capacity of the PCN to form and congeal was also based on the fact that there was an unusual point of political weakness in the Liberal Party. Usually broad-based "oppositional" coalitions would form around the main opposition party, but on this occasion the Liberals and the NDP were running "neck and neck" in the polls and the Liberal leader, John Turner, was viewed to be especially weak.

Even the effort to construct an electoral and political alliance between the CLC and the New Democratic Party has not borne fruit since the majority of individual workers do not vote for the NDP. At the same time this overt alliance with the NDP has made successive federal Liberal and Conservative governments suspicious of the CLC and all the more unwilling to consult with the CLC, much less enact policies favourable to it. The CLC's role in the great free trade debate was symptomatic of its posture in the 1980s. It declined an invitation to be a part of the free trade consultative process, but then attacked it from within the Pro-Canada Network. It wanted access and influence, but it did not want to become an instrument of the state.

The Provinces as Interest Structures

The importance of federalism in Canadian policy formation has already been set out in Chapter 2's survey of Canada's key institutions. While a separate chapter on the policy process of federal–provincial relations could certainly be amply justified, we have included the provinces as an interest structure for several reasons. We draw brief attention to these reasons here, but many of these themes will re-emerge in our later examination of major policy fields.

The first aspect of provinces as interest structures is that in their policy engagements with Ottawa, any given province may not arrive at the policy table as an unified entity. The provincial executive structure is also a mélange of departments working out policy compromises, often extremely loose ones, within the provincial state. And while the temptation may be to regard most policy issues as policy battles (for jurisdiction, credit, or blame) between Ottawa and any given province, the underlying realities may be quite different. For example, when federal and provincial finance ministers confront each other over the cost of shared programs or revenue raising, there may well be real conflict and tension involved. However, those same ministers may be silently but knowingly in league with one another when it comes to attempting to control their own health departments or subsidy practices by their industry ministries.

A second feature of the role of provincial policy structures is to appreciate the diverse patterns of both conflict and alliance-building that occur in relations between and among federal and provincial departments. For example, the federal and Alberta provincial energy ministries were at loggerheads with one another in both the 1973–74 and 1979–80 periods, but during these same periods, Ontario and federal energy ministries were in broad agreement and worked closely with each other. Quebec's energy department was meanwhile tactically selective, sometimes supporting their Ottawa counterparts but becoming extremely testy when it came to matters such as hydro-electric power.

For a further example, consider the case of federal and provincial environmental departments. For most of the 1970s and 1980s, these departments shared a mutual alliance of common misery, as governments at both levels gave them short shrift. In this context, they both needed each other to get things done. There certainly were environmental disputes, for example, between British Columbia and Ottawa over the use of the Fisheries Act, but the structural relations were more supportive of each other than was the case with energy policy.

The third provincial structural imperative is the need to appreciate the differences in the policy process between organizing for multilateral policy negotiations as opposed to bilateral ones or for issues involving regional groupings of provinces. The structures needed to deal with intricate 10 versus 1 negotiations, such as those involving the multibillion-dollar Established Programs Financing (EPF) arrangements or the 1986–87 free trade negotiations, are very different from those involved in forging the energy accords of 1985 or regional development agreements with each province.

None of the above is intended to give short shrift to any of the traditional aspects of federalism that influence policy-making. The question of which level of government has jurisdiction and in what specific ways clearly affects the design of policies. For example, forestry policy, that is, policies dealing with Canada's largest export industry, are provincially dominated. So are education policies. Federal efforts to structure its capacity to influence these areas have been largely resisted by the provinces. Trade policy, until recently, has been largely a federal area of expertise and structural presence.

Nor should one forget that federal–provincial policy relations, and the fate of many particular policy initiatives, can be profoundly influenced by the changing partisan composition of provincial Cabinets. The Mulroney free trade initiative was in part possible because the prime minister could call on the presence of a sea of Conservative provincial Cabinets anxious to support him or at least not to offend a new national like-minded government. Three years later, the party composition had changed. Had free trade been introduced during this later period, its fate may have been very different, and it may not even have reached the agenda phase of policy development, let alone been successfully negotiated.

Finally, it is essential to appreciate that provincial structures as interests play a key role in the dynamics by which many policies and programs were altered and downsized in the 1980s. Here the patterns are also quite complex. For example, federal programs were often downsized, thus leaving new pressures on the provinces to take up the policy slack. The provinces in turn did the same thing regarding the local or municipal level. But at the same time, provincial departments were often allies of their federal counterpart departments and thus resisted some efforts to cut back. Thus, the intricate structure of provincial and federal bureaucracies and programs also served as a bulwark against further cuts.

All of these points suggest that it is useful and important to see the provinces as policy structures, similar to interest groups, even while recognizing that they are constitutionally recognized as governments in a federal system with governing powers in their own right.

Policy Communities and Consultation

Policy communities are a network of private and public entities that have a continuing stake in, and knowledge about, any given policy field or issue.[14] Consisting of interest groups, the main governmental departments with policy jurisdiction, and consultants and experts in academe and private institutes, such communities of policy interest are a key part of understanding how policy is made. The presence of such a community can greatly facilitate policy action, while its absence may make coherent policy impossible. Such communities have a sense of policy history, are repositories of technical knowledge, and have dealt with each other over many years.

In the Ottawa jargon, such communities are often referred to as the stakeholders. In some respects, the Mulroney period turned stakeholder consultation into a new art form, especially since, as a political party long out of power, the Tories wanted to build their own networks and alter some of the traditional communities. While we comment more specifically on the dilemmas of consultation below, we are first interested in conveying why the concept of policy communities is an important element of structure. Examples from the transportation, trade, and environmental policy fields are useful in this regard.

In transportation policy, the Conservatives sought to deregulate the transportation system. Captured in their policy document *Freedom to Move*, the changes in the railway sector involved a deliberate effort to break up the old policy community. This was a community dominated by producer groups such as the main railway companies, CNR and CPR, and agencies such as the Canadian Transport Commission. The Mulroney Conservatives forged new relationships with a coalition of transportation user groups.[15] While this coalition was forming in part of its own accord, it required considerable nurturing and support from a transportation minister, Don Mazankowski, who wanted to reach beyond the traditional network.

In trade policy, the situation was more complex. For most of the post–World War II period, trade policy had been virtually "above" politics. The various international rounds of negotiation under the General Agreement on Tariffs and Trade (GATT) were the preserve of a tiny band of experts committed to the multilateral traditions of Canadian trade policy. The trade policy community was more like a club than a community.[16] The Conservatives' decision to proceed with a broad bilateral free trade deal with the United States in 1985 broke this club first through the persistence of a few key people, but also through the formation of a wider network of players. Trade became politicized again as it had been in the 1930s and in earlier periods of Canadian history. Indeed, as the free trade initiative took hold, the federal government sought to institutionalize this broader trade community through devices such as funded centres for trade policy at various universities. Opposition political parties also found that they had to mount their own trade policy network. The net effect is that the trade policy community of the 1990s is very different than it was in the 1980s.

Finally, consider the situation surrounding the environmental policy community.[17] For most of the 1970s, environmental groups and environmental departments surprisingly did not regard themselves as allies. Moreover, the environmental community could scarcely be considered to include business. Environmental groups in this early period were often advocates of a no-growth policy, and their views were especially antithetical to energy and resource companies. During the 1980s, however, two developments changed the nature of the environmental policy community. First, the federal environment department, especially under the Mulroney Conservatives, engaged in a series of consultative exercises that brought business and environmental interests increasingly into the same room. Both groups began to moderate their views of each other. Second, the structure of groups in both halves of the community was changing. Among environmental groups, there was now a wider array of national and local groups. In the business community, there were now firms and sectors that had a vested pro-environment position because they wanted to make money out of the newly emerging environmental technologies.

Thus, in different ways, the student of public policy must track the changing nature and complexity of policy communities. New networks emerge out of the changing structure of the economy as well as out of deliberate strategies by governments to encourage new communities into existence or to break up old ones. Clearly it is but a small step to connect policy communities and interest groups to demands for continuous and special consultation in policy-making.

Often, governments are charged with a failure to consult, or to consult adequately, with interest groups and interests that are affected by a particular decision or policy. Alas, the purposes of consultation in a democratic setting are many. The politics of consultation means different things to different interest groups, not to mention governments, regions, and classes in Canadian political life. Formal consultation can be and has been used:

- to learn, to be informed, and to *understand* in the best democratic and human sense of the word;
- to secure or conclude an agreement;
- to agree or disagree;
- to delay;
- to co-opt interests and/or to facilitate "voluntary" compliance;
- as a symbolic act to show concern, or as a substitute for other more substantive action.

Because consultation serves many purposes and the motives and expectations of the parties engaged in consultation often differ, it is not surprising that there is frequently much talk about failures or weaknesses in consultative exercises. The rhetoric of "failed consultation" is standard fare in politics, and one of the truly scarce political skills is the art of differentiating bogus from legitimate claims in this regard.

The need to talk, to consult, and to learn is central in democratic government. However, consultation is made particularly difficult in Canada because there are different ideas and bases of political and institutional legitimacy, and these compete. First, Canada is a federal state in which legitimacy rests on a regional base, a geographic base, and a cultural/ethnic base. This requires consultation of a costly but usually necessary kind. Second, legitimacy resides in a Cabinet held accountable in theory and sometimes in practice by a popularly elected House of Commons. Third, legitimacy rests in part on interest group participation. It is accorded in proportion to the real power and influence exercised by major economic interests. Big business ranks at the top, but agriculture and, to a certain extent, unions share this base of legitimacy.

These bases of legitimacy intersect and overlap in numerous ways and so are often difficult to disentangle. There can be no doubt that the competing bases affect both the appearance and the reality of consultation in Canada. It is next to impossible for any single, formal consultative body adequately to embrace all these bases, and efforts to do so are destined to disappoint. Worse still, such efforts may add to the disillusionment with governmental and private institutions that already prevails.

It is also evident that consultation is not a uniform game in which the rules are the same for all the players. Numerous multilateral and bilateral bargains are struck. The "interests" involved are not just monolithic ones such as "government," "industry," and "labour," but must be seen more realistically to include:

- big business and small business;
- foreign-owned business and Canadian-owned business;
- organized labour and unorganized labour;
- public sector unions and private sector unions;
- agriculture and consumers;
- strong provinces and weak provinces;
- established professions and professions that would like to be established;

- those who have expertise and those who do not;
- those who have and those who have not.

Even this list does not encompass all the players and does nothing to alert us to the problem of the inequality of access to the consultative process. It tells us nothing, moreover, about informal consultation. It *does* alert us to the complexity of governing, to the need to be suspicious of exaggerated claims for new consultative eras, and to the potential costs of excessive consultation.

Conclusions

It can be seen that there is clearly a legitimate role for interest structures and policy communities in the policy formulation process. Such structures are needed to identify ideas, to *learn* about problems, and with luck and goodwill, to achieve *some* solutions. It is equally clear that no single consultative mechanism can adequately embrace the federal–provincial, parliamentary, media, producer interest group, and public interest group elements of the political system. There will always have to be a number of forums.

Finally, it is evident that too much consultation can result in enormous costs, including economic costs. Too much consultation can also produce increasing cynicism about the capacity of democratic government to take concrete action when required.

Notes

1. A. Paul Pross, ed., *Pressure Group Behaviour in Canadian Politics* (Toronto: McGraw-Hill Ryerson, 1975), 7. See also A. Paul Pross, *Group Politics and Public Policy* (Toronto: University of Toronto Press, 1986), and Robert Presthus, *Elite Accommodation in Canadian Politics* (Toronto; Macmillan, 1973).
2. Pross, *Pressure Group Behaviour in Canadian Politics*, ch. 1.
3. See Phillip Slayton and Michael J. Trebilcock, *The Professions and Public Policy* (Toronto: University of Toronto Press, 1978).
4. See David Langille, *From Consultation to Corporatism? The Consultative Process Between Canadian Business, Labour and Government, 1977–1981* (Ottawa: M.A. Research Essay, Department of Political Science, Carleton University, 1982).

5. Richard W. Phidd, "The Agricultural Policy Formulation Process in Canada," paper presented to the Canadian Political Science Association Meetings (Montreal: June 2–4, 1980).
6. See Mancur Olson, *The Logic of Collective Action* (Cambridge, Mass.: Harvard University Press, 1965). For a critique of this view as applied to trade unions, see Leo Panitch, "Trade Unions and the Capitalist State," *New Left Review* no. 125 (January–February 1981), 21–43.
7. Douglas Hartle, *Public Policy, Decision Making and Regulation* (Montreal: Institute for Research on Public Policy, 1979), 66.
8. See R. M. Rickover, "The 1977 Bank Act: Emerging Issues and Policy Choices," *Canadian Public Policy* 2, no. 3 (Summer 1976), 368–79; and D. E. Bond and R. A. Shearer, *The Economics of the Canadian Financial System: Theory, Policy and Institutions* (Toronto: Prentice-Hall, 1982).
9. See G. Bruce Doern and Glen Toner, *The NEP and the Politics of Energy* (Toronto: Methuen, 1984), ch. 5, and G. Bruce Doern and Brian W. Tomlin, *Faith and Fear: The Free Trade Story* (Toronto: Stoddart, 1991), ch. 5.
10. See David R. Harvey, *Christmas Turkey or Prairie Vulture?* (Montreal: Institute for Research on Public Policy, 1981), and Howard Darling, *The Politics of Freight Rates* (Toronto: McClelland and Stewart, 1980).
11. See Grace Skogstad, *The Politics of Agricultural Policy-Making in Canada* (Toronto: University of Toronto Press, 1987).
12. See William D. Coleman, *Business and Politics* (Montreal: McGill-Queen's University Press, 1988).
13. See Doern and Tomlin, *Faith and Fear: The Free Trade Story*, ch. 9.
14. See Pross, *Group Politics and Public Policy*, ch. 6.
15. See Margaret Hill, *Freedom to Move: Explaining the Decision to Deregulate Canadian Air and Rail Transport* (M.A. Research Essay, School of Public Administration, Carleton University, August 1980).
16. Doern and Tomlin, *Faith and Fear: The Free Trade Story*, ch. 3.
17. See Glen Toner, "Whence and Wither: ENGOS, Business and the Environment," paper presented at conference, Carleton University, February 8, 1990.

Process I: The General Policy Process

Process is the third element needed to understand how Canadian public policy is made. A process is a regularized cycle of behaviour that policy actors to some extent have to work through or around. In this chapter we look first at the general policy process, in short the overall routine that characterizes the development and consideration of individual policy proposals within the executive-bureaucratic structures. The second glimpse involves a discussion as to why "routines" and "systems" confront the more complex dynamics, realities, and uncertainties of politics and governing, thus revealing why governments have difficulty doing first things first, why notions of a single rational policy process have severe limitations, but why, simultaneously, governments still have to try to plan.

The Simple Model of Rational Policy Stages

We must first assume that a policy or a decision is proceeding through the Cabinet system in an orderly manner, one policy field or proposal at a time. In this sense we will be visualizing, temporarily at least, a rational policy process. Ideally, and to a certain extent in practice, a policy problem goes through several stages.[1] These stages include:

- identification;
- definition;
- alternative search;
- choice;
- implementation; and
- evaluation (feedback and learning).

They encompass the main features of a rational process of thought and action to solve a problem or reach a goal.

The identification of a problem involves the persistent articulation of a concern or issue. It can emerge from an external demand (a general one to "provide jobs" or a particular one to restore railway service in a given locality) or internally, from the executive-bureaucratic arena itself (for example, from a previous study) or from a combination of both external and internal sources.

The definition stage involves a process in which "the problem" is shaped or confined to more practical limits. It is "defined" into what policy-makers and advisers believe to be its real meaning. This would involve discussion and elaboration of the ideas inherent in it, of the objectives to be met, and of the consequences to be avoided.

Closely tied to the definition stage is the search for, and analysis of, alternative ways of solving the problem. Ideally, all major alternatives would be assessed as to their costs and benefits and likely efficiency and effectiveness. This would involve a search for alternative instruments (exhorting, spending, taxing, regulating) or mixtures of instruments. Often it will include a consideration of the option of doing nothing and/or of maintaining the status quo.

It is at the definition and search for alternative stages that bureaucratic influence is perhaps at its maximum. The deputy minister, assistant deputy minister, and other key senior policy analysts in the sponsoring department and in other departments involved in the problem are engaged in continuous meetings and telephone discussions as they "massage" and analyze the problem. But they do this in concert with their own ministers who are also talking to each other as politicians. Ideas and facts are present in abundance at this stage even though they may be glibly buried in the rhetoric and/or terminology of short-term politics and analysis. Indeed, they meld into what Vickers has called the "appreciative system" of decision-makers. These stages are also the point where it is most difficult to separate the myths, realities, and perceptions of the relative influence and power of bureaucrats and ministers. This is also a crucial feature of policy formulation.

At the stage when actual choice occurs, the question of resource allocation ceases to be theoretical. Real resources (money, personnel, political goodwill, time, etc.) are committed or rejected. The implementation stage follows suit and may or may not involve new legislation by Parliament. Some decisions and policies can be carried out under existing legislative authority or permission and thus are implemented through an order-in-council, a regulation, a guideline or a rule, or an expenditure of funds. Others may require new legislation in the form of an overall new or amended statute or as an expenditure appropriation or tax through the annual passage of the Estimates or Supplementary Estimates or through "ways and means" legislation following a budget speech. Implementation also involves the behaviour of *both* public officials and private citizens. Since it occurs over time, this stage is usually the longest and most permanent. The intent of implementation is to produce results in a reliable, predictable way to meet the ideas and objectives sought.

Finally, it would be both necessary and desirable to evaluate the results to see if the objectives had been met. In the broadest sense it is assumed, ideally, that the policy-maker wants to learn and obtain feedback so that corrections can be made.

Even though it is recognized that these stages are not always discrete and watertight but are normally a series of iterative events, it is nonetheless intuitively appealing to visualize the policy routine in this way and to practise policy-making according to its precepts. It is in this important sense that the rational model retains its appeal.

Cabinet Papers and the Paper Flow

One of the formal ways in which the policy process in the government of Canada nominally conforms to the simple policy stages model is in the requirements placed on ministers and officials for the submission of proposals to Cabinet or its committees. The types, content, and paper flow of Cabinet documents partly conform to a rational model. It must be stressed, of course, that Cabinet documents are only a *written* form of policy advice. They tell us nothing of the perhaps even more crucial *verbal* dimensions of the policy formulation process, let alone much about the dynamics of the process. These aspects are discussed in later chapters. In the meantime, however, it is instructive to review the content of Cabinet papers in relation to the simple policy stages model and as a main element of the general routine of policy formulation.

There are two broad types of Cabinet papers: *Cabinet documents* and *other Cabinet papers*. The former includes memoranda to Cabinet, draft bills, agendas and minutes of Cabinet and Cabinet committees, committee reports, and records of decisions. These papers are deemed to contain a "confidence of the Queen's Privy Council" and are internal to Cabinet.[2] The papers are secret in order to encourage frank discussion among ministers and to ensure that, once policy is decided, differences among ministers are kept private and Cabinet solidarity is maintained. Other Cabinet papers, such as the discussion paper, are not secret documents, though they may be kept confidential as circumstances dictate. For the limited purposes of this chapter, we focus briefly on two papers—the discussion paper and the memorandum to Cabinet, including the presentation of the latter in the Mulroney era as a short *aide-mémoire*.

The memorandum to Cabinet and the discussion paper are the main documentary vehicles through which a minister brings an issue to Cabinet. In essence, the memorandum contains specific recommendations, summarizes the nature of the decisions, and discusses delicate political, including partisan, considerations. It is not supposed to exceed five pages in length. The discussion paper, on the other hand, can be of widely varying lengths. Avoiding a discussion of recommendations and partisan political sensitivities, it provides an extensive discussion of alternatives, background issues, and trends suitable for both ministers and officials. Begun in 1977, this dual system was introduced to ensure that ministers "are not burdened with briefing material ... beyond what is necessary for political choice."[3] As we see below, even greater brevity was sought in the Mulroney era with the introduction of an even briefer *aide-mémoire* and with a downplaying of the use of the discussion paper.

The main headings for material to be examined in the discussion paper are summarized below[4]:

- the origins and dimensions of the problem, including relevant statistical information;
- the impact on various segments of society and on the achievement of government objectives;
- the possible solutions;
- the positions of provincial governments, interest groups, and others; and
- conclusions.

The much shorter memoranda to Cabinet are decision documents whose headings, again greatly shortened in the Mulroney era, are[5]:

- Background
- Options
- Considerations
- Conclusions

However, it is the "executive summary" of the memorandum to Cabinet that assumed even greater importance during the Mulroney era. It became an *aide-mémoire* in part out of the need to channel decisions through the more day-to-day oriented Operations Committee of the Cabinet headed by Don Mazankowski, the deputy prime minister. The relevant headings in these summary pages are[6]:

- Issue
- Recommendation
- Rationale
- Possible Adverse Consequences
- Departmental Positions
- Political Consultations
  - Caucus
  - Party/Other
- Communications
  - Plan
  - Major Theme
  - Response to Criticism

The greater reliance on even shorter, more political documents must be related to several features of the Mulroney period. First, given severe fiscal restraint for much of the period, and given its desire to separate itself from the perceived excessively rational approach of the previous Trudeau government, the Mulroney government cut the number of memoranda to Cabinet going before ministers virtually in half. Second, many Mulroney ministers, influenced by the telecommunications revolution of the 1980s, were not readers, and felt far more at home with visual slide-show presentations in Cabinet. These kinds of presentations increased considerably in the 1980s. Indeed, it can probably be said that most ministers in any Cabinet are not readers. They much prefer the telephone and the face-to-face meeting complemented by very short memos. Third, the increased political nature of the executive summaries, especially reflected in greater emphasis on the communications plan, was the product of deeply felt Conservative angst about the reception their policies would get as a new government denied power for most of the previous twenty years. The communications gurus in the Prime Minister's Office were determined to overcome any hostile press and to face the usual sea of critics that any given policy or decision might generate.

The listing of these document headings does not in itself show how decisions are actually made. They convey no sense of whether ministers have time to read documents or to understand them. But these documents as a whole do contain roughly the same kinds of information and the same sequence of treatment implied in the simple policy stages model. Identification, definition, alternative search, and choice are all explicitly present. Implementation and evaluation are less explicitly present, although the documents contain information and analysis of past decisions and programs.

The adequacy of the implementation and evaluation stages of the general policy process raises numerous interesting questions about how evaluations are conducted, who does them, and about the state of social knowledge. We return to these questions. At this elementary stage it is worth stressing, however, that these latter stages have been the object of particular criticism in recent years. The Auditor General of Canada and the Office of the Comptroller General have been extremely critical of the failure, in their view, of the government's overall managerial responsibility to "complete the rational cycle," so to speak—that is, to conduct and utilize formal evaluations of programs to see if past implementation is "efficient and effective" and to change or discard programs and policies if they have not measured up.

It is instructive at this point to take note of the possible headings that do *not* appear in these documents. There is no explicit heading for "scientific and technological factors," or "foreign policy considerations," or "effects on low-income Canadians." Some would argue that these headings should be "flagged" as well in an ideal policy process. This is not to suggest that these items do not show up in one form or another under other headings, but they indicate the range of "considerations," that is, processes and ideas that are part of the agenda. On this last point it is essential to note the undertaking made by the Mulroney Cabinet in 1990 that *all* policies of the government would be subject to prior environmental assessment. This has the potential to be quite a radical change, not only in the documentation it requires, but also in the actual policy choices. It is too soon, however, to assess the effects of this environmental undertaking.

The Cabinet documents outlined above are intended to inform a *collective* Cabinet of the proposals being made to it by one (or more) of its *individual* ministers. It is estimated, however, that there are typically from three to four hundred Cabinet memoranda submitted annually to Cabinet and many fewer discussion papers. At the same time, there are other kinds of voluminous written materials that cross ministers' desks. As a result, there has been a constant concern about both the quantity and quality of ministerial briefing material and how it is prepared, and hence the increased use of the *aide-mémoire* format.

The Limits of the Simple Policy Stages Model

Ministers and senior officials must adhere in a formal way to some kind of a simple policy stages model, primarily because they must attempt to manage, coordinate, and control the overall policy and decision process. Most of this book, however, testifies to the inherent limits of the simple policy stages model. This is not because ministers and other politicians are inherently "irrational" while the rest of us make decisions wisely. The limits of the simple policy stages model flow from the unique rationality of politics and government, which in turn is founded on relationships between ideas, structure, and process. Thus, to appreciate the limits of the systems and routines enunciated above, we need to return to the basic concepts introduced in earlier chapters.

First, it is essential to stress that public policy is almost never made "one policy field at a time." While there may be periods of time when Cabinet attention is focused on energy policy, medicare, the status of women, or policies for small businesses, political, bureaucratic, and economic realities are such that the agenda is almost always filled with several concurrent policy concerns.

This untidy agenda is aided and abetted by the persistent presence of the ideologies and dominant ideas discussed in Chapter 3. Concern for efficiency, individual liberty, equity, stability, redistribution, national unity, and regional sensitivity exists in virtually every major policy field. These concerns are voiced by ministers, political parties, the caucus, as well as by interests, interest groups, and other governments in Canada and abroad. This is not to suggest that these dominant ideas are expressed in an even-handed, pluralistic way. At various times one or more ideas may have more powerful advocates and friends with greater access to the apex of governmental power. The point is that the dominant ideas are almost always present in some significant way regardless of the effort of government or certain ministers and senior officials to define and control the policy agenda.

The simple policy stages model also fails to take account of the existence of the several processes generated by the basic governing instruments. These processes are examined in Chapter 7. Thus, the tax process, though related to many substantive policy fields (fiscal, energy, regional, and social policies) has, in part, a life of its own, centred in the Department of Finance. A tax community exists that is concerned about the revenue and tax system and the tax process. Moreover, the tax decision process has been dominated by secrecy founded on a normative concern for ensuring that private interests could not gain from prior knowledge of tax measures. In a similar way the regulatory process and the expenditure process constitute separate but obviously related processes with constituencies that are concerned about the overall integrity and the specific benefits and protections these instruments confer, and that advocate regulatory reform or expenditure reform. It is important to stress that these instrument-based processes are not neutral processes. They are normatively valued and are the object of policy dispute, both in aggregate terms and in specific policy situations and fields.

The single policy process concept also breaks down for reasons that theorists of incrementalism have long appreciated. The need to narrow the range of alternatives and to confine the definition of a problem is a product of the political need to obtain a consensus and of an appreciation that only finite resources and information are available.

It is essential to appreciate in this context that there can be "policies without resources" to support them. Resources include money (taxes and spending), personnel, time, and political will. Many governments find it necessary to enunciate policy to express their concern about, and support for, a particular constituency or group, since this is usually preferable to expressing no public concern whatsoever. But it does not mean necessarily that the policy will be given full or complete resource support. Thus, only some money may be provided, or only limited enforcement of regulations may be supplied.

Another phenomenon that makes the simple policy stages model inappropriate is the frequent emergence of major physical capital-intensive *projects* (such as pipelines or airports) on the policy agenda.[7] Canada began its continental existence with such a project, the construction of the Canadian Pacific Railway. Since then, there have been other dominant projects—the St. Lawrence Seaway, the Trans-Canada Pipeline of the mid-1950s, the Olympic Games, the Alaska Pipeline, and the Hibernia project to name a few.

A large physical *project* has a high probability of triggering interests and ideas in several policy fields concurrently than does a normal policy initiative. Because each project is partly unique and occurs at different times, it "tests" these policy fields in different ways each time. Although efforts will be made to "be fair" to each project and to treat them equally, there will also be a need to "be reasonable," in short, to strike a new composite policy deal every time. The kinds of policy fields that can be and have been involved concurrently in large projects include energy and resources, economic and fiscal, social and environmental, labour relations and employment practices, regional policy, foreign policy, and trade and technology. Each of these are under the custody of different ministers and officials in numerous departments, agencies, and boards of several levels of government, federal, provincial, local, and foreign.

If several policy fields are involved, it follows that several policy instruments are likely to be involved to ensure that the right, or at least the acceptable, mix of public and private behaviour occurs in relation to each project and, over time, in relation to all or most projects. Thus, packages of spending grants and subsidies, verbal understandings, procurement activity, taxes or tax breaks, regulations (including administered prices), and direct public investment through crown or mixed enterprises could be involved. These packages are not easily assembled, partly because there are always disputes (that is, politics) about how much of the "carrot and the stick" or the "iron hand in the velvet glove" is necessary to achieve the many purposes of the project. Moreover, the custodian departments and boards must constantly decide when a project arises how much of an exception, if any, the project should be to their normal ongoing policies and policy responsibilities. Such judgments must be made in the context of legal as well as political and financial constraints. These judgments become all the more difficult as more and more megaprojects queue up at the governmental trough. Which ones deserve the most support and on what grounds? Which ones should come on stream first, and why?

For several reasons, then, the simple policy stages model has severe limitations. Our appreciation of these limits is not yet complete, since we also need to relate the above features to the larger priority-setting process, the process by which governments try to decide to do first things first.

Priorities, Mandates, and the Problems of Doing First Things First

Governments do attempt to set priorities and to make "the policy process" manageable. On an annual or regular basis these priorities may be formally expressed in the throne speech, the budget speech, international economic summit meetings, and speeches on the tabling of expenditure estimates. Periodically, the prime minister may give special speeches on particular critical issues (for example, during the Meech Lake crisis in 1990). Thus, there is no shortage of occasions when governments attempt to communicate with the electorate about what things should be done first. A government does this not only for purposes of internal management, but also to provide reassurance to its supporters and to those who might support it at the next election.

Priority-setting is a two-edged sword. On the one hand, it is a process intricately tied to the government's mandate. The electoral platform of the governing party in Canadian politics does not have the entrenched nature or apparent coherence that electoral "manifestoes" have in British politics, but nonetheless the prime minister will try to convey to, and with, his or her ministers a clear sense of the party's and the government's mandate. For example, in the first Mulroney government, ministers and the bureaucracy were constantly urged and required to relate their proposals to the economic renewal statement tabled in the fall of 1984. During the second Mulroney government, the prime minister sought to keep ministers' eyes fixed on continuing deficit reduction polices, as well as controversial measures such as the second stage of tax reform and the Meech Lake Accord.

If mandates are one cutting edge to determine what is at the top of the agenda, there must equally be a process for relegating items of low priority. One could liken this to the planet Pluto in distant orbit. Governments must have ways to throw low-priority items into "deep orbit," never to be seen or heard again. In this sense, the overall policy process is intended not only to make policy, but also to prevent policy from being made.

But the task of maintaining and sustaining the priority list over a significant period of time is notoriously difficult because the domestic and international environment is always undergoing change. Once again, we must ask why this is so since it will tell us why there are limits to the simple and orderly policy stages model. Undoubtedly, the strongest incentive against the rational setting of, and adherence to, priorities is found in the inexorable ticking of the electoral clock. A political party without power cannot make policy. Therefore, at best, the ideal political planning cycle extends only to about three years, since electoral preparations are likely to neutralize the fourth year.

There is, of course, a paradox here because there is inherent in democracy a view that a general form of rational behaviour is occurring. That is, it is assumed that a particular political party is elected with a mandate and that it will "keep" (implement) its major election promises. Even when the public is aware of the inflated bidding war inherent in electoral promises, it seems to expect that at least the major promises and priorities will be implemented.

But this quasi-rational expectation about a government's priorities is confounded by two other equally powerful forces: the need to survive politically and the obligation of the government to *govern*, and hence to reach decisions and set priorities in relation to the host of demands and situations that have impact on it *between* elections. Political survival is a powerful instinct. Most politicians would prefer to be in power rather than in the opposition. The accoutrements of public office—salary, prestige, status, and influence—are valued and coveted. To retain them, political parties in power are often prepared to change priorities to help sustain the coalition of voter support that will preserve them in office. Rarely are these self-interest motivations totally separate from the need to govern and deal with dominant ideas. Thus, self-interest and purposeful *governing* responsibilities are inextricably linked.

Priorities are difficult to sustain because of the inevitable limits of information and knowledge. Many policies fail because we lack theory (that is, a knowledge of causal relations), and we lack knowledge about what is required to change human behaviour in desired ways. Interests do not always want to "behave" properly. Policies rarely fail merely because we lack clear objectives. Because of the limits of knowledge, governments must constantly adjust priorities and policies. In short, they must constantly try to *learn* and adjust to the power of other institutions.

A scarcity of resources also accounts for shifting priorities. Many priority concerns and policy fields have inadequate resources of time, money, personnel, and political will. Some have more resources than are needed. There is therefore a constant pressure to change priorities to increase the resource support for neglected areas.

In this context it is also necessary to appreciate the source and intensity of policy initiatives and demands. There are obviously external as well as internal demands and pressures, both for change and to sustain the status quo. External demands can emanate from other countries (foreign policy concerns), from other levels of government in Canada, as well as from interest groups and opposition political parties. Internal demands can come from ministers themselves, political advisers and staff, senior bureaucrats, policy and planning branches, and from line departments equally anxious to expand empires and to do "good things."

The relative predominance of these sources of initiative and demand not only affect and change priorities, but also raise normative concern about where the power to initiate *should* rest. Are some outside interests too powerful? Are ministers controlled by bureaucrats? Is the policy and priority-setting process a "top-down" one or a "bottom-up" one, the latter implying an inordinate influence by the line ministers and departments rather than by the prime minister and central agencies or, alternatively, of excessive influence by bureaucrats over ministers?

To this confusing tug and pull of "interests," institutions, and ideas, one must add a point stressed in earlier chapters, namely the largely media-induced tendency of politicians to believe that they must "be seen to be doing something." The media's attention span *is* short. It does thrive on new announcements and on personalities, and on who is "winning" and "losing." It criticizes priorities, but never has to allocate resources. It thrives on the latest reactions to the monthly ritual of unemployment and cost-of-living statistics and to Gallup polls. This adds a further dimension of pressure to change the priority list or, alternatively, to add to the priority list until it becomes a veritable "wish list" of political goods.

Finally, it must be noted that priorities change in form, but perhaps only partly in substance, because of the perceived need to put old priority wine into new bottles. Thus, old priorities may have to be expressed in new ways partly to show that new things are being tried and/or to disassociate current efforts from past failures. These changes are rarely just "window dressing" because policy circumstances do in fact change over time.

Conclusions

One might be tempted to ask in retrospect why a chapter devoted to the general policy process ends by systematically picking apart the very notion that there is a general policy process. One cannot avoid this paradox. The reality is that there are several policy processes operating concurrently. A full understanding of the making of public policy demands that one examine the dynamics of policy-making. At the same time the government of the day must manage "the policy process" as a whole and seek to impose order upon it despite the extreme difficulty of doing this successfully. Thus, we have focused initially on the formal Cabinet documentation required and on the vague, often implicit, rational and democratic expectation that the government will implement its major promises—in short, that it will set priorities and seek to carry out its mandate.

Notes

1. See for example, C. O. Jones, *An Introduction to the Study of Public Policy* (New York: Wadsworth, 1970).

2. See Richard French, "The Privy Council Office: Support for Cabinet Decision Making," in Richard Schultz, O. M. Kruhlak, and J. T. Terry, *The Canadian Political Process* (Toronto: Holt, Rinehart and Winston, 1979), 369–72.
3. Ibid., 370. See also Canada, Privy Council Office, *Cabinet Paper System* (Ottawa, 1977), Parts I and II.
4. Canada, Privy Council Office, *Guidance Handbook for the Preparation of the Memorandum to Cabinet* (Ottawa: Privy Council Office, 1984), 5.
5. Ibid., 6.
6. Ibid., 6.
7. See G. Bruce Doern, "Mega Projects and the Normal Policy Process" (Ottawa: School of Public Administration, Carleton University, 1982).

CHAPTER 7

Process II: The Expenditure, Tax, and Regulatory Processes

A second element of process emerges from an appreciation of the role of governing instruments. Governments make and implement policy through a set of instruments—exhortation, expenditure, taxation, regulation, and public enterprise—each of which to some extent constitutes a separate policy process. That is, though operating within the confines of the larger Cabinet documents and priority-setting process examined in the previous chapter, there are also subordinate processes that often take on a life and rhythm of their own.

In this chapter we introduce these processes, especially the expenditure, tax, and regulatory processes, but the larger purpose here is to develop a conceptual understanding of the basic instruments for making public policy. (A more detailed look at how these processes function inside the Canadian executive structure is found in Chapters 11 and 12.) The three main subordinate processes vary in their purpose, in the number of ministers and departments involved, and in some of the norms that accompany them.

The expenditure process deals with the way in which tax dollars are allocated to meet new and existing policy and program obligations. It includes a cycle of activity to determine the basic fiscal framework of the government and the policy reserves (money for new initiatives, if any). It also encompasses a process of bargaining and haggling between line ministers and central treasury authorities. These political skirmishes can be over both expansion and contraction of the expenditure pie; in recent years, mainly the latter. Finally, the process includes parliamentary scrutiny and approval of the spending choices, including the auditing by Parliament's agent, the Auditor General of Canada. In the expenditure process, all ministers are involved to some extent.

The same cannot be said about the tax process, the process through which the government seeks to obtain its revenue and to influence the growth and shape of the macro economy. It is focused on one minister, the Minister of Finance, whose tax decisions (and some of their expenditure consequences) are revealed in the annual budget speech. The tax process involves a high degree of secrecy as to its final content, although it is preceded by a formal pre–budget consultation process, especially with business interests.

The regulatory process deals with the promulgation of rules of behaviour backed up by the sanctions of the state. In its purest form, it involves delegated legislation (rules emanating from powers granted in existing statutes). But generically it can also include rules achieved through changes to the parent statute itself. For example, in the last decade, major changes in transportation regulation occurred in both delegated legislation and in statutory amendments. In the regulatory process most ministers are involved, but so also are numerous independent regulatory bodies such as the National Energy Board and the National Transportation Agency. Until the Mulroney era, the regulatory process did not have as routinized a decision process as has existed for both spending and taxation. The Mulroney Conservatives established an Office of Privatization and Regulatory Affairs (OPRA), in effect a central agency for reviewing regulatory and privatization proposals from line departments and agencies.

Instruments as Means versus Ends

The mere use of the word "instruments" suggests that they are "devices" or "techniques." In short, they are seemingly the "means" through which the "ends" of political life are achieved. In part, of course, this is what they often are. But to view these basic instruments to be merely matters of technique would be a great mistake. The instruments are also *ends* in themselves. They are the object of political dispute, are embedded with ideas, and are valued because they fundamentally affect the *process* and *content* of policy-making. In democratic politics, process always matters.

Why are instruments also ends? Why are they normatively valued? The first clue to answering these questions is to understand the connection between the types of instruments noted above and the degrees of *legitimate coercion* involved in governing.[1] Figure 7.1 displays these characteristics. It shows the instruments arranged, albeit somewhat artificially, along a continuum starting with minimum or almost nonexistent coercion and extending to maximum coercion. Thus, exhortation involves an effort to ensure support and compliance through persuasion, discussion, and voluntary approaches. At the other end of the continuum taxation, regulation, and public enterprise (especially the nationalization of a firm) are all more coercive because they involve setting rules of behaviour backed up directly by the sanctions (penalties) of the state. *In theory*, all three of these are "regulatory" in a broad sense in that taxes are rules of behaviour regarding the extraction of income and wealth from private citizens and institutions, and public enterprise involves rules of behaviour regarding the ownership of shares and assets by the state. In practice, of course, we tend to distinguish between these instruments, with public ownership usually being seen as the most coercive and interventionist.

In the middle of the continuum one finds public expenditure. It is only moderately coercive in that governments, when they spend, are distributing the funds as benefits or services (grants, transfer payments, etc.). Actual coercion occurs when the revenue is extracted from the taxpayer, but when it is spent, the coercive edge has disappeared or is at least blurred since the question of who pays and who benefits is not always easily determined.

In policy formulation, the choice of instrument(s) is itself valued precisely because judgments about the degree of coercion and the object of coercion *are* replete with values. For example, there is probably a liberal democratic presumption that it is preferable to be

FIGURE 7.1   The Instruments of Governing

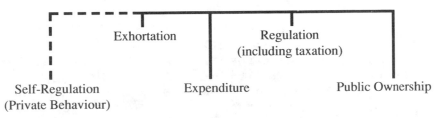

persuaded to change one's behaviour or to be offered an expenditure incentive than to be required to change (that is, regulated). Moreover, while broad policy "objectives" are something to be achieved in the future, instrument choice is real and operates in the "here and now." We comment later in this chapter and again in Chapter 12 on the particular characteristics of each type of instrument and the dynamics they create, but it is first necessary to deal further with some general issues concerning governing instruments.

Instruments and the Growth and Contraction of Government

Data on the growth of particular policy instruments provide an aggregate snapshot of what government is doing. Such data often become the surrogate under which many claims and counterclaims are made about the efficacy of policy or about how much government intervention is good or bad for Canadians. For much of the post–World War II period, growth, in the context of a broad liberal demo-cratic consensus, was seen as good. But beginning in the 1970s and surging in the 1980s, the neoconservative view took hold and argued that too much spending, taxation, regulation, and public enterprise constituted the main problem. This led to numerous actions to con-strain public spending, to deregulate, and to alter the tax system. When looking at the instrument data in this section, one must fully appreciate that these are but a rough profile of change over time. Ultimate judgments of policy efficacy—of good or ill—require more in-depth analysis of individual policy fields.

Expenditure Growth and Deficit Reduction

The growth of expenditure is the most visible sign of governmental expansion. As a percentage of Gross National Product (GNP) the expenditures of all levels of government have grown from 36.1 per-cent in 1946 to 36.4 percent in 1970. By the late 1980s the figure was over 48 percent.[2] Of equal interest is the comparison of expenditures by level of government. The data show that provincial government and local government expenditures have expanded the most rapidly, especially during the 1960s and 1970s. It is important to note, however, that these figures do not convey the degree to which some of the provincial and local increases were triggered by federal fiscal transfers and grants in fields such as health, education, and welfare. Also, the overall data on the growth of expenditures do not convey the different claims that different expenditures make on the economy. Thus, transfer payments (made to individuals who then decide how to spend it) have grown more rapidly than exhaustive expenditures, that is, those that use up goods and services, including labour, directly.

When federal expenditures are looked at by envelope or broad policy fields, as in Table 7.1, the pattern for the 1980s is fairly stark. The biggest change by far has been the growth of public debt charges, which has gone from 16.5 percent of total federal outlays in 1980 to 24.5 percent at the end of the decade. Economic and regional spending has shown the largest decline. Other expenditures have changed only marginally. Total federal expenditures as a percentage of Gross Domestic Product (GDP) were 16.6 percent in 1980, rose to 23.4 percent by 1985, but then declined to 20.8 percent in 1989. These latter data lend credence to the claim that the Mulroney Conservatives have significantly restrained expenditure growth. The growth of program spending (that is, exclusive of the debt charges) has declined as a share of GDP. The decline in economic and regional spending shares could also be said to reflect a Tory desire to reduce the state's role, especially in the form of grants to industry.

As for the debt itself, the data indicate in absolute terms the mushrooming of the budgetary deficit from $11.5 billion in 1980 to $32.3 billion as the Mulroney Conservatives took office in 1984. It is little wonder then that reducing the deficit became Finance Minister Michael Wilson's main priority. In absolute terms the deficit still

TABLE 7.1 Federal Expenditures by Envelope (As Percentage of Total Outlays)

Envelope	1980	1990
Fiscal Arrang.	7.0	6.0
External Affairs	2.7	2.6
Parl./Govt. Services	4.2	3.5
Defence	8.5	8.4
Economic & Regional Development	14.9	10.6
Social	45.9	44.1
Public Debt	16.5	24.5

Source: Calculated from Public Accounts, various years.

hovered around the $30-billion mark as the 1990s began, but as a percentage of GDP the Tories had managed to wrestle it down from a figure of 8 percent in 1985 to 4.4 percent five years later.[3]

Revenue Growth, Taxes, and Tax Expenditures

Government revenues and the taxes and charges that produce them have also increased greatly. Total government revenues as a percent of GNP grew 31 percent between 1947 and the end of 1970s, most of the growth occurring between the mid-1960s and the mid-1970s. Nontax revenues have increased quite significantly and were a major factor in the intense energy and resource policy and fiscal struggle between Alberta and the federal government in the late 1970s and early 1980s. Taxes on individual income have increased, while taxes on corporations have declined as a percentage of GNP. As a percentage of total taxes, provincial and local taxes have increased to virtually equal federal taxes. This compares to about a 60–40 split in favour of the federal government in the early 1960s. There has also been an increasing reliance on personal income as opposed to corporate income tax.

Federal revenue data for the 1980s, as shown in Table 7.2, also indicate some of the shifts, particularly in the later Mulroney years as the decade ended. Personal income tax went from 40.6 percent of revenues in 1980 to 53.9 percent in 1989. Corporate taxes as a share fell by over five percentage points. The share of indirect taxes will undoubtedly escalate in the 1990s with the passage in 1990 of the Goods and Services Tax. As a percentage of GDP, federal revenues have increased under the Conservatives, bumping up from 14 percent in 1984 to about 16 percent, on average, for the rest of the 1980s.[4]

TABLE 7.2   Federal Revenue Sources
(As Percentage of Total Revenues)

Source	1980	1989
Personal Tax	40.6	53.9
Corporate Tax	16.8	11.0
Indirect Taxes (e.g., sales, duties)	24.8	24.6
Other Revenue (e.g., fees, some energy taxes)	17.6	10.3

Source: Calculated from Public Accounts, various years.

Another feature of the growth of the tax system was the debate that emerged about so-called tax expenditures.[5] Tax expenditures arose when the government chose to forego revenue by providing, for some public policy reason, a tax deduction or credit—in short, a tax break to individuals and companies. This issue crystallized in relation to corporate tax breaks in the 1972 election when NDP leader David Lewis coined the phrase "corporate welfare bums." Later analysis in the 1970s began to show that tax expenditures for individuals and corporations were growing at a faster *rate* of increase than regular expenditures. Moreover, because richer taxpayers were better able to take advantage of these tax breaks, the net effect of this growing use of tax expenditures was to make the tax system less progressive. As we discuss in greater detail in Chapter 16, the debate over tax expenditures helped in eliminating many of these loopholes in the 1980s when the tax reform process led to the conversion of many of them to tax credits.[6]

Regulatory Growth and Deregulation

Because it is inherently a less quantitative phenomenon and was not a particular concern of social scientists in Canada until the 1970s, the growth of regulation has only been seriously assessed since the late 1970s.[7] Regulation does involve increases in government spending, but its real impact is on *private* budgets as people and companies spend to comply with regulations set by government. This accounts for its relative lack of visibility *within* government, even though many outside of government were instinctively aware of great regulatory growth. A second aspect of recording the growth is simply one of appreciating the scope of regulation even in the abstract. Table 7.3, derived from an Economic Council of Canada study, shows the scope of policy fields involved.

The Economic Council study also documented the growth of federal and provincial regulatory statutes by decade until the end of the 1970s.[8] Statutes are, of course, only a crude measure of output, but other measures confirmed the overall growth pattern. These included the growth in the number of statutory instruments and regulations made pursuant to statutes. Despite problems in all these measures of "output" (rather than of outcome or effects), it was evident that the 1970s represented a period of remarkable growth at the federal and provincial levels.

Much of the growth in the 1970s was in the area of so-called social regulation—health, safety, and fairness—as opposed to earlier eco-

TABLE 7.3   The Scope of Regulation in Canada

- **Communications**
  Broadcasting
  Radio (AM, FM)
  Television
  Telecommunications
  Telephone
  Telegraph
  Satellite
  Cable TV

- **Consumer Protection/Information**
  Disclosure (product content labelling, terms of sale, etc.)
  False and Misleading Advertising
  Sales Techniques (merchandising)
  Packaging and Labelling
  Prohibited Transactions (e.g., pyramid sales, referral sales)
  Weights and Measures

- **Cultural/Recreational**
  Residency Requirements
  Language (bilingualism)
  Canadian Content in Broadcasting
  Horse Racing

  Gambling (lotteries)
  Sports
  Film, Theatre, Literature, Music (e.g., Canadian content)

- **Energy**
  Nuclear
  Natural Gas
  Petroleum
  Hydro-electric
  Coal

- **Environmental Management**
  (a) Pollution Control
      air
      water
      solid waste disposal
  (b) Resource Development
      minerals
      forestry
      water
  (c) Wildlife Protection
      hunting
      fishing
      parks/reserves
      endangered species

  (d) Land Use
      planning/zoning
      development approval
      subdivision
      strata-title
  (e) Weather Modification

- **Financial Markets and Institutions**
  Banks
  Nonbanks
  Trust Companies
  Management Companies
  Finance Companies
  Credit Unions/Caisse Populaires
  Pension Plans
  Securities/Commodities Transactions
  Insurance

- **Food Production and Distribution**
  (a) Agricultural Products Marketing
      pricing
      grading
      storage
      distribution
      entry
      supply
  (b) Fisheries (marine, freshwater)
      price
      entry
      quotas
      gear

- **Framework**
  Competition Policy
  Anti-dumping Laws
  Foreign Investment Review Act
  Bankruptcy Laws
  Corporation Laws
  Intellectual and Industrial Property
  Copyright
  Industrial Design
  Patents
  Trade Marks
  Election Laws
  Contributors
  Spending
  Reporting

- **Health and Safety**
  - (a) Occupational Health and Safety
  - (b) Products—Use
    - explosives
    - firearms
    - chemicals
  - (c) Product Characteristics
    - purity
    - wholesomeness
    - efficacy
    - accident risk
  - (d) Building Codes
  - (e) Health Services
    - nursing homes
    - private hospitals
    - emergency services
  - (f) Animal Health
  - (g) Plant Health

- **Human Rights**
  - Anti-discrimination legislation in respect to hiring, sale of goods or services, etc.
  - Protection of privacy, personal information reporting

- **Labour**
  - Collective bargaining
  - Minimum wage laws
  - Hours of work, terms of employment

- **Liquor**
  - Characteristics (e.g., alcoholic content)
  - Distribution and Sale

- **Professions/Occupational Licensure**
  - Certification/Licensure

- Registration
- Apprenticeship

- **Transportation**
  - Airlines (domestic, international)
  - Marine (domestic, international)
  - Railways
  - Intercity Buses
  - Taxis
  - Pipelines
  - Trucking (inter and intraprovincial)
  - Urban Public Transit
  - Postal Express

- **Other**
  - Rent Control
  - Metrication
  - General Wage and Price Controls

Source: Economic Council of Canada, *Responsible Regulation*, 1979, ch. 6. Reproduced with the permission of the Chairman of the Economic Council of Canada, 1991.

nomic regulation.[9] Another area of growth was in agricultural marketing boards as producers sought to stabilize and protect their incomes. We have much more to say about economic versus social regulation later. The point to stress here is simply to note the pattern of growth and the proxy nature of its measurement.

This growth and proliferation were among the factors that prompted the Mulroney Conservatives to launch a regulatory reform strategy in 1986. While this strategy is examined in Chapter 12, one feature of it deserves mention in our initial inventory of the expansion or contraction of the state. This is that by 1990 the government argued it had significantly reduced the rate of production of new regulations. In 1986, there were 1140 regulations approved. This total dropped to 653 in 1988 and to 585 in 1989.[10] In addition, significant measures were introduced to deregulate the oil and gas, transportation, and banking sectors. The issue of whether all of this constitutes a reduction in the role of government as opposed to a realignment of its role is a topic for later chapters.

Crown Corporations and Privatization

The effort to chronicle the growth of crown corporations as a further instrument of policy is also fairly recent and produces mixed results.[11] Recent federal estimates indicate that there are well over four hundred government-owned or controlled crown corporations. The Clark government's 1979 crown corporation bill, however, was premised on distinguishing this total universe of nondepartmental organizations, which included regulatory agencies, advisory councils, and "mixed" or "joint" ventures, from "true" commercial crown corporations that are wholly owned, directly or indirectly, by the federal government. Accordingly, it was envisioned that the bill would especially apply to about 178 crown corporations (69 percent parent companies and 109 wholly owned subsidiaries). By a similar gradual process of definitional elimination (especially to exclude agencies that functioned much like regular departments of government), the Vining study of provincial crown corporations concluded that there were about 205 provincial enterprises.[12] Needless to say, there are genuine problems in determining the total number of enterprises. This has been one factor leading to a concern about the need for better systems of accountability and to efforts to sell or privatize public enterprises.

There are several ways in which the size and growth of public enterprise could be viewed. Richard Bird has shown that in 1961 the recorded *sales* of such enterprises were 30.4 percent of government revenues, but only 21.3 percent in 1975.[13] As a proportion of Gross

National Expenditure, public enterprise sales decline from 8.7 to 8.3 percent. Employment trends followed a similar path.

Vining's data compare provincial crown corporation *assets* along several dimensions. They have fixed assets equal to 36 percent of total corporate assets. The total assets of provincial crown corporation assets represent 33 percent of federal assets and 49 percent of provincial assets. Vining also compares the growth in the number of provincial crown corporations with asset growth. He concludes that 72 percent of all crown corporations were created since 1960, but only 11 percent of total assets in 1980 were created since 1970.[14]

Within the federal crown corporation sector, several points should be noted about absolute size and the relative patterns of growth, whether expressed in assets or employment. The first is to appreciate the obvious differences in absolute size. Canadian National Railways, for example, dwarfs all other crown corporations in employment (though not in rate of growth in employment), and it is by far the largest of the nonfinancial service crown corporations in assets. When it comes to asset growth, however, it is clear that the most rapidly expanding crown corporation sector in the 1970s was in financial services. The Bank of Canada, the Canada Mortgage and Housing Corporation (CMHC), the Export Development Corporation (EDC), the Federal Business Development Bank, and the Farm Credit Corporation increased their assets, on average, by over 100 percent in the 1970s. Employment growth rates have also been highest in this sector.

As was the case with regulation, the Mulroney era has brought with it significant changes in the state-owned sector. While the Conservatives did not privatize with the gusto of their Thatcherite counterparts in Britain, they nonetheless sought to prune the federal stable of public enterprises.[15] The Mulroney government privatized Air Canada, Teleglobe Canada, Canadair, and de Havilland as well as several less well known entities. In addition, it put tremendous financial pressure on virtually all of its remaining companies by requiring them to obtain private funding or by forcing them to increase charges to their customers. While the size of the state-owned sector as measured in assets has not declined by much during the Mulroney period, there is little doubt that some key entities are no longer in the public domain. Similar practices have also occurred at the provincial level, especially in Saskatchewan, British Columbia, and Quebec.

Exhortation and Symbolic Outputs

As to exhortation, this is the least studied instrument of all. We have more to say about it in Chapter 12 where we link it to symbolic policies.[16] It is perhaps sufficient to note that exhortation devices have also grown. They include an entire array of ways in which political authorities show concern or respond to demands by making a speech, studying the problem, holding meetings and engaging in consultation, reorganizing agencies, and so on.

The above inventory of instrument growth is important background information. In the aggregate it shows growth without a doubt, but accompanied also by significant efforts to shrink the state in the Mulroney period. However, these data do not show the myriad interactions among instruments. Arguments about why growth or contraction has occurred and whether it is good or bad are the stuff of politics. On this point theory and ideology become hopelessly mixed. Evidence does not necessarily matter. Explanations range from the expansionary habits of bureaucrats, to federal–provincial and party competitions, the phenomenon of rising expectations and the so-called "overload" of governments, to the fiscal crisis of the state caused by the internal contradictions of capitalism.

Instruments and Ideas

Instruments and ideas are inseparably linked. We can see this in two different illustrative ways: by looking at the social and economic content of the major instruments and by using three brief case studies to give more specific examples.

The first way can be briefly stated. Each of the major instruments has been subject to a debate in which the dominant social and economic ideas are central. Thus, the expenditure process involves controversy over social versus economic priorities and over whether certain subsidies are an "investment" or "welfare." The tax system is embroiled in debate about the *equity* of the system among taxpayers at the same income level, the *efficiency* of the system as an aid to investment and growth, and its degree of *progressivity* or *regressivity*. Regulation, as we have seen, has been routinely (and often artificially) divided into economic versus social regulation. Disputes also rage as to the commercial versus public policy and/or social role of crown corporations, and of the social consequences when they are privatized.

A second way to relate ideas to instruments is to consider three cases from different policy fields: energy policy, social policy, and charitable foundations. The energy policy example concerns the 1980 National Energy Program (NEP). The social policy example concerns means-tested grants versus a tax-based child tax credit, and the example of charitable foundations concerns the tax treatment of such organizations.

Under the NEP the federal government changed the energy policy instruments in a major way. Prior to the 1980 NEP, the energy policy "incentives" were conferred primarily through the tax system in the form of deductions and depletion allowances. Companies could take advantage of them if they had a healthy cash flow and were taxpayers. When conferred through the tax system, the incentives were much more in the control of the company, partly because the revenue remained in its hands and partly because tax information is confidential. The NEP shifted most of the incentives from the tax system to direct expenditure grants. The grants were given under guidelines and regulations administered by energy officials in the Department of Energy, Mines and Resources.

The purpose of the change in incentives was related both to energy purposes and to questions of power and control. The energy purposes were reflected in the fact that the grants could be targeted better on Canadian firms, many of which had an inadequate base to take advantage of tax incentives. The grants were also to be applicable to firms that explored in the Canada Lands. In terms of power the grants were *intended* to make the oil and gas industry more visibly dependent upon the federal government—hence the use of visible grants rather than less visible tax breaks. The change in instruments was not a matter of mere technique. It was charged with normative controversy. This was starkly reinforced when the Mulroney Conservatives came to power. One of their major policy acts was to take down the NEP regime in the name of nonintervention, efficiency, and a pro–western Canada policy.

The second case illustrates similar issues, but in a different policy field. In social policy many programs for low-income Canadians are delivered through grants with means-tested conditions of eligibility attached. The recipient must apply for the grant in a visible way with the discretionary decision (within rules) residing with the government official concerned. Contrast this with a social policy formulated to deliver a benefit through the tax system such as the federal child tax credit. Here the benefit can be obtained in the relative privacy of one's home when filling out a confidential tax form. Once again, the different use of instruments is not a matter of mere technique, even though our example has shifted from the oil company to the individual "welfare" recipient.

The third case involves charitable foundations. Charitable foundations greatly prefer to be assisted or encouraged by government through tax exempt status rather than through grants from government. Again, the concern here is with control and power as well as with ideas of charity, gift-giving, and voluntarism. Policy concerns, therefore, turn not just on the desire to encourage voluntary and philanthropic activity in society, but also on where the balance of decision-making power resides.

Numerous other examples could be cited where instrument choice is a critical issue. In research and development policy there are policy conflicts over the grants versus tax breaks issue. Indeed, it can be said that business generally prefers tax breaks to direct grants because of the issue of control and power and the freedom to use resources as it sees fit.

The examples discussed above should also alert us to a problem in dealing with the relationship between coercion and governing instruments, namely the *perception* of coercion and hence of degrees of government intervention in private decision-making. It will be recalled that we earlier located expenditure grants in the middle of the continuum and characterized it as only moderately coercive. But the degree of coercion is not a judgment made only by those who govern. It is also a matter of perception by those who are the object of governing. The three cases suggest that grants may involve greater and more visible control by government than benefits conferred by the tax system. These differing *perceptions* of coercion are also an object of further dispute, and make policy formulation an even more difficult exercise.

Theories of Instrument Choice

We have stressed that, ideally, the intent of a policy is to obtain or sustain a desired form of human behaviour over a long period of time. The use and choice of instruments over time is intricately connected to the problems of obtaining democratically desired behaviour in the face of an uncertain future. As a policy issue or field evolves over time, it could be expected that governments might need to use all or most instruments. What instruments or mix of instruments will it take? Which ones will yield policy success? Which ones will be acceptable? To whom? Will exhortation and persuasion produce the desired effect? The latter, frequently heard statements are merely metaphorical versions of the problem of instrument choice.

It is useful to inquire into what we know about the use of instruments over time. It is one thing to have a typology or a continuum of instruments, but can research provide any generalization about instrument use over time? The general answer is that no fully satisfactory generalizations exist. By reviewing two or three attempts to generalize, one can show the severe problems of conducting research into such a question and at the same time show why the need to raise such questions is important.

One hypothesis has been suggested by Doern and Wilson. It states that "politicians have a strong tendency to respond to policy issues (any issue) by moving successively from the least coercive governing instruments to the most coercive."[17] This hypothesis is a plausible one, but it would be difficult to test it satisfactorily in the real world. One has to know, for example, when a policy issue is "new," and how long a period of time passes before one sees the continuum of hypothesized behaviour unfold. It is also not easy to deal with the question of whose perception of coercion is involved, the government's or that of the persons, voters, or groups who are the object of policy.

Moreover, one could certainly think of some policy issues where decision-makers use regulation first rather than last. Stanbury's analysis suggests that politicians too readily practise the adage that "there ought to be a law" and easily reach for the regulatory political gun first.[18] But here again, one must ask what "first" means. What events, decisions, and nondecisions *preceded* the decision to regulate? Was regulation really used first? A regulation can be promulgated and announced to satisfy a general public interest group demand in a symbolic way without unduly harming the more cohesive producer groups who will be given elaborate procedural protections and who can afford to participate in them. In this case regulations are almost symbolic gestures only. But each situation has to be explored on a case-by-case basis. Politics, after all, is a dynamic process and involves exchange relationships between governors and governed across several policy fields.

Consider, finally, the effort by Trebilcock, Prichard, Hartle, and Dewees to construct a broader alternative hypothesis of instrument choice, one that tries to be more dynamic.[19] Their hypothesis (or rather a series of "axioms") is rooted in the premise that all or most political behaviour will be guided by the calculus of vote maximization. They then conclude (based on this assumption) that instrument choice, interwoven with the choice of actual policy objectives, will be determined by intricate cost-benefit calculations regarding the relationship between marginal swing voters in swing constituencies, and political parties competing for their votes (in the next or most recent election).

The point of this brief excursion into the theory of instrument choice is not to downplay the attempt to grapple with it, but to show

how difficult it is to generalize about the use of instruments over time and to show how attempts to theorize about such choices are inevitably couched in the researcher's a priori model of human behaviour. Nonetheless, an understanding of policy formulation will continue to require us to ask questions such as: Why and when do governments regulate as opposed to spend? Why and when do governments choose to use public ownership as opposed to taxation?

Instrument choice is also influenced by ideology, by the nature and source of demands for change, and by constitutional-legal and structural variables. Recent studies of decisions to create crown corporations show that in nine of the eleven cases examined crown corporations were created *after* other instruments had been tried and found wanting.[20] They were used as a last resort, a practice that could be viewed as consistent with a liberal ideology. Moreover, evidence indicates that NDP governments have a far stronger tendency to create such enterprises than other parties at the provincial level.

That instrument choice is influenced by the nature of the demand for change is also logical. For example, Telesat Canada, a mixed public and private enterprise, became the principal federal satellite policy instrument in the late 1960s as a compromise solution to two types of explicit instrument demands. Private interests were demanding a private corporation, and some federal government departments wanted a full-fledged crown corporation. A mixed enterprise was the final result, its purpose being to manage a dispute over a new technology and its effects on an old one.

Constitutional, legal, and administrative factors are also central to the choice of instruments. Most policy problems do not, in substantive terms, obey the artificial boundaries of federalism. Therefore, there is constant political competition to solve problems, to obtain credit, and to deflect blame. But in legal terms, federalism does impose limits on instrument choice. Provincial governments cannot tax by any mode or means. The federal government can. A provincial government may create a crown corporation in part to avoid federal taxation. The federal and provincial governments must be legally precise and certain when they regulate in a given area because they must have the power to "make laws" in the field concerned. Spending powers, on the other hand, are far less legally constrained, and the federal government has not hesitated to use federal dollars aggressively. Exhortation is, of course, available to either level of government without *legal* constraint.

Legal and jurisdictional factors may also be important among government departments and agencies in the same level of government. For example, statutes may confer the main spending authority on the line department (the Ministry of Transport) but confer major regulatory powers on an independent agency (the National Transportation Agency). Tax powers concerning transportation, meanwhile, rest with the Department of Finance. This legal reality creates problems of policy coordination, and contributes to the inevitable political logrolling and bargaining among ministers and officials, not only within the transportation policy field, but between transportation and other policy fields.

Policy Instruments and Implementation

Finally, it is important to see the connections between instrument choice and the implementation of policy. We have already indirectly spoken of implementation in our earlier reference to the problems of sustaining changes in human behaviour. We now wish to draw attention to two particular features of implementation as they relate to the choice of governing instruments.

The first feature is portrayed in Figure 7.2. It shows a finer breakdown of the main instruments first identified in Figure 7.1. In a very real sense this chart is a portrait of an important part of the world of policy implementation. Implementation involves a series of activities and actions that are derived from the basic instrument list. Thus, the choices can become even more subtle—particular *types* of grants, regulations with varying *degrees* of penalty, different *kinds* of public enterprise, etc.

The figure, however, does not reveal a second equally important connection between policy implementation and instruments. One is tempted to define implementation—getting things done—in relation to the actions of officials and bureaucrats. But implementation also involves *private* behaviour to ensure that things get done in desired ways. Many public policies can only be "implemented" when a governing instrument or combination of instruments produces or induces the appropriate *private* behaviour. Thus, police services are very dependent upon people "calling the cops." Energy policy is dependent on consumers availing themselves of grants to aid them in switching from oil to gas or electricity. And accelerated capital cost allowances are intended to induce greater capital investment and thus "implement" a fiscal policy objective. The willingness of private decision-makers to play their implementation role is, however, a function of several normative concerns, including their view of the legitimacy and acceptability of the policy, of the instrument, and of the decision-making power it implies.

FIGURE 7.2 A Secondary Categorization of the Instruments of Governing: Finer Graduations of Choice

Exhortation	Expenditure	Regulation	Public Ownership
• Ministerial Speeches • Conferences • Information • Advisory and Consultative Bodies • Studies/Research • Royal Commissions • Reorganizing Agencies	• Grants • Subsidies • Conditional Grants • Block Grants • Transfer Payments	• Taxes • Tariffs • Guidelines • Rules • Fines • Penalties • Imprisonment	• Crown Corporations with Own Statute • Crown Corporations under Companies Act • Purchase of Shares of Private Firm • Purchase of Assets • Joint Ownership with a Private Firm • Purchase of Private Firms' Output by Long-Term Contract

Conclusions

Policy instruments generate further important elements of the process aspects of public policy-making and implementation. Operating within the larger Cabinet policy- and priority-setting process are several subordinate but also partly independent policy processes. The expenditure process, the tax process, and the regulatory process in particular must be understood on their own terms. This is all the more necessary given the strong tendency in the last decade to restrain the state across all policy instruments through expenditure cutbacks, tax reform, deregulation, and privatization.

Notes

1. Theodore Lowi, "Four Systems of Policy, Politics and Choice," *Public Administration Review* (July–August 1972), 298–310.
2. Richard M. Bird, *Financing Canadian Government: A Quantitative Overview* (Toronto: Canadian Tax Foundation, 1979), 8–9.
3. See Katherine Graham, ed., *How Ottawa Spends 1990–91* (Ottawa: Carleton University Press, 1990), 297.
4. Ibid., 294.
5. Allan Maslove, "Tax Expenditures, Tax Credits and Equity," in G. Bruce Doern, ed., *How Ottawa Spends Your Tax Dollars 1981* (Toronto: James Lorimer, 1981), ch. 7.

6. See G. Bruce Doern, "Tax Expenditures and Tory Times: More or Less Policy Discretion?" in Katherine Graham, ed., *How Ottawa Spends 1989-90* (Ottawa: Carleton University Press, 1989), 75–107.
7. Economic Council of Canada, *Reforming Regulation* (Ottawa: Minister of Supply and Services, 1981), and G. Bruce Doern, ed., *The Regulatory Process in Canada* (Toronto: Macmillan, 1978).
8. Economic Council of Canada, *Reforming Regulation*, and Economic Council of Canada, *Responsible Regulation* (Ottawa: Minister of Supply and Services, 1979); W. T. Stanbury, ed., *Government Regulation: Scope, Growth, Process* (Montreal: Institute for Research on Public Policy, 1980).
9. See Economic Council of Canada, *Responsible Regulation*, ch. 2.
10. See the Honourable John McDermid, "Making it Work," Notes for an Address to the Conference on Regulation, Ottawa, May 4, 1990, 3.
11. See Allan Tupper and G. Bruce Doern, eds., *Public Corporations and Public Policy in Canada* (Montreal: Institute for Research on Public Policy, 1981); Marsha Gordon, *Government in Business* (Montreal: C. D. Howe Research Institute, 1981); R. Prichard, ed., *Crown Corporations in Canada: The Calculus of Instrument Choice* (Toronto: Butterworths, 1983); and W. T. Stanbury and Fred Thompson, eds., *Managing Public Enterprises* (New York: Praeger, 1982).
12. Aidan R. Vining, "An Overview of the Origins, Growth, Size and Functions of Provincial Crown Corporations," study prepared for the Institute for Research on Public Policy (Vancouver: University of British Columbia, 1979), 18.
13. Bird, *Financing Canadian Government*, 4.
14. Vining, "Overview of the Origins," 19–20.
15. See Allan Tupper and G. Bruce Doern, eds., *Privatization, Public Corporations and Public Policy in Canada* (Halifax: Institute for Research on Public Policy, 1988).
16. See Murray Edelman, *The Symbolic Uses of Politics* (Champaign-Urbana: University of Illinois Press, 1967), and Murray Edelman, *Politics as Symbolic Action* (New York: Academic Press, 1971).
17. See G. Bruce Doern and V. Seymour Wilson, eds., *Issues in Canadian Public Policy* (Toronto: Macmillan, 1974), 339.
18. W. T. Stanbury, *Government Regulation*, ch. 1.
19. M. Trebilcock, R. S. Prichard, D. Hartle, and D. N. Dewees, *The Choice of Governing Instruments*, study prepared for the Economic Council of Canada (Ottawa: Minister of Supply and Services, 1982).
20. Tupper and Doern, *Public Corporations and Public Policy in Canada*, 19.

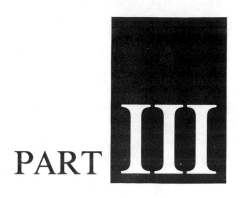

PART

PUBLIC POLICY AND RESOURCE ALLOCATION

- Prime Ministers, Political Power, and Policy Preferences
- Priorities and Priority-Setting
- Bureaucracy and Policy Formulation
- Public Policy and Public Expenditure
- Taxation, Regulation, and Other Instruments
- Knowledge, Information, and Public Policy

CHAPTER 8

Prime Ministers, Political Power, and Policy Preferences

An understanding of the dynamics of resource allocation to meet policy goals—resources of power, money, time, political will, and organizational capacity—must start at the centre. It is prime ministers, their characters, values, styles, and preferences, that set the tone and agenda for governments. As head of the governing political party, the prime minister must both lead and hold his or her partisans together. As leader of a country, the prime minister must strive to symbolize in his or her leadership both the problems to be faced and the solutions to be offered. At the same time, in many areas, the prime minister lacks power in the sense of having only a limited ability actually to solve problems if broader policy circumstances, including the power of other leaders, interests, and countries, conspire against the position adopted. He or she may also decline to invest power in policy fields that simply do not interest or concern the leader as much as other fields do.

In this chapter we survey the key policy preferences of several recent Canadian prime ministers from Brian Mulroney back to John Diefenbaker.[1] Where such views can be discerned, we also survey their views about the general policy process and the management of the policy process within government. In comparing political leaders in this way, we are obviously spanning a broad historical period with different social, political, and economic circumstances. This makes comparison difficult but not uninstructive, particularly if the comparisons attempted here are not viewed in isolation.

Problems in Evaluating Power and Policy Preferences

Several characteristics and problems arise in assessing a prime minister's policy preferences and influence in the policy process. The major ones examined here are: the concept of fixed versus variable power; the relationship between longevity in power and the rhetorical labelling of regimes; the personal and career background of prime ministers; the prime minister's control of the Cabinet agenda and the power to appoint ministers and senior officials.

Fixed or Variable Sums of Power

There has always been an implicit controversy over the kind of power a prime minister possesses. Is power a kind of fixed sum that a leader "acquires" on election and that is then dissipated, spent, or invested (but that invariably reduces over time), or is it a sum that can be augmented and replenished? According to the former notion, a prime minister's power is at its maximum in the first year or two of a mandate, and hence this is the optimum time to act and to change the policies most needing change. If the leader did not act early, the pressures, accumulated grievances, and challenges to his or her personal authority would invariably mount and failures would increasingly become part of political memory. The contrary view is that a prime minister's power can be replenished most obviously through re-election (especially with a majority), through the successful handling of a crisis situation, or simply through strong leadership and successful policies.

It is not difficult to see that these differing views of the kind of power possessed by a political leader are hard to analyze and agree upon. One obvious and blunt indicator is sheer longevity in power and electoral success. But the importance of investing and spending power also affects the conduct of public policy and priority-setting in other ways. For example, Prime Minister Pearson's "60 days of decision" concept in 1963 could be viewed as being based on an explicit strategy corresponding to the "fixed sum of power" concept.

Major initiatives were to be taken early by a new government with a fresh, albeit minority, government mandate. In contrast, the first Trudeau government from 1968 to 1972 seemed to operate from the opposite premise. The strategy in part seemed to be to think carefully and plan a course of action in the first year, take action in the second and third year, explain one's actions in the fourth year, get re-elected, and repeat the cycle again.

Alas, political strategies are based on more than just the notion of fixed or expandable concepts of power. Pearson's "60 days of decision" approach was also motivated by the Liberals' desire to contrast his government's decisiveness with the previous Diefenbaker government's alleged indecisiveness.[2] Similarly, the new Trudeau government of 1968 wanted to display its rational planned orderliness as a contrast to the perceived chaotic untidiness of the last years of the Pearson government.[3]

Longevity and the Perception of Regimes

It is elementary to observe that longevity in power affects a prime minister's approach to policy. A regime begins to collect political baggage, an amalgam of credits and debits and friends and enemies that form the political record. Prime ministers become entrenched defenders of what they and others view as their chief policy successes. They try to distance themselves from their past failures, hoping as always that the electorate has a bad memory and short attention span. Above all, longevity produces the inevitable labelling of regimes, the application of an overall brand name by journalists, opposition parties, and others as a code word to sum up the regime's successes or failures. These labels do not always coincide with policy fields per se, but rather convey views about the prime minister's overall approach and/or personality. Thus, the Mulroney leadership has had to struggle to overcome the corruption and "sleaze" factor. Trudeau governments earned the epitaph of being technocratic and arrogant. The Pearson regime was first viewed as being innovative and decisive, but later characterized as almost hopelessly disorganized. These labels are not always wholly accurate or even fair, but the reality is that they stick and prime ministers have to live with them.

Regimes also acquire labels expressed in terms of policy fields as well. We see this in greater detail in the next section of this chapter. One interesting illustration of this kind of perception was the persistent view that Prime Minister Trudeau was simply not interested in the economy. Language policy and the Charter of Rights were his chief interests, while economic policy assumed a distant second place. While the evidence in Chapter 9 does not fully support that view of the

Trudeau regime, the more general point to be made in relation to prime ministerial policy preferences is that virtually all recent occupants of the office, except perhaps Brian Mulroney, have leaned to the social policy side of the policy continuum. This is partly because party leadership conventions seem to prefer leaders who display, or are perceived to have, a preference for the "softer" human issues on the not unrealistic expectations that this is where the "votes" are.

Career Experience and Personal Leadership Style

The tautological adage that people "are what they have been," or alternatively, that a leopard "cannot change its spots," obviously has some relevance to understanding how prime ministers behave, their policy preferences, and the strengths and limitations of the skills they bring to high office. These behaviour traits also become bound up in judgments about how charismatic a leader is. In this context the media play a decisive role. Prime ministers in the television age face a two-edged sword in this regard. Easy access to, and manipulation of, the media can be a decisive attribute of the exercise of leadership by a prime minister. At the same time constant daily visual exposure can also breed familiarity and contempt as prime ministers utter the "same old line" or "yesterday's speech."

It is evident and natural that career experience influences a prime minister's policy preferences, views of political power, and at the same time limits his or her skills in some ways. Prime Minister Trudeau came to political power almost directly from an academic career. He had written about government and political philosophy, and his views were known on such topics as nationalism and federalism, human rights, and French–English relations in Canada.[4] He had limited parliamentary experience; nor had he worked in a large organizational setting or acquired managerial experience.

In sharp contrast, Prime Minister Clark was a product of party politics and was familiar with the insides of party machinery, local constituency politics, and the frustrations of parliamentary life on the opposition side.[5] Clark also lacked any significant experience in managing a large organization. Moreover, he did not have the intellectual range or communication skills of Trudeau. Clark was utterly victimized in the 1979–80 period by the so-called "wimp factor," a combination of media exaggeration of his alleged physical gangliness, periodic nervous speech habits, and general youth and inexperience.[6]

Prime Minister Diefenbaker was also a political outsider and, in addition, a proverbial lone wolf. A small-town prairie lawyer, Diefenbaker had suffered numerous political defeats and saw himself as constantly battling his political enemies, whether they were Bay Street financiers or came in the form of leadership threats from within his own Cabinet. Long years in parliamentary opposition had ensured that Diefenbaker would never be an "organization man" interested in or concerned about the machinery of government.[7]

In contrast to all of the above, Prime Minister Pearson had considerable experience in Ottawa as a deputy minister, minister, and diplomat. He was not a constituency politician. As a historian by education and a diplomat by experience, he was not, however, embued with a fascination with bureaucracy.[8] Possessed of an infectious amiability and legendary diplomatic skills, Pearson was both liked and at the same time often viewed as the consummate incrementalist who "muddled through" to a satisfactory, if temporary, consensus. He lacked the charisma and overall leadership skills of either Diefenbaker or Trudeau.

The regional origin and political base of a prime minister are of critical importance in defining policy ideas and preferences. Brian Mulroney and Pierre Trudeau are Quebeckers, and each has been concerned about Quebec's place within Confederation. John Diefenbaker and Joe Clark had their political base in western Canada, and it affected their emphasis on regional, agricultural, resource, and energy policy. Lester Pearson was from Ontario and brought a special concern about English Canada's relation to French Canada.

Prime ministers are obviously not totally imprisoned by their past accumulated traits. There is obviously a certain amount of "on the job" training and learning as experience is gained, crises are surmounted, and failures and mistakes are absorbed and stored in some corner of the political brain. Sooner or later, however, a prime minister must learn to manage the governmental and political leviathan he or she heads. A prime minister is never fully trained for the job in advance, but must survive in an environment where ideas are in conflict, the guideposts are vague, the advisers and the advice numerous and contradictory, and the future never as clear as the many critics believe it to be.

Controlling the Agenda and the Power of Appointment

Within the Cabinet and executive-bureaucratic arena, two of the major levers and/or points of prime ministerial control over policy are the Cabinet agenda itself (including the agenda of the Priorities and Planning Committee of Cabinet) and the power of appointment of ministers and senior officials. These powers are an amalgam of legal, constitutional, and prerogative powers, and are backed ultimately by the prime minister's power to dissolve Parliament and call an election. This latter power cannot be used or threatened very frequently, but then again it may not have to be because ministers and others are aware of its potential use.

The prime minister (along with key advisers) tries to exert as much control as possible over the Cabinet agenda, namely the issues to be considered, the order of consideration, and the relegation of lower-order problems for "further study." Such control is never fully exercised. In the past there has always been concern about the capacity of other ministers to conduct what, in football parlance, is called the "end run," that is, the tactic of disobeying the agenda-setting rules to bring a pet project or even an urgent project directly to Cabinet without "proper" prior assessment. In the simpler Cabinet committee and central agency days of the 1940s, 1950s, and early 1960s, it was often believed that "end runs" were too frequent. In part, of course, end runs were simply evidence of the influence of other line ministers who in those days did not have to run the minefield of the more elaborate central agency and Cabinet committee system constructed in the late 1960s and early 1970s.

The issue of Cabinet "end runs" and agenda control raises some interesting paradoxes when one attempts to assess the power of a particular prime minister or of different prime ministers at different times. Consider, for example, a comparison between Prime Minister Trudeau and Prime Minister Mackenzie King. It is probable that most people would argue that Trudeau was more powerful than King due to his greater command of the media and the centralization of power in central agencies, including the PMO. When one considers the agenda-setting process in the two eras, however, one may be inclined to reach a different conclusion. In King's day the Cabinet agenda and the central machinery was a more fluid and uncertain affair.[9] King's fellow ministers did not necessarily know what the agenda was. Where there is uncertainty in a relationship, there is a greater opportunity for the exercise of power, in this case by Mackenzie King who controlled the process. In contrast, in the Trudeau era the agenda-setting process and the Cabinet committee apparatus had become heavily bureaucratized; that is, the relations between ministers and the prime minister had been made more rule-ridden and *predictable*. The more predictable the process, the less room there is for arbitrary discretion. In this sense Trudeau may have had less power than often thought because he also had to obey the rules of the policy game he wanted his ministers to obey. It is also true, however, that more than any other minister, a prime minister can disobey whatever rules of procedure he or she puts in place and design others to suit his or her needs.

The power of appointment is also a crucial basis for a prime minister's influence on policy and reflects a central role as the bridge between the Cabinet and the public service as a whole. It is also closely tied to the power to reorganize departments and the overall machinery of government. The appointment of ministers and senior public servants is a prerogative that most leaders protect carefully. Peter Aucoin has developed the concept of positional policy, a concept that alerts us to the fact that overall policy for a given period of time in a given department or agency is set, not just by what the head of the agency does or says, but by the prior choice by the prime minister of the person whom he or she appoints and the organizational restructuring that may, on occasion, accompany such appointments.[10] This is perhaps the most human interpersonal dimension of politics and public policy, since it involves the complex calculus and chemistry of friendships and loyalties, competence and representativeness, patronage and purpose, and vanity and pride.

There is little science to the appointment process.[11] It is the art of judgment personified. Prime ministers face a welter of often contradictory principles and must face up to their own knowledge, toughness, and/or weaknesses in dealing with friends, enemies, and with many people they do not know well. Louis St. Laurent was known to keep his own counsel on appointment matters and made them expeditiously. John Diefenbaker discussed them with colleagues and had difficulty making up his mind.[12]

The potential conflicting principles and ideas inherent in appointment criteria are numerous. At the Cabinet level there are the issues of regional representativeness, competence, knowledge and experience, and the need to choose from the often limited personnel produced somewhat capriciously by the electoral and party process. At the senior official level there is the need to maintain some sense of a career public service, while at the same time ensuring that public service and agency appointees are sensitive to, and supportive of, the government's preferences in the policy field concerned. At both levels there are needs to balance the concept of turnover versus tenure.[13] By increasing the turnover of ministers, prime ministers may enhance their power over their colleagues simply by a visible exercise of their appointment power. It can also enable them to weed out weaker ministers and put a new public face to their government. It allows them to put a minister in place with specific instructions about what they, as prime minister, want done. On the other hand, increased tenure can augment a minister's knowledge of his or her responsibilities, enhance familiarity with a powerful clientele or region of the country, or even ensure that a Cabinet enemy is isolated and preserved in a safe place. By increasing the tenure of ministers and simultaneously increasing the turnover of deputy ministers, the prime minister may feel he or she can enhance political control of the public service. Correspondingly, a deputy kept in a department while several ministers rotate in and out may also enhance a political leader's policy purpose.

Not surprisingly, in the face of this array of principles practice varies in infinite ways both in the same prime minister's tenure in office and among prime ministerial regimes. For example, in the Mulroney era, macroeconomic policy has enjoyed considerable success. It is both a cause and an effect of the long tenure of Michael Wilson as Minister of Finance and relative stability at the deputy ministerial level as well. At another extreme, in the Trudeau era there were several ministers of consumer and corporate affairs, reflecting an unwillingness to proceed further with changes to competition policy that were strongly opposed by the business community.[14] In this instance the several ministers were offered as veritable sacrificial lambs while they maintained a holding operation for a year or two. Between these extremes are a host of other permutations and combinations of "policy-making by appointment."

It is evident, of course, that not all appointees perform as expected in ministerial or other realms. For example, it is doubtful that the Diefenbaker government's appointment of Mr. Justice Hall in the early 1960s was premised on the assumption that he would produce a report that was enthusiastically supportive of compulsory medicare. Nor was the appointment of Justice Berger by the Trudeau government expected to yield the controversies resulting from his later report on energy and the northern environment.

Appointments also raise issues, especially at the ministerial level, but at other levels as well, about how to deal with political deadwood or incompetence, or simply with persons who, for many reasons, are no longer suited to their current tasks. As human beings, prime ministers are reluctant to deal ruthlessly with fellow partisans and politicians. They have an appreciation of how hard it is to get good people to commit themselves to the risks of a political career. This is why the Senate and other agency appointments assume an importance out of all proportion to the role of these institutions per se. Prime ministers search inevitably for substitutes for the ignominy of the political firing.

All of the above elements affect the prime minister's efforts to formulate policy, set priorities, maintain power, and manage the policy process within government and in the country at large. It is in this context that our survey of prime ministerial policy preferences must be viewed.

The Policy Preferences of Prime Ministers

The profiles presented here are brief. They are intended to illuminate the importance of the general preferences of Prime Ministers Mulroney, Trudeau, Pearson, and Diefenbaker, both on policy issues and, where it can be discerned, on policy structures and processes. It is essential to stress again the difficulties of making these comparisons due to factors such as the widely varying periods of tenure in office. It must also be emphasized that no political leader is fully consistent in the application of the principles or ideas he or she most cherishes. Often, a leader is also reacting to the perceived excesses or weaknesses of predecessors in office or of the leaders of the opposition political parties.

Prime Minister Mulroney

Perhaps the leading political characteristic of Prime Minister Brian Mulroney is his intense partisanship. While all leaders are partisans to some extent, Mulroney came to power after a career spent in Conservative backroom machinations in Quebec where Tories had for decades been shut out of power and influence. Unlike Pierre Trudeau, he was not known for his penchant for ideas. He was more akin to the back-slapping verbal politician who always seemed to be campaigning regardless of whether there was an election or not.[15] He was permanently on the telephone, trying to find out what people thought and what was going on.

His personal style has cast him into the mould of a brokerage politician, more interested in the clash of interests and the search for consensus than in grand ideas and rational planning.[16] He brought to office a mild ideological instinct to restrain the role of government, and he certainly had no compunction about engaging in bureaucracy-bashing. But these instincts were just as likely to emerge from partisan urges as ideological ones. This was because the Liberal Party had been in office virtually continuously since 1963 and twenty years of Liberal dominance had made Mulroney suspicious of anything Liberal, be it the technocratic style of the Trudeau years, the suspected Liberal sympathies of senior civil servants in Ottawa, or the province- and region-bashing inherent in Liberal policies such as the National Energy Program. All of these suspicions were embedded as well in a fierce partisan desire to replace the Liberals as the dominant governing party, not only in Ottawa, but especially in his own Quebec base of power.[17]

The notion of a brokerage style prompted Mulroney to do away with most of the horizontal coordinating machinery and the elaborate paper flow of the Trudeau years. He wanted to deal with ministers bilaterally and in different combinations, freed from the "processitis" of the Trudeau era. This view was also extended to interest groups and to provincial governments as well. In the former arena, new forms of consultation would be the norm and in the latter, "national reconciliation" would be practised and preached.

In some respects, these instincts were also a part of the Mulroney personality. A garrulous and cheerful man who liked to be liked, Mulroney genuinely thought that governing and policy should proceed in ways that were less combative than in the 1980 to 1984 Trudeau government. But this approach also sowed the seeds of its own contradictions. After initially governing this way, the Mulroney system found itself practising the politics of trivial pursuit. In short, it was unable to manage the numerous smaller issues that, when badly handled, can weaken a government. As a result, in 1986 it established a system that gave new importance to the role of the deputy prime minister, who chaired a new Operations Committee of the Cabinet. It became the true nerve centre of the Mulroney regime. Don Mazankowski became his especially trusted "Mr. Fix It" or, in the view of some, the "Minister of Everything."[18]

But juxtaposed against this partly truthful image of the Mulroney brokerage policy style, a style that otherwise suggests care and caution, was a policy record that included some very historic and risky endeavours. For a man without ideas, Mulroney went for concepts that overturned much of the post–World War II consensus. His free trade, Meech Lake, and tax reform initiatives were all extremely divisive and risky.[19] Indeed, as Colin Campbell points out, Mulroney shifted from a broker politician to "a highly risky brand of survival politics—so dangerous, in fact, that the stakes involved the very character of the Canadian nation."[20]

Mulroney, however, is not an unthinking, flighty glad-hander. While a hands-on politician to the core, he worked extremely long hours reading Cabinet papers to inform himself of the issues. But his instinct for partisan battle was always finely honed and ready to take charge of his more cerebral moments.

Prime Minister Trudeau

Prime Minister Pierre Elliott Trudeau is unique among the prime ministers surveyed not only because of a much longer tenure in office, but also because prior to entering politics he wrote extensively about his philosophy of politics. Four basic philosophical premises anchored the Trudeau view of public policy in general. These, in turn, had an impact on his policy preferences. The four premises are an opposition to narrow nationalism, a belief in the view that governments exist to support and defend individual rights, a belief in the need to countervail powerful policy tendencies, and a belief in rationality as opposed to emotion as a guide to human behaviour.

Trudeau's famous articles on nationalism and French Canadians clearly reflect his opposition to what he viewed as narrow cultural nationalism.[21] Trudeau did not oppose a broader nationalism, but strongly criticized one whose boundaries reinforced a purely cultural definition of such nationalist sentiment. This view not only propelled Trudeau into federal politics, but strongly influenced the view of Canada he espoused and enshrined both in the Official Languages Act, which institutionalized bilingualism, and later in the Charter of Rights and constitutional reform passed in 1982. He stoutly rejected the two-nation view of Canada and sought to ensure that French Canadians would feel at home in any province and not just in Quebec.

Trudeau's belief in the freedom of the individual as the ultimate purpose that the state exists to serve was expressed by his very early proposal for a Charter of Rights. The Charter itself was not achieved until 1982 after Trudeau's unforeseen return to power, but there can be little doubt that it will continue to affect both the nature of government and public policy.[22]

There are, of course, contradictions between Trudeau's first two premises and the third, his devotion to the theory of counterweights in which government would shift its weight and direction to counteract evolving excesses, be it in centralized federalism, market power, or dependence on other states. While the notion of counterweights can be a philosophical premise of a decidedly woolly nature, it appears to have guided his thinking in the decision to impose wage and price controls in 1975 and in the new nationalism directed against the provinces in 1980 and 1982.[23]

Finally, there is the Trudeau preference for rationality. Trudeau's view of rationality only partly converges with the concept of a rational model outlined in Chapter 6. Radwansky characterizes Trudeau's view in two ways. First, it introduced "an element of intolerance into the system which was otherwise designed to encourage diversity."[24] Second, it produced an insistence by him on the need for cold, unemotional stances in politics. Trudeau did strive to make the policy process within the Cabinet and executive structures more rational. Indeed, if there is one overall perception of his era in power, it is that of a technocratic government. That he was not very successful in being rational should not be surprising, but we will reserve further judgment on this question until Chapters 9 and 10. It is useful to note, however, the apparent contrast between Trudeau's fascination with rational structures and his often dogmatic and argumentative public persona and the accounts of his actual conduct of Cabinet meetings. Several ministers have publicly and privately attested to his fair-minded, almost Socratic and consultative behaviour in guiding Cabinet meetings.

Prime Minister Pearson

Prime Minister Lester B. Pearson presided over five years of minority government, but this difficult political liability was compensated by the opportunity to govern during a period of economic buoyancy.[25] He also had to respond to and manage extremely delicate changes in the relations between English and French Canadians, as the national impact of Quebec's Quiet Revolution began to be felt for the first time. As it is with every Canadian political leader, Pearson's policy preferences and ideas were partly his own and partly the product of the times and of the views of the political party he headed. Although political party platforms per se usually bear only a tenuous re-semblance to what governing parties actually do, the early 1960s were an exception. The Liberals' 1960 Kingston policy conference had clearly helped set the Pearson agenda, particularly in the social policy field.

Pearson himself was best known for his views and skills in foreign policy, where he had won a Nobel Prize. His two governments, however, were most identified with the major initiatives they took in the social policy field, including the Canada Pension Plan, medicare, a major expansion of federal financing for higher education, and major initiatives in employment training. His government also introduced collective bargaining in the federal public service. In addition, the Pearson government forged ahead with the establishment of the Maple Leaf as Canada's flag. In the delicate area of relations between English and French Canadians, the Pearson regime enunciated the concept of "cooperative federalism," witnessed the work of the Royal Commission on Bilingualism and Biculturalism, and saw the passage of legislation to allow Quebec to opt out of certain joint programs in exchange for tax points.

It is clear that Pearson strongly supported and preferred these largely social policy initiatives. Though not Kennedy-like in style or manner, he was influenced by the social buoyancy of the Kennedy era in the United States. This was perhaps best symbolized by his support for the creation of the Company of Young Canadians. One cannot underestimate, however, the degree to which Liberal policy thinkers, including Walter Gordon, Pearson's first Minister of Finance, forged their social views on the assumption and belief that the economy would be a buoyant one and that the social programs were affordable without the need to impose overly burdensome new taxes. The economy was in a sense taken for granted by Pearson. This was partly reflected in the lack of attention he personally gave economic issues and the difficulties his government encountered over selected economic issues such as in labour relations and strikes and foreign investment, especially in the first Walter Gordon budget speech.[26]

As to structure and process, the Pearson views and record present a mixed package. We have already referred earlier in this chapter to Pearson's quixotic "60 days of decision" approach, his antidote to Diefenbaker's indecisiveness. As a man with extensive Ottawa experience, Pearson was not especially enamoured of the need to reorganize the Cabinet, at least not until near the end of his tenure in office when he established the Cabinet Committee on Priorities and Planning. He did support the vague "planning" notions inherent in the establishment of the Economic Council of Canada and the Science Council of Canada, but these bodies were attributable much more to the views of advisers and ministers such as Maurice Lamontagne, who saw them, equally vaguely, as hybrid Canadian versions of French-style "indicative planning."

Matheson's analysis of the Pearson habits in the actual conduct of Cabinet stresses the looseness of the prime minister's approach, something that later appalled Pierre Trudeau when he was Minister of Justice in the Pearson Cabinet.[27] While an easy-going amiability is perhaps congruent with Pearson's personality and diplomatic habits, it is nonetheless important to recall again the perpetual minority government status of his five years in power, a political condition even less conducive to orderliness and discipline, assuming such a condition can ever exist in any Cabinet.

Prime Minister Diefenbaker

Prime Minister John Diefenbaker was a western Canadian populist and a charismatic leader. He and the Progressive Conservatives came to power in 1957 and formed a minority government after twenty-two years of Liberal rule. In a very real sense, Diefenbaker arrived as the embodiment of an eclectic set of grievances held by those who had not fully shared in the heady prosperity of the postwar years. He had successfully labelled the tired St. Laurent–C. D. Howe Liberals as an arrogant, smug, and uncaring government. Diefenbaker's minority regime of 1957–58 was therefore characterized by a spate of what were essentially a diffuse set of social, often regionally defined, measures.[28] Thus, changes in old age security benefits, support for hospital construction, improved equalization payments for poorer provinces, increased agricultural support payments, and special rural development initiatives were begun, the latter being the precursor of Canada's later explicit "regional development" policies.

Some of this social energy was also later reflected in the early years of the massive Diefenbaker majority government elected in 1958. By then Diefenbaker had spoken passionately of his views of "One Canada" and his "northern vision," including a "roads to resources" program. The former was symbolized in the federal Bill of Rights passed in 1960, which defined Diefenbaker's view of the un-hyphenated Canadian. The northern vision never materialized, partly because it was never clear what it meant. Diefenbaker embodied ideas, but had little intellectual discipline or inclination to think them through.

Diefenbaker's strong views about "One Canada" undoubtedly adversely affected his ability to deal effectively with French Canada, including the large contingent of Quebec MPs in his own caucus. It was an idea that screened out other possible forms of accommodation. This prospect was not aided by another aspect of his vision, his foreign and trade policy view that Canada could reduce its excessive dependence on the United States by diverting a higher portion of its trade to Britain, the mother country.

The persistence of Diefenbaker's nationalism was also reflected in his view of whether Canada should accept nuclear warheads as part of its BOMARC missile bases, as the Americans were pressuring his government to do.[29] This issue ultimately brought down his government. Though Diefenbaker's indecision on this matter was a product of many factors, there is little doubt a major one was his ingrained instincts not to be, and not to be *seen* to be, catering to American pressure. But his nationalism and latent anti-Americanism, not surprisingly, were exercised in a selective way. For example, despite the symbolism of the historic 1956 "Pipeline Debate," a debate that forged Diefenbaker's public persona, there was little reluctance in 1961 to devise a National Oil Policy, which was strongly supported by the American government. This was the policy that divided the Canadian oil market at the Ottawa Valley, with points west served by Canadian sources of supply and points east by foreign U.S. multinational sources of supply.[30]

Diefenbaker's views were also influenced by his perpetual concern over the loyalty of his colleagues and his lack of knowledge or interest in certain policy fields. His views of the serious dispute between his government and James Coyne, the Governor of the Bank of Canada, were in part due to a simple lack of interest in monetary affairs and in part because of Diefenbaker's mistrust of his own Minister of Finance, Donald Fleming. Fleming had finished second to him in the Tory leadership race and had close connections with the Toronto business and financial community, which Diefenbaker also suspected.

Prime Minister Diefenbaker's overall conduct of the Cabinet was also reflected by a frequent lack of trust of his colleagues. Andrew Johnson's extensive study of the Diefenbaker Cabinet, in comparison with the previous St. Laurent Cabinet, draws out the different features of each period and hence of the two prime ministers. He characterizes the Diefenbaker regime as "collegial" in the extreme, while St. Laurent fostered a "pluralistic" Cabinet in which he trusted ministers to take initiatives.[31] While these differences cannot all be attributed to personality, they are certainly partly due to this reality.

As we noted earlier in the chapter, Diefenbaker was not an "organization man." He was a small-town prairie lawyer who had defended society's outcasts in court. He was a politician used to years of opposition politics. Structure did not interest him greatly. He was concerned enough about a perceived "Liberal-dominated" public service to "consider" wholesale changes at the deputy ministerial level, but did not act on this concern. He appointed businessman J. Grant Glassco to head a Royal Commission on Government Organization, but it was left to the Pearson government to deal with its results.

Conclusions

Prime ministers are different. They do have more power than their colleagues. They do have different policy preferences, career experiences, and definitions of Canada's future as they see it. They possess the normal range of human strengths and weaknesses. They reflect different attitudes to knowledge and analysis—from the intellectual and cerebral Trudeau to the gut political instincts of Mulroney and Diefenbaker. At the same time they are propelled by ideas and conditions not wholly within their power to change. Like their ministers, they are pulled by the idea of cabinet government in two directions at once, the need for collective legitimacy and coordination and the need to delegate and allow for the individual decisiveness of other persons, some of whom are often as ambitious and skilled, as well as flawed, as they are.

Notes

1. For other general reviews see Leslie Pal and David Taras, eds., *Prime Ministers and Premiers* (Scarborough: Prentice-Hall, 1989); W. Matheson, *The Prime Minister and the Cabinet* (Toronto: Methuen, 1976), chs. 6, 7, and 8; T. Hockin, ed., *Apex of Power*, 2nd ed. (Toronto: Prentice-Hall, 1977), chs. 21, 23, and 24; and Andrew Johnson, "The Structure of the Canadian Cabinet," unpublished Doctoral Thesis, Oxford University, 1980.
2. See Peter C. Newman, *The Distemper of Our Times* (Toronto: McClelland and Stewart, 1968), ch. 2. See also Denis Smith, *Gentle Patriot: A Political Biography of Walter Gordon* (Edmonton: Hurtig, 1973), chs. 7, 8, and 9; and Lester B. Pearson, *Mike* (Toronto: Signet, 1976), ch. 4.
3. See George Radwanski, *Trudeau* (Toronto: Macmillan, 1978), chs. 3 and 8; and G. Bruce Doern and Peter Aucoin, *The Structures of Policy Making in Canada* (Toronto: Macmillan, 1972), ch. 2.
4. See Radwanski, *Trudeau*, Richard Gwyn, *The Northern Magus* (Markham, Ont.: Paperjacks, 1980), and Pierre Elliott Trudeau, *Federalism and the French Canadians* (Toronto: Macmillan, 1968).
5. See Jeffrey Simpson, *Discipline of Power* (Toronto: Personal Library, 1981), and David Humphreys, *Joe Clark: A Portrait* (Ottawa: Deneau and Greenberg, 1978).
6. Simpson, *Discipline of Power*, ch. 3.
7. On Diefenbaker, see Peter C. Newman, *Renegade in Power* (Toronto: McClelland and Stewart, 1963); John G. Diefenbaker, *One Canada* (Toronto: Macmillan, 1975); and George Grant, *Lament for a Nation* (Toronto: McClelland and Stewart, 1965).
8. Newman, *Distemper of Our Times*, chs. 3, 4, and 5; and Pearson, *Mike*, chs. 4 and 8.
9. Johnson, "Structure of the Canadian Cabinet," ch. 2, and J. W. Pickersgill, *The Mackenzie King Record*, Vol. I, 1939–1944 (Toronto: University of Toronto Press, 1960), 6–8.
10. On the excesses of reorganization, see G. Bruce Doern and Peter Aucoin, *Public Policy in Canada* (Toronto: Macmillan, 1979), chs. 3, 8, and 11.
11. Pearson, *Mike*, ch. 8.
12. Johnson, "Structure of the Canadian Cabinet," ch. 4; and Matheson, *The Prime Minister and the Cabinet*, ch. 8.
13. The 1979 Lambert Royal Commission focused on this point but treated it in a very narrow and unsatisfactory way since it applied only managerial criteria to it and not political criteria. See Royal Commission on Financial Management and Accountability, *Final Report* (Ottawa: Minister of Supply and Services, 1979), ch. 10.
14. See W. T. Stanbury, "Consumer and Corporate Affairs: Portrait of a Regulatory Department," in G. Bruce Doern, ed., *How Ottawa Spends Your Tax Dollars 1982* (Toronto: James Lorimer, 1982), ch. 8.

15. See Jeffrey Simpson, "The Lessons of Power," *Maclean's*, November 1988, 47–59.
16. See Peter Aucoin, "Organizational Change in the Machinery of Government: From Rational Management to Brokerage Politics," *Canadian Journal of Political Science* 19, no. 1 (March 1986), 3–27.
17. See Andrew B. Gollner and Daniel Salee, eds., *Canada Under Mulroney* (Montreal: Véhicule Press, 1988).
18. See Charlotte Gray, "Check It With Maz," *Report on Business Magazine*, October 1988, 146–54.
19. See G. Bruce Doern and Brian W. Tomlin, *Faith and Fear: The Free Trade Story* (Toronto: Stoddart, 1991), ch. 12.
20. See Colin Campbell, "Mulroney's Brokerage Politics: The Ultimate in Politicized Incompetence," in Gollner and Salee, eds., *Canada Under Mulroney*, 328.
21. Trudeau, *Federalism and the French Canadians*.
22. See Robert Sheppard and Michael Valpy, *The National Deal* (Toronto: 1982), and Peter H. Russell, "The Effect of a Charter of Rights on the Policy Making Role of Canadian Courts," *Canadian Public Administration* 25, no. 1 (Spring 1982), 1–33.
23. See Radwansky, *Trudeau*, ch. 7; and G. Bruce Doern, "Liberal Priorities 1982: The Limits of Scheming Virtuously," in Doern, ed., *How Ottawa Spends Your Tax Dollars 1982*, ch. 1.
24. Radwansky, *Trudeau*, 121–22.
25. See Newman, *Distemper of Our Times*; and Robert Bothwell, Ian Drummond, and John English, *Canada Since 1945* (Toronto: University of Toronto Press, 1981), chs. 26, 27, and 28.
26. See Smith, *Gentle Patriot*, chs. 8 and 9.
27. Matheson, *The Prime Minister and the Cabinet*, 167.
28. See Newman, *Renegade in Power*, chs. 4 and 5; and Bothwell et al., *Canada Since 1945*, chs. 21 to 25.
29. See Peyton V. Lyon, *Canada in World Affairs, 1961–1963* (Toronto: Oxford University Press, 1968).
30. See John N. McDougall, *Fuels and the National Policy* (Toronto: Butterworths, 1982), chs. 5 and 6.
31. Johnson, "Structure of the Canadian Cabinet," 371–76.

CHAPTER 9

Priorities and Priority-Setting

The federal Cabinet has several major occasions when it attempts to inform Canadian citizens about priorities and about what the government stands for. These include speeches from the throne, budget speeches, speeches on the tabling of expenditure estimates, international economic summit meetings, and crisis speeches by the prime minister. From time to time political party conventions and the electoral hustings provide additional vehicles for this essential act of political communication and policy-making.

These priorities affect the fate of particular individual policy fields. It therefore follows that one cannot understand or explain the drift or evolution of a single policy field except in relation to the broader cluster of priorities present in any given time period. Some policy fields are persistently high on the priority list (for example, inflation or unemployment), while others bob up and down like pistons on an engine (for example, policies for research and development). Still others manage to squeeze their way onto the agenda, but only to its outer fringes (for example, occupational health or policies for native peoples).

The purpose of this chapter is to offer a critical review of priorities and priority-setting in greater detail. This is done by taking two portraits of priorities over two time periods. The first portrait is historical and encompasses Canada's history since 1867. The second view focuses on priorities since 1974 and includes an analysis of the formal expression of priorities in the throne speeches and budget speeches of the Trudeau and Mulroney governments. This will help set the scene for our analysis in Chapter 11 of the formal annual priority-setting and expenditure process.

Looking Back: Priorities and Political Memory

Priorities always look clearer in the past than in the future. Hindsight has its much advertised advantages. The main reason for reviewing priorities in a historical perspective is that political systems have memories. Both policy successes and failures become a part of political institutions, partisan allegiances, regional identities, and the overall collective political and social composition of Canada. While certain decades may have been dominated by one or more overall priority concerns, they also communally produce a historical list of achievements, grievances, and perceptions of grievances that affect the priorities of subsequent decades. Some of these unresolved grievances persist to the present day. In this section we briefly review national priorities in seven time periods, 1867 to 1914, 1914 to 1929, 1930 to 1945, 1945 to 1957, 1957 to 1970, 1970 to 1982, and 1983 to the early 1990s. Needless to say, these dates are somewhat arbitrary since history can rarely be chopped up quite this conveniently. For our limited purposes, however, the periods help to highlight major events and trends.

1867 to 1914: The National Policy

This period can be characterized as being dominated by Sir John A. Macdonald's National Policy.[1] The National Policy was, in fact, an array of policies intended to create an industrial base in Ontario and Quebec under a protective tariff, unite the country from sea to sea by building the Canadian Pacific Railway, and settle the West to develop its resources and to supply the eastern industrial heartland and also to head off encroaching American interests anxious to exploit the Canadian frontier. The National Policy was national and regional policy rolled into one. It was an act of defiance against the "efficiency" of the north–south axis of North America. It embraced tariff policy, transportation policy, and immigration policy. It was achieved through an English–French Canadian political alliance within the Conservative Party that survived, initially at least, both financial scandal and the hanging of Louis Riel.

Though challenged by the Laurier government and a brief flirtation with free trade, the National Policy essentially survived intact. It helped create the modern Canadian industrial structure, centred in Ontario and Quebec, but truncated in shape in the sense of having to serve a small Canadian market with limited export potential for manufactured goods. It was also a resource-based policy dependent on the resources of the hinterland, both to serve the industrial heartland and to export abroad.

1914 to 1929: The Attack on the National Policy

Those Canadians who increasingly saw themselves regionally, and even in terms of economic classes, as the victims of the National Policy made some political headway in the 1914 to 1929 period. The period can therefore be seen as a period of attack against the National Policy. Aided by the massive changes induced by World War I, including the conscription crisis and the continuing rapid settlement of the West, the period produced major challenges to the previous national consensus.[2] Prairie populism rose in opposition to eastern financial and industrial power. Provincial governments, thought initially to be minor appendages to a centralized federal government, began to exercise influence because of the need to build and finance the social, economic, and educational infrastructure of an increasingly industrialized, urbanized, and less agricultural and rural population. Hydro facilities, schools, and highways had to be built, and minimum social insurance programs had to be created to assist those who were the casualties of the market. Increased labour militancy resulted as well from a struggle for basic recognition of labour's rights—rights that were, in the main, not achieved until World War II.

1930 to 1945: Depression and War

Depression and World War II traumatized this period of Canadian and global political life. It emblazoned on the consciousness of post–World War II political leaders a desire to avoid future wars and depressions, but did not produce results in the specific period between 1930 and 1945. It was essentially war itself that ended the depression and put labour, capital, and land back to productive use.[3] Though made infinitely worse by the depression, the period was nonetheless initially a continuation of the pattern of challenge to the National

Policy by those who were not its beneficiaries. It produced yet another wave of prairie populism and eventually yielded the agrarian and labour alliance that later became the Co-operative Commonwealth Federation (CCF), the predecessor to the social democratic NDP. In the midst of World War II, the political left enjoyed its greatest electoral success until that time, forming a government in Saskatchewan and the official opposition in Ontario.

Despite the growing protest against the status quo, there was, in the 1930s, no equivalent level of national leadership or reformist social philosophy in Canada to that of Roosevelt's New Deal in the United States. Canada's national politics continued to be influenced by the inevitable delicacy of French–English relations, relations that soured badly in the midst of another conscription crisis during World War II.

World War II resurrected and greatly expanded Canada's industrial base, but left it centred in Ontario and Quebec. Canada's natural resources again became valuable to a Western alliance desperately in need of an expanded and secure resource supply base. Since the cooperation of labour would be essential to the war production effort, the period saw the first extensive national recognition of labour's right to bargain collectively and to strike.

1945 to 1957: Keynesianism and the Second National Policy

This period is often viewed to be one in which a Second National Policy was assembled to dominate federal priorities in the postwar decade. Such a policy was forged, it is often suggested, by the Keynesian doctrine, which created an acceptable economic and social rationale in a capitalist economy for increased intervention by the state.[4] Thus, governments had to construct both a permanent infrastructure of programs that would stabilize the economy in the postwar era, and also strategically alter aggregate taxing and spending activities to ensure that economic investment and consumer demand was maintained. While Keynesianism helped legitimize the idea of this kind of macro intervention, it was not the only normative basis for intervention in Canada. The post–World War II reconstruction program was also influenced by the strength of populist and left-wing political pressure, by the prewar and wartime use of public enterprises, and by the general social welfare concepts articulated in the United Kingdom by the Beveridge Report and its Canadian equivalents.

It is probably fair to characterize this period in terms of the emergence of a Second National Policy, but it is an error to associate it fully with Keynesian economics. Keynesian fiscal policy has never been fully practised in Canada, and certainly not in this period. Moreover, other than the new array of social welfare programs launched in the post–World War II period (family allowances, expanded old age security programs, etc.), the core of Canada's economic policies during this period were not forged by a Keynesian Department of Finance, but rather by a Department of Reconstruction, Defence Production, and later Trade and Commerce headed by C. D. Howe.[5] Howe's policies were essentially to use tariff and tax policies to encourage foreign equity investment in Canada. The result was to produce continued prosperity until the late 1950s, but also to reinforce the age-old pattern of Canada's truncated industrial structure first put in place by Macdonald's National Policy.[6] But by the end of the 1950s it was dominated by foreign ownership.

The period was also characterized by Liberal Party dominance and by the dominance of the federal government over the provincial governments.[7] The latter was reflected in the tight postwar tax agreements that centralized fiscal control in Ottawa. Liberal Party dominance was assured by the renewed English–French accommodation, evident in the King–Lapointe, King–St. Laurent, and St. Laurent–Howe–Pearson leadership alliances within successive Liberal Cabinets, and by the Liberals' successful portrayal of the Tories as the anti-Quebec party.

1957 to 1970: The Heyday of Social Programs

We have already examined key features of this period in Chapter 8 when we surveyed the Diefenbaker and Pearson regimes. We will also examine in some detail the priorities of the latter part of this period, in the early Trudeau years, in the next section of this chapter. It is essential here to highlight certain general attributes of this period as a whole. In general we characterize it as the heyday of social policy. This was first reflected in the regional definition of social policy and other grievances that led to the election of the Diefenbaker government. The quasi-populist basis of the Diefenbaker appeal was reflected in the spurt of reforms in 1957 and 1958, which included agricultural and rural development programs, hospitalization grants, and old age pension increases. It was evident in the loosening of the federal fiscal reins through more generous tax agreements with, and equalization payments to, the provinces.[8]

The second round of change occurred in the mid-1960s when the Pearson government launched several major social policy initiatives, including the Canada Pension Plan, medicare, further old age security increases, the Canada Assistance Plan, and federal assistance to higher education and employment training.[9] Much of this was accompanied by buoyant expectations about a growing economy. The economy was buoyed by the expansionary consumer demand of the postwar baby boom, as well as by extensive immigration in the 1950s and 1960s. The growing economy would produce increased revenues even without the need for massive tax increases, and hence the social programs were affordable, both those launched by Ottawa and still others launched by increasingly expansionary and aggressive provincial governments.

The early Trudeau years promised more of the same, albeit sold under the label of "the Just Society." Where the Pearson Liberals offered a quantum jump in social welfare, Trudeau offered a qualitative leap, promising a renewed effort to reduce regional disparities and to improve linguistic, cultural, environmental, and individual rights.[10]

1970 to 1982: The Slow Rediscovery of Scarcity

The period from the early 1970s to 1982 is perhaps best characterized as one in which there was a grudging and belated rediscovery of scarcity. As declining economic growth and high inflation rates exerted their deadly double influence, politics, policy, and the allocation of resources became increasingly a zero-sum game. Gains for one group, region, or class increasingly became a visible loss for another group, region, or class. The OPEC oil crisis and the continuing pressure of the environmental movement initially taught Canadians more about scarcity in its even broader ecological dimensions. By the early 1980s social policy programs were under attack as beleaguered debt-ridden governments sought to redeploy scarce tax dollars to shore up the industrial base of the economy or to reduce huge deficits.

Despite these realizations, the decade of the 1980s began with a remarkably aggressive and interventionist agenda by the revived Liberal government of Pierre Trudeau. Its content, centred on the National Energy Program, is examined later in the chapter, but it should be noted that it decidedly set the scene for the pro-market counteragenda enunciated and later largely put into place by the Mulroney Conservatives.

If the period as a whole involved the slow rediscovery of scarcity, it ended abruptly and resoundingly with the effects of the 1982 recession. The recession was largely policy induced and partly reflected the efforts by the Reagan administration to break the back of high inflation with a monetarist policy. Its effects on Canada were devastating. The loss of over 300 000 manufacturing jobs brought back memories of the 1930s and jolted Canada and the Western world into a search for new options.

1983 to the Early 1990s: The Neoconservative Agenda

The most coherent agenda available was that which gained the label of neoconservatism or simply the "new right." Comprising a mixture of monetarism, expenditure cutbacks, deregulation, and privatization, the agenda was centred in the theory and early practices of both the Thatcher Conservatives in Great Britain and the Reagan Republicans in the United States. In both countries the agenda was also linked to supply-side tax cuts for upper-income earners and to expansionist defence policies to counter the Soviet threat.[11]

With the "new right" agenda already firmly underway by 1983, it was selectively borrowed and adapted in Canada, first by the Trudeau Liberals in their last two years in power and then more fulsomely by the Mulroney Conservatives. The Canadian version of this agenda is brought out in greater detail below. It included the Canada–U.S. Free Trade Agreement, expenditure restraint, deregulation, and privatization, accompanied by appropriate amounts of bureaucracy-bashing. But such policies were leavened by the need to consider the realities of Canada's regional makeup.[12] Thus, while bureaucracy-bashing might strike a resonant cord in all regions, spending cuts were worrisome to Atlantic Canada.

If the Mulroney agenda was decidedly pro-market in its orientation, it was also decentralist vis-à-vis federal–provincial relations. This was most symbolized by the Mulroney government's efforts to obtain support for the Meech Lake Accord. The failure to achieve agreement led to a severe constitutional crisis. However, the agenda of the late 1980s and early 1990s was not simply one of economic priorities and an attempted rolling back of the boundaries of the state. Other issues were percolating in ways that defied conventional post–World War II definitions of problems. Thus, issues as broad, important, and emotive as abortion, AIDS, environmental policy (including global warming), drugs, and an aging population struggled for their place on the public agenda.

In terms of the seven periods, however, it is possible to see the dominant concerns of each era. Depending upon one's metaphorical preference, they show a different ebb and flow, or a different phase in the swing of the pendulum between different aspects of public policy, politics, and ideas: in short, between creating economic wealth and redistributing it regionally and among income groups, between economic policy and social policy, between national policy and regional equity and sensitivity, between the centralization and decentralization of federalism, and between those who benefit from technological and other kinds of change and those who attempt to stabilize and protect their lives from the adverse effects of such changes.

Hindsight allows us to see priorities with greater clarity. But the priorities of the past have also been forged in vastly different political times. For example, the role of mass communication, especially television, is only a recent phenomenon. The early decades were not characterized by democratic mass suffrage and by democratic methods of choosing leaders. For these and other reasons, not the least of which is that it is part of Canada's more recent political memory, we need to have a second portrait of priorities, one in which all of the general modern conditions of democratic politics are present.

Priorities in the Trudeau and Mulroney Eras: Throne and Budget Speeches

The priorities of the Trudeau and Mulroney governments should ultimately be viewed in the context of the broad historical priorities sketched above. But the priorities are also noteworthy because they were devised by governments headed by prime ministers who, as we have seen in Chapter 8, had quite different approaches to policy-making. Pierre Trudeau openly enunciated a philosophy whose intent was to make public policy processes more rational. He was critical of what he perceived to be the disorganized nature of the previous Pearson government. Brian Mulroney, on the other hand, disavowed this kind of technocratic approach and sought to practise a brokerage style of policy-making.

We review the priorities and the priority-setting process since 1974 in a dual way. We survey them chronologically in each prime ministerial period in office, but in each period we will also compare selected throne speeches and budget speeches, particularly to illustrate the continuous difficulty in meshing general priorities with economic priorities. But when comparing the general internal documents on priorities with throne speeches and budget speeches, it is essential to remember that we are not comparing totally analogous documents or policy occasions. They each deal with different time periods. The internal priorities exercise and the documents it produces is centred in the Priorities and Planning Committee of the Cabinet, chaired by the prime minister. It is intended to drive the *internal* decision and resource allocation process and operates annually. The speech from the throne is a *public* document intended to convey the government's overall legislative and policy plans to Parliament as well as to communicate a general view of priorities to Canadians. Throne speeches are not necessarily given on an annual basis, but rather to open a new session of Parliament. The budget speech presents the Minister of Finance's (and the government's) view of the state of the economy and the fiscal and other policy measures needed to manage the economy effectively. Budget speeches are prepared in relative secrecy even within the Cabinet. They usually occur annually, but in some years there have been two budget speeches per year. We will defer until later chapters the detailed analysis of the machinery of priority-setting and resource allocation and will refer here only to selected major developments since 1974. It is sufficient to stress, however, that our brief chronological review of these years shows the difficulty of coordinating the priorities reflected in these several priority-setting documents and time frames.

1974 to 1979

Following the return to a majority Trudeau government in 1974, efforts were made to enhance the legitimacy of the priority-setting process among ministers and their officials. This included more elaborate ministerial meetings, as well as the submission from departments of their plans regarding how they would contribute to and implement the priorities. An effort was also made in the mid-1970s to make the priority list more explicit and detailed.

   The crux of the problem was highlighted in an internal Cabinet report dated January 30, 1975. It noted:

> Over the past few years, the government has established a set of priorities which were meant to guide government activities and the allocation of resources — not only resources in terms of dollars and man years but also resources in terms of the time of the House of Commons, the Cabinet, and policy analysts. In the past two years this statement of government priorities has taken the form of a set of policy thrusts and major objectives. The process has been useful and has resulted in significant progress being made in many areas. However, the process has not been too successful in bringing a concerted effort to bear on the achievement of the government's priorities, nor have the priorities been related to the bulk of the ongoing activities of the government. One of the main problems with the priorities as stated in the past is that they have led to consideration of only new government activities and of

the need for new resources, with little attention being paid to possible shifts in the resources already deployed throughout the government. This problem should be substantially overcome by Cabinet's decision to carry the process one step further by requiring responses to the Government's Priorities from each department and certain agencies.[13]

As a result, the priority exercise of 1974–75 involved a small group of officials from the Privy Council Office (PCO) and the Prime Minister's Office (PMO) interviewing each minister. As Richard French points out, these interviews revolved around two questions posed to each minister in the newly elected Cabinet: "What does the government have to do during its mandate to win the next election?" and "What do you want to be remembered for having done, should the government lose the next election?"[14] This produced a list of priorities. Departments were then asked to indicate how they could contribute to these priorities. After each area on the list was discussed in detail with departmental officials, an overall memorandum was prepared and discussed at the Cabinet's Meech Lake retreat. This document identified five themes and sixteen priority policy areas as follows:

I. A more just, tolerant, Canadian society including:
   —social security
   —native rights
   —law reform
   —bilingualism
   —labour–management relations

II. With a greater balance in the distribution of people and the creation and distribution of wealth between and within regions including:
   —demographic and growth patterns
   —transportation
   —national industrial and regional development

III. Which makes more rational use of resources and is sensitive to the natural and human environment including:
   —conserving our natural resources, particularly energy resources
   —maximizing the use of Canada's agricultural and fisheries resources
   —diversity of lifestyles and mental and physical health

IV. Accepting new international responsibilities, particularly with regard to assisting developing countries, including:
— sharing of resources
— alleviating international crises

V. With an evolving federal state capable of effective national policy as well as sensitive, responsive and competent government at all levels including:
— federal–provincial relations
— communications
— Parliamentary reform[15]

It is instructive to note that nowhere in this document was the growing concern for inflation and unemployment reflected. By the fall of 1975 the priority exercise had disintegrated, replaced by the wage and price control program and a "law and order" package devised by a handful of officials and ministers in Finance, the PCO, and the PMO. As Richard French aptly concluded, the Cabinet planning system "was at the point of collapse" due to the disparity between the actual pressures on the government and the abstract phrases of the planning document.[16] The content and process of the 1975 priority-setting exercise is all the more remarkable because the previous throne speech of September 30, 1974, did stress the serious international economic situation. The priorities were inflation and restraint, ameliorated by the need to soften the impact of soaring oil prices.

While the income control program was being put in place late in 1975 and early in 1976, priorities lurched in yet another direction. By the October 12, 1976 throne speech, the priority item was national unity and language policy, a priority precipitated by an air traffic control strike and the bitter dispute over language policy and air safety.[17] The dispute resulted in Prime Minister Trudeau's national television address prior to the Olympic Games, which described the crisis as being equal to the conscription crisis of World War II.

The 1976 throne speech also reflected the growing influence of neoconservative criticism of the growth of government. While leaning to the right, the Liberals portrayed themselves as having a middle-of-the-road view of the role of government. This was also reflected in the publication of two philosophical position papers, *The Way Ahead* and *Agenda for Cooperation*, both of which addressed issues regarding the "post-incomes control" society and the need to fundamentally restructure the economy.[18]

By the fall of 1978 and the new throne speech of October 1, the major themes of the 1976 speech were even more entrenched. The election of the separatist Parti Québécois government in Quebec resulted in a new round of proposals for constitutional renewal. The growing popularity of the Progressive Conservatives under Joe Clark, expressed in both polls and by-elections, strengthened the neoconservative emphasis in Liberal priorities (for example, expenditure restraint, public sector wage restraint, and industrial expansion). This included a sudden "two billion dollar expenditure cut" exercise ordered by Trudeau in August 1978.[19] This exercise was carried out through processes entirely separate from the "normal" priority-setting routine. It was a prime ministerial "lightning bolt" that hit while most ministers were on their August vacations.

The economic policy emphasis on anti-inflation policy is evident in the two 1974 budgets of John Turner and the 1976 budget of Donald Macdonald. The content, however, is quite different. Turner opposed controls and promoted priorities and policies that would encourage the supply of new goods and services. Following the 1974 election that returned the Liberals on an anticontrols mandate, Turner attempted an elaborate but unsuccessful consultative process with business and labour to bring down prices.[20] When the Macdonald budget was brought down following Turner's resignation, wage and price controls were a fait accompli. The Macdonald budget focused on the need for major underlying structural policies, including energy conservation, expenditure growth not to exceed the growth of the GNP, and gradual reductions in the rate of monetary expansion.

The Chrétien budget of November 1978, the last budget prior to the 1979 election that saw the defeat of the Liberals, witnessed a continuation of the 1976 themes about structural reform of the economy, but couched the budgetary priorities in terms of "laying the basis for future growth." It contained a pre-election mixture of neoconservative restraint with social measures such as the child tax credit, as well as investment tax credits with higher rates earmarked for economically depressed regions. Even though the budget speech had been preceded by the August budget cuts exercise and the formation of the Board of Economic Development Ministers to coordinate and devise an industrial strategy, Chrétien pointedly expressed his scepticism in the budget speech about the search for a single, grand industrial strategy.

1980 to 1984

The Liberal throne speech of April 1980 gave testimony to the Liberals' new aggressive post-election position. Reacting against the Clark government's "community of communities" and neoconservative view of Canada, the Liberal throne speech asserted that Canadians wanted more effective government, not less government, and that they wanted someone to speak for Canada. It promised constitutional renewal, an expanded Petro-Canada, steps to achieve 50 percent ownership of the petroleum industry and a strengthened mandate to enable the Foreign Investment Review Agency (FIRA) to review foreign investment more vigorously.

The 1980 throne speech did not, however, reveal the degree of aggressiveness and initial coherence of the overall *internal* strategy devised by senior ministers, advisers, and officials.[21] The basis of the strategy can be summarized briefly.

- There was a fundamental belief among senior Liberals that the national government could not restrict itself to acting merely as a referee between competing interests of the Canadian "communities." They profoundly rejected the short-lived Clark government's "community of communities" concept of Canada.
- The Trudeau Liberals concluded that their plans and policies had to be designed, wherever feasible, to reassert federal presence and visibility. Such a presence and identity was to be fostered by actions and decisions in which the federal government dealt *directly* with individual persons, businesses, and other social institutions rather than channelling its support *through* the provincial governments.
- Federal ministers were increasingly tired of reacting to the initiatives of provincial governments and of being perceived as a mismanaged, debt-ridden, and remote government, while the provincial governments basked for most of the 1970s in the political glory of balanced budgets, perceived competence, and sensitivity and closeness to "their" people.
- With the Quebec referendum "settled," the Liberals turned their attention westward to try to forge some kind of a new political coalition that would strengthen their representation, legitimacy, and power in the West. This search was premised on a strategic political view that they would have their best electoral prospects if they tried to woo the left-of-centre NDP voter. They would also have to latch on to the western resource boom, influence its direction, and be *seen* to be influencing it in significant ways.

The federal identity approach or the "new nationalism" was centred in the Constitution with its Charter of Rights and the National Energy Program. In addition to these high-risk initiatives, the 1980 plan envisioned three other large, aggressive initiatives—an industrial strategy, a Western Canada Fund to help build Liberal support in the otherwise barren Liberal electoral territory, and major changes in social programs, especially the federal–provincial arrangements for financing health and education. The nationalism and federal identity focus, carried out on several policy fronts concurrently, was intended to be conflict oriented and to assert federal jurisdiction.

In terms of resource allocation the Liberal expenditure plans gave a clear indication, if carried out, that economic development and energy expenditures would receive the top priority, and social expenditures would be given a low priority. The Trudeau Liberals retained the full-scale envelope system begun by the Clark government, including the publication of five-year expenditure plans. This system was intended to bring the priority-setting machinery closer to a possible resolution of the problems identified earlier in the 1970s, namely, the need to link policy choices directly to resource allocation and the need to link new expenditures to ongoing or "A-base" expenditures. The prime minister, however, abandoned the Clark experiment with an inner Cabinet because of the obvious tensions it had created among Clark ministers excluded from the inner group.

The budget speeches of the early 1980s reflected the usual range of coherence and incoherence with overall priorities. Finance Minister Allan MacEachen's first budget in the fall of 1980 was the NEP budget. It contained radical changes to the structure of oil and gas industry incentives, from tax incentives to direct grants favouring Canadian firms. The second MacEachen budget of November 1981 diverged from overall priorities in some respects. On the one hand it asserted the need to fight inflation, reduce the deficit, and to stick to a tough monetary policy and high interest rates. On the other hand, it experimented with a quasi-social policy of closing off loopholes or tax expenditures and reducing the highest marginal tax rates. Tax expenditures increasingly favoured the rich. The 1981 budget, however, did not redistribute the additional revenues obtained to low-income Canadians, but rather shuffled them around to other middle- and higher-income Canadians. The budget produced a political disaster in an economy sinking into depression. It was widely perceived to be one that produced neither good economic nor social policy.[22]

The June 1982 budget was designed to recover from the previous budgetary debacle. It was produced by yet another aberration from the overall priority-setting process, a small ad hoc group of ministers. The budget produced the plan for the "Six Percent Society." The focus was on an anti-inflation attack anchored on a policy of statutory control of public service wages. All three MacEachen budgets contained some underlying continuity of concerns over inflation and the deficit, but in other respects they revealed the normal political need to respond to often contradictory short- and medium-term realities and perceptions of realities.

1984 to 1988

The first Mulroney government throne speech and its first two budget speeches, along with an important autumn 1984 economic renewal statement, all pointed to a considerable coherence to early Conservative priorities.[23] In part, the coherence was reflected in the dominance of the economic agenda, which in turn was unmistakably under the control of the Department of Finance headed by Michael Wilson.

The Conservatives' four main themes were: economic renewal, national reconciliation, social justice, and constructive internationalism. Economic renewal was cast in only mildly ideological language. The Conservatives spoke of the need to "remove government obstacles to growth" and to "encourage private initiative and competitiveness." The budgets set in train a determined long-term deficit reduction strategy centred initially on expenditure cuts. The national reconciliation theme reflected a desire to end the combativeness of the last Trudeau years and to practise a new form of consultation with the provinces. This was to be initially practised in the energy field where a series of energy accords were concluded, each intended to exorcise both the memory and the content of the Liberals' National Energy Program. The social justice theme involved an array of particular items such as day-care studies, but it also included a promise to reform the unemployment insurance program to make it more of an economic insurance instrument than a welfare policy instrument. Last but not least, the concept of constructive internationalism became a code word for the Conservatives' desire to build closer economic ties with the United States. This did not yet show up in the form of a free trade agreement, but it did mean a much more cooperative posture toward the Reagan administration.

By the fall of 1986, the Mulroney agenda seemed to be getting reasonable applause on the economic front, but as for its overall political strategy, the government was increasingly portrayed as being in disarray. Several scandals and ministerial conflict of interest problems revealed a government that seemed not to be in charge of its day-to-day agenda. The throne speech of October 1, 1986, sought to re-establish some credibility by including promises to introduce new conflict of interest rules, new tax reform initiatives, a drug strategy, and new regional policy agencies for Atlantic Canada and the West. Tax reform, though in concert with a "new right" agenda, was primarily forced higher up the agenda by the fact that, quite suddenly, in the summer of 1986, the Americans had reformed their income tax system by reducing marginal tax rates and eliminating several tax loopholes.

The later budgets of the first Mulroney term were dominated by the need to show that the overall deficit strategy was on track.[24] As the 1988 election approached, the strategy turned more on tax increases than expenditure cutbacks. Indeed, special spending initiatives were needed for the depressed oil and gas business and for hard-pressed prairie farmers. In addition, a special pre-election set of expenditure initiatives was mounted.

As the 1988 election drew near, however, the issue of the Canada–U.S. Free Trade Agreement became the dominant priority. The government had committed itself to seeking a broad free trade deal in the fall of 1985, but the negotiations in 1986 and 1987 seemed to be going nowhere and were costing the government support as the controversy about a hypothetical agreement rose.[25] When the deal was finally signed in early January 1988, it was evident that it would be the major, though certainly not the only, election issue.

1988 to Early 1990s

The fact that the free trade agreement had become the dominant priority was symbolized by the first post-1988 election throne speech of the re-elected Mulroney Conservatives. It simply said that the free trade legislation would now be passed and was the shortest speech in recent memory. It was not until the April 1989 throne speech that the contours of the second Mulroney mandate were revealed. The agenda was headed by three items that reveal the struggle between intended and unintended priorities. The first was a promise to introduce what became the national Goods and Services Tax (GST), a major new sales tax. It was viewed as the second stage of tax reform, but its forceful advocacy by the Department of Finance was also due to its view that consumption taxes were a more economically productive tax and hence would complement free trade and other structural changes to the economy.[26] It would also be a prolific revenue raiser and was consistent with the overall deficit reduction strategy.

The second priority was yet another undertaking to reform unemployment insurance. The government had backed away from earlier promises on this delicate social policy issue because of regional opposition and concern in its own caucus. Now, with a new second mandate, it felt it could move even on this front.

Lastly, there was the environment. This had not been a planned Conservative priority in the 1984–88 agenda, in part because it went against the grain of deregulation and other pro-market policies. But by 1988, the government was swept along, as were many other Western governments, by public demand that environmental issues be dealt with. The specific impetus for renewed public concern built up in the late 1980s after a series of international incidents that ranged from the Chernobyl nuclear meltdown in the Soviet Union to the drought and severe heat of the summer of 1988, which some scientists attributed to global warming. In any event, by December 1990 the Conservatives had tabled an ambitious $3-billion Green Plan.[27]

While a new agenda was thus set, it was continuously jarred by the ongoing need in successive Wilson budgets both to keep increasing taxes and to cut spending. Each of the 1989, 1990, and 1991 budgets continued this trend, with the 1991 budget influenced by the unexpected costs of the Gulf War. The spirit of the Mulroney government was also rudely jarred by the failure to achieve the Meech Lake Accord. When the accord failed in the summer of 1990, the government had to recircle the wagons to restore its own confidence in itself and in its standing with the Canadian public. This depression in the psyche of Canadians and of their government was all the more noticeable in the early 1990s because of the comparative euphoria otherwise being felt elsewhere about the revolution that had occurred in Eastern Europe in late 1989 and 1990 and in the Soviet Union in 1991.

Conclusions

We have taken two portraits of priorities, one capturing a 115-year period and the other almost two decades of the Trudeau and Mulroney regimes. When looking at whole decades in the distant past, priorities seem clearer. When priorities deal with the future, politics and uncertainty are the constant companions. Governments are caught between a rock and a hard place. If they try to stick to a medium-term view, they may be guilty of arrogant rigidity and of being insensitive to present needs. If they engage in too many ad hoc short-term responses, they are accused of failing to plan or failing to create a "climate for investment." Neither rationality nor incrementalism is good enough.

Throne speeches have evolved from quite philosophical documents in the early Trudeau years to somewhat more prosaic ones in the later Mulroney period. All, however, contain the veritable wish list of "priorities" for different constituencies and regions, an act of essential political communication. The trends in substantive priorities show the tendency for continuous movement across the middle of the political stage, a "to-ing and fro-ing" between a relative focus on social priorities (1968, 1970) and economic priorities (1972, 1974), between left (1980) and right (1978), and between fiscal restraint (1985, 1989) and bursts of political spending (1988). They also show the rightward movement of overall priority agendas from the Trudeau to the Mulroney years. Despite this tendency, certain subjects are persistently at or near the top of the priority list (inflation, national unity), while others move on and off the list (competition policy, immigration, women's issues) on the fringes of politics.

The expression of general public priorities is partly an act of political theatre. This does not necessarily make it unreal or a meaningless charade. However, public priorities expressed in throne speeches do not usually equate well with internal resource allocation processes, including those expressed in budget speeches. The machinery has to be constantly changed to get a better fit between internally expressed priorities and actual resource decisions. Various ways have been tried. Indeed, there have been several occasions where the prime minister and his senior advisers deemed it necessary to concoct special priority-setting devices. The wage and price controls priority of 1975, the August budget cuts of 1978, the National Energy Program of 1980, and the "Six Percent Society" initiatives early in 1982 all emerged from special machinery that disobeyed the normal priority-setting rules.

Budget speeches also reveal the varied and episodic links between nominal economic priorities and the broader throne speeches. They raise the oldest "chicken versus the egg" question about priorities. Should the economic framework and fiscal posture largely set the scene for overall political priorities, or should it be vice versa? A review of several budget speeches shows their obvious economic tone, but reveals them to be profoundly political documents as well. As is the case with several of the themes raised in this chapter, we examine these concerns in greater detail in Chapter 11 and in our detailed analysis of policy fields in Part IV.

Notes

1. See Donald Creighton, *John A. Macdonald: The Old Chieftain* (Toronto: Macmillan, 1955), ch. 6; W. L. Morton, *The Kingdom of Canada* (Toronto: McClelland and Stewart, 1963), chs. 18 and 19; and Vernon Fowke, *The National Policy and the Wheat Economy* (Toronto: University of Toronto Press, 1957).

2. See Donald Smiley, "Canada and the Quest for a New National Policy," *Canadian Journal of Political Science* 8 (March 1975), 40–62; W. L. Morton, *The Progressive Party in Canada* (Toronto: University of Toronto Press, 1950); and M. J. Brodie and Jane Jenson, *Crisis, Challenge and Change: Party and Class in Canada* (Toronto: Methuen, 1980), chs. 4 and 5.

3. See Blair Neatby, *The Politics of Chaos: Canada in the Thirties* (Toronto: Macmillan, 1972); David Lewis, *The Good Fight* (Toronto: Macmillan, 1981), chs. 6, 7, and 8; and Reginald Whitaker, *The Government Party* (Toronto: University of Toronto Press, 1977), chs. 1 and 14.

4. Robert Campbell, *Grand Illusions: The Keynesian Experience in Canada*; A. Armitage, *Social Welfare in Canada* (Toronto: McClelland and Stewart, 1975); L. Marsh, *Report on Social Security for Canada—1943* (Toronto: University of Toronto Press, 1975); and Robert Bothwell, Ian Drummond, and John English, *Canada Since 1945* (Toronto: University of Toronto Press, 1981), chs. 9, 15, and 17.

5. Richard W. Phidd and G. Bruce Doern, *The Politics and Management of Canadian Economic Policy* (Toronto: Macmillan, 1978), chs. 7 and 8; and Bothwell et al. *Canada Since 1945*, ch. 7.

6. Glen Williams, "The National Tariffs: Industrial Underdevelopment Through Import Substitution," *Canadian Journal of Political Science* 12 (1979), 333–68.

7. See Whitaker, *The Government Party*, ch. 5, and Donald V. Smiley, *Canada in Question*, 3rd ed. (Toronto: McGraw-Hill Ryerson, 1981), ch. 6.

8. See Bothwell et al., *Canada Since 1945*, ch. 27; Peter C. Newman, *Renegade in Power* (Toronto: McClelland and Stewart, 1963). See also our survey of this period in Chapter 8.

9. See Richard Simeon, *Federal-Provincial Diplomacy: The Making of Recent Policy in Canada* (Toronto: University of Toronto Press, 1982); Kenneth Bryden, *Old Age Pensions and Policy Making in Canada* (Montreal: McGill-Queen's University Press, 1974), ch. 8; and Malcolm Taylor, *Health Insurance and Canadian Public Policy* (Montreal: McGill-Queen's University Press, 1978).

10. See Bothwell et al., *Canada Since 1945*, chs. 31 and 32; and George Radwansky, *Trudeau* (Toronto: Macmillan, 1978). See also our review in Chapter 8.

11. See Desmond S. King, *The New Right* (London: Macmillan, 1987).

12. See Andrew B. Gollner and Daniel Salee, eds., *Canada Under Mulroney* (Montreal: Véhicule Press, 1988).

13. "Responses to the Government's Priorities," unpublished Cabinet Discussion Paper (Ottawa: January 30, 1975), 1.

14. Richard French, *How Ottawa Decides* (Ottawa: Canadian Institute for Economic Policy, 1980), 77.

15. Quoted in ibid., 79–80.

16. Ibid., 83–84.

17. See Sandford F. Borins, *Language of the Sky* (Montreal: McGill-Queen's University Press, 1983).

18. See Canada, *The Way Ahead: A Framework for Discussion* (Ottawa: Minister of Supply and Services, 1976); and Canada, *Agenda for Cooperation* (Ottawa: Minister of Supply and Services, 1977).

19. French, *How Ottawa Decides*, ch. 6; and G. Bruce Doern and Richard W. Phidd, "Economic Management in the Government of Canada: Some Implications of the Board of Economic Development Ministers and the Lambert Report," paper presented to Canadian Political Science Association, Saskatoon, May 1979.

20. See Allan Maslove and Eugene Swimmer, *Wage Controls in Canada* (Montreal: Institute for Research on Public Policy, 1980), ch. 1.

21. See G. Bruce Doern, ed., *How Ottawa Spends Your Tax Dollars 1981* (Toronto: James Lorimer, 1981), ch. 1.

22. See G. Bruce Doern, ed., *How Ottawa Spends Your Tax Dollars 1982* (Toronto: James Lorimer, 1982), chs. 1 and 2.

23. See Michael Wilson, *A New Direction for Canada* (Ottawa: Department of Finance, November 8, 1984). For analysis, see Michael J. Prince, ed., *How Ottawa Spends 1986–87* (Toronto: Methuen, 1986), ch. 1.

24. See Katherine Graham, ed., *How Ottawa Spends 1988–89* (Ottawa: Carleton University Press, 1988), ch. 1, and Katherine Graham, ed., *How Ottawa Spends 1990–91* (Ottawa: Carleton University Press, 1990), ch. 1.

25. See G. Bruce Doern and Brian W. Tomlin, *Faith and Fear: The Free Trade Story* (Toronto: Stoddart, 1991).

26. See Allan M. Maslove, "The Goods and Services Tax: Lessons from Tax Reform," in Graham, ed., *How Ottawa Spends 1990–91*, 27–48.

27. See G. Bruce Doern, "Shades of Green: Gauging Canada's Green Plan" (C. D. Howe Institute, Commentary, Toronto, 1991).

CHAPTER 10

Bureaucracy and Policy Formulation

The role of the bureaucracy in policy formulation flows logically from the three basic ways in which bureaucracy manifests itself in policy matters.[1] Bureaucracy is first a set of structures—an array of departments and agencies—that have legally defined mandates and that push and pull policies and ideas in both horizontal and vertical directions. Bureaucracy is also a system of delegation that immediately creates an impetus for "bottom-up" policy initiatives emanating from departments that possess their own agendas reinforced and challenged by their own policy communities. And last but hardly least, bureaucracy is a set of senior officials—the mandarins of Ottawa—who exercise influence, positively and negatively, as they interact on a day-to-day basis with cabinet ministers.

All of these manifestations of the bureaucracy's role in policy formation attracted particular attention during the Mulroney Conservative era because, in a significant way, the Mulroney regime campaigned against the Ottawa-centred bureaucracy and sought to put the stamp of its own control on an institution perceived by Conservatives to be too long under the tutelage of a Liberal-dominated Ottawa system. This effort at asserting control was reflected in several initiatives, ranging from the introduction of a system of ministerial chiefs of staff, and an insistence on new interest group consultation processes, to public service staff reductions and the promotion of privatization.

In this chapter all of these features of the great, grey mass of the state are examined so as to understand how ideas, structure, and process are linked in the formation of Canadian public policy.

The Horizontal and Vertical Tug and Pull

One instinctively thinks of government in terms of a hierarchy. The prime minister and Cabinet are poised on top and the line departments reside below, their functions extending out vertically to serve particular constituencies, regions, and groups with suitable policies, goods, and services. Observers point with some fondness to the 1940s and 1950s when powerful line ministers such as C. D. Howe and Jimmy Gardiner and their deputies held sway. Central agencies were "lean and thin" and there was a clear track to the full Cabinet to gain approval for proposals. The problems of horizontal coordination were taken care of by the small personal network of highly educated super-generalist mandarins and their political bosses.[2]

The evolution of departmental mandates and central agencies since the mid-1960s has produced a system where such a simple hierarchical organization chart creates a decidedly distorted view of reality. The federal bureaucracy might be better portrayed as a matrix, in which almost half of the departments exist to coordinate the other half.[3] In short, there has been a significant increase in the number of departments and ministries whose mandates extend horizontally across the government to coordinate some particular crosscutting normative idea or purpose. Each of these ideas or purposes, individually and separately, is quite desirable. The key question that arises is what effect the horizontal-vertical maze has on policy formulation and coordination.

The most recognizable departments are the traditional central agencies. Thus, the prime minister, the President of the Privy Council, the Minister of Finance, the President of the Treasury Board, the Minister of Justice, and the Secretary of State for External Affairs all deal with broad horizontal responsibilities and values. With the exception of the Department of Finance these portfolios do not directly possess large operating budgets. They have inherently high policy influence because of the formal authority they possess and because they afford their occupants the highest number of strategic opportunities to intervene in almost any policy issue if the occupant wishes. They deal with the traditionally most basic horizontal or crosscutting dimensions of government policy, namely, overall political leadership and strategy, foreign policy and the foreign implications of domestic policy fields, aggregate economic and fiscal policy, the basic legal and judicial concepts and values of society, and the overall management of government spending programs and personnel.

A series of hybrid horizontal ministries were experimented with at various times in the last two decades. The first two were the Ministry of State for Science and Technology (MOSST) and the Ministry of State for Urban Affairs (MSUA) whose mandates were intended to cut across all other departments.[4] Science and Technology was a horizontal dimension to the extent that it is, more or less, an input in all policy fields. Urban Affairs sought to define a policy field in terms of a spatial concept—the city—and dealt on a cross-governmental basis as well. The influence of these portfolios was supposed to be based almost totally on knowledge and research. They were to "persuade" other departments by the quality of their advice on these subjects. Reliance on this base of influence proved to be insufficient since knowledge is *not* power. Both ministries were eventually abolished.

Other hybrid ministries have been created as well, albeit none with the innocent "knowledge is power" basis for their existence that MOSST and MSUA had. Thus, ministers of state for federal–provincial relations and for small business were created. The experiment with coordinative policy ministries reached a new and more significant plateau with the establishment of the ministers of state for economic development and social development to support Cabinet committees of the same name. These latter ministries were also abandoned for reasons set out in Chapters 11 and 12.

There is a third type of department with a horizontal mandate that might at first glance escape our attention, but should not. These administrative coordinative departments include National Revenue, Public Works, and Supply and Services. The Public Service Commission would ordinarily be mentioned here as well, except that it is not headed by a minister.[5] It has an overall role to preserve, on Parliament's behalf, the merit principle in government recruitment, hiring, and promotions. The above-mentioned portfolios are usually perceived to be among the least influential of Cabinet positions. They are most likely to be perceived as administrative "nuts and bolts" departments needed to keep government operating. In recent years their functions have been viewed more and more by some as "common service" agencies. This implies a nonpolicy function, although frequently the occupant of these portfolios will quite appropriately refuse to accept such a designation. The portfolios deal with budgets that are quite modest, but the mere fact that they deal with the means of government, for instance, buildings, real estate, supplies, tax and revenue collection, implies a latent and sometimes manifest coordinative role, especially when it is suggested that the government use its procurement powers as a lever in industrial and regional policies. These activities are also closely related to traditional but nonetheless important ideas such as probity, fairness, and honesty in government in the acquisition of such goods, services, and resources.[6]

We have already accumulated almost fifteen ministers whose departmental mandates are broadly horizontal in nature. This leaves some fifteen to twenty vertical constituency departments (for example, agriculture, fisheries, environment, corrections, regional and industrial development). Alas, even some of these (for example, environmental and regional) have at various times aspired to play horizontal coordinative roles as well.[7] Generally speaking, however, this group includes the portfolios that normally have the largest budgets and represent the "vertical" dimension of government in that they tend to extend outward to deliver programs to their respective constituencies, including many of the interest groups discussed in Chapter 5. In recent years this cluster has come to include a second type of smaller ministry of state, namely those created to assist other ministers, with program and/or policy responsibilities. These include Fitness and Amateur Sport, Mines, and Multiculturalism. Within this cluster are the group of portfolios that, generally speaking, are second in order of general influence, ranking behind the traditional horizontal coordinative portfolios identified earlier. The largest parts of the budgets of these portfolios represent existing ongoing programs, but within these programs there are often large but varying amounts of discretionary spending. The occupants of these portfolios therefore possess a fairly strong constant base of influence. This base can be augmented or reduced when the policy field in their portfolio becomes the object of political review, criticism, or controversy. Occupants of these portfolios likely have mathematically fewer opportunities to intervene in another policy field or portfolio, at least in comparison with the traditional and perhaps even with the new horizontal coordinating portfolios. Ministers obviously possess some opportunities to intervene because of their Cabinet committee memberships, but these occasions are still less frequent, generally speaking, than the traditional coordinative portfolios.

The classification of portfolios presented above captures in a stark manner the genuine way in which bureaucratic structure of this kind affects policy formation and coordination. To state even loosely that half the portfolios exist to coordinate the other half is to suggest that the system may well only produce a form of acute policy and organizational constipation. The ministry structure, it could be argued, is mesmerized by the relationship of everything to everything else. There are too many coordinators and not enough "doers."[8]

Here again we also have evidence, this time in organizational form, of the absence of a tidy "means-ends" chain in political life. Each horizontal *and* vertical mandate is purposeful and can be defended separately. Cumulatively, however, the purposeful mandates may intersect to produce an unmanageable state.

It is possible that policy and departmental organization has evolved in recent decades so as to replace one weakness of government with another. We have moved from the heyday of the line ministerial czar when the vertical dimensions were dominant to the heyday of the grand coordinators. Remember that cabinet government, by definition, always pulls ministers in both a horizontal and vertical direction. The trick is to devise some reasonable balance and to know when one has achieved it. This daunting task is clearly an art and not a science.

Another feature that emerges from a serious look at bureaucratic structure is the degree to which departments are the custodians of dominant ideas. In our discussion of the dominant ideas of Canadian political life in Chapter 3, we suggested that one could, in the abstract, envisage a simple political system in which there would be separate departments of efficiency, equity, redistribution, income stability, national unity, and regional sensitivity. In effect, the classification of departments analyzed in this chapter carries this notion forward, albeit in a much more complex way. Obviously, departments are the custodians of certain policy ideas. These include not only the dominant ideas listed above, but numerous other ideas as well, such as honesty and probity in financial transactions, environmental well-being, and law and order.

While there are certain insights to be gained from the identification of ideas with organizational units, in either the simple or complex version, there are obviously dangers in using these typologies. First, there is a sense in which the typologies imply that all the dominant ideas and public policy fields are reflected in an even-handed "pluralistic" way, or that government departments are a fully accurate microcosm of Canadian society. We have already suggested in previous chapters that the concern for redistribution is not well or persistently "represented" in the organization of government. This is true when expressed at the level of the dominant ideas examined in Chapter 3. It is also reflected in more particular terms when one looks at individual departmental mandates. For example, there are many more departments whose overt mandate is to look after particular industries and producer groups (for example, Industry, Science and Technology; Energy, Mines and Resources; Fisheries; Agriculture) than to look after labour. Indeed, even the Department of Labour does not generally regard itself as a pro-labour agency.[9] It tends to see itself as a defender of a system of labour–management *relations*, and hence as a neutral referee overseeing the collective bargaining process. Thus, it is clear that there is a structure of power within the Cabinet and its organizational units that goes beyond the simple pecking order of vertical and horizontal Cabinet portfolios described above.

The typology of portfolios should not be used to reach the conclusion that no coordination exists or that the horizontal-vertical maze is a portrait of perpetual stalemate. Policies *are* enunciated. Resources *are* allocated that favour some groups, classes, and regions over others. In short, some coordination occurs because *power* is exercised by some ministers, officials, organizations, and interests over others. In a host of other situations a more episodic but incrementally stable form of coordination occurs through numerous bargains, accommodations, and compromises where ministers, officials, and interests satisfy themselves with small victories, while they prepare to struggle through the next round of adjustments.

Departments and "Bottom-Up" Policy Initiatives

The policy process is profoundly influenced by a simple human organizational need—the need to delegate and to specialize—in short, to chop policy into chewable organizational and analytical chunks. This need is aided by a political desire to disperse political power or to avoid an excessive concentration of power. At the same time this delegation creates a steady flow of "bottom-up" policy initiatives. We have already spoken of two ways in which this delegation is reflected at the macro governmental level. The first way is through the delegation of tasks to ministers grouped in Cabinet committees and in the mandates assigned to the departments that they head. The second way is the delegation of tasks to a host of quasi-independent agencies, boards, commissions, and crown corporations. Thus, at the macro level, a prime minister must not only manage his or her ministers, but also the huge amalgam of quasi-independent units. The same problem exists for the individual minister at the micro departmental and portfolio level, where the minister's domain may consist not only of his or her own department, but of a stable of other agencies as well. An appreciation of policy formulation requires an understanding of the constraint this places on both ministers and on those interests that are advocating change or otherwise seeking to influence policy outcomes.[10]

The most important constraint is that ministers may not be in a legal position to order the quasi-autonomous agency to change policy or to do some specific act without gaining further parliamentary authority. Regulatory agencies and crown corporations have defined legal spheres of competence. Though ministers may try to persuade such a board or agency to behave according to their or the government's wishes, it is not always legally or politically easy to take back what has been delegated. All public policy proposals must traverse a minefield of existing statutes. The rule of law implies that governments must obey present laws even while they may be trying to change them.

There is also a profoundly human element that reinforces the legal spheres of influence, namely the morale and esprit de corps of the quasi-independent unit. They have been given tasks to do and possess the expertise to do them. There is an inevitable price to be paid when ministers too frequently take back the authority delegated to these bodies. It is to be remembered, of course, that ministers in their relations with such agencies are pulled in two directions at once. They are likely to be blamed by the opposition parties and the media for decisions that go awry regardless of whether the regulatory board or the crown corporation made them or not. They are expected to "manage" their portfolio, not just their department. They are potentially damned if they do and damned if they do not.

Obviously, the situation in this regard can vary greatly among ministers. For example, the Minister of Transport and the Minister of Energy, Mines and Resources have a large stable of units within their ministerial bailiwick.[11] The former includes not only the Department of Transport, but bodies such as the National Transportation Agency (NTA), Canadian National Railways (CNR), Via Rail, and the St. Lawrence Seaway Authority. The latter's domain encompasses the National Energy Board, the Atomic Energy Control Board, Petro-Canada, and Atomic Energy of Canada Limited. Other ministers such as Consumer and Corporate Affairs or Supply and Services have in this sense less complicated organizational entities to manage.

Arising out of these organizational and policy complexities, the main ministerial departments have a correspondingly important initiating role in the policy process. Aided by their own policy branches, by their own reviews of the adequacy of existing programs, by the pressure of "their" policy communities, and by normal bureaucratic self-interest, the line departments press for new or changed policy and for more resources. They also press for the status quo and against some of the proposals that emanate from other departments. It should not be assumed, however, that line departments are an automatic or easy conduit for the needs and "wants" of the interest groups most interested in their activities. As we stressed in Chapter 4, much time is spent by ministers and deputy ministers listening to such groups, to keep relations in good repair, to obtain information and intelligence, and to find out what they oppose and will not tolerate. But these demands and concerns must clearly be juxtaposed by the department against the horizontal pressures emanating from other parts of the government and from other interests and jurisdictions, including the provinces and other countries.

There is ultimately no fully satisfactory way to generalize about the relative influence of the "bottom-up" versus "top-down" sources of policy initiation. These judgments are governed by both perception and by much disputed evidence, both as to the period being considered (1950s and 1960s versus the 1980s) and in relation to different policy fields. It is nonetheless safe to say that departments, their ministers, and senior officials are important players in the policy process, sometimes confidently pushing forward new initiatives, while in other cases reacting to the favourable or unfavourable initiatives that come from the top or from other departments.

The Senior Bureaucracy and Policy Influence

The starting point for dealing with the senior bureaucrats' role in policy-making is the idea of the policy-administration dichotomy. This concept must be examined both as an idea and as a description of reality. As an idea, indeed as a constitutional principle, the implications of the policy-administration dichotomy are clear: elected ministers should make policy and public servants should implement it loyally, efficiently, and effectively. It evokes a sharp distinction between ends and means. While there is much evidence to suggest that senior bureaucrats such as deputy ministers and senior staff advisers do more than just implement, there can be little doubt that the belief in the policy-administration idea is an essential and powerful normative standard against which we judge the democratic policy process.[12]

Many governments at the federal and provincial levels have been concerned about how best to ensure that the policy-administration dichotomy is not only preached but practised. Both the Diefenbaker and Clark Conservative governments were exercised by this question when they assumed power after many years of Liberal dominance.[13] In general, however, they did not act forthrightly on their concerns, preferring instead to rely on the entrenched officials. The Mulroney Conservatives, however, have been much more determined in this regard. They have paid close attention to patronage appointments and have attempted to restructure the system to reduce the influence of senior officials, especially in their first few years in power in the 1984 to 1986 period.

The above concerns reflect the policy-administration debate at a general macro governmental level. But the heart of the practical concern resides also in the day-to-day relations between a minister and his or her deputy minister. Ministers must ultimately allocate their time, energy, and preferences among several aspects of their role. These aspects include their role:

- in general policy development;
- in defending themselves and the government in the House of Commons, especially in question period;
- in cultivating media relations;
- as a special regional minister;
- in developing relationships with the caucus and the party;
- as MP for their own constituency;
- in Cabinet and in several Cabinet committees; and
- as titular manager of a department where sometimes little things can get them into as much trouble as matters of "high policy."

The specific allocations of time and energy vary greatly according to the personality and abilities of the minister, policy interests, electoral status (a safe or unsafe seat), and the type and size of the department involved. He or she is assisted by a personal political staff who are concerned not only about how well the minister does in real terms, but also about the minister's image and future political prospects. Some ministers are more interested in their next Cabinet portfolio than in their current one.

Into this world of ministerial politics enters the deputy minister (and, to a significant extent, other senior bureaucratic and political advisers, especially in the central agencies). The deputy is usually someone the minister did not have a hand in choosing, but the deputy must nonetheless become an alter ego to the minister. The deputy is responsible for the general management of the department, but must also serve as policy adviser, sensitive to, and fully cognizant of, the political constraints and concerns of the minister. The deputy has a constitutional duty to warn and to advise the minister. There are also obligations to serve the rest of the government in a collective sense, just as the minister must.

Several other important points about modern ministerial–deputy ministerial relations should be emphasized. First, it has become increasingly difficult to speak of an integrated Cabinet with full governing responsibility. While most departments, agencies, and crown corporations nominally report to or through ministers, there are different kinds of reporting relationships and hence different degrees to which ministers feel themselves to be responsible and deputies consider themselves to be accountable.

Second, because many ministers often prefer to allocate their time to their policy and political party duties, and since many have a distaste for administrative and managerial matters, administrative matters are increasingly the concern of deputy ministers. The evolving relationship between ministers and their deputies is often less of a superior to a subordinate, but much more a matter of mutual dependence.

A third point raised in recent years concerns the consequences of the turnover of both ministers and deputy ministers. The general argument in the late 1960s was that a higher turnover rate and shuffling of deputy ministers would enhance control of the senior public service by the Cabinet because deputies would be less entrenched. However, any potential benefits were largely obviated as Prime Minister Trudeau at the same time shuffled cabinet ministers with increasing frequency. Many senior public servants argue that this "musical chairs" approach had a negative impact on management and, moreover, had caused both ministers and deputy ministers to adopt a "low profile/low risk" approach to their responsibilities to ensure their own survival. These patterns were exacerbated by numerous reorganizations of existing portfolios and the creation of others, each making it more difficult to pinpoint accountability and easier to evade responsibility.

Finally, it is essential to point out that deputy ministers must in some respects cater to at least three masters: their minister, the prime minister by whom they are appointed (on the advice of the Secretary to the Cabinet), and the Treasury Board and Cabinet committees that exercise general managerial and expenditure authority. They must also pay heed to the activities of agents of Parliament such as the Federal Human Rights Commission, the Official Languages Commissioner, and the Auditor General of Canada.

Deputy ministers thus face conflicting pressures.[14] In addition to their normal roles as policy advisers and general managers, they have been deluged in the last decade with a seemingly endless stream of reforms and directives, each of which separately may have been desirable, but which cumulatively have often distracted them from their primary departmental responsibilities. These reforms include the introduction of collective bargaining and new budgetary systems. Deputy ministers properly point out that as long as they are subject to conflicting and/or vague instructions from ministers, the Cabinet, the central agencies, the special agencies of Parliament, and the many statutes they must administer, there can be no simple concept of accountability.

Views about the influence of bureaucrats on public policy are also affected by the broader and increasingly unfavourable perceptions of bureaucracy and the public service in general. A study of the image of the public service in Canada concluded that over the decades of the 1970s and 1980s the perception of Canadians regarding the fairness and promptness of government has improved, although the public service is still viewed as less able than the private sector to carry out its responsibilities.[15] It also concluded that increased contact with specific parts of the public service, even when favourable, does not spill over into a favourable overall view of the public service. A public opinion poll conducted in the midst of the deep 1982 recession concluded that there was a desire to see some measure of punishment of the civil service, and public service unions, because they were not giving the public what Canadians considered to be value for their money.[16] Later, the Mulroney government frequently played on these resentments. In its second term it sought to improve the morale of civil servants and to foster, through study initiatives such as Public Service 2000, a more positive view of the bureaucracy's role.

It must be remembered that in the 1960s, 1970s, and 1980s the bureaucracy itself increasingly became the *object* of public policy. This was true not only with regard to wage controls and restraints (1975 to 1977, 1982 and 1991) and macro fiscal policy, but also in the introduction of collective bargaining, language policy, human rights legislation, freedom of information laws, "value for money" auditing, and the decentralization and relocation of government agencies. Problems and controversies regarding these policies in the face of growing economic malaise have helped alter the once more favourable or at least more neutral perception of the public service.[17]

It should also be emphasized that the growth of public service unions and militancy was a significant force in the 1970s. Unions such as the postal workers and the Canadian Union of Public Employees (particularly in provincial and local government levels) became the most radical part of the general labour movement in Canada and assumed an even larger proportion of the membership of the Canadian Labour Congress.[18] Quebec's public service unions became very powerful with close alliances to the state, especially under the Parti Québécois. Many of these unions associated themselves closely with the fate of certain public policy fields—especially social programs in education, pensions, and health, and in the transportation services. Thus, despite prohibitions against the right to bargain about matters of public policy, the collective bargaining process inevitably embraced public policy concerns in these fields.

But the core of the concern about the role of senior public servants and senior advisers in policy formulation centres on their role in initiating policy ideas and proposals, analyzing and "massaging" policy proposals, and in blocking or frustrating the plans or ideas of elected politicians. It is evident that bureaucrats have a considerable capacity to initiate policy. In part the political system expects and encourages them to do so when it berates them on those occasions when they have failed to plan, to estimate costs and effects adequately, and when legislators leave wide discretionary powers in their hands or assign such powers to separate boards and agencies.

The reality of decision-making in a complex Cabinet-bureaucratic structure is that policies are not always clear, frequently conflict with each other, and must be constantly reinterpreted as they are applied to single cases or projects. It is not always clear whether the dominant policy is found only in the statute that governs a program or department, the Cabinet's latest directive, a minister's speech made over the weekend, or a combination of all of these. Analysts and advisers at and below the deputy ministerial level are constantly meeting in departmental, interdepartmental, and federal–provincial settings to determine what ministers want or what "their" minister's preference is. As Cabinet documents and memoranda are drafted, advisers attempt to add the right nuance of meaning to particular features of a proposal. Data and estimates may be challenged or questioned. Interdepartmental concerns are raised. Questions of timing and cost are identified. All of this is done with advisers engaged in constant discussions "up the line," to the minister through his or her deputy minister, and across departmental lines through other ministers, departmental officials, political aids, and central agency officials. Frequently, there is also contact with outside interests and with provincial governments. Though senior advisers may see the end product of this iterative process as a polished Cabinet document, the reality is a mixture of a verbal and written exchange of views. The volume of written documentation, however, is beyond the human bounds of any minister or deputy to digest fully, and thus a premium is increasingly placed on verbal advice.

The degree and extent of this analysis and massaging varies greatly, of course, but the paradoxes of the process must be appreciated when judging the bureaucrats' overall policy role, both normatively and descriptively. Consider briefly two examples of bureaucratic influence, one concerning a macro policy initiative, the Canada–U.S. free trade decision, and the other a micro policy decision, the famous "tuna case" that led to the resignation of the then Fisheries Minister, John Fraser. Space allows only a perilously brief account of each decision, but nonetheless it is sufficient to illustrate the dilemmas of interpreting senior official–ministerial relations of influence and power.

In the case of the free trade decision, there is little doubt that most of the Ottawa mandarinate strongly opposed the free trade initiative when it first surfaced in 1984–85.[19] But the role of one official, Assistant Deputy Minister Derek Burney, was pivotal. Burney was virtually the lone ranger of free trade in the External Affairs bureaucracy. He kept nudging the issue forward, ensuring that it was not pushed aside. In insisting that ministers be presented with a full array of options, including free trade, he was doing his constitutional job, but also riding through and around the opposition of other senior External Affairs officials.

Some opponents in External Affairs, and in other government departments, resisted Burney's free trade crusade because they had genuine doubts about the wisdom of putting all of Canada's economic eggs in the American basket. Others were simply playing the Ottawa game of winners and losers. They made a judgment that the free trade issue would fail politically and set out to block a losing cause. Burney, however, pressed on and helped persuade the prime minister to back the risky free trade initiative.

As for the micro example, the "tuna case," the problem was one that has numerous parallels across the government in areas where technical judgments must be made about health and safety. Fraser was a respected minister in the recently elected Mulroney government. It would appear that he was simultaneously anxious both to show that he was in charge of his new department and to assist a local firm for which some Atlantic Canada caucus members were strenuously lobbying. The problem concerned fisheries inspectors who had ruled that some of the tuna products produced in the struggling company's plant were rancid or unhealthy.

The minister decided not to accept the advice of his deputy and his field inspectors that a health hazard existed. The issue surfaced in the House of Commons, and after relentless pressure the minister was forced to resign, ultimately for failing to uphold health and safety policy. In this case, a decidedly small political decision exploded in the minister's face. Ninety-nine times out of one hundred it is in ministers' best interests to listen to the advice of their officials. Officials, in turn, do their duty by giving their best technical judgment in the context of carrying out the intent of a law. They may also be doing ministers a great political favour by keeping them out of political trouble in parliamentary question period.

Obviously between a macro decision like free trade and micro decisions like the "tuna case" there are a large array of other middle-level policy choices as well. Each one contains its own type of ministerial–deputy ministerial story as to how the relationships of influence and power occur.[20] It should not be surprising, then, that virtually every minister privately and sometimes publicly displays his or her anecdotal saga about the great idea that was sabotaged by the senior bureaucracy or by the prime minister's "henchmen." In each of these it is difficult, if not impossible, to determine why a given ministerial initiative or pet project may have been changed or stalemated. Was there a difference in values and priorities whereby a deputy was able, by a process of wearing down the minister, to impose a decision? Was the deputy, on the contrary, merely playing his or her proper constitutional role in warning the minister of the pitfalls of the proposal or the possible contradictions between it and the law? Was the proposal in reality dismissed not by the minister's bureaucracy, but by other ministers whose concerns and priorities were different?

Flora MacDonald's brief account of her nine-month ministerial experience as Secretary of State for External Affairs shows the empirical woolliness of the bureaucratic influence question.[21] Her article describes the many ways in which bureaucrats furnish "entrapment devices" for ministers (for example, delayed recommendations, multiple deputy ministerial committees, bogus "options"). It describes the difficulties she had in establishing alternative advisory networks of academics and of her personal political staff. She is careful to say that the problem does not arise from the overt partisanship of senior public servants, but rather from the fact that public servants regard themselves to be above the partisan battle. She quotes approvingly other experienced politicians on this score, from Tony Benn to Henry Kissinger. But nowhere in her account is there a specific example of a policy blocked or an initiative frustrated. The article leaves the impression of a *feeling* that a problem exists. This should not be surprising, since both perception and reality have real effects on behaviour and on the views expressed on this kind of complex subject.

A particular manifestation of the larger issue of relations between elected and appointed officials is the often fine line needed to distinguish partisan political advisers from senior bureaucrats who are also known to be personal confidants of the prime minister or other key ministers. No political system can avoid the presence of relationships of personal trust, loyalty, and confidence. Those who enjoy such confidence are almost by definition influential and have frequent access to key ministers. Overall strategic approaches to policy are not forged by a simultaneous discovery of the approach by over thirty ministers. Leadership of a strategic kind is the catalyst, and senior partisan and bureaucratic advisers are positioned to be a part of that leadership.

Michael Pitfield is without doubt the official who most elicited concern in the Trudeau era about the public service–partisan dilemmas. Pitfield was a senior adviser who encouraged Trudeau to seek the prime ministership, agreed with and helped shape Trudeau's view that government had to be more rational, and fostered the Trudeau era's fascination with systems and reorganization. He served as a Deputy Secretary in the PCO, Deputy Minister of Consumer and Corporate Affairs, and then at an unprecedentedly young age, Clerk of the Privy Council, Ottawa's pre-eminent public service position. Pitfield genuinely strived for an improved Cabinet system and was one of the few to operate as Trudeau's intellectual equal, but he was often rightly perceived as being excessively preoccupied with process. This does not mean that he did not influence the substance of policy as well. For example, Pitfield eventually became a strong advocate of the wage and price controls program launched in 1975. He also helped foster a group of Pitfield PCO graduates who later became deputy ministers and assistant deputy ministers of various departments in Ottawa.

The quintessential example of the political official in the Mulroney era is Derek Burney. Burney had been a career foreign service officer in the Department of External Affairs. When the Mulroney government came to power in 1984, Burney was an assistant deputy minister. In 1984–85 most deputy ministers in Ottawa were being kept at arm's length because of their suspected Liberal sympathies. Burney, however, had direct access to Prime Minister Mulroney because he helped organize the prime minister's first visit to Washington, and did it well. A personal rapport and trust developed between Mulroney and Burney, in part through happenstance and in part through Tory desires to reach below the top levels of official Ottawa to find sympathic allies in the bureaucracy. Burney further showed his credentials by being one of the very few in External Affairs who kept the free trade option before the new government during its review of trade policy.

As a result, Burney had a special influence on Mulroney. In 1986, when the government was floundering and seemingly rudderless, Mulroney called on Burney to become his right-hand person in the

Prime Minister's Office. It was from this position that Burney was also called on to rescue the free trade negotiations with the United States when they were on the verge of collapse in the fall of 1987. After the 1988 election, Burney left the PMO and took up a civil service position as Canada's ambassador in Washington.

There is a certain inevitability to the existence in any prime ministerial regime of a small cadre of quasi-civil service, quasi-partisan, key advisers who exercise influence and upset the pure models of either a neutral public service marching to the beat of the policy-administration dichotomy, or ministers operating in spendid isolation without the occasional whiff of the Machiavellian interloper. In the Pearson era, for example, it is possible to argue that Tom Kent, Pearson's chief adviser in the PMO, exercised an even more profound influence than his Trudeau-era successors ever dreamed of. Kent had been a major idea man at the Liberals' 1960 Kingston conference, which set the agenda for the major Pearson social welfare reforms of the mid-1960s. While his influence later waned, he also became Deputy Minister of Regional Economic Expansion and later head of the Cape Breton Development Corporation. The Pearson Cabinet also included several former senior public servants including Mitchell Sharp, Maurice Lamontagne, and Pearson himself.

None of the above is intended to argue that there are no problems regarding the power of bureaucrats and key advisers. It is a perpetual and genuine democratic concern. Part of the problem at the federal level undoubtedly arose from the sheer fact of Liberal Party dominance for much of the post–World War II period. But beyond a certain point there are limits as to whether any permanent solutions exist, since each reform suggested to solve the problem has its disadvantages as well and a capacity to produce its own excesses. Americans complain as much about bureaucratic Washington despite the power of the American president to appoint officials well below the deputy ministerial or equivalent level.

To generalize about the respective kinds of influence that ministers, deputies, and key senior advisers exercise, it is necessary to discuss evidence in a large number of particular policy fields and to characterize the relationships more precisely, taking into account the factors outlined above.[22] An article by Andrew F. Johnson conveys something of what is required. He reviews the development of unemployment insurance in the 1970s. He characterizes the role of Bryce Mackasey, the minister responsible for introducing a new scheme of unemployment insurance in 1971, as that of a major change agent, particularly in carrying out what Johnson calls the "surveillance" and "legitimation" functions necessary for major policy reforms. Mackasey's successors, Robert Andras and Bud Cullen, began to routinize the program, and thus their legitimation and surveillance skills became increasingly unnecessary and inconspicuous. The role of bureaucratic experts was correspondingly minor in the first phase of reform and larger in the second phase. The overall relationship was essentially one of mutual dependence.

Conclusions

The bureaucracy is both a set of structures and a hierarchy at the peak of which sit senior officials such as deputy ministers and key political advisers. Out of this central reality of officialdom three key features of policy formation have been examined. First, the structure of departments, including their legal mandates, tugs and pulls policy-making in both horizontal and vertical directions as numerous values clash and contend. Second, the delegation of tasks to departments ensures that a continuous series of "bottom-up" policy initiatives occurs in the Ottawa policy system aided both by departmental self-interest and by pressure from relevant policy communities. And finally, policy is always at least partly the outcome of day-to-day relations between senior officials and ministers as they each seek to play their prescribed administrative and political roles in the face of a changing agenda.

Notes

1. J. E. Hodgetts, *The Canadian Public Service* (Toronto: University of Toronto Press, 1973), chs. 5 and 6. See also O. P. Dwividi, ed., *The Administrative State in Canada* (Toronto: University of Toronto Press, 1982); and V. Seymour Wilson, *Canadian Public Policy and Administration* (Toronto: McGraw-Hill Ryerson, 1981), chs. 9, 10, and 11.
2. See J. L. Granatstein, *The Ottawa Men: The Civil Service Mandarins, 1935–1957* (Toronto: Oxford University Press, 1982).
3. See G. Bruce Doern, "Horizontal and Vertical Portfolios in Government," in G. Bruce Doern and V. S. Wilson, *Issues in Canadian Public Policy* (Toronto: Macmillan, 1974), ch. 12.
4. See Peter Aucoin and Richard French, *Knowledge, Power and Public Policy* (Ottawa: Science Council of Canada, 1974).
5. W. D. K. Kernaghan, ed., *Public Administration in Canada*, 4th ed. (Toronto: Methuen, 1982), ch. 5; and Hodgetts, *The Canadian Public Service*, ch. 12.
6. See Douglas J. McCready, "The Department of Supply and Services: Efficiency Canada?" in G. Bruce Doern, ed., *How Ottawa Spends Your Tax Dollars 1982* (Toronto: James Lorimer, 1982), ch. 9.

7. Doern, "Horizontal and Vertical Portfolios."
8. See H. L. Laframboise, "Here Come the Program-Benders," *Optimum* 7, no. 1 (1976), 40–48.
9. See Eugene Swimmer, "Labour Canada: A Department 'Of' Labour or 'For' Labour," in G. Bruce Doern, ed., *How Ottawa Spends Your Tax Dollars 1981* (Toronto: James Lorimer, 1981), ch. 5.
10. See John Langford, *Transport in Transition* (Montreal: McGill-Queen's University Press, 1970); and Peter Aucoin, "Portfolio Structures and Policy Coordination," in G. Bruce Doern and Peter Aucoin, eds., *Public Policy in Canada* (Toronto: Macmillan, 1979), ch. 8.
11. See Langford, *Transport in Transition*, and G. Bruce Doern, "Energy, Mines and Resources and the National Energy Program," in Doern, ed., *How Ottawa Spends Your Tax Dollars 1981*, ch. 2.
12. See Wilson, *Canadian Public Policy and Administration*, ch. 4, and K. Kernaghan, "Politics, Policy and Public Servants: Political Neutrality Revisited," *Canadian Public Administration* 19, no. 3 (Fall 1976), 431–56.
13. On the Clark government's concerns, see Jeffrey Simpson, *Discipline of Power* (Toronto: Personal Library, 1981), ch. 5.
14. On the role of the deputy minister, see Royal Commission on Financial Management and Accountability, *Final Report* (Ottawa: Minister of Supply and Services, 1979), chs. 9 and 10, and Gordon Osbaldeston, "Job Description for DMs," *Policy Options* (January 1988), 33–38.
15. See David Zussman, "The Image of the Public Service in Canada," *Canadian Public Administration* 25, no. 1 (Spring 1982), 63–80, and David Zussman, "Walking the Tightrope: The Mulroney Government and the Public Service," in Michael Prince, ed., *How Ottawa Spends: 1986–87* (Toronto: Methuen, 1986), 250–82.
16. Reported in *The Globe and Mail*, July 15, 1982, 1.
17. See Sharon L. Sutherland and G. Bruce Doern, *Bureaucracy in Canada: Control and Reform* (Toronto: University of Toronto Press, 1986).
18. See E. Swimmer and M. Thompson, eds., *Public Sector Industrial Relations in Canada* (Montreal: Institute for Research on Public Policy, 1983).
19. See G. Bruce Doern and Brian W. Tomlin, *Faith and Fear: The Free Trade Story* (Toronto: Stoddart, 1991), ch. 2.
20. For other case studies see Gordon F. Osbaldeston, *Keeping Deputy Ministers Accountable* (London: National Centre for Management Research and Development, 1988).
21. Flora MacDonald, "The Minister and the Mandarins," *Policy Options* 1, no. 3 (September/October 1980), 29–31. See also Mitchell Sharp's critique of the MacDonald article in Paul W. Fox, ed., *Politics Canada*, 5th ed. (Toronto: McGraw-Hill Ryerson, 1982), 476–79.
22. Andrew F. Johnson, "A Minister as an Agent of Policy Change: The Case of Unemployment Insurance in the Seventies," *Canadian Public Administration* 24, no. 4 (Winter 1981), 612–33.

CHAPTER *11*

Public Policy and Public Expenditure

The public expenditure process is undoubtedly the most central and visible way in which public policies are translated into concrete actions and levels of commitment. The annual process of deciding where scarce dollars will be spent is vital to ministers, departments, and the policy communities that benefit from government programs. Indeed, for most of the past decade, the struggle has been to minimize or prevent cuts in public spending.

Spending dynamics can be understood in a number of ways, each of which presents a different configuration of the interplay among ideas, structure, and process. One way is to trace substantive priorities and trends in each of the main categories of spending: social, economic/industrial, and foreign and defence. This essential approach was looked at in Chapter 7 and will be taken up again in Part IV when we look at policy fields. Another way is to examine the expenditure process as a continuous contest of wills between guardians and spenders, in short, between those in the political executive charged with overall control of expenditure totals and those whose instinct and job is to spend. In both cases, they are defenders of important sets of ideas. The structures and processes of budgeting are intended to constrain and channel their struggle over the practical meaning of public policies. It is this latter approach that is the main focus of this chapter. We first describe the overall resource allocation process. We then examine the evolving nature of basic criticisms of the resource allocation process. The third section of the chapter highlights key features of the expenditure process per se. Finally, we look at the issue central to the Mulroney period, the battle over expenditure control to help reduce the federal deficit.

Main Features of the Overall Resource Allocation Process

What does the overall allocation system look like? It is helpful to view two general portraits of it. The first is portrayed in Figure 11.1 and shows in simple terms the elementary parts of the revenue and expenditure halves of the resource allocation system. The revenue inputs include taxes, tariffs, royalties, and user fees and charges. The ideas that govern the process of revenue generation include the familiar ones of efficiency (Will the tax system promote initiative and risk taking?), equity (Will taxpayers at similar income levels be treated equally?), stability (Will the tax system produce a "climate for investment"?), and redistribution (Will the system redistribute income from rich to poor?). The revenue side also raises concerns about the adequacy of the total revenues to meet the government's needs, the size of deficits and surpluses, and the simplicity and ease of revenue collection. On the output side, taxes reappear in the form of tax expenditures that serve as policy incentives. Expenditures of many kinds are generated, including transfers to individuals, grants (conditional or unconditional), subsidies, investments, and the purchase of goods, services, and personnel. The contending ideas inherent in the expenditure and tax expenditure outputs are the same, as we have stressed throughout the book.

Figure 11.2 therefore presents a second, somewhat different snapshot of its most recognizable features, the overall priority-setting mechanisms, the fiscal framework, and the expenditure process.[1] The latter two in particular combine to form some kind of desired balance or relationship between revenues and expenditures. Until the late 1970s the overall resource allocation process operated on about an eighteen-month time frame, that is, about eighteen months prior to the start of the federal government's fiscal year (April 1). Thereafter an attempt was made to extend the time frame to a four- or five-year period, but in reality, as we see in this chapter, it is a series of annual

FIGURE 11.1 **The Revenue-Expenditure Components
of the Resource Allocation System**

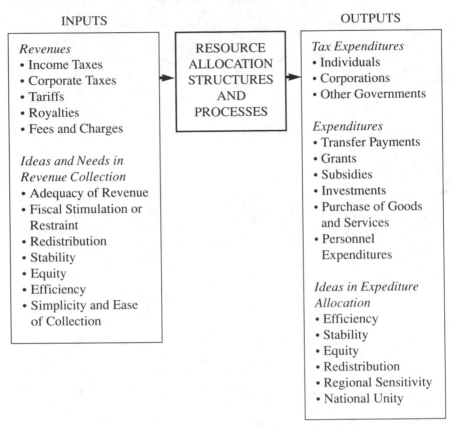

INPUTS   OUTPUTS

Revenues
- Income Taxes
- Corporate Taxes
- Tariffs
- Royalties
- Fees and Charges

*Ideas and Needs in
Revenue Collection*
- Adequacy of Revenue
- Fiscal Stimulation or
  Restraint
- Redistribution
- Stability
- Equity
- Efficiency
- Simplicity and Ease
  of Collection

RESOURCE
ALLOCATION
STRUCTURES
AND
PROCESSES

Tax Expenditures
- Individuals
- Corporations
- Other Governments

Expenditures
- Transfer Payments
- Grants
- Subsidies
- Investments
- Purchase of Goods
  and Services
- Personnel
  Expenditures

*Ideas in Expediture
Allocation*
- Efficiency
- Stability
- Equity
- Redistribution
- Regional Sensitivity
- National Unity

rolling resource-allocation exercises. The above features will be described in order.

Overall Priorities

Chapter 9 has shown that there are several mechanisms that help
produce or express priorities, including throne speeches and budget
speeches. These are not all necessarily annual in nature. The prime
minister and the Cabinet must, however, have some annual mechanisms to help guide the allocation process and to express the ultimate
political judgment of the government. In Ottawa this has centred on
the Cabinet Committee on Priorities and Planning, chaired by the
prime minister and advised primarily, though certainly not exclusively, by the Department of Finance, the PMO, and the PCO.

FIGURE 11.2 A Simplified View of the Overall Internal Federal Resource Allocation System

	Fiscal Framework and Revenue Budget	Overall Priorities	Expenditure Budget
COMPONENTS	Fiscal stimulus or restraint; short versus medium term based on judgment about state of the economy	• overall social/economic priorities and political judgment • short-term responsiveness versus long-term "planning"	"A" Budget (ongoing expenditures) "B" Budget (new initiatives) "X" Budget (cancellation or reduction) Statutory and Controlled versus Discretionary Spending
PRIMARY UNITS INVOLVED	Department of Finance	• Priorities and Planning Committee of Cabinet • PCO, PMO • Cabinet Committees and Secretariats	• Priorities and Planning Committee • Cabinet Committee on Expenditure Review • Treasury Board • Operations Committee

The Fiscal Framework

Priorities must be forged in the context of some judgment about the fiscal position and revenue needs and capacity of the government and the economy. The Department of Finance has historically been the lead agency in carrying out this difficult task. The setting of the fiscal framework has involved the development of a formal "economic outlook" document detailing the government's view of the current and likely future state of the economy. It sets out the Keynesian judgment about the fiscal balance, namely the degree to which the fiscal position should help stimulate the economy (with deficits), restrain it (with surpluses), or be in some generally balanced position. This kind of annual to eighteen-month Keynesian fine tuning has been thrown into disrepute due to the evidence of a declining economy in the 1970s and criticism from monetarists and others.[2] It is viewed by these critics to be more a part of the problem than the solution. In the late 1970s and 1980s an effort was made to extend the fiscal framework into a longer time frame, into a document setting out the "medium-term track" of the economy. Needless to say, the fiscal framework is judgmentally and politically loaded. Moreover, there are significant problems in the art of forecasting the Canadian and world economies, the behaviour of investors and consumers, and other governments' revenue and expenditure decisions.

The Expenditure Budget

The development of an annual expenditure budget, to be presented to Parliament as the Estimates, is both a product of, and a contributing factor in, the overall priority-setting process and the fiscal framework. The dual relationship is shown by the inevitable existence of a so-called "A" and "B" budget and of the different legal and political constraints involved in the control and discretion of budgetary expenditures. The "A" budget refers to those expenditures of an ongoing nature needed to maintain existing programs or to fund them at new levels caused by changes such as population growth. The "B" budget refers to expenditures on new initiatives or programs and is also often called the "policy reserve." Increasingly, the level of scarcity is such that an "X" budget must be created, one that identifies items in the "A" base that can or should be eliminated in whole or in part either to achieve restraint or, more typically, to be reallocated to some new "B" budget initiative.

The issues of what is ongoing or new, and desirable or expendable, are political by their very nature.[3] The political past and the possible future are closely linked. The expenditure process is therefore a central and visible part of policy formulation. Many expenditures are statutory, fixed for a period of years, or without a time limit. These include large social programs involving federal–provincial transfers, conditional grants, and tax agreements. On an annual basis, significant change is difficult, legally and politically. Some basic kind of certainty and level of past commitments must be maintained. At the same time circumstances change and so must budgets.

Decisions about the expenditure budget are made by several Cabinet committees. The Priorities and Planning Committee sets out the key expenditure decisions. The Expenditure Review Committee has become the focus for expenditure cuts. Individual Cabinet committees have influenced or actually determined allocations within their policy field, but not in recent years. The Treasury Board and other agencies exercise influence through their roles in approving "A-base" expenditures and advising on issues of efficiency, controlling personnel establishments (person-years), collective bargaining, administrative policy (for example, on contracts), and evaluations. Bargaining, logrolling, and mutual backscratching are central to the budget process. This is why it has been characterized as being essentially incremental in nature and why it is always the target for "rational" reform.

Evolution and Criticisms of Overall Resource Allocation Process

It is not difficult to see why the overall resource allocation system is subject to diverse and continuous criticism. The system has evolved in response to changing ideas about politics and economics and to different rankings of the institutional, substantive, and procedural ideas that should be maximized at any given time. Some of these changes can be linked, especially in retrospect, with changes in structure. For example, prior to the Glassco Commission on Government Organization in the early 1960s, the Treasury Board functioned virtually as a staff arm of the Department of Finance. This symbolized a view that the revenue and expenditure process should be intricately and closely coordinated "under one roof," so to speak. Following Glassco, the Treasury Board was separated from the Department of Finance, not because of problems with fiscal policy per se, but because of the Glassco Commission's concern about the better "management of government," the need it expressed to let departmental managers "manage." This symbolized the greater separation of the expenditure process from the fiscal process and framework. Other developments also contributed to this process, including the changes in the Cabinet and the central agencies examined in Chapter 4 and the changing ideas and conflicts inherent in economic policy and economic management.

By the late 1970s the system was judged by some to have resulted in too great a separation of the revenue and expenditure elements. There was a need to link more explicitly and carefully the policy decisions of the Cabinet with its resource allocation decisions. This led to the envelope system examined in the last part of this chapter. Before examining it, however, one must appreciate in greater detail the general criticisms of the overall resource allocation system as it had evolved until the late 1970s. This is especially important because no "system" is permanent or cast in stone. The underlying ideas in conflict are, however, fairly constant and recurring. They reappear in different permutations and combinations as ideas about "process" and about policy fields, and values are ranked differently at different times by the same government or political party or by different governments. The main criticisms are centred on a concern for imposing greater coordination and discipline between policy ideas and the availability of resources; increasing ministerial control over bureaucrats in the policy and decision process; and increasing the time frame of decisions and the capacity to plan. Contained within these concerns are other particular problems, including the need to improve the capacity to estimate revenues, the need to evaluate programs, especially the seemingly sacrosanct "A-base" of expenditures, and the need to provide ministers with better analytical support and policy analysis in a timely, economical way. These concerns are analyzed briefly below.

The Integration of Policy and Resource Allocation

The overriding criticism of the system as it had evolved in the 1970s was that policy determination and resource allocation were not adequately linked. A new system was needed so that ministers in the various Cabinet committees would have to face the fiscal consequences of their own decisions directly. Under the pre-1979 system, Cabinet committees could all too easily approve policy ideas, leaving the resource implications to be dealt with primarily by the President of the Treasury Board and/or the Minister of Finance. Thus, only two ministers had an institutional responsibility to say "no." This reinforced the pro-spending instincts of ministers, especially in the early 1970s when there was economic prosperity and a decided lack of concern about costs.

In short, then, there was a growing belief that government lacked discipline, that expenditures were out of control, and that excess spending was itself the major cause of inflation and the growing economic malaise of the late 1970s and early 1980s. Closely related to this was the concern about the apparent political sanctity of the "A" budget expenditures and the failure to evaluate ongoing programs. All of these themes were stressed in the Auditor General's criticisms in the 1970s,[4] by the Lambert Royal Commission on Financial Management and Accountability in 1977, and by the Clark and Mulroney Progressive Conservative governments.

The Need for Greater Ministerial Control

The need for greater control of decisions by ministers was inherent in the concern for coordinating policy with resource allocation. However, greater ministerial control can mean different things. It means in part greater control over bureaucrats, but it also implies a desire to make ministers more accountable to each other collectively. Once again, the Cabinet system pulls ministers in two directions. Ministers are expected to be held individually responsible, but by having ministers more involved in the resource trade-offs of all departments, as they were in the envelope system of the early 1980s, they are in fact less and less in individual control of their own department.

Nonetheless, on balance, the evolving criticism in the late 1970s focused on the need to decentralize decisions in the policy Cabinet committees in recognition of the need to delegate and the need for the Cabinet Committee on Priorities and Planning to focus on major strategic issues or overall priorities and on a longer-term view of policy and resource allocation. A necessary corollary to this system was that there had to be changes in the analytical support for the Cabinet committees *as a collectivity*. With the arrival in power of the Mulroney Conservatives, the meaning of ministerial control changed. As we see below, it was the "ministry," the Cabinet as a governing entity, that needed more control of spending. This led to the abandonment of the envelope system.

Lengthening the Time Frame of Decisions

If policy was to be better linked to resources, and if ministers were to exercise control, it followed that neither could happen unless a longer-term "planning" period was envisioned. One immediate problem of the pre-1979 system was to ensure that ministers *collectively* (as opposed to just the Treasury Board) were constantly aware of how their *current* decisions were going to affect the availability of resources in the medium-term *future* (about three to five years). They also had to have better cost estimates and projections, especially for large capital projects. The dilemma here, as we have seen in the analysis of priority-setting previously, is that political-electoral incentives conspire to create a "short-term" game, while allocative realities are such that longer-term consequences are inevitable, not only because of scarcity itself, but also because of the need to make choices between expenditures on current consumption and on longer-term capital development.

The Expenditure Process

When dealing with expenditure dynamics per se, three basic characteristics of the process deserve emphasis. First, it is a highly quantified process. The ideas and priorities of political life can be translated into the common denominator of dollars. This produces at least some kind of comparability, much more so, as we will see in Chapter 12, than occurs in the regulatory process. Quantification does not itself eliminate policy controversy, but it helps to bring the process to somewhat more manageable proportions.

Second, the expenditure process is characterized by the active participation, bargaining, and logrolling of numerous ministers and officials. The bargaining is somewhat more peaceful and politically enjoyable if the participants are bargaining over a growing expenditure pie, as was the case in the 1960s and 1970s. In conditions of severe restraint where there are "X budgets" to be carved from the expenditure base, the expenditure process is almost by definition more conflict oriented. The fact that expenditure bargaining, at least over details, goes on over several months in a typical year is also important politically since it allows ministers and officials "to win some" and "lose some" and thus generate some sense of political peace and fair play. In a large, unwieldy Cabinet and bureaucracy this is a by-product of no small importance.

The third feature is that the expenditure process has a highly visible and well-recognized point of central agency coordination, again much more so than the regulatory process. Historically, this has been the Treasury Board, but in recent times the central point of coordination has been the Priorities and Planning Committee, the Expenditure Review Committee, and the Treasury Board together.

In addition to the broad criticisms referred to in the previous section, there have been continuous series of reforms of the expenditure process, motivated by diverse ideas about what constituted improved accountability and policy outcomes.[5] These ideas emerged from both the political left and the political right, with the latter gaining the upper hand in the 1980s and 1990s. The left of centre political ideas were reflected in the advocacy of increased expenditures, especially in social programs and in a reluctance to support measures to promote better program evaluation. Critics on the left were aware of, and even concerned about, some expenditure waste, but were unwilling to be a part of a general attack on government expenditures or processes. They were also unwilling to support any general attack on universal social programs, raising the age-old question of the unfairness and regressivity of means tests and deterrent or user fees to low-income Canadians. They did support measures such as the indexation of some social programs such as old age security payments as a protection against inflation.

The right of centre political criticism of the expenditure process took many forms and had many specific targets. The most persistent has been the criticism of the Auditor General, Parliament's expenditure watchdog. The Auditor General has been particularly skilful in using the media to help build a political constituency critical of spending itself and of the expenditure process. The Auditor General sold the concept of "value for money" auditing and secured new powers for the office. Instead of just auditing for control purposes to detect illegal and improper expenditures, the Auditor General's office would audit to see if government departments had the proper "system" in place to evaluate programs so that value for money could be determined. In short, it was believed by some that the proposed system would lead to the discovery of the government's "bottom line," the equivalent to business profit measures and calculations of return on investment.

Much of the Auditor General's simple line of argument was echoed by the Lambert Royal Commission on Financial Management and Accountability created in 1976 in response to the Auditor General's criticisms. To a somewhat lesser extent the criticisms were also reflected in the early work of the Comptroller General of Canada, an official at the deputy ministerial level who reports directly to the President of the Treasury Board. The Comptroller General's task is to ensure that departments have the systems in place and that they actually carry out program evaluations.

All of the above was a nominally apolitical development clothed in the ethos and language of rational managerial reform and couched in the need to allow Parliament to be "restored" to its alleged former heights as controller of the public purse. In reality the ideas were anything but apolitical. They reflected small "c" conservative ideas about, and criticisms of, the growth of government expenditure and the perceived expansionary appetites of bureaucrats and their alleged inability to manage properly.

Some of this line of criticism was undoubtedly valid. For example, there is little doubt that there were serious problems and inadequacies in the federal system for estimating and managing large capital projects and for managing the government's cash flow. Beyond these genuine problems, however, there was a deceiving and far from politically neutral simplicity to the argument. It was that, underlying the call for rational evaluation studies and better management, there existed a discoverable bottom line to government activities, analogous to and as quantitatively endowed as the profit motive was to the private sector. There was little inclination among such reformers to acknowledge the multivalued and therefore "multi-bottom" line nature of political life and of public programs. Reform lay in "getting the systems right."

The professional conservative reformers of the expenditure process had a natural ideological constituency in the broader political system. The Progressive Conservative Party, both federally and in several provinces, supported the expenditure reform concepts. The larger political debate of these issues was also joined to the popularity of "bureaucracy-bashing." Growing expenditures, coupled with media exposure of a few expenditure boondoggles, unpopular public service strikes in high-visibility industries (for example, postal workers and air traffic controllers), and the perceived insensitivity of distant Ottawa "bureaucrats" created an easy political target. Expenditure reform became allied with proposals and promises to cut or freeze the growth in the public service, and to eliminate or reduce the scope of collective bargaining.

Also important during this period was the link between monetarism and criticisms of expenditure growth. These ideas, as we saw in Chapter 9, were reflected in budget speeches and included the government's commitment to hold federal expenditure increases to the trend line rate of increase in real GNP. This resulted in an immediate reduction in the rate of expenditure increase, but not in the actual achievement of the overall commitment.

Linked to these developments, but a much more subtle reflection of them, were reform proposals to increase the use of user fees and charges and to increase revenue dependency. The central concept was simple — make citizens who use particular services pay more for them. These ideas were influenced in part by the application of public choice theory to the behaviour of bureaucrats. Rational bureaucrats, it is argued, have a natural tendency to expand and oversupply goods and services or to produce output inefficiently because they are not subject to market discipline and competition. By charging for services and/or making departments more dependent on their own revenue sources (that is, rather than on the revenues provided by the broader tax base and "given" to them by central budget agencies), bureaucrats would be more sensitive to consumer needs and demands, and to input costs. The idea of user fees was also revived because of the sheer need for more revenue in the face of growing deficits. Fees became a new way to "tax" without calling it taxation and sometimes without having to go through the more visible political pain of a tax change, including a formal budget speech.

User fees also tended to be paraded in a very misleading way as a neutral managerial tool. It is evident, however, that such fees are chock full of conflicting values. They embrace not just the "nuts and bolts" problems of airport fees, highway tolls, and charges for passports, but include deterrent fees for visits to doctors and hospitals, higher tuition fees, and special charges on oil consumers. Because they are often flat charges regardless of the income of the payers, they become a regressive policy instrument, in short, of reverse redistribution in social policy terms.

The Battle Over Expenditure Control

The concerns over resource allocation as a whole and over the expenditure process in particular crystallized in the Mulroney years. But a final way of appreciating the nature of the battle, and of how its spender–guardian dynamics is a surrogate for battles over efficiency, equity, and other ideas, is to look somewhat more closely at two spurts of expenditure reform. These are the envelope system begun in 1979 and abandoned in 1984 and the Mulroney expenditure control approach that began in 1984 and extended into the 1990s.

Some features of the envelope system have already been referred to earlier, but the essence of the system requires an examination of Figure 11.3. It shows how, in the early 1980s, various packages (envelopes) of spending were assigned to particular Cabinet standing committees.[6] Figure 11.3 is also relevant in that one feature of the envelope system is always present, no matter what later budgetary systems might be called in the latest Ottawa jargon. This is that governments always have to have some way in which to characterize and shift their expenditure aggregates. Public expenditure data are still presented in envelope categories, as we show in Chapters 15 and 16.

However, the real key to the envelope system in use from 1979 to 1984 was that each Cabinet committee, backed by a significant sup-

FIGURE 11.3 Cabinet Committees and Their Resource Envelopes: 1979–1984

PRIORITIES AND PLANNING	ECONOMIC AND REGIONAL DEVELOPMENT		SOCIAL DEVELOPMENT	FOREIGN AND DEFENCE	GOVERNMENT OPERATIONS
FISCAL TRANSFERS	ECONOMIC DEVELOPMENT AND ENERGY	• Industry and Technology • Agriculture, Fisheries & Forestry • Regional Economic Expansion • Transportation • Communications • Labour, and Consumer and Corporate Affairs	SOCIAL AFFAIRS • Employment & Immigration • National Health and Welfare • Indian Affairs and Northern Development • Canada Mortgage and Housing • Veterans Affairs • Secretary of State • Environment	EXTERNAL AFFAIRS AND AID • External Affairs • Foreign Aid	PARLIAMENT • Senate • House of Commons • Parliamentary Library
PUBLIC DEBT	ENERGY • Energy, Mines and Resources • Home Insulation Program • Oil Import Compensation Program		JUSTICE & LEGAL • Justice • Solicitor General	DEFENCE • National Defence	SERVICES TO GOVERNMENT • Executive • National Revenue • Post Office • Public Works • Supply & Services • Statistics Canada

Source: Privy Council Office.

porting secretariat, had de facto control of its own reserve for new policy initiatives. As suggested earlier, this was because the system was seen as a "policy and expenditure management system" in which all ministers would, in a sense, be their own guardian. Each committee was forced, within limits, to be both its own spender and guardian.[7] It was hoped that this would make ministers more disciplined because they would always have to match their policy wishes and desires directly with the reality of the amount of money in their envelope. Someone, of course, controlled the total reserve available for all the envelopes, but within the envelopes ministers were free to spend and guard as they saw fit.

The system eventually broke down for a number of reasons and was abandoned by the Turner Liberal government and then buried by the Mulroney Conservatives. The system required an extensive amount of analytical paper flow and seemingly endless meetings. At its core, however, it failed because it was difficult for ministers to be their own controllers. It did not necessarily produce a more rational sense of "quality control" between policy and expenditure decisions. Rather, it seemed to increase the amount of conflict among ministers because they had to guard each other directly rather than being guarded by a small band in the form of the Treasury Board or the Department of Finance. In essence, then, the Trudeau Liberals who operated the system for most of its four years of existence did not in any pure sense see the envelope system as a way of reducing public expenditure, but rather as a way of managing the relations between policy choices and expenditure management. The Mulroney Conservative agenda was quite different. In their first term the Conservatives began a determined effort to reduce a deficit that hovered near $30 billion annually. For the most part, this was done through a general political determination rather than through changes in structure.[8]

The Mulroney government's struggle to stick to its fiscal framework and to maintain a tight control on public spending reached a new plateau after the 1988 election. Early in 1989, it announced a new Cabinet structure that gave additional emphasis to the control function and even nominally identified it directly with the prime minister himself.[9] The Priorities and Planning Committee of Cabinet was given formal responsibility to approve all new government spending, indeed any significant spending even if it involved existing resources. More significantly, an Expenditure Review Committee was established, chaired by the prime minister. Its job was to conduct ongoing reviews of all expenditure programs. De facto, it became the expenditure-cutting star chamber.

Meanwhile, it was made clear in the new system that the other standing policy committees of Cabinet would have no expenditure role. The Treasury Board would approve routine ongoing expenditure programs, except for major ones. Effectively, these changes strengthened the guardians against the spenders and certainly put the final nail in the coffin of whatever remained of the old envelope system. Envelopes continued to exist for purposes of a basic functional classification of spending, but not as a functioning budgetary decision process.

Two years later, in 1991, the Mulroney government ratcheted the control system another notch, both practically and symbolically. The February 1991 budget speech contained measures that would seek a *legislated* control of public spending.[10] The legislation imposed mandatory limits on annual spending for a five-year period. Flexibility was provided only to meet a very limited number of contingencies defined in the legislation. By legislating these controls, the government was in part admitting that markets needed further reassurance that its deficit reduction plans would in fact be carried out. It was also attempting to force the opposition parties to say where they stood on the overall issue of expenditure control by putting the issue in legislated form.

The main declaration of victory that the Conservatives were able to make about public expenditure control was that they had significantly reduced *program* spending. Program spending includes controllable nonstatutory spending, but does not include debt costs, which continued to grow. Program spending from 1970 to 1984–85 had averaged 13.8 percent annually during the Liberal years, but had been reduced to an average growth of 3.7 percent during the Mulroney years.[11] Despite these efforts—and there is no doubt that they were painful for many departments and interests—Canada's level of public spending for the 1980s as a whole still went up, mainly because of debt costs. But general federal government outlays as a percentage of GDP declined from 46.8 percent in 1984 to 44.2 percent at the end of the decade.[12]

Expenditure politics within the Cabinet is usually portrayed in basic terms of the clash between spenders and guardians, but some interpretations of the expenditure process place additional emphasis on the regional nature of ministerial competition within the Cabinet and how this ultimately overwhelms the guardians of the public purse. Donald Savoie's gloomy assessment of the prospects of control is based on an analogy he draws with a group paying for a meal.[13] Group members have agreed to split the tab equally. As a result, there is no incentive for control because no one "wants to miss out on the best food while having to pay for someone else to eat it." In this sense interregional competition for federal dollars produces a continuous "spending by comparison." If Quebec gets something this month, then Alberta must get its "good meal" next, and so through the provincial-regional list, endlessly repeated.

Conclusions

The public expenditure process both influences and reflects the content and shape of general and specific policy initiatives. The contest of wills between spenders and guardians gives concrete meaning to the ideas inherent in policy formulation. The expenditure process is tied to the larger resource allocation process, at the centre of which is the annual determination of the fiscal framework. Accordingly, it must first be understood in relation to evolving criticisms of overall resource allocation. The nature of the expenditure process has witnessed an increasingly intense battle of control over public expenditure between spenders and guardians. Program expenditure has been controlled during the Mulroney years, but total expenditure has still risen because of increased debt charges.

Notes

1. See G. Bruce Doern, Allan Maslove, and Michael Prince, *Budgeting in Canada* (Ottawa: Carleton University Press, 1988); Donald Savoie, *The Politics of Public Spending in Canada* (Toronto: University of Toronto Press, 1990); and Douglas Hartle, *The Expenditure Budget Process in the Government of Canada* (Toronto: Canadian Tax Foundation, 1978).
2. See Thomas J. Courchene, *The Strategy of Gradualism* (Montreal: C. D. Howe Research Institute, 1978), and Arthur W. Donner and Douglas D. Peters, *Monetarist Counter-Revolution* (Ottawa: Canadian Institute for Economic Policy, 1979).
3. See Aaron Wildavsky, *The Politics of the Budgetary Process*, 3rd ed. (Boston: Little, Brown, 1979).
4. See Sharon L. Sutherland, "The Office of the Auditor General of Canada: Watching the Watchdog," in G. Bruce Doern, ed., *How Ottawa Spends Your Tax Dollars 1981* (Toronto: James Lorimer, 1981), ch. 6.
5. See Doern, Maslove, and Prince, *Budgeting in Canada*, ch. 2.
6. Treasury Board, "Policy and Expenditure Management System: Envelope Procedures and Rules" (mimeo copy, dated July 1, 1981), 1–2.
7. See Richard Van Loon, "Stop the Music: The Current Policy and Expenditure Management System in Ottawa," *Canadian Public Administration* 24 (Summer 1981), 175–99.

8. See Savoie, *The Politics of Public Spending in Canada.*
9. Katherine Graham, ed., *How Ottawa Spends 1989–90* (Ottawa: Carleton University Press, 1989), ch. 1.
10. Canada, *The Budget* (Ottawa: Department of Finance, February 26, 1991), 12.
11. Ibid., 12–13.
12. Organization for Economic Cooperation and Development (OECD), *The Public Sector: Issues for the 1990s* (Paris: OECD, 1991), 38.
13. Savoie, *The Politics of Public Spending in Canada*, ch. 1.

CHAPTER *12*

Taxation, Regulation, and Other Instruments

Taxation and regulation are the two other main ways in which public policy receives concrete expression. Within the executive policy process as a whole, the tax process and the regulatory process to a considerable extent lead lives of their own and exhibit different features and dynamics than the expenditure process examined in the previous chapter. The best testimony to the fact of policy change in the latter half of the 1980s in Canada is that, with the mere mention of the words taxation and regulation, one must almost immediately speak of tax reform, deregulation, and privatization. This was not the case even in the early 1980s in Canada, but reflects changes brought by the Mulroney era and by the larger Thatcherite–Reagan legacy that made economic liberalism the new orthodoxy. Privatization in particular became the watchword, and thus the use of state enterprise as a policy instrument was constrained.

Our focus in this chapter is mainly on the tax and regulatory policy processes, but reference will also be made to state enterprise and to exhortation, the other policy instruments referred to initially in Chapter 7. As in the previous chapter, it is best to digest these important features of public policy in small doses. Figure 12.1 is intended to help guide the way. It is a slightly more complex version of the figure used to introduce Chapter 11 and shows the full array of outputs, not just expenditures, by adding taxation, regulation, public enterprise, and exhortation. Table 12.1 provides a more detailed look, not only in a static way, but also with reference to the influence of the reform ideas advanced since about 1970 for each of the main instruments. We refer to this table throughout the chapter in our analysis of ideas, structures, and processes. First, the basic dynamics of each instrument-based process are characterized. Then we show how each process, separately, has been the subject of pressures for reform. The ideas advocated through such pressure embrace a broad ideological spectrum of political debate.

The Tax Process and Tax Reform

The basic characteristics of the tax process within government can be readily identified.[1] It is a partially quantitative process, not in the across-the-board sense as in the expenditure process, but certainly in the sense that decisions about tax revenue are based on some well-established but by no means wholly accurate bases of calculation, estimation, and analysis. In sharp contrast to the expenditure process, however, the tax process has a focused centre of ministerial power and very limited room for interministerial bargaining. In part this is due to the convention of budget secrecy, a norm devised in the late 19th century to prevent persons from benefiting personally through advance knowledge of tax (then, usually, tariff) changes. Around the

FIGURE 12.1   Resource Allocation and Governing Instruments

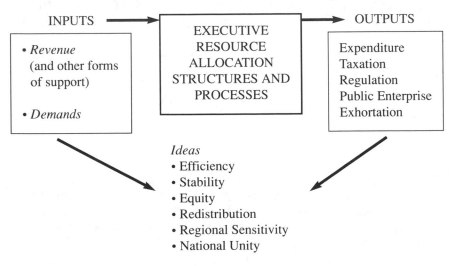

TABLE 12.1   Instruments and Policy Processes: A Profile of Characteristics and Reform Ideas

	Expenditure	Taxation	Regulation	Public Enterprise	Exhortation
Basic Characteristics	• Quantified • Multiminister and departmental participation and bargaining • Recognized central agency point(s) of coordination	• Partially quantified • Focused ministerial power (Finance) • Limited bargaining due to secrecy and limits on ability to consult private interests • Recognized central agency	• Limited quantification • Multiminister and departmental agency participation • Limited bargaining over content of regulations, but considerable bargaining over severity of enforcement • No easily recognized central agency until Mulroney period	• Limited quantification • Multiminister and agency involvement • Independent sources of revenue • No easily recognized central agency until Mulroney period	• Nonquantified • Multiminister "leadership" and involvement • Numerous discrete acts of persuasion and information • Production of policies "for show" or to express symbolic concern • No recognized central agency

Continued

	Expenditure	Taxation	Regulation	Public Enterprise	Exhortation
Reform Ideas and Events Since 1970	• Auditor General's call for value for monetary practices • Lambert Report • Call for program evaluation • Indexing of social expenditures • Spending growth limits to trend line GNP increases • Reduce size of civil service • Charging for services • Envelope system • Cabinet Committee on Expenditure Review • Legislative limits on public spending	• Carter Commission: "A Dollar is a Dollar" • 1972 "Corporate Welfare Bums" tax debate • Indexation of tax system • Tax expenditure debate • Budget consultation • Lower marginal rates • The deficit • Simplify the tax system • Envelope system • Wilson tax reforms: phase I and GST phase	• Increased public participation and hearings • Socioeconomic impact statements • Deregulation • Reducing the paper burden • Guidelines approach • Economic Council of Canada reports • Envelope system • Regulatory reform strategy • Deregulation of oil and gas, air and rail transport, and telecommunications	• PCO Blue Report of 1976 • Lambert Report • Privatization • Single window concept • Expansion of public enterprise • Open policy subsidization • Crown Corporations Act • Privatization of crown corporations (e.g., Air Canada, de Havilland, Canadair)	• Information Canada • Growth of monitoring and advisory agencies • Advocacy advertising • Varying numbers of studies and royal commissions • New consultative exercises

concept of budget secrecy has been built a subtle fortress that has preserved the powers of taxation in a remarkably centralized way. Only the Minister of Finance and, in the very last stages, the prime minister are privy to the budget's content.

Two aspects of the tax process deserve particular comment: the power of the Department of Finance and the issue of the extent of tax bargaining. First, the focused power of the Department of Finance over ongoing *tax* decisions remains undiminished since 1970. As to the extent of tax bargaining, the conclusions vary somewhat. David Good's analysis of the tax process characterizes it broadly as the "politics of anticipation."[2] He refers here particularly to the relations between the minister (and senior tax officials) and outside groups. Secrecy and other related norms prevent the former from actually bargaining with these outside interests and hence tax policy-makers rely more on intelligent "anticipation." To a certain extent this is a reasonable characterization, especially when contrasted with the expenditure process. On the other hand, one has to be careful in utilizing the concept of anticipation in too general a way since anticipating other actors in the policy process is an inevitable part, in *some* degree, of all decision-making.

Although the tax process is normally the preserve of the Minister of Finance, there are occasions when other senior line ministers can secure the inclusion of tax breaks in the budget speech.[3] Often these kinds of line ministerial initiatives follow from the cancellation of direct expenditure programs after which the ministers involved pressure the Minister of Finance to supply a substitute, usually less expensive program. The child tax credit of 1978 emerged from such a process following cuts in family allowance payments. Once launched, the child tax credit was expanded and became the precursor to later progressive redistributive tax-based social policy. In the Mulroney era, the Cape Breton tax credit was forged after pressure from the Minister of Regional Industrial Expansion who was trying to compensate for the cancellation of heavy water production subsidies at two plants in Cape Breton. Clearly, however, there are fiscal and political limits to how often such measures can be conceded by the Minister of Finance. But this does not mean that ministers will not stop trying to shop for political goods.

Despite these subtleties, it can be said with considerable emphasis that the tax process differs from the expenditure process in significant ways and to a significant degree. Not unexpectedly, then, it has become the *object* of debate to reform it. Undoubtedly, the most sweeping early event was the debate that ensued in the late 1960s and early 1970s in the wake of the Carter Royal Commission on Taxation. One tax expert has succinctly observed that the tax system is "anything but systematic."[4] The work of the Carter Commission in the late 1960s was the first major effort to examine the tax system in any coherent way. Its clarion call was that in a fair tax system a "dollar is a dollar" and, therefore, income and wealth should be defined broadly. The Carter Commission also supported the need to reassert "ability to pay" as a cardinal principle of a progressive tax system and suggested ways to simplify the system, eliminate loopholes, and therefore enable the reduction of marginal rates.[5]

An elaborate "White Paper" process followed the Carter report involving extensive consultation with interest groups. While some changes, such as the taxation of capital gains, followed in the wake of the White Paper, the White Paper process itself showed the power of specific interests with a vested interest in the status quo to wear down the decision process. As a result, the Carter impetus quickly faded.

Tax content and the tax process were simultaneously the object of political attack from the political left and the political right. The 1972 election, which produced a minority Liberal government, was noteworthy primarily because of the campaign by the NDP leader, David Lewis, against "corporate welfare bums." This was the precursor to the larger tax expenditure debate of the mid and late 1970s. The debate not only asserted the concept of corporate welfare and the use of tax breaks by corporations, but also painted a portrait of the declining share of the tax burden borne by corporations. The debate was successful enough that Finance Minister John Turner, when offering a new capital cost allowance to corporations, coupled it with a promise to report back to Parliament on whether corporations had actually used the tax break to help generate more jobs and/or had used it for other purposes.

Another reform concept, one embracing support from the political left and right, was the indexation of the tax system against inflation. Conservative opposition leader Robert Stanfield pressured the government into adopting indexation in 1973 by appealing to the unfairness and lack of fiscal integrity caused by the "painless" infusion of new revenue into government coffers. The extra revenue flowed in because inflation was pushing taxpayers into higher income brackets with higher marginal tax rates. The government, Stanfield argued, was profiting from inflation without having to endure the political discipline of increasing taxation in an open parliamentary way. The indexation issue was itself used in other ways in the ongoing debate about taxes and economic management. Thus, when Canadian Conservatives urged the Trudeau Liberals in 1981 to emulate the initially large Reagan tax cuts in the United States to promote supply-side economic growth, the Liberals argued that this was unnecessary in Canada because indexation since 1974 had resulted in tax cuts every year. The Americans had not indexed their tax system against inflation. Similarly, indexation was viewed in Canada as a way to provide automatic benefits so that weaker groups in society such as the aged were not held hostage to unseemly short-term partisan politics, having to "beg" annually for protection from inflation. This did not, however, prevent the government from capping the indexation percentage in 1982 as part of its campaign to keep inflation to 6 percent in 1982–83 and 5 percent in 1983–84 and to save money in the face of ballooning deficits.

Tax reform and the reform of the tax process gradually broadened in the mid and late 1970s to embrace virtually all of the Carter issues. Increasingly, however, they were debated at a time of serious and evident economic malaise. One manifestation was the formal debate about tax expenditures.[6] The Americans had begun in 1976 to publish an annual report on tax expenditures showing the cost of new tax benefits granted. As we saw in Chapter 7, increased research in Canada began to show the sharply growing use of tax expenditures, its regressive effects, and the growing complexity and costliness of the tax system that resulted. In 1979, Conservative Finance Minister John Crosbie published the first tax expenditure account with his budget. He justified the reform on the need to open the tax process and to broaden political scrutiny. The information in the tax expenditure account is very general in nature and is not tied to corresponding spending programs. Its publication, however, shows the evolution of an idea that ultimately can be traced to the Carter Commission and the "corporate welfare bums" debate of 1972.

The degree to which the tax process was subject to a tax expenditure debate was further revealed in 1981. In his November 1981 budget, Finance Minister Allan MacEachen unexpectedly announced that he would be closing off several tax "loopholes" on the grounds that they favoured the wealthy.[7] He coupled these changes with a general lowering of marginal rates at the upper-income levels, thus favouring those who wanted a somewhat more simplified tax system without high rates that sapped initiative and risk-taking. While the budget was virtually replaced six months later and suffered from many problems, it showed again the political staying power of those who benefited from the current tax system. Ideas clashed. A supposedly egalitarian "cut out the loopholes" budget was charged, among other things, with being an attack on enterprise and initiative, in short, on efficiency. In addition, suddenly there were concerns, mainly from the business community, that the budget process had broken down and had to be reformed. More and better consultation was needed to ensure that the Department of Finance did not lose touch with reality again. It was argued by some that the norms of secrecy were too pervasive and Finance had become too "academic."

The need to reduce budget secrecy and improve consultation had arisen before 1981, but never as vociferously.[8] The 1981 budget was perceived by business interests to be antibusiness, and therefore the process was wrong. The contrast between the 1981 experience and the Carter and post-Carter tax process is instructive. In the Carter–White Paper process there was much consultation. Concern was expressed by business interests that the process would create uncertainty. In the end, however, only business interests could afford to participate in the elongated consultative process. In the 1981 debate over the Mac-Eachen budget the tax reform process was too swift. Finance had acted irresponsibly. After the budget, business interests marshalled their resources and through intensive lobbying succeeded in having the budget proposals watered down. In this case, Finance had acted first and consulted later. In the Carter exercise, it had consulted first and acted later. The result was not noticeably different in either case.

Unlike the abortive MacEachen reforms of 1981, the Conservative tax reforms engineered by Michael Wilson were thought through with considerable care, but with alternative tilts to the ideas of efficiency and equity as well as the need to reduce the deficit.[9] Wilson's first major tax initiative that had reform implications was his introduction of a lifetime capital gains in his first budget. This was unambiguously a gesture to signal the government's desire to award capital and to promote enterprise. But the Wilson reforms of 1986–87 were clearly large-scale reforms. Following similar major American changes in 1986, the federal changes reduced the number of bands in the progressivity of tax rates and eliminated a number of tax expenditure deductions and converted still others into redistributive tax credits. Depending on which aspects one focused, the first phase of reform could be seen as being pro-efficiency and favouring the rich (lowering upper-income tax rates) or pro-equity and equality oriented (converting breaks to credits that were refundable to those not paying taxes).

While both stages of the Wilson tax reforms were accompanied by considerable consultation, there is little doubt that it was the second phase that produced the political storm. The phase from 1988 to 1991 that saw the introduction of the Goods and Services Tax (GST) to replace the little known but economically distorting federal manufacturer's sale tax produced a battle royal.[10] Massively unpopular, the GST contained the same mix of ideas that any tax battle ultimately involves, but in this case the fight became a surrogate struggle over the whole Mulroney agenda. The GST was sold as an economically efficient tax, first because it got rid of the inefficient manufacturer's sale tax and because it taxed consumption rather than investment. Its legion of critics regarded it as a regressive tax because, despite certain exemptions and credits, it was a flat tax. To others it was simply a revenue grab or an unprincipled reach into provincial jurisdiction. Regardless, the tax took effect in 1991 as the Mulroney government rammed it through Parliament, including an unprecedented use of additional Senate appointments to get it through the Liberal-dominated upper house.

The Regulatory Process and Deregulation

In Chapter 7, we traced the growth of regulation, including the attempt to differentiate between economic regulation and social regulation. We noted the numerous points of intervention that exist along the production cycle where governments have regulated or are contemplating regulation. We stressed the large number of line departments and special quasi-independent agencies and boards involved in regulation. When viewed in this way, regulation is both visible and omnipresent.

Within the confines of government, however, the regulatory process has been until the Mulroney era a much less visible and focused activity than either the tax or expenditure processes.[11] This is partly due to the fact that the regulatory process in general has been far less quantitative in nature than either taxes or spending. Regulations obviously result in the allocation of resources, but these are, in the main, private resources, not governmental resources, though the latter are affected as well. Regulations are a form of tax. These allocations are therefore hidden, at least in the eyes of regulators and ministers. Moreover, annual regulations are not aggregated into a kind of "regulatory budget" of public *and* private resources and reviewed by a super central agency. It is argued by some that this hidden nature, and the unequal scrutiny of regulation, compared to other instruments is a major reason why it is used frequently. The burden of regulatory reform in the Mulroney era, as we see below, is to alter this state of affairs by requiring more prior quantitative analysis and review of proposed regulations.

The regulatory process is not totally devoid of quantitative assessment and central review. Quasi-independent boards such as the National Transportation Agency, the National Energy Board, and the Canadian Radio-television and Telecommunications Commission (CRTC) have elaborate processes for prior analysis, including formal hearings.[12] A form of central review occurs because both the federal and provincial governments have regulation or statutory instrument statutes.[13] These acts typically require that all formal regulations (subordinate legislation), but not necessarily all "guidelines," be vetted by a registrar or similar official. These assessments are based on such tests as whether the regulation flows properly from the enabling powers of the parent statute, whether it contravenes the Charter of Rights, whether it imposes a tax, and other similar concerns. One should not lose sight of the fact that the normal informal processes of Cabinet discussion, ministerial and official telephone calls, and behind-the-scenes communication are also a part of the regulatory decision process.

In general, however, regulation is an activity carried out in a disaggregated, decentralized way by many ministers and officials and special agencies. In this way the process is similar to the expenditure process, but not the tax process. The regulatory process is in a sense even more decentralized than the expenditure process because *within* line departments, as well as at the central governmental level, there is often no single point of ongoing regulatory review by the minister and deputy minister as there is with expenditures.

The problem of securing greater review both by the central agencies of the government and of the departments is not just a product of its hidden nature or lack of quantification. It is also due to the persistent problems of knowing what a regulation is as distinct from a standard or a guideline. For example, in Chapter 7 we defined regulation in a somewhat narrow way as rules of behaviour backed by the direct sanctions and penalties of the state. Thus, regulation occurs when the more coercive powers of the state are used to back up norms of conduct. In this political sense both statutes or legislation as well as so-called subordinate legislation would be regulatory in nature and would be distinguishable from other instruments of governing such as spending, taxation, or exhortation.

Government officials, however, will often use regulation to denote only subordinate legislation, that is, "regulations" that are made pursuant to a parent statute and that go through legally prescribed steps including publication in the federal or provincial *Gazette*. Similarly, "standards" in fields such as health and safety regulation are usually viewed by officials as statements arising as subordinate legislation, setting out upper or lower health and safety limits or setting out procedures that must be followed. In this sense they are rules of behaviour backed up by sanctions that apply if the standards are not met.

However, these are not necessarily the same as guidelines. In the health and safety field, for example, guidelines are often viewed to exist because of the presence of greater scientific uncertainty, or because it is agreed that there is no safe threshold limit, that is, a point of measurement within which something is "safe" and beyond which something is "unsafe."[14] But regulation defined as "guidelines" does not occur purely because of differences in scientific and technical precision. Guidelines also have political qualities and embody ideas that many groups prefer.

Strict regulations (rules of behaviour) and standards carry with them the notion of equality of treatment and equality before the law, a powerful and important idea in Canada and in other Western societies. Guidelines, on the other hand, suggest flexibility and a capacity to recognize that circumstances and situations are different or unique. Both of these combine to suggest a defence of fairness and equity.

As if these distinctions were not confusing enough to the lay person, they do not complete the picture. The fact is that "standards" are often in reality applied flexibly, and "guidelines" are often obeyed as if they were standards. As in so many other aspects of political life, language and the words used, though rarely clear, matter a great deal. In the words "regulation," "standard," and "guidelines," we have code words for two closely linked but overriding ideas of democratic society. Governments are enjoined simultaneously to treat people in equivalent situations equally and to treat people who are not in equivalent situations unequally (that is, to be fair and reasonable). Both of these ideas are equally desirable and, in a broad sense, form a consistent philosophical and democratic concept. In practice, however, they are often in conflict.

The regulatory process is therefore, for several reasons, not nearly as uniform or ritualistic a process as the expenditure or tax process. It has, however, been the object of reform pressures. Again, the ideas for reform reflect both the left and right of the political spectrum. To appreciate the nature of the reform ideas listed in Table 12.1, however, one must understand in greater detail the attempt to differentiate social regulation from economic regulation.[15]

Economic regulation is the older, familiar form of regulation. It tends to be specific to a particular industry (for example, communications, transportation, energy) and focuses on regulating entry to the industry, ownership, rates of return, and sometimes, prices. It is "economic" because government intervention was, in part at least, premised on the need to overcome market imperfections such as monopoly and oligopoly. It was originally the product of the criticism of capitalism by liberal progressives early in this century and of a desire to "restore" competitive forces and efficiency, or at least prevent things from getting worse. In Canada such regulation was also based on a desire to prevent incursions from the American giant and therefore embodied nationalism. Regulators in these sectors were later usually accused of being captured by the industries they were intended to regulate.

Social regulation, on the other hand, is a more recent phenomenon, primarily a product of another phase of liberal criticism of capitalism in the 1960s and early 1970s during a period of economic prosperity.[16] Social regulation cuts across industries and deals with "health, safety, and fairness." Thus, it intervenes even more directly in the production technology and processes of firms and in their marketing practices. The volume of environmental, occupational health, and consumer product regulations increased markedly in the 1970s. In terms of economic theory the state is supposedly intervening in social regulation because of the need to deal with "externalities" or the effects of market transactions on third parties. Social regulators, it was argued by some, tended not to be as easily "captured," since there were several industries among their industrial clientele. Moreover, particularly in the United States, they seemed to pursue their regulatory tasks with considerable missionary zeal.

Since the mid-1970s, during a period of economic malaise, social regulation in particular has become a target of conservative political interests in both the United States and Canada. In this respect it became merely one of many targets, as interests and experts sought to discover the causes (and perhaps the villains) of high inflation and sluggish economic growth. To trace the evolution of this criticism and its effects on regulatory reform, it is necessary to appreciate the existence of two broad phases of social regulation in the 1970s.

During the first phase, social regulations required private firms (especially in the environmental and occupational health fields) to undertake major capital-intensive investments and expenditures. In general (although even here there is dispute), this first regulatory wave produced a quantum jump in environmental improvements. However, as the second phase of regulation-mandated capital investments was being proposed in the mid-1970s, circumstances were different. First, economic times were much more difficult, but equally important, the second wave of capital-intensive regulation could only produce, so it was argued, much smaller marginal gains in health and safety. Critics argued that social regulators were being unreasonable, unfair, and inefficient. Regulators reached for the heavy regulatory guns when other solutions might have been more useful and more cost-effective as well.

The issue that perhaps best symbolized this line of argument was the frequent dispute over the use of masks in occupational health situations. Masks were much less expensive than installing new production processes and were preferred by employers. Regulators, pressured by labour unions, argued that by focusing on masks the responsibility for the hazard was being placed on the worker. Besides, they argued, such a control program could not be implemented. There were thousands of workers, and enforcement was impossible. Since there were fewer firms, one could monitor them more easily for compliance purposes. In short, it was more appropriate to change production technologies. Nothing illustrates more distinctly the close connection between political ideas, economic costs, assumptions of human behaviour, and the real world of regulatory implementation than the case of the dispute over workers' masks.

As the search for solutions to the economic malaise continued in the late 1970s, social regulation became more intensely scrutinized. This began first in the United States where regulators were required in 1975 to prepare "inflation impact statements" for proposed regulations.[17] Studies also began to appear outlining the annual and aggregate private sector costs imposed by social regulation and its effects in lost production and jobs. An antiregulation movement became a part of the larger antigovernment ethos, which culminated in the election of the Reagan administration, a regime bent on reducing spending, taxes, and regulations—in short, on having less government.

The Canadian version of this general line of argument followed somewhat later and in more muted tones, but it occurred nonetheless.[18] During the period of wage and price controls, between 1975 and 1978, the committee of ten federal deputy ministers (DM 10) launched the initial trial studies that led to the adoption of the federal Socio-Economic Impact Assessment (SEIA) process in 1978. The Progressive Conservative premier of Manitoba, Sterling Lyon, easily persuaded the first ministers' conference in 1978 to launch a major study by the Economic Council of Canada into regulation (social and economic). In 1979 the Ontario and British Columbia governments began their own deregulation and regulatory review programs. In 1980 and 1981 a special Parliamentary Task Force on Regulatory Reform held meetings and issued its report. The politically weaker nature of the Canadian regulatory reform process as compared to that in the United States can be seen by the fact that the Economic Council's study generally advocated a form of deregulation in several sectors, but advocated *stronger* regulatory action in social regulation fields.

In terms of regulatory decision-making within government, the regulatory reform debate has produced some differences in the formal decision process. The federal SEIA process was launched by Cabinet directive in August 1978. It applied to "major" new proposed regulations in the health, safety, and fairness field under sixteen specific federal statutes. "Major" regulations were understood to be those that were likely to impose private sector costs in excess of $10 million. Proposed regulations imposing lower costs were exempt from the SEIA process.

Under the SEIA process, federal departments were required to prepare and publish, for comment by affected interests, a socioeconomic impact statement on the likely costs and benefits of the proposed regulation. There was no requirement, if costs exceeded benefits, that the regulation could not proceed. Rather, the intent was to produce more systematic "second sober thoughts" and to consult interests more formally and deliberately. Only a few proposed regulations went through a full SEIA cycle after 1978, and eventually SEIA was cancelled by the Mulroney Conservatives.

It should be noted that earlier in the 1970s regulatory reform was influenced more by the political left, which pressed for greater public participation in the regulatory process. This usually meant participation by public interest groups, some of which received, and still receive, public funds to enable them to participate on a reasonable financial footing. As stressed in Chapter 5, such groups clearly suffered from the "free rider" problem and became dependent on the state for funds.

Certain producer interest groups, on the other hand, practised their own brand of regulatory reform. Agricultural producer groups succeeded in creating more marketing boards to stabilize their incomes.[19] This was possible in part because the highly decentralized regulatory process allowed agriculture departments to agree with their producer clientele groups without much worry about central agency intervention. The continuing influence of agricultural producer interests was reflected in the reaction to the Economic Council of Canada's regulation studies. The Economic Council was extremely critical of the inflationary impact of marketing boards and suggested a form of deregulation. Agricultural interests and the Minister of Agriculture, Eugene Whelan, dismissed the report with contempt, and there seemed little doubt that no one was prepared to risk angering the agricultural lobby at this time.

When the Mulroney Conservatives came to power in 1984, they embarked upon a series of changes that altered both the substance and processes of regulation over the next eight years. First, they adopted a formal regulatory reform strategy centred on rationalizing the central regulatory decision process by giving a review mandate to the regulatory affairs wing of a new Office of Privatization and Regulatory Affairs (OPRA). Second, the Conservatives deregulated several areas of the economy at least to some extent. These included the oil and gas sector, transportation (air and rail), and telecommunications. Third, they expanded regulation in the growing and all-pervasive area of environmental regulation, especially in their 1990 Green Plan.

The Mulroney government's regulatory reform strategy emerged partly out of the Nielsen Task Force review on government programs.[20] Among other things, it pronounced the failure of earlier experiments such as the SEIA process and roundly criticized the absence of any sensible and accountable regulatory decision process. One element of the reform strategy accordingly focused exclusively on process. This included: the requirement for a Federal Regulatory Plan to be published annually setting out proposed departmental regulations; more openness and comprehensibility in the way regulations are published in the *Canada Gazette*; and a requirement for all regulatory proposals to be accompanied by a regulatory impact analysis statement (RIAS). The overseeing of these reforms was centred in OPRA and was given ministerial clout by the appointment of the federal government's first minister responsible for regulatory affairs. A Citizen's Code of Regulatory Fairness was also published. Finally, there was an undertaking to subject all regulatory programs to a regular process of evaluation.

The Mulroney regulatory agenda was not accompanied by any clarion call for deregulation.[21] Rather, the procedural reforms were sold in terms of the need to "regulate smarter." But though there was no ideological fervour for deregulation, the Conservative years certainly saw several initiatives to deregulate. Interestingly, when these occurred, they did so largely without reference to the new rationalized regulatory decision process. Thus, oil and gas deregulation, changes to banking and securities, and air and rail deregulation all took effect. While some of these changes had domestic roots, more often than not deregulation occurred or was thought to be necessary because of deregulation that had already taken place in the United States (air and rail) or in Europe (banking and securities). While some reduction in regulation undoubtedly happened as a result of these changes, there were other areas where regulation increased. The main example here was the expansion of regulation in the environmental field—in short, in the realm of social regulation—where public opinion was demanding tougher action and where past regulatory action by the Department of the Environment was seen to have no teeth.[22]

Overall, then, the Conservatives can take some credit for being the first federal government to have thought seriously about the regulatory process as a whole. At the same time, the government has had to absorb criticism that some of its deregulation initiatives have left the weaker regions of Canada more vulnerable, given that certain kinds of regional and social policies have been delivered in fact through cross-subsidization of regulatory instruments.

The Public Enterprise and Privatization Process

It is awkward even to speak of a public enterprise and privatization process. A process of sorts exists, but it is not one that is as well recognized by outsiders or practitioners as is the tax, expenditure, or even regulatory process. In Chapter 7 we showed that there are certainly still a large number of crown corporations and mixed or hybrid enterprises. The public enterprise process, in fact, shares many of the features of the regulatory process. It is highly disaggregated and involves many ministers and officials. It is not a very quantitative process, at least at the centre of government, nor has it been characterized by focused central agency review, at least not until the Mulroney Conservatives established the Office of Privatization and Regulatory Affairs mentioned earlier.

The central aspect of the public enterprise process concerns the actual operations of such companies, including their capital investment decisions and the approval of their corporate plans.[23] A further characteristic of the operations process is that those enterprises with a commercial function (for example, Air Canada, Canadian National Railways) have their own sources of revenue. Though reformers in the late 1970s and 1980s sought to secure some greater overall process of coordination and accountability of the total stable of public corporations, especially the large commercial ones, this effort had numerous inherent limitations. The reality is that there are a plurality of processes in which public corporations must interact. We will highlight only three of them, since much of the basis for the existence of these diverse processes flows logically from the analysis in previous chapters. The three related processes are the public corporation's "home" policy portfolio or ministry, the regulatory process, and the process of economic management.

While all crown corporations are influenced by the general state of the economy and the nature of the general political agenda, they are ultimately domiciled in a "home" policy field or ministry. Thus, they respond to, and attempt to influence, the nature of energy, transportation, or communications policy, as the case may be. They are also under pressure, however, not only from central agencies of government, but from other closely adjacent policy ministries. For example, environment departments have sought to influence the way decisions are made about the location of major projects planned by public corporations. Eldorado Nuclear Limited's proposed refinery site near Saskatoon was abandoned following an unfavourable environmental assessment panel report. The CBC has been under interdepartmental as well as community pressure regarding advertising directed at children.

Even within its own home ministry, a public corporation, especially at the federal level, may be only one of a small stable of crown corporations competing for funds, capital, and ministerial attention. The energy, transportation, and communications ministries are characterized by the presence of a stable of enterprises. From the point of view of the senior management of any particular crown corporation at any particular time, the crowded stable can be either a curse or a blessing. A minister preoccupied with other concerns can be a distinct asset, since the corporation may well be then left alone to do its job. In other circumstances, the lack of ministerial time and attention may prevent desired actions or funding from being achieved.

Crown corporations are always involved, in part at least, in an interdepartmental and ministerial tug of war. If a crown corporation is in political trouble, its minister will bear the brunt of parliamentary and media criticism regardless of the formal arm's length reporting relationship. Controversy over whether a minister or the Cabinet as a whole should have the power to issue directives to crown corporations is a reflection of this political reality. Regardless of their stated mandate, crown corporations are increasingly subject to the vagueness of their own minister's priorities as well as to the pressure to have the crown corporation, often at the behest of other ministries, function as the model public corporate citizen. In the latter role it is expected to be sensitive to the need to favour Canadian suppliers, support regional policies, practise proper language policies, adopt progressive environmental and occupational/labour relations practices, adopt federal wage guidelines, and so on.

The role of crown corporations in the regulatory process involves many of the same issues enunciated above, since in practical terms regulation is merely one other way in which benefits/subsidies can be secured for oneself or sanctions imposed on others. Canadian regulatory bodies under the cabinet-parliamentary system have never been as "independent" as their American counterparts. Moreover, regulatory bodies are not always viewed by their own members as being purely regulatory in nature since some of them engage in the use of other instruments. Regulators cannot help but take into account the fact that they are merely one part of an array of public institutions created to politically/governmentally "manage" an industry or policy field. They are often part of the same stable of agencies reporting to their minister as is the crown corporation they are regulating.

A question arises, therefore, about whether crown corporations get special regulatory treatment in comparison with their private sector competitors. Nominally, in a strict legal and procedural sense, they do not. In a practical political sense, however, they are intended to get a special deal, but the degree of discriminating treatment varies greatly, is partly a function of the eye of the beholder, and is the product of widely varying degrees of discretion exercised by regulators, the Cabinet, the courts, or all three. For example, Atomic Energy of Canada's nuclear facilities were, until the early 1980s, not formally licensed by the Atomic Energy Control Board, a special deal of no small initial advantage to the company, but now an indirect source of its malaise in the public eye. Similarly, until deregulation occurred in the mid-1980s, Air Canada was the favoured child of the Canadian Transport Commission (the CTC, since changed to become the National Transportation Agency) among the airlines, as mandated by public policy and successive Cabinets.

Crown corporations are a central element of general federal and provincial economic management policies and processes. They have been established in part to create jobs, or save jobs, to increase resource trade and domestic "value added," to promote Canadianization, and to resist foreign capital, especially from south of the border. Crown corporation decisions that have an impact on these areas are, of course, in one sense "evaluated" all the time within the company and policy field ministries and departments. There are, however, grounds for concern about the degree to which some of the aggregate investment impacts, especially of the largest public corporations, are incorporated into the central processes of economic management. Obviously, the Department of Finance and the Treasury Board Secretariat have some notion of the annual capital demands of major federal corporations (and some major provincial ones), but there are only the most haphazard mechanisms in place to determine, with sufficient advance knowledge, the capital and other economic plans of these major enterprises on a longer-term basis.

This invariably raises the question of economic planning and industrial policy in a liberal federal state. Crown corporations merely provide another prism through which the importance of the planning issue emerges. The domestic and foreign borrowings and capital requirements of these firms, the proposals and practices to endow them with Canadian sourcing mandates, the pricing, subsidizing, and regulatory preferences accorded them, and the effort to utilize them as opportunities to develop indigenous technology when added together constitute important dimensions of central economic management.

In many respects, when the Mulroney Conservatives came to power in 1984 they decided to eschew all these policy conundrums that had accompanied the stable of government enterprises. They knew that many crown corporations were still popular among Canadians, so they by no means came to office with a bold Thatcherite desire to privatize. But they were determined to prune selectively and to subject all such enterprises to more market-based incentives. After being accused of a timid beginning, the Conservatives eventually changed the nature of the decision process concerning the crown corporations and also sold some significant companies.[24]

The process changes centred on the establishment in 1986 of the full-fledged Cabinet Committee on Privatization and Regulatory Affairs and on the announcement of a policy whereby each existing enterprise would be assessed as to whether or not it should continue. If an enterprise had no sustainable public policy role, the presumption would be that it should be sold or wound up. In effect, there were now two crown corporation decision processes, one for approving corporate plans and one that reviewed their very existence.

The Conservatives' early sales involved some very minor companies as well as some well-known and controversial "lame ducks" such as Canadair and de Havilland.[25] Later, healthy and larger companies such as Teleglobe Canada and, above all, Air Canada were sold. As well, undertakings were made to sell the most controversial of all, Petro-Canada. In each sale, the policy process took ministers into varying quagmires of past and future policy obligations and guarantees, ownership issues, competitive versus negotiated bids, and related changes to regulatory regimes.

As was the case with regulation, there is little doubt that the Mulroney years have witnessed a significant shaking up of the comfortable post–World War II assumptions about the role of public enterprise in Canadian public policy. A larger central presence scrutinized such investment choices. This was not done with a Thatcherite vengeance, but rather was more like a determined country gardener getting rid of troublesome undergrowth in a garden too long untended.

Exhortation and Symbolic Politics and Policy

If the notion of a public enterprise process is an uncomfortable one, then the designation of an "exhortation process" may seem grotesque, both conceptually and grammatically. It is the element of the larger public policy process that is perhaps the least analyzed in any systematic way. We have placed it last in our analysis of instrument-based subsidiary policy processes not because it is the least important—the reverse may well be true—but because it seems to become a residual category into which one puts everything that does not quite fit into the other processes examined above. We have combined the notion of governing by exhortation with the notion of symbolic politics both to reflect the breadth of this category and to demonstrate the analytical problems inherent in it.[26] These two concepts must first be discussed before attempting to define the overall process.

To govern by exhortation is to engage in a whole series of potential acts of persuasion and voluntary appeals to the electorate as a whole or to particular parts of it. In this sense many would view exhortation as democratic government in its highest and most ideal form. It would be equated with the essence of leadership and of democratic consent, of legitimate government in its most pristine form. The concept could be equated even more broadly to governing based on an appeal to common values. It would be government without coercion.

There can be little doubt that governing would be impossible, not to mention undemocratic, if there were not a significant element of exhortation defined in this broad way. At the same time, there is little doubt that exhortation is not a wholly reliable way to ensure that public policy goals are achieved in the long run, since several main ideas compete for attention and since human beings respond to other instruments and incentives as well.

The notion of symbolic policies or politics must be added to the concept of governing by exhortation because it adds the additional dimension of perception.[27] Symbolic politics does not just embrace an appeal to national symbols such as a flag or the national anthem; it implies an array of ways in which governments express symbolic concern. Such concern is often expressed because to show no concern at all may be both uncaring and inhuman or, somewhat more basely, politically unwise. Moreover, symbolic concern may be expressed because there is genuinely no solution to the problem at hand. Thus, concern can be shown symbolically, as opposed to taking more concrete actions, by making a speech expressing concern, by studying the problem, by holding meetings and discussions and consulting interests, by reorganizing a department or creating a new one such as the Ministry of State for Small Business, or by making available certain kinds of information so that people affected are better able to take their own action as individuals or in collective groups and associations.

Symbolic actions may also be needed to assuage and placate those with concerns that, for any number of valid or invalid reasons, are simply ranked at the lower end of the government's priority list. It is in this sense that action that we might otherwise wish to classify under one of the other instrument lists may at times be *perceived* to be a symbolic act, that is, an act perceived by the interest concerned to be an *insufficient* response or an act designed merely to buy time. Thus, groups that want action may get a royal commission instead. Or, alternatively, those that say "there ought to be a law" get their regulation passed, but it is then only feebly enforced.

It is not difficult to see that the excessive use of symbolic politics and of exhortation can easily lead to the alienation of citizens from the state and from democratic government. It can bring government and politicians into disrepute. Not all of this dissatisfaction is necessarily directed against "the system." Some may well be channelled as support for opposition political parties, which collect and marshal these grievances.

There is already some considerable evidence that symbolic politics has already reached an epidemic proportion. This has been suggested in earlier chapters when we linked the role of the media to the increasing need for politicians to be *seen* to be doing *something*. This has resulted in an even greater need for policies "for show" or for an increased series of symbolic acts. These may well increase even further in direct proportion to the increased scarcity of *real* expenditure, tax, and regulatory resources.

The concept of governing by exhortation and symbolic politics is also directly related to ideological and other ideas. At one level it is an essential and desirable feature of democratic politics. People probably prefer to be consulted and persuaded rather than coerced, legitimately or otherwise. At the same time, small "c" conservatives see the symbolic malaise as simply further evidence of the inherent limits of state activity and of the need to appreciate that government cannot and should not do everything, since it creates a virtually immoral dependence on the state rather than on individual responsibility or community initiatives. In many respects sections of the political left agree with this critique of modern government, even while simultaneously advocating such things as more state regulation.

With these explanations and issues in mind, it should now be possible to characterize the exhortation process, at least to some degree, again with the aid of Table 12.1. The first point to note is that it is the least quantitatively based process of all those identified in this chapter. Second, it involves virtually all ministers and senior officials engaged in a series of numerous acts of persuasion, consultation, speeches, and the like. It involves, accordingly, policies "for show" as well as activity that is the epitomy of democratic leadership and democratic consent. Finally, it is evident that the exhortation process is not visibly anchored in any one central agency. The creation in the early 1980s of a Cabinet Committee on Communications may be a step in this direction, but even it has only a limited role in relation to the way exhortation is defined here. It was established not only to improve the communication of federal policies, but to support the campaign to ensure the visibility of federal initiatives vis-à-vis the provinces. The Mulroney Conservatives enhanced the status of the communication function even more.

Table 12.1 shows a sampling of the reform ideas that can be broadly viewed to be a part of this process. All have been subject to dispute and criticism, and each demonstrates the fine line between a reform idea that is viewed as the epitomy of democratic virtue by some and, at the same time, as the quintessential example of democratic vice by others. For example, Information Canada was created in the early Trudeau years. It was heralded with metaphorical fanfare as an example of the new cybernetic view of government. Government needed good information about citizen preferences coming "in" and good information about public policies going "out." It quickly became perceived as a propaganda agency. This same issue was revived in the early 1980s when the Trudeau Liberals engaged in aggressive advocacy advertising of their policies in the print and television media.[28] So also did the Mulroney Conservatives in their major policy initiatives such as free trade and the GST. The latter were intended to "inform" people since it was felt by some that the media would not adequately and fairly report on these policies. Another example of governing by exhortation was the emergence of monitoring and policy advisory agencies. They included bodies such as the Petroleum Monitoring Agency and the Food Prices Review Board. They were established to produce information of a more independent kind. The logic of both was that exposure to this information would exert pressure on the industries concerned and help improve public understanding. We comment further on this kind of information in Chapter 13.

Finally, Table 12.1 contains an old Canadian friend, the royal commission or other analogous studies and task force inquiries.[29] Such acts of exhortation or symbolic politics can be both an input to policy and a policy output, a device to buy time. Again, they can be, and have been viewed as, either essential acts of democratic life or a bane to democracy. Other acts and forums of consultation and advice could just as easily be noted here as well. Some of these have already been analyzed in Chapter 5.

Conclusions

The tax and regulatory processes, as well as those that we have labelled the public enterprise and exhortation processes, involve a different set of dynamics than does the more familiar expenditure process. The degree of quantification of policy values, the number of ministers and agencies involved, and the degree of central structural presence varies widely across these different realms of policy expression. With respect to tax reform, regulation, and privatization, there can be little doubt that major changes occurred in the Mulroney era.

In Chapters 11 and 12 we have reviewed the policy and resource allocation process in some detail, and with greater realism than our initial portrait in Chapter 4 or even our historical review of priorities in Chapter 9. These chapters illustrate the connections and mutual influence of ideas, structures, and processes and why it is virtually impossible to secure any lasting agreement on what constitutes the ideal policy structure and resource allocation system. In the early 1980s, Ottawa had its envelopes and, in the 1990s, a special expenditure review committee and new central regulatory review machinery. Specific structural titles may change, but the underlying imperatives do not: how to deal with contending ideas; how to plan without calling it planning; how to be responsive, but not spend recklessly; how to centralize, delegate, and decentralize at the same time; how to keep bureaucrats under control, but at the same time get better analysis and advice; how to ensure both individual and collective ministerial responsibility while catering to powerful individual egos and personalities; and how to link social, economic, and foreign policies and actually change private behaviour in a democratic way.

Notes

1. See Robin W. Boadway and Harry M. Kitchen, *Canadian Tax Policy* (Toronto: Canadian Tax Foundation, 1980); David Good, *The Politics of Anticipation: Making Canadian Federal Tax Policy* (Ottawa: School of Public Administration, Carleton University, 1980); and Douglas Hartle, *The Revenue Budget Process of the Government of Canada* (Toronto: Canadian Tax Foundation, 1982).
2. Good, *The Politics of Anticipation*, ch. 2.
3. See G. Bruce Doern, "Tax Expenditures and Tory Times: More or Less Policy Discretion?" in Katherine Graham, ed., *How Ottawa Spends 1989-90* (Ottawa: Carleton University Press, 1989), 75–106.
4. See John Bossons, "The Analysis of Tax Reform," in L. H. Officer and Lawrence B. Smith, eds., *Issues in Canadian Economics* (Toronto: McGraw-Hill Ryerson, 1974), 303.
5. On the general aspects of tax reform, including the Carter reforms, see Irwin Gillespie, "Tax Reform: The Battlefield, the Strategies, the Spoils," paper presented to Conference on "The Limits of Govern-

ment Intervention," School of Public Administration, Carleton University, Ottawa, October 1982.

6. See Allan Maslove, "Tax Expenditures, Tax Credits and Equity," in G. Bruce Doern, ed., *How Ottawa Spends Your Tax Dollars 1981* (Toronto: James Lorimer, 1981), ch. 7.

7. See G. Bruce Doern, ed., *How Ottawa Spends Your Tax Dollars 1982* (Toronto: James Lorimer, 1982), ch. 1.

8. See Canada, *The Budget Process* (Ottawa: Minister of Finance, April 1982), and Hartle, *The Revenue Budget Process*, chs. 4 and 5.

9. See Allan Maslove, *Tax Reform in Canada: The Process and Impact* (Ottawa: Institute for Research on Public Policy, 1989).

10. See Allan Maslove, "The Goods and Services Tax: Lessons from Tax Reform," in Katherine Graham, ed., *How Ottawa Spends 1990-91* (Ottawa: Carleton University Press, 1990), 27-48.

11. See Economic Council of Canada, *Responsible Regulation* (Ottawa: Minister of Supply and Services, 1979).

12. See G. Bruce Doern, ed., *The Regulatory Process in Canada* (Toronto: Macmillan, 1978).

13. See Robert D. Anderson, "The Federal Regulation-Making Process and Regulatory Reform, 1969-1979," in W. T. Stanbury, ed., *Government Regulation: Scope, Growth, Process* (Montreal: Institute for Research on Public Policy, 1980), ch. 4.

14. See G. Bruce Doern, Michael Prince, and Garth McNaughton, *Living with Contradictions: Health and Safety Regulation and Implementation in Ontario* (Toronto: Royal Commission on Matters of Health and Safety Arising from the Use of Asbestos in Ontario, 1982), ch. 1.

15. Economic Council of Canada, *Responsible Regulation*, ch. 4.

16. See Paul H. Weaver, "Regulation, Social Policy and Class Conflict," *The Public Interest* 50 (Winter 1978), 45-64; and Doern et al., *Living with Contradictions*, ch. 1.

17. See Fred Thompson, "Regulatory Reform and Deregulation in the United States," in Stanbury, ed., *Government Regulation*, ch. 5.

18. See W. T. Stanbury and Fred Thompson, *Regulatory Reform in Canada* (Montreal: Institute for Research on Public Policy, 1982).

19. See J. D. Forbes, R. D. Hughes, and T. K. Warley, *Economic Intervention and Regulation in Canadian Agriculture* (Ottawa: Economic Council of Canada and Institute for Research on Public Policy, 1982).

20. See Canada, *Regulatory Reform: Making It Work* (Ottawa: Office of Privatization and Regulatory Affairs, 1988).

21. See Richard Schultz, "Regulating Conservatively: The Mulroney Record, 1984-1988," in Andrew B. Gollner and Daniel Salee, eds., *Canada Under Mulroney* (Montreal: Véhicule Press, 1988), 186-205.

22. See G. Bruce Doern, "Social Regulation and Environmental-Economic Reconciliation," in G. Bruce Doern and Bryne Purchase, eds., *Canada at Risk: Canadian Public Policy in the 1990s* (Toronto: C. D. Howe Institute, 1990), 100-115.

23. Allan Tupper and G. Bruce Doern, eds., *Privatization, Public Corporations and Public Policy in Canada* (Halifax: Institute for Research on Public Policy, 1988).

24. See William T. Stanbury, "Privatization and the Mulroney Government, 1984–1988," in Gollner and Salee, eds., *Canada Under Mulroney*, 119–57.
25. See G. Bruce Doern and John Atherton, "The Tories and the Crowns: Privatizing in a Political Minefield," in Michael Prince, ed., *How Ottawa Spends 1986–87* (Toronto: Methuen, 1986), 129–75.
26. See Murray Edelman, *The Symbolic Uses of Politics* (Champaign-Urbana: University of Illinois Press, 1967).
27. See Douglas Hartle, *Public Policy, Decision Making and Regulation* (Montreal: Institute for Research on Public Policy, 1979), 33–35.
28. See W. T. Stanbury, "Government Expenditures: The Critical .001 Percent Advertising," in G. Bruce Doern, ed., *How Ottawa Spends Your Tax Dollars 1983* (Toronto: James Lorimer, 1983), ch. 5.
29. See V. Seymour Wilson, "The Role of Royal Commissions and Task Forces," in G. Bruce Doern and Peter Aucoin, eds., *The Structures of Policy Making in Canada* (Toronto: Macmillan, 1971), ch. 4; and Liora Salter and Debra Slaco, *Public Inquiries in Canada* (Ottawa: Science Council of Canada, 1982).

C H A P T E R *13*

Knowledge, Information, and Public Policy

The policy formulation process is characterized by both an active trade in information and knowledge and by strategies for strenuously withholding information and knowledge. In some areas of policy there is too much information and knowledge, and in many other areas of policy there is a great scarcity. In this chapter we take the examination of policy formulation into the world of knowledge and information, a world about which it is difficult to generalize, but that is absolutely essential to understand. Like so many other axioms, the commonly heard "knowledge is power" thesis needs examination and qualification. Knowledge is an amalgam of facts and values produced both by intellectual-analytical processes and by social interaction among decision-makers, their "advisers," and interests in and out of government. It involves ideas about knowledge and about the language and rhetoric of public debate. It involves numerous types and sources of information. Information, moreover, is both an output of policy and an input to policy development.

In the first part of this chapter we examine different types of knowledge and information focusing in particular on several pairs of dichotomous categories: verbal versus written information, facts versus values, causal knowledge versus uncertainty, voluntary versus compulsory information, and input versus output information and knowledge. In the second part we examine different sources of knowledge and information, from the so-called "hard" statistics collected by agencies such as Statistics Canada, to softer kinds of data that come in the form of political intelligence and "street smarts" supplied by sources such as Members of Parliament, party officials, or local radio hotline shows. Finally, we conclude with some observations about why knowledge is not necessarily power, and why more research and analysis, though often desirable, does not necessarily produce better policy.

Types of Knowledge and Information

Verbal versus Written

The first type of distinction to make about information and knowledge in the policy process is that between written and verbal. Ministers and senior officials are besieged by a constant flow of paper, memoranda, statistical data, and reports. Bureaucracies thrive on the written word. We drew particular attention in Chapter 6 to the importance of Cabinet background papers, memoranda to Cabinet, and *aides-mémoire*. The volume of written information has developed to the point where no minister can read, let alone digest, all the material. The interdependence among policy fields increases this load on both ministers and deputy ministers because there are greater obligations to be prepared to deal with the proposals of other departments, as well as one's own.

Increasing paper flow and the need to interact with more central agencies have placed an even greater premium on the verbal transmittal of advice, knowledge, and information. Verbal person-to-person communication via meetings, telephone calls, and the luncheon circuit has perhaps always been the central human dimension of politics. It therefore places a premium on who has access to ministers and who controls their schedule. For the prime minister, this may be a handful of senior officials and advisers who meet with the prime minister every day. For individual ministers, it is the deputy minister and his or her senior political staff. Indeed, there is nearly always some tension between the minister's partisan political and bureaucratic advisers in the kind of access and expertise they each possess.

Facts versus Values

The crucial relationships between advisers and decision-makers raise a very old concern regarding knowledge and information, namely the alleged facts versus values dichotomy.[1] Some scholars of decision-making have tried to distinguish between advising on facts and on values. Indeed, a "policy and decision science," for many of its advocates, is premised on the clear possibility of separating the two.[2] Others, such as Sir Geoffrey Vickers, argue that no such distinction can ultimately be made. Vickers refers to the "appreciative system" of decision-makers and advisers, in effect an amalgam of values and facts, preferences and experience.[3] Similar conclusions are reached by other students of policy-making.[4] The concept of incrementalism is basically in agreement with this view in that small adjustments are the norm because knowledge is limited and ends may not be seriously reviewed lest such a debate ruins the chance for consensus. This view also suggests that there is an inevitable link between policy analysis and policy advocacy.

There is no easy guide through the maze of relationships, concepts, and ways of viewing the adviser–advisee relationship and the facts–values controversy. Consider, for example, the debate about what policy analysis is or should be and about what policy analysts in government do. Wildavsky distinguishes between intellect versus interaction as forms of analysis.[5] The former involves "cerebral cogitation" and calls for the need for causal knowledge, "theories of society to predict the paths of the complex sequences of desired action and power to sustain this effort."[6] Such knowledge is by definition limited. Social interaction in markets and in other social forums is also a form of analysis. Social interaction among decision-makers and others "gives analysis a historical outlook made up of the past pattern of agreements, including agreements to disagree until next time."[7] Policy analysis consists of enabling the "recognition, reformulation and resolution of problems."[8]

When policy advisers and analysts describe what they do, the picture is never very clear. The task involves partly facts and partly values. It involves partly the application of pet theories and partly "seat of the pants" experience.[9] It embraces an amalgam of analysis and advocacy. Often the process is characterized as "fire-fighting," merely surviving to deal with the same old policy problem over and over again. Analyses of Canadian decisions and relations between decision-makers and advisers are often not very helpful. This is partly because few studies have been carried out, but even where they exist it is clear that it is an extremely difficult area to study.[10] To obtain a sufficient subtlety in understanding the advisory role, one needs detailed case studies; but unique case studies do not allow for much generalization. If, on the other hand, one attempts broad-based surveys of decision-makers' attitudes, one obtains questionable generalizations because the studies lack the subtlety that everyone knows exists in real decision-making situations. In the final analysis, we are left with a limited number of illustrative Canadian glimpses of the facts–values relationships in different public policy fields. We will note two of these in quite diverse fields. The first concerns the role of economists as advisers, and the second concerns scientists and brings us into the realm of professional knowledge interests.

While one is tempted to stereotype all economists, this is not always very helpful. It is possible to show the influence of different economists who adhere to different basic schools of thought, policy paradigms, or policy ideas. Economists are recruited in increasing numbers to the upper echelons of government, but it is their adherence to particular schools of thought that shows up in advice and in some, but certainly not all, policies and decisions. For example, the team of analysts working in the federal Ministry of State for Economic and Regional Development (MSERD) in the early 1980s were primarily economists with a basic microeconomic view of the world and of what constitutes economic development.[11] They were suspicious of intervention and enthusiasts for the need for cost-benefit analysis. These views gained some momentum and were reflected in decisions to eliminate subsidies that were viewed by the economists as a form of social welfare. The question that one has to ask, however, is whether it is their ideas that are having an effect or whether it is the broader flow of events and ideas and the lessons of the previous years of experience that are producing change. And what of the previous decade? Industry, Trade and Commerce and the Department of Regional Economic Expansion (DREE) were also well populated with microeconomists during the 1970s, many of whom advocated similar views, but often to little or no avail.

In a similar way one can analyze the role of Keynesian economists and monetarists.[12] The former held sway in the Department of Finance for much of the 1950s and 1960s, and the latter began to exercise influence at the Bank of Canada in the mid and late 1970s. Even in the heyday of a Keynesian finance department, however, it cannot be said that a Keynesian policy was followed. Keynesianism was nonetheless the dominant paradigm or prism through which fiscal policy was viewed, and its transmitters were economists. The rise of monetarist thought was also transmitted by economists who enjoyed their moments in the economic policy sun.

The complexity of the facts–values interplay as revealed in economic advice is also reflected in the debate on a policy field that is much less frequently in the policy limelight, namely agricultural policy.[13] Agricultural marketing boards and income stabilization measures run counter to a microeconomist's view of economic efficiency. But farm producer groups have succeeded politically in sustaining support for the idea of stabilizing producer incomes by appealing to the existence of market and climatic vagaries and uncertainties in people's most essential need, the food basket. Indeed, their views were often supported by agricultural economists, a group often reared in different concerns and traditions than mainline economists. In the 1990s, however, the attack against marketing boards grew as food product producers in Canada increasingly argued that such boards would soon put them out of business. This was because, under Canada–U.S. free trade, Canadian food manufacturers would face greater U.S. competition from firms whose input costs were lower because the United States did not use marketing boards.

The role of scientists in policy formulation shows a similar variety of possible professional relationships in the facts–values and adviser–decision-maker web.[14] Scientists are even more likely to be viewed as experts than are economists, partly because scientific theories are perceived to be harder edged and more technical. Hence, there may be a greater tendency for the lay person to defer to scientific opinions. On the other hand, even though scientific advice is an important part of many policy fields, scientists are generally not deputy ministers or central agency advisers. Thus, they are often one step removed from access to decision-makers. Moreover, because of their training in scientific methods and in rational calculation, scientists often view themselves to be apolitical. Things that are not technical are viewed by them to be emotional or irrational, a defiance of "the facts." These labels have certainly characterized the debate and interaction between scientists and others engaged in policy fields such as nuclear power and environmental and occupational health and safety.[15]

Scientists are, of course, not a monolithic group either. They are divided by different interests in basic versus applied research, and they operate in different disciplines and fields, from physics, biology, and geology, to engineering. They are as prone as economists or any other knowledge group to speak *ex cathedra* and to advise about a subject that is not in their area of technical expertise, but rather is in the realm of broader values and ideas.

The facts–values dimension of knowledge and information must also be related to the issue of the presentation of alternatives. The classic rationally ideal model of the adviser, indeed of the ministerial–civil servant relationship, is that the adviser's obligation is to generate and suggest alternative means to meet a given policy purpose or goal. Many advisers conscientiously try to supply alternatives. Many, however, do not. Indeed, the processes of interagency "massaging" of ideas and the constant meetings prior to a formal decision being made often induce the adviser to produce a consensus. If alternatives are presented, they are often of necessity "strawmen" alternatives that can be triumphantly knocked down on the way to the previously arranged consensus. Moreover, ministers are not always interested in having alternatives since it may imply a need to decide and take risks, something not all ministers are willing to do, or often are allowed to do, by their Cabinet colleagues.

Causal Knowledge versus Uncertainty

The essence of good public policy-making is to change or sustain desired behaviour in reliable, predictable ways. It therefore often requires a capacity to change private behaviour. It must, in short, deal with causality or theory. But there is only a limited supply of causal knowledge in the sphere of social relations, and even it is in considerable dispute. Moreover, people do not always behave in expected ways. Interests can often resist change and act in opposition to "the facts." There is usually considerable uncertainty not only about results in a single policy field, but even more so when policy fields intersect, as they invariably do. Thus, the policy process must be thought of in relation to the existence and limits of causal knowledge.[16] In this sense it can be said that if there is no theory, there is unlikely to be successful practice.

The issue of causal knowledge must also be linked to the limits of program evaluation. Full-blown program evaluations imply a capacity to link observed actions with discrete effects and results. Few program evaluations can meet this ultimate test. Results, moreover, are time related. Is the program to be judged over one year or over five or ten years? Information and program evaluation studies will be and should be viewed with a critical eye. The political system learns, that is, "evaluates," in many ways. Formal evaluation studies are only one form of knowledge.

At the same time, it is evident that policy-makers should not ignore the packages of partial causal knowledge that do exist. For example, even though there is no agreed theory of accident causation in the health and safety field, governments have constructed policies based on partial theories and ideas about what will work. The basic theory of Keynesian policy was adopted in general, though not practised in detail or consistently. The assertions of different theories of inflation, including monetary theories, have partly influenced anti-inflation policies. Contending theories and models of penal reform in the corrections field have been tried and usually found to be wanting as ideas, and public opinion has ebbed and flowed between tough law-and-order measures to reformist self-help and humanitarian measures. This notion of partial causal knowledge should be linked to our discussion of the role of policy paradigms. These are ways of viewing and acting on policy problems that are often entrenched in the education of professionals in different policy fields.

Uncertainty in the use of information is also evident in the constant need to forecast future events based on past data and on hypothesized relationships among variables. This need is unavoidable, and yet the perils are evident. Transportation policy must be based on estimates of future traffic patterns and use preferences whose estimation is in turn based on a host of other economic and social variables. Energy policy is dependent upon calculations of future oil and gas reserves and consumer behaviour in the use of different energy forms. Pension policy, education policy, and other policy fields are dependent upon demographic projections.

It is worth remembering in this context that the use of formal forecasting and econometric models is a relatively recent phenomenon in the federal government.[17] Though some basic survey activities were begun in the 1940s, other models were not developed until the late 1960s and early 1970s. Controversy surrounded major models such as the CANDIDE model. Although there are now several private sector modelling efforts on the economy, it is a matter of no small importance to stress that *within* the federal government there has never been a process, through formal modelling or otherwise, to generate an agreed portrait among the central agencies of what the medium-term, three-to-five-year state of the Canadian economy was likely to be. Some degree of progress in this state of affairs was made in the early 1980s and coincided with the emergence of the Ministry of State for Economic and Regional Development. An annual "medium-term track" document began to be prepared that supposedly represented a consensus of views, but it was a very shaky consensus indeed.

This does not mean, however, that such a consensus forecast portrait will govern all or even most policy decisions. The macro realities and the micro pressures are always in a state of tension. For example, the free trade decision of the mid and late 1980s was partly premised on a wide variety of modelling and forecasting. Such studies all pointed in the same direction and showed economic gains for Canada, but the magnitude of the gains varied widely depending upon various assumptions. Yet the decision to proceed with negotiations had little to do with these projections per se. The decision was based as much on a fear of growing U.S. protectionism as on a faith in liberalized markets.[18]

Voluntary versus Compulsory Information

The acquisition and use of information and knowledge in the policy process frequently involves sharp controversy over the idea of whose privacy will be invaded to obtain and use the information. The evolution of several policy fields shows a history of the increasingly compulsory nature of information acquisition. Initially, policy may be based on voluntarily supplied data, but gradually data become statutorily required. Not surprisingly, many object on ideological grounds to this growing compulsion and state involvement. In some cases, special monitoring agencies have been created to collect, publish, and interpret the data. Several examples can be cited to show the importance of the voluntary versus compulsory controversy. They have arisen in energy policy, education, environmental regulation, and occupational health, to name only a few.

In energy policy, a major controversy in the 1970s arose over the degree to which the federal government depended upon the oil and gas industry for information both on oil and gas reserves in the ground and on industry financing. The response to the former problem was in part to strengthen the Department of Energy, Mines and Resources' forecasting abilities and in part to create Petro-Canada as a so-called "window on the industry." As to industry finances, the powers of the Petroleum Monitoring Agency compelled the production of information that could not otherwise be gleaned, let alone legally published, from corporate tax returns.

A second example can be found in education policy. The federal government transfers billions annually to the provinces, both in grants and tax points, as part of the Established Programs Financing Arrangements. In the early 1980s when these arrangements were being renegotiated, the federal government concluded that several provinces were diverting money to other noneducational areas. The federal government indicated it was no longer prepared to tolerate this and wanted a new system of compulsory information and reporting to ensure it would not happen in future. Provincial governments opposed this concept on the grounds that it violated their jurisdiction over education.

Similar sensitivities have occurred regarding the compulsory testing data on chemicals that companies are required to submit for new chemical products under the federal Canadian Environmental Protection Act. In this instance, companies raised the principle of protecting commercial secrets or commercial privilege from competitors. In an analogous way, many workers and unions have objected in principle to the publication and use of employee medical records as a way of learning about and combatting occupational health problems. Here, individual privacy was the principle asserted to be balanced against a broader concept of public good.

Information and Knowledge as Input and Output

It is evident from the above examples that information and knowledge are both an input to the policy process and an output. We have more to say in the next section about the sources of information, but it is essential to stress this obvious presence on both sides of the policy system. Information and knowledge are necessary to identify and characterize a particular state of affairs. Analysis takes place in both of the ways to which Wildavsky alludes, that is, by intellectual cogitation and by social interaction.

Information is also an output. As our discussion in Chapter 12 of the issue of symbolic politics and exhortation showed, information and knowledge are produced so as to help influence private behaviour in certain desired ways and to show concern. Economists refer to the high "transaction costs" that face many groups and individuals in making decisions. A justification for government involvement is provided where government-supplied information becomes a public good to help overcome these costs. Thus, information is compelled or otherwise produced in fields such as consumer protection and securities regulation to enable decision-makers to make more informed market choices. Another example of growing importance in the 1990s is the publication of summaries of environmental assessments of all federal policy choices. These summaries are intended both to inform Canadians, but also to offer symbolic reassurance that environmental values are being taken into greater account in Cabinet.

As we saw in Chapter 12, information output can become propaganda as governments use resources for advocacy advertising and partisan advantage. It is necessary to add that some of the input information coming to government from interest groups can also be characterized as a form of propaganda or advocacy, depending upon the adjective applied. The different characterizations of information and knowledge on both the input and output sides are one of the reasons why freedom of information legislation presents problems that go well beyond the motherhood concepts inherent in such legislation. The federal legislation passed in 1982 endorses the principle of freedom of information, but also creates other major exceptions where the legislation will not apply. These exceptions are widely defined and include information for federal–provincial relations, for the scientific testing of data that might be subject to misleading interpretations, for matters of commercial privilege, for foreign policy relations and national security, and for information involved in Cabinet deliberations and policy development.[19] In each case a counter-idea is marshalled to sustain the need for an exception to the idea of freedom of information.

Major Sources of Information

One way of looking at the sources of information and knowledge is to range them along a continuum from "hard" to "soft." The former suggests official statistical, quantitative, and scientific data, perhaps including public opinion polls. At the soft end of the continuum there exist many kinds of political intelligence, usually much less quantitative and much more judgmental and interactive, emanating from ministers, their political staff, the party caucus, party professionals, the media, individual citizens, and opinion leaders. This way of viewing information and knowledge would be quite valid were it not for the frequent implications that "hard" means quantitative and therefore good data, while "soft" means nonquantitative and therefore less than good data. The fact is that democratic policy-making must have both *hard* (that is, good) quantitative and statistical data, and *hard* (that is, good) political intelligence. This necessity should be kept in mind as we review the major sources of information and knowledge.

The purpose of the brief profiles of these sources is a simple one, to make the student of policy formulation aware of their existence and of some of the issues and characteristics involved in their use. In fact, we have already begun this process in the previous chapter when we noted the public documentation emanating from each of the tax, expenditure, and regulatory processes.

The Media

The mass media, especially newspapers and television, is arguably the most important source of policy information. Ministers and their office staffs are rabid readers of the press and watchers of television coverage. The mass media's role as an information source is especially important in a daily agenda-setting sense. This is because media coverage is directly linked to the daily tactical battle in the House of Commons during question period. Items that the mass media regards as important easily become items on which opposition critics will focus. This in turn can lead to actions by ministers and departments that would not have been predicted in their own preferred agendas. Beyond this tactical role, the mass media is also a source of general information for the public and for interest groups engaged in continuous lobbying activities. In the 1980s and early 1990s, the reactions and reporting of the business press also became a significant source of information and pressure.

Official Statistics

Public policy is influenced by both the content and the timing of the release of statistical and other data on major economic and political aspects of Canadian society, much of it collected by Statistics Canada. On the question of timing, it is of no small importance to note the effect of the release of monthly data on the Consumer Price Index (CPI) and unemployment levels. Their release induces a political ritual equivalent to the proverbial dance of the seven veils. The government is routinely raked over the coals by the opposition political parties in the media and in the House of Commons and urged to do "something" about inflation or unemployment, or both, The government routinely defends its economic wisdom while privately confessing to itself that it will have to do "something" and "soon." It can be easily argued that the mere release of these data contribute pressure to further "fine tune" the economy or to produce policies "for show," as we have previously put it. This is not necessarily an argument against publishing such data (the Rhinoceros Party once advocated eliminating unemployment by abolishing Stats Canada!), but it does illustrate the connection between information, the media, and parliamentary politics.

The contents of these official major statistics (and others like them) also deserve understanding since beneath the data are disputes both about methodological issues and ideas. Consider first the CPI. The CPI is considered by many to be a "cost of living" index.[20] It has important resource allocation implications since it is tied to an increasing number of collective wage agreements through "cost of living allowance" or "COLA" clauses, to the indexation of some pension and social program benefits, and to the indexation of the tax system. But the CPI is not a totally reliable measure of changes in living costs. It is, in fact, an index of retail prices. Statistics Canada publishes other price indices, the most important of which is the Gross National Expenditure (GNE) implicit price deflator, which includes price changes for all goods and services traded in the economy and counted in the National Accounts. But the CPI clearly gets the lion's share of the political and media attention.

The CPI, in fact, measures the changes in prices for a basket of four hundred goods and services purchased by individuals and families living in large cities with a population of more than 30 000. In the index several prices are grouped together and weighted in their importance relative to the proportion of family income spent on the various goods and services in the basket. The weights stay the same for a decade or so at a time. Food prices are also shown separately, as well as included in part of the overall CPI. As a result, the CPI may not be a good guide to what is happening to particular groups of citizens such as pensioners, low-income Canadians, or single women with children.[21]

Statistical data on the unemployment rate present similar methodological and policy dilemmas, as well as problems of political visibility. Problems arise because the composition of the labour market, and of the unemployed, has changed dramatically in the 1970s and 1980s. Moreover, Canada has experienced labour market changes that have been markedly different than other countries. This was especially the case in the higher level of growth in the labour market and in higher levels of unemployment due to seasonal/climatic factors. These issues in turn affect the vague and highly politicized debate about what constitutes a reasonable measure of full employment.

Statistics Canada does not, as some countries do, estimate the number of unemployed by looking at the number receiving unemployment benefits. It conducts a monthly survey of about 55 000 Canadian households. There are continuous disputes, certainly in the realm of political rhetoric, about the failure of this measurement approach to capture the hidden unemployed. This is further exacerbated by the fact that there is often more than one worker in a family or household. The increased number of employed women or wives looking for work leads to different political interpretations of how serious unemployment is, especially as a measure of hardship.[22]

Data on the CPI and unemployment rates are obviously not the only statistical information whose timing and content evoke political dispute. Data on the size of the federal deficit, energy and resource reserves, environmental pollution levels, crime rates, and various measures of the money supply, to name other examples, also influence the process and content of public policy.

Public Opinion Polls

All of Canada's political parties employ pollsters to help them gauge public opinion for immediate electoral purposes and between elections as well.[23] The periodic publication of Gallup and other polls produces a similar tribal ritual to that described above for the announcement of CPI and unemployment data. Line departments and agencies have also used poll data in their own policy fields. Thus, there have been numerous polls: to gauge the "work ethic" and other values deemed to be important for programs such as unemployment insurance; to assess support for federalism versus separatism among citizens of Quebec; to gauge the popularity of free trade and the Meech

Lake Accord; to assess attitudes about the bureaucracy; and to gauge support for abortion laws and capital punishment.

Indeed, many departments subscribe to regular quarterly public opinion reports supplied by private firms. In addition to supplying views about particular policy fields, the polls survey the overall mood of the country, including the perceptions that Canadians have about their confidence in the future. Since the late 1970s the "communications plan" section of Cabinet documents has regularly included brief paragraphs setting out recent polling data on the subject at hand. The importance of such data is difficult to gauge precisely, partly because the degree to which ministers actually read Cabinet documents is not verifiable and partly because ministers are themselves often sceptical of polls and have greater confidence in their own political intelligence.

Interest groups, businesses, and unions have also used polls not only to assess particular policies, but to gauge how they are perceived by the public. Private polls by Gallup and others have shown important changes in public perceptions of different institutions. For example, in the early 1970s businesses and then unions were more feared and distrusted than government. By the end of the 1970s and in the mid-1980s government was the most distrusted.

Polls used for policy purposes, though not necessarily for electoral purposes, are almost always used with great caution and as a supplement to many other sources of information. Polls have inherent weaknesses in particular policy fields or as devices to help set priorities. This is because most polls are rarely tied to the *costs* of those preferences. They are therefore the political equivalent of "having your cake and eating it too." Despite this, they continue to be used. In addition, publicly financed polls raise important questions about who owns the information. Opposition parties argue that results should automatically be made public, a view difficult to dispute. The governing party meanwhile asserts that such polls are another form of advice to the government and that there is no obligation to make the polls public. In the context of elections, polls are undoubtedly of greater importance, particularly because they capture immediate moods of the electorate. Moreover, such polling data are usually given to only a small handful of persons and thus become an important instrument of power.

Political Intelligence

The sources of political intelligence about the views, concerns, and preferences of Canadians are numerous and utterly essential to policy formulation. In the immediate political arena outside the Cabinet and the party, the main sources are Parliament and the media. Parliament is composed of the opposition political parties and the government's own caucus. Both are a constant source of information and views about general priorities and specific policy fields. The opposition's views are expressed in a decidedly public way, while those of the caucus usually arrive in the private confines of weekly caucus meetings and numerous telephone calls and private discussions. It is these forums that provide the regional views about the impact of current policies and programs. The individual Member of Parliament has a communications network in his or her constituency that no bureaucrat or journalist can match. This is not to argue that these views are always listened to or that regional opinion is faithfully reflected in policy. Ministers who do not cultivate their relations with their own party caucus or who are chained to their Ottawa desks can quickly lose touch with this kind of political intelligence.

We have already mentioned several facets of the mass media's role in the policy process. In terms of political intelligence, the media provide an additional source of editorial opinion, especially that of the key political columnists. While the mass media hardly offers a consistent set of views or even necessarily accurate information, it is nonetheless so critical in the development of political careers that its many views are listened to, if not necessarily agreed with. There is, of course, an intense mutual distrust between a "free press" and politicians. This has been evident in the 1980s and 1990s in the increasing use of advocacy advertising by governments to market their policies and, hence, themselves. The mass media is often critical of this practice, but at the same time willingly pockets the profits from the advertisements.

Cabinet Documents and Papers

We have referred at length to the Cabinet's internal paper flow in Chapter 6 and in the brief analysis in this chapter of written versus verbal information and knowledge. We include these documents as an important source of information in this brief inventory of sources precisely because they are one form of documentation in which some (but not all) of the other sources are synthesized, summarized, and interpreted for ministers by bureaucrats and political staffs.

Other Jurisdictions

The sheer volume of information and knowledge transmitted (and also withheld) by other jurisdictions is both awesome and unwieldy. Federal–provincial, international, and public sector–private sector information is traded constantly in numerous forms and modes of communication. Of equal significance is the frequent withholding of information between and among sectors. This practice is caught up in the compulsory versus voluntary aspects of information discussed above, but is also influenced by a number of principles such as commercial privilege, the sensitivity of international relations, and national security, not to mention partisan distrust among ministers in different governments and among officials.

One example of the conflicting pattern of information exchange is found in environmental data. In a field such as the pretesting of chemicals, federal and provincial governments separately collect some of the same data from the same companies. The sharing of data is not permitted for fear of a breach of commercial privilege. In this instance, "duplication" is hailed by companies as an administrative virtue. In other instances, these same companies would complain bitterly of federal–provincial duplication and the growing paper burden of government. In the latter instance, duplication is a bureaucratic sin. Similar problems exist, incidentally, in the exchange of data among countries in this field and in others.

Specialized Policy Analysis Units

A further source of information, knowledge, and advice is found in the burgeoning and relatively recent (post mid-1960s) emergence of a policy analysis industry. Within the government these specialized units include numerous policy and planning branches established in many departments.[24] In part these units were created out of genuine desire to improve analysis and to lengthen the time frame of decision-making and planning. The units, however, were also established by departments as a protective device against the growing central agency "planners." Not surprisingly, the units have a very ambivalent role to play. Some do genuine research, while others are merely firefighters engaged in the short-term analytical trench warfare that often characterizes interdepartmental relations.

Other manifestations of this policy analysis industry are found in governmental advisory bodies such as the Economic Council of Canada and the Science Council of Canada, as well as the several private and university research bodies such as the Conference Board of Canada, the C. D. Howe Research Institute, the Fraser Institute, the Institute for Research on Public Policy, the Ontario Economic Council, and the Centre for Policy Alternatives. These bodies reflect ideas from almost the entire ideological spectrum and produce numerous reports and studies.[25] Most studies are dutifully reported by the media, read by *some* bureaucrats in relevant departments, and discussed at conferences and seminars. It is doubtful that most are read by ministers and senior officials, who generally lack the time. These specialized units are nonetheless an important feature of the knowledge and information network.

Conclusions

The analysis of some of the characteristic dichotomies of information and knowledge—written versus verbal, facts versus values, causal versus uncertain, voluntary versus compulsory, input versus output—and our brief descriptive inventory of the major sources of information show the general need to be more careful about the usual "knowledge is power" thesis. It is essential to appreciate that knowledge and analysis embrace both intellectual thought and processes of social interaction. It is this fundamental reality that places limits on the utility of formal evaluation studies, and yet it makes public policy theory and practice not polar opposites, but closely interconnected endeavours.

Notes

1. See Herbert A. Simon, *Administrative Behavior*, 2nd ed. (New York: Free Press, 1965), ch. 3.
2. See Yehezkel Dror, *Design for Policy Sciences* (New York: Elsevier, 1971).
3. Sir Geoffrey Vickers, *The Art of Judgement* (New York: Basic Books, 1965), ch. 4.
4. See Aaron Wildavsky, *Speaking Truth to Power: The Art and Craft of Policy Analysis* (Boston: Little, Brown, 1979).
5. Ibid., ch. 5. See also Arnold J. Meltsner, *Policy Analysts in the Bureaucracy* (Berkeley: University of California Press, 1976).
6. Wildavsky, *Speaking Truth to Power*, 120.
7. Ibid., 139.
8. Ibid., 123.
9. See Leslie A. Pal, *Public Policy Analysis*, 2nd ed. (Toronto: Nelson, 1992).
10. See G. Bruce Doern and Brian W. Tomlin, *Faith and Fear: The Free Trade Story* (Toronto: Stoddart, 1991), ch. 2.
11. Sandford F. Borins, "Ottawa's Envelopes: Workable Rationality at Last," in G. Bruce Doern, ed., *How Ottawa Spends Your Tax Dollars 1982* (Toronto: James Lorimer, 1982), ch. 3.
12. See David C. Smith, ed., *Economic Policy Advising in Canada* (Montreal: C. D. Howe Research Institute, 1981).

13. See Richard W. Phidd, "The Agricultural Policy Formulation Process in Canada," paper presented to the Canadian Political Science Association Meetings, Montreal, June 2–4, 1980.

14. G. Bruce Doern, *Science and Politics in Canada* (Montreal: McGill-Queen's University Press, 1972); G. Bruce Doern, *The Peripheral Nature of Scientific and Technological Controversy in Federal Policy Formation* (Ottawa: Science Council of Canada, 1981). See also Dean Schooler, Jr., *Science, Scientists and Public Policy* (New York: Free Press, 1971).

15. See Liora Salter and Debra Slaco, *Public Inquiries in Canada* (Ottawa: Science Council of Canada, 1981); and Doern, *The Peripheral Nature of Scientific and Technological Controversy in Federal Policy Formation.*

16. Wildavsky, *Speaking Truth to Power*, ch. 15.

17. Mervin Daub, "Economic Forecasting in the Federal Government" (Ottawa: Ministry of State for Economic Development, 1982).

18. Doern and Tomlin, *Faith and Fear: The Free Trade Story*, ch. 2.

19. John D. McCamus, *Freedom of Information: Canadian Perspectives* (Toronto: Butterworths, 1981).

20. See Wayne Cheveldayoff, *The Business Page* (Ottawa: Deneau and Greenberg, 1980), ch. 9; D. J. Desjardins, "Sharpening a Public Policy Tool: The CPI," *The Canadian Business Review* (Summer 1982), 36–38; and M. C. McCracken and E. Rudick, *Toward a Better Understanding of the Consumer Price Index* (Ottawa: Economic Council of Canada, 1980).

21. Cheveldayoff, *The Business Page*, 108–10.

22. Ibid., 129.

23. See Richard Johnson, *Public Opinion and Public Policy in Canada* (Toronto: University of Toronto Press, 1986).

24. Michael Prince, "Policy Advisory Groups in Government Departments," in G. Bruce Doern and Peter Aucoin, eds., *Public Policy in Canada* (Toronto: Macmillan, 1979), ch. 10.

25. See Pal, *Public Policy Analysis.*

PART IV

PUBLIC POLICY AND THE OVERARCHING POLICY FIELDS

- Foreign versus Domestic Policy
- Macroeconomic and Industrial Policy
- Social and Labour Market Policy

CHAPTER *14*

Foreign versus Domestic Policy

Everyone involved in the study and practice of public policy cannot avoid the practical task of having to put public policy into manageable categories or policy fields. Thus, the final way in which we look at policy formation is by examining three overarching policy fields. We begin with foreign policy and then look in Chapters 15 and 16 at economic and industrial policy and social and labour market policy.

As these fields are examined, it is essential to keep in mind several important realities regarding the analytical task involved. First, the notion of a policy field is comforting, but often illusory. It is comforting and necessary to view fields as if they had finite boundaries and definitions, but it is illusory in that there is slipperiness among policy fields and in defining what precisely is being included in the field by various authors and practitioners. This is true not only in examining Canada, but also in comparing Canada to other countries. Second, policy fields are usually complicated entities in that they consist of numerous ideas, structures, and processes. Moreover, an inquiry into them requires an appreciation of many statutes and program elements. Third, it is next to impossible to make sense of a policy field without an appreciation of its history. Fourth, it is vital to distinguish between the rhetorical flourish of debate about policy fields and the actual set of policies and programs in place and the effects they may be having on different political interests. There is usually a slowness and lag between what is said about policy in a given field and what is actually happening.

Foreign policy is an essential starting point for looking at policy fields. Foreign policy is the set of positions and actions Canada takes regarding the larger world of which it is a part. These positions have always had to intersect with domestic policy issues, but foreign policy is even more compelling for the 1990s because developments suggest a steadily increasing influence for international factors on domestic policy. Indeed, some suggest that Canada and most middle-sized countries are increasingly policy-takers rather than policy-makers.[1] In short, it is argued that in the interaction between foreign and domestic policy, international imperatives are more and more in the ascendancy and Canadians have little choice but to learn how to adapt to continuous international change.

As we look at the ideas, structures, and processes of foreign policy and how they have altered domestic policy formation, several elements of what is frequently referred to as globalization must be highlighted. First, the astonishing developments in computer and communications technology have transformed the world economy. Capital, money, and financial instruments can now move around the world in milliseconds.[2] The degree of mobility of capital, which was always greater than that of labour, has escalated several-fold. This, in turn, has profoundly altered the division of labour and production among countries and within countries, with Western countries being more and more concerned about divisions between good and bad jobs, the former seen as high-technology manufacturing jobs and the latter often portrayed as low-paying, low-education service jobs.

A second development, though with roots preceding the 1980s, is the emergence of major international trading blocs.[3] Instead of just liberalized trade among countries, there is now a set of three major blocs of nations, both trading with and erecting some barriers between each other. Thus, the European Community, a North American bloc, and a Japan–Pacific Rim bloc have emerged. These blocs have forged arrangements that greatly alter and usually reduce the domestic policy flexibility of national governments in exchange for actual or hoped for economic gains. Europe's 1992 program to complete the formation of a true common market, the Canada–U.S. Free Trade Agreement, and negotiations with Mexico for a North American pact all significantly change the balance between domestic and foreign policy influences.

The 1980s ended with yet another compelling change, namely the revolution in Eastern Europe and the collapse of the Soviet

Communist Empire. The end of the Cold War led to the euphoria of democratic advance in Eastern Europe and the reunification of Germany. But heady optimism was quickly dashed by the dangers of the Gulf War and its aftermath and the uncertainty of just what kind of new order would replace the familiar Cold War orthodoxy.

Thus, uncertainty and change, and the growing feeling in the Canadian psyche that Canada was at risk in this unfamiliar world, became an increasingly important reality in the formation of all public policy.[4] These changes are especially relevant for understanding the evolution of foreign policy ideas, structures, and processes in the Mulroney period, but they in turn must be traced through the key elements of the Trudeau period and of earlier post–World War II developments as well.

Foreign policy is fundamentally a territorial definition of policy.[5] Like other territorial or spatial definitions such as regional policy, it is therefore bound to cut across most or perhaps all of the domestic policy fields, albeit some fields more than others. Foreign policy is therefore a composite product of Canada's domestic policy ideas, structures, and processes, and is influenced by those of other states in the world community.

Of critical importance in Canada's foreign policy is our economic dependence on foreign trade, which accounts for about 25 to 30 percent of Canada's economic activity. Much of Canada's trade is in resource products, augmented by a very limited and truncated range of manufacturing products. The great majority of Canada's trade is with one country, the United States. Related to this economic reality is the extensive foreign ownership of Canada's economy, again primarily by American multinational enterprises. These economic realities, despite several efforts to construct counterweights to the north–south continental axis, have produced the inevitable problems of dependence. In the more extreme view this dependence is characterized as a virtual state of economic colonialism.

In Canada's early history the essence of foreign policy was to secure the real and symbolic levers of independence from the United Kingdom. These were largely achieved by the beginning of World War II. The not unimportant residue of the British connection in foreign policy is found in Canada's continuing support for the Commonwealth, an institution that, in its modern form, provides an important link as well to countries of the Third World. In the post–World War II era, however, Canada evolved more and more into the American axis. This was partly a product of war and postwar defence arrangements, and the official encouragement of foreign equity ownership and investments, but it was also a cultural phenomenon, propelled by the power and influence of Canadian exposure to the

American media and by the geographic proximity of Canada's neighbour.

A further historical product of considerable importance to Canada's foreign policy was the country's emergence after World War II as a significant middle power on the world stage, a power of even greater influence in the immediate postwar era because of the weakened state of Western Europe. It was in this era that Canada's foreign policy developed a highly articulate commitment to internationalism, the latter epitomized by the chief architect of this view, Lester B. Pearson.

Ideas: Nationalism, Internationalism, and Continentalism

The central ideas of Canada's foreign policy are therefore a composite of the ideas embedded in domestic policy, but often clothed in the language of international relations and the territorial definition of such policies. Certainly, nationalism, or national independence and sovereignty, is a central idea sometimes preached and sometimes practised. It is evident in such symbolic decisions as establishing a national flag and in support for international sporting and cultural events and exchanges. More concretely, it is evident in policies such as rigid and even discriminatory immigration polices, the aggressive 1980 National Energy Program, the foreign ownership limits on broadcasting and banking, and the review and screening role of foreign investment by Investment Canada.

The opposite of the nationalist idea is internationalism on the one hand and continentalism on the other.[6] The former usually evokes more positive connotations. It embraces policy support for the Western defence alliance centred in the North Atlantic Treaty Organization (NATO), for the work of the United Nations, for the General Agreement on Tariffs and Trade (GATT), for humanitarian immigration policies, for the reduction of nuclear weapons and proliferation, for the international redistribution of wealth through development aid to Commonwealth and other Third World countries, and for commitments to international peace-keeping functions in at least some of the world's trouble spots. Internationalism can also embrace the Canadian role as diplomatic intermediary between the United States and Europe, and perhaps between the rich North and the poor South. Internationalism in these numerous contexts is thus an amalgam of ideas including equality, equity, and the preservation of world peace.

Continentalism, on the other hand, evokes a less favourable view, an idea to avoid rather than support. It initially evokes a concern for Canada's stock of wealth in its natural resources and the American desire to utilize them, but it can also include American domination of the Canadian economy and of Canadian cultural life. Nonetheless, continentalist policies have been explicitly or implicitly pursued, albeit usually clothed in the positive terms of economic development and efficiency. These policies include those on encouraging foreign investment, the Autopact, defence production sharing arrangements, energy policy in the 1960s and early 1970s, and trade policy generally, including the Canada–U.S. Free Trade Agreement.

Somewhere between internationalism and continentalism, Canadian foreign policy has also lent support to the idea of finding a counterweight to the dominance of the Canadian–American relationship.[7] This has been attempted and defined in various ways. For the Diefenbaker government it was a failed attempt to reassert a stronger trade relationship between Canada and the United Kingdom. For the Trudeau government it was an attempt in 1972 to devise a so-called "Third Option" between the status quo (Option One) and closer integration with the United States (Option Two). In part, this implied seeking greater ties with Western Europe and Japan as a counterweight, a policy that was not achieved.

The hydra-headed territorial imperatives of nationalism, internationalism, and continentalism obviously produce a panoply of interdependent and sometimes contradictory objectives. Numerous policy fields inject themselves into the foreign policy arena, including defence policy, immigration policy, trade policy, foreign investment policy, foreign aid policy, agricultural policy, mineral policy, and energy policy, to name only a few policy fields. The best way to see foreign policy objectives in practice is to briefly trace one or two foreign policy cases or issues. The first concerns the Trudeau government's early foreign policy review. The experience of the Trudeau era in foreign policy is instructive particularly because Prime Minister Trudeau placed such an initial emphasis on altering in a "rational" way the perceived thrust of the Pearson era, a foreign policy labelled by Trudeau as being both reactive (that is, unplanned) and internationalistic (that is, insufficiently attuned to national self-interest).

Trudeau's review of foreign policy led to a White Paper in 1970 that outlined six policy objectives.[8] These were: fostering economic growth; safeguarding sovereignty and independence; working for peace and security; promoting social justice abroad; enhancing the quality of life; and ensuring a harmonious natural environment.

Though fostered by Trudeau's strong penchant for rationality, the presumed changes in objectives were not without some foundation in the changing geopolitics of the world community in the early 1970s. There were clearly, for example, growing problems arising out of oil pollution from supertankers and sea-based transport of resources through Canada's Arctic waters, satellite communication, and a depleting fisheries stock off Canada's coasts. The social justice and quality of life objectives were partly a product of genuine concern expressed by other states and partly a reflection of Trudeau's domestic policy objectives, especially in the early 1968 to 1971 period.

The formal reordering of priorities by Trudeau undoubtedly reflected some genuine concern about emerging world issues, but these changes were not as starkly in opposition to the Pearsonian concepts as either Trudeau or his critics of the day believed. This is because Trudeau's nationalism was in fact a particular form of internationalism. As Michael Tucker suggests, Trudeau saw Canada as a kind of "mentor state," taking initiatives on behalf of the world community. His openings to Communist China and his movement away from NATO were seen as messages the larger world wanted to hear from Canada.[9]

The connection between foreign and defence policy also raises questions about the degree to which Trudeau succeeded in developing a more planned and less reactive foreign policy. The logic is that the clearer one is about objectives, the more assertive one can be—in short, the more one can do first things first. The evolution of defence policy within this set of reordered priorities in the 1970s is of considerable interest in this regard. In the Trudeau plan, Canada's defence policies were to become more oriented toward North America, moving away from the European focus through NATO. This view and the logical ambiguities behind it brought Prime Minister Trudeau and his chief foreign policy adviser of the day, Ivan Head, into a sharp conflict of views with senior officials in the Department of External Affairs. The differences were not merely a reflection of narrow bureaucratic infighting, but also of differences in ideas and the logical relationships between objectives and ideas.

Thordarson's analysis shows how the Trudeau view misunderstood the connection between Canada's military commitment to NATO in Europe and Western Europe's view of Canada.[10] NATO was far more than a defence pact. It was rooted in broader foreign policy considerations, both economic and human in the broadest sense. Thus, officials in the Department of External Affairs argued that it was not defence policy that produced foreign policy as Trudeau believed, but the reverse. When NATO defence commitments were reduced in real dollars in the early 1970s, Western Europe took this as a signal of Canada's reduced overall foreign policy interest in Europe, despite efforts to forge new links with Europe in matters of trade. NATO was an essential part, moreover, if one was to secure a counterweight to U.S. influence.

By the end of his tenure as prime minister, Trudeau had partly contradicted and partly ignored the precepts of his policy White Paper. As Kim Nossal points out, by 1984 he discovered "by turns, the utility of Canada's military alignments, the usefulness of peacekeeping, and the helpfulness of helpful fixing."[11] But in the early 1980s, the foreign policy of the Trudeau era also reached its nationalist zenith. Following the 1980 election, the Liberal government launched the National Energy Program and promised a strengthened Foreign Investment Review Agency (FIRA) as well as more aggressive industrial policies.

The Mulroney Shift: Free Trade, Constructive Internationalism, and Entrepreneurial Nationalism

In many respects, the foreign policy of the Mulroney Conservative government was forged out of opposition to the early 1980s nationalist binge by the Trudeau Liberals.[12] It therefore focused on Canada–U.S. relations. As opposition leader, Mulroney adopted a strong pro-American stance and cultivated a relationship with President Ronald Reagan and senior Republicans. On issues such as the shooting down of the KAL-007 airliner, Mulroney took the American line that it was cold-blooded murder as a counterweight to Trudeau's opinion that it was an accident. During the election, Mulroney promised exuberantly that Canada would be a "super ally" and would give Washington the benefit of the doubt in criticism.

Once in power, the foreign policy statements were broadened to embrace what the Conservatives called a policy of "constructive internationalism." But it was clear that the main policy thrust was to repair the damage caused by what they saw as the excesses of Trudeau nationalism. Thus, in short order, the National Energy Program was abandoned and the Foreign Investment Review Agency was changed to Investment Canada, with its review powers reduced. With these two initiatives, Mulroney confidently declared that Canada was "open for business." The first of his "Shamrock" summits with President Reagan also promised the examination of a comprehensive trade agreement between Canada and the United States. This eventually led to the Canada–U.S. Free Trade Agreement and, with it, a quantum change in the nature and depth of Canada's economic and political relationships with the giant to the south.

There is no doubt concerning the thrust of foreign policy ideas and actions in the early Mulroney years, but even in this setting foreign policy could not be structured too cosily with the Americans.[13] Like Trudeau, Mulroney had to abandon or change some of his electoral posturing and temper his anti-Soviet and pro-American stance. He distanced himself somewhat from U.S. positions on Star Wars technology, Central America, and South Africa. He also made sure that he challenged the Americans publicly and frequently in the long battle over acid rain. Initially, he had tried the "constructive internationalist" approach with the Americans on the issue of acid rain, but then grew increasingly frustrated at the Reagan regime's intransigence.

In the decisive battle over free trade, the ideas of sovereignty, nationalism, and continentalism took on a somewhat different character that they had in earlier debates on Canada's foreign policy. The Mulroney Conservatives began to articulate a form of "entrepreneurial nationalism,"[14] in short, an inbred confidence in the Canadian business community's capacity to compete. The pro–free trade coalition portrayed the anti–free traders as being defenders of a "little Canada" with narrow notions of sovereignty and protection. The antidote to negative continentalism was not state-led sovereignty and intervention, but rather a new desire to show that Canadians could compete with the best and need not fear the larger global world.

Structure: The Institutionalization of the Canada–U.S. Relationship

The structures of foreign policy-making embrace several departments and agencies, ranging from the Department of External Affairs (DEA) to the International Joint Commission. These include entities such as the Prime Minister's Office, the Department of Finance, the Department of National Defence (DND), the Canadian International Development Agency (CIDA), and the international sections of many other line departments such as environment and energy. Increasingly the provinces have also asserted foreign policy roles. Any list of foreign policy structures must also include international agencies such as the United Nations, NATO, GATT, the World Bank, and the International Monetary Fund.

The central locus for Canadian foreign policy, however, is without doubt the Department of External Affairs. Accordingly, it is essential to appreciate the main phases of DEA's evolution.[15] In the period from World War II to the late 1960s, DEA was clearly the leading agency, its role reinforced by its close connection to the prime minister, a fusion most epitomized by Lester Pearson's years as prime minister, but also in the earlier St. Laurent–Pearson era when Pearson was Secretary of State for External Affairs. The Diefenbaker era provided an aberration of this close relationship, but even in this period DEA's foreign policy supremacy among Ottawa departments was not seriously challenged.

During the Trudeau era, DEA's role changed significantly. This was because initially its senior officials disputed the basis of Trudeau's rational foreign policy constructions, including, as we have seen, the downgrading of the economic and diplomatic implication of the NATO defence alliance. DEA's role also declined because of the emergence in the Trudeau era of other central agencies, including the Prime Minister's Office where Ivan Head resided. Moreover, the more that the international economic order created stress, the more other line departments and agencies defended their turf and the policies within them. These fields involved expertise that DEA did not necessarily possess. Thus, issues such as the law of the sea and acid rain required the involvement of the Department of the Environment; immigration issues involved the Department of Employment and Immigration; nuclear exports brought in Atomic Energy of Canada and Industry, Trade and Commerce; foreign aid involved the Canadian International Development Agency; energy policy involved Energy, Mines and Resources, Petro-Canada, and the National Energy Board; and grain exports involved the Department of Agriculture and the National Wheat Board. This is not to suggest that other agencies were not part of foreign policy in earlier periods, but now there were more of them and they were struggling in an international and domestic economy that was less hospitable than the 1950s and 1960s.

Moreover, provincial governments and their agencies and crown corporations were far more assertive in the foreign policy field. This was true not only in respect of Quebec in relations with France and other francophone nations, but also of western Canadian provinces in resource exports, tariffs, and crown corporation borrowings in foreign capital markets, and of Atlantic Canada in the fisheries, law of the sea, and offshore resources. Even an issue such as regional development incentives was viewed increasingly as a nontariff barrier to international trade under GATT and consequently a concern to all provinces.

In the early 1980s the DEA role evolved in still a different direction. Foreign policy organization and process was affected by the reorganization of DEA itself when its trade policy functions were increased in 1982 through the transfer to DEA of the Trade Commissioner Service previously located in the Department of Industry, Trade and Commerce. The addition of a trade presence in External Affairs was intended to strengthen the economic capacity of the department, especially with a view to getting the economic relationship with the Americans right. This relationship was seen as being "wrong" by key economic players in the wake of the Liberals' National Energy Program and promised changes to strengthen the Foreign Investment Review Agency.

It would be tempting to see a direct causal link between this structural change and the eventual adoption of a free trade strategy at External Affairs. In fact, however, the link is at best indirect.[16] The department did complete an extensive trade policy review. It broadly endorsed Canada's previous multilateral trade policy approach, but also included a suggested sectoral free trade approach with the Americans. The Minister of State for Trade, Gerald Regan, picked up the sectoral approach as his personal brief and pushed the issue. The fact that a sectoral approach got nowhere with the Americans in the 1983–84 period helped prompt a search for even wider options. The business community, led by the Business Council on National Issues, was urging a "comprehensive" trade agreement, as was Derek Burney, a senior official in External Affairs. Burney was virtually alone among the External Affairs mandarins in wanting a free trade approach. It took the coming to power of Brian Mulroney, plus other factors such as the support of Alberta Premier Peter Lougheed and the work of the Macdonald Royal Commission on the Economic Union and Development Prospects for Canada, to produce a sufficient catalyst for change.

While the latter years of the Trudeau government had witnessed several reorganizations at External Affairs, each attempting to "beef up" traditional diplomacy with more economic clout, these experiments were largely abandoned in the Mulroney period, with one significant exception. To conduct the free trade negotiations with the United States, the prime minister established a separate Trade Negotiator's Office (TNO). The TNO was set up partly because Simon Reisman, the chief negotiator, insisted on it, but also because the Department of Finance wanted to blunt some of DEA's economic ambitions.[17] Though officials from other departments were seconded to the TNO, Reisman's own combative style of operation ensured its independence. For a considerable period, the TNO became a policy juggernaut in Ottawa, a veritable central agency itself with its negotiating mandate cutting across several departmental mandates, from energy to agriculture.

In the case of the TNO, structure did influence policy. The formation of an independent TNO helped determine the nature and breadth of the agreement sought and the tactics used. Had the structure been more inherently interdepartmental, the agreement's content would likely have been less bold and the tactics for bargaining less risky. Simon Reisman knew this and thus opted for a structure he could more fully control. He also insisted, despite his reporting relationship to Trade Minister Pat Carney, that he would take instructions only from the prime minister and Cabinet.

A further structural change that affects the whole of the Canada–U.S. foreign and trade policy relationship emerged out of the free trade agreement itself. Chapters 18 and 19 of the agreement will result in a significant institutionalization of Canada–U.S. policy-making and dispute-settlement activities.[18] Chapter 18 provides for a Canada–U.S. Trade Commission composed of each country's trade ministers. The commission will function through processes modelled on the procedures used under the General Agreement on Tariffs and Trade. It provides for a process of continuous notification, information provision, consultation, referral to the commission, and use of panels and other dispute-settlement machinery.

Chapter 19 of the free trade deal provides for dispute settlement on matters involving countervail and antidumping. This structural provision went to the very core of the free trade agreement because Canada's main concerns when the negotiations began were the increasing use by American business interests of countervail measures against alleged Canadian subsidy-supported exports. Given that the two sides could not agree on a subsidies code, the free trade agreement provided for a dispute-settlement process limited to judicial review of procedures. Henceforth, bilateral panels can be used to replace review by domestic courts. While this provision is being used, a period of five to seven years was also set aside to attempt to negotiate a subsidies code.

While it is too early to gauge the exact effects of these new structures of foreign and trade policy-making, one clear consequence is that the foreign policy structures between Canada and the United States are now more bureaucratic. Whereas in earlier periods Canada could make bilateral foreign policy between prime minister and president or embassy to embassy, the array of institutions is now more elaborate. Department to department arrangements have, or course, always prevailed in fields such as energy and immigration and through institutions such as the International Joint Commission, but even these will be somewhat less flexible because of the additional requirements for prior consultation.

In addition, one other lesson was learned in the aftermath of the free trade era, and this is that the U.S. Congress, and not just the U.S. administration, will be a key arena for bilateral foreign policy-making.[19] The battles over the free trade agreement itself, over the softwood lumber dispute, and over acid rain have taught many Canadian foreign policy players and interests that they have to lobby the Congress aggressively and with increasing skill and resources if Canada is to make its presence felt in a Washington increasingly preoccupied with a much larger and more complicated world.

If bilateral foreign policy-making is more structurally constrained, so also is multilateral foreign policy-making, but here the pattern of structural change is somewhat different and perhaps slower in adapting to the new imperatives of globalization. In the immediate post–World War II era, the Western world engaged in a spate of creative international institution-building, in large part from a desire to avoid a repetition of the disastrous combination of depression and war that occurred in the 1930s and 1940s. Thus, key structures such as the United Nations, GATT, the World Bank, the International Monetary Fund, and NATO were established and contributed greatly to postwar security and prosperity. In the 1970s and 1980s, two other institutions of a less formal nature were forged, namely the annual G-7 economic summit meetings of the leaders of the seven leading Western industrial nations and the G-7 meetings of their Ministers of Finance to manage exchange-rate policy.

While these institutions have largely stood the test of time, the overwhelming changes of the 1980s—especially in financial markets, but also in relation to other global issues such as the environment and Third World poverty—seemed to put them on the defensive. In short, in the 1980s era of deregulation, privatization, and pro-market policies, there was a vacuum of correspondingly needed new international institution-building. It is likely in the 1990s that such a new phase will occur in part to deal with the consequences of unbridled markets. As the 1990s began, the search for such structures was already evident in areas such as banking and capital markets and environmental protocol-setting.

Process: The New Globalizing Dynamics

Many of the changes in the foreign policy process flow from the shifts in ideas and structure. But equally, process can cause changes in policy. The multiple influences of process can be seen in several developments, four of which are briefly highlighted. These are: the relationships between priority-setting and international summitry; the constraints on domestic policy instruments by the free trade agreement and GATT commitments; the impacts of U.S. deregulation processes and policies on Canadian processes; and the character of public spending processes in the foreign policy field.

To some extent, it has been possible in the past to keep foreign policy priorities somewhat separate from domestic priorities. This separation is less and less possible because of several of the changes already noted above. It is also less possible because of the greater and more visible presence of summitry itself. The increased number of summit occasions and the extensive coverage by the mass media make it increasingly difficult for domestic political leaders to say one thing for domestic consumption and another abroad. Summits are a vehicle for putting pressures on domestic agendas, especially for smaller countries such as Canada.[20] Fiscal, monetary, environmental, and social policies are increasingly given an international test of relevance and comparative progress, both substantively and as an exercise in symbolic political expression. Even a casual reading of throne speeches and budget speeches in the latter part of the 1980s reveals this clearly. Accordingly, the priority-setting process of the 1990s will undoubtedly see an even greater convergence and melding of foreign policy imperatives on the domestic policy agenda-setting process.

The logic of recent changes also suggests that, in broad terms, all of the instrument-based policies and processes will be constrained by international obligations. Tax decisions, regulatory processes and spending, and the use of state enterprise are all constrained more than they were in the 1960s and 1970s. Indeed, the intent of most international regimes, especially economic regimes, is to "discipline" domestic policy urges in the name of a hoped for larger international public interest. Thus, losses of sovereignty and the independent, unfettered use of a policy instrument are expected to result in some larger sense of policy capacity achieved through other countries also losing some of their sovereignty and through international collaborative action.

Canada's future capacity to use its spending instrument to subsidize will undoubtedly be constrained,[21] even though a formal subsidies code was not agreed to in the free trade agreement. Canadian governments will probably restrain themselves out of a fear of being countervailed, either under the free trade agreement or via GATT provisions. The actual effect of this lessened use of subsidies will vary, as our next chapter on economic and industrial policy shows.

It should be emphasized that constraints on Canadian policy instruments did not need the free trade agreement to become noticeable. Consider, for example, the impact of U.S. deregulation processes and how they produced varied outcomes on the Canadian regulatory process. American deregulation of its airline industry did not yield an immediate Canadian counterpart. It took almost a decade for parallel domestic interests to produce a Canadian version of airline deregulation. In the rail sector, however, the effect was more immediate. When the U.S. deregulated its railway freight traffic there was an immediate impact on the two main Canadian railways in the form of lost business that seeped southward. The pressure for deregulation mounted quickly and was given special impetus by the Mulroney government's first Transport Minister, Don Mazankowski.

Another example of changing foreign policy and domestic policy processes came in an area where the regulatory process was becoming more complex, but where the pressure was for more, not less, regulation. In the environmental policy arena, multilateral and bilateral processes were increasingly interwoven, as tactics in one area were used to secure leverage in another. In negotiations on acid rain, Canada tried to use alliances with the Nordic countries to extract greater leverage over the United States. But in other areas of environmental hazard, such as NOx and VOCs protocols, Canada found itself pressured to undertake change faster than many of its domestic interests were prepared to go.[22] As environmental hazards became more and more interlocked, the processes for securing domestic and foreign consensus became even more intricate and time consuming.

A final example where process influences the nature of policy formation and debate can be seen from a basic look at the very character of public spending within the External Affairs envelope of funds. This envelope consists of DEA's own spending plus that of the Canadian International Development Agency and the Department of National Defence. Development spending and defence spending share a common feature in public debate that is rarely applied as frequently to any other policy field. This feature is that policy is often debated through the rhetorical use of percentage targets.[23] Thus, development aid will be judged to be good or bad depending upon whether there is upward or downward movement in the percentage of GNP Canada is planning to spend on such assistance compared to other countries. The government can often buy itself time and support simply by promising that support will be at a higher target level a few years later. Similarly, defence spending was often debated in the 1980s on a comparative table gauged to how much of a percentage increase, in real dollars, was being committed to NATO. The politics of target percentages in these realms of foreign policy seem to characterize the policy process in part because public opinion has greater difficulty grasping either distant aid programs or technologically complex, but infrequent, weapons choices. The targets become a convenient shorthand for complexity.

The extent to which foreign policy spending is composed of personnel and capital expenditures versus grants must also be appreciated, and thus the limited room for manoeuvring that such spending affords in the short to medium term. This is all the more true when, as in recent years, there have been cuts in real spending. DEA's own expenditures in the External Affairs envelope are overwhelmingly personnel oriented, and thus there is little room for change. The greatest area of discretion is in CIDA's far larger budget, and it is here that discretion has been primarily exercised, both in changing Canada's commitments to developmental aid and, since these expenditures involve extensive domestic contracting, in promoting industrial development in Canada. The defence envelope is large, but also contains little room for manoeuvre. It is also highly personnel oriented and, in addition, involves a heavy capital equipment and weapons component that cannot be changed easily in the short run. Moreover, when decisions over major weapons procurement do arise every few years, they immediately involve several departments because of their military and economic effects. As to other policy fields with foreign policy implications, it follows that DEA and its minister cannot actually allocate resources in these fields since they are lodged in the other envelopes.

One final attribute of the foreign policy process that deserves comment is the secretiveness of many aspects of international relations and the conduct of such relations at a very personal leader-to-leader or diplomat-to-diplomat level. While federal–provincial and intra-Cabinet relations also turn on heavy doses of secrecy and personal chemistry, it is fair to say that foreign policy trades on these characteristics to an even greater degree. It is not, however, a totally closed process. It must be emphasized that many of the interest groups examined in Chapter 5 continuously attempt to influence foreign policy both in Canada and in countries whose decisions might affect them favourably or unfavourably.

Conclusions

Foreign policy reflects Canadian positions and actions regarding the larger world. It is vitally concerned with important ideas such as nationalism and sovereignty, internationalism, and continentalism.

While it has always had an important impact on domestic policy agendas, the influence of foreign policy and of international imperatives on domestic policy fields escalated greatly in the 1980s in the wake of globalizing pressures and events. In the 1990s, few domestic policy fields will be developed without the influence of international factors and institutions. The Canada–U.S. Free Trade Agreement, in particular, institutionalizes the Canada–U.S. policy process to an unprecedented extent. However, international influences have also increased because of the entrenchment of summitry and the need to build new multilateral institutions to deal with the effects of a decade of pro-market policies and the stunning increase in the mobility of financial capital.

Notes

1. See Richard Simeon, "Globalization and the Canadian Nation State," in G. Bruce Doern and Bryne Purchase, eds., *Canada at Risk: Canadian Public Policy in the 1990s* (Toronto: C. D. Howe Institute, 1990), 46–58.
2. See Thomas Courchene, "Global Financial Developments: Implications for Canada," in James McRae and M. Desbois, eds., *Traded and Non-Traded Services* (Halifax: Institute for Research on Public Policy, 1988), 243–54.
3. See Michael Hart, *A North American Free Trade Agreement: The Strategic Implications for Canada* (Halifax: Institute for Research on Public Policy, 1990).
4. See Richard Gwyn, "Canada at Risk," in Doern and Purchase, eds., *Canada at Risk: Canadian Public Policy in the 1990s*, 116–24.
5. See Kim Richard Nossal, *The Politics of Canadian Foreign Policy*, 2nd ed. (Scarborough, Ont.: Prentice-Hall, 1989), ch. 1.
6. See Peyton V. Lyon and Brian Tomlin, *Canada as an International Actor* (Toronto: Macmillan, 1979), ch. 3.
7. See Andrew Axline, Maureen Molot, J. Hyndman, and Peyton Lyon, eds., *Continental Community: Independence and Integration in North America* (Toronto: McClelland and Stewart, 1974).
8. See Bruce Thordarson, *Trudeau and Foreign Policy* (Toronto: Oxford University Press, 1972), chs. 6 and 7.
9. See Michael Tucker, *Canadian Foreign Policy* (Toronto: McGraw-Hill Ryerson, 1980), 10.
10. Thordarson, *Trudeau and Foreign Policy*, ch. 5.
11. Nossal, *The Politics of Canadian Foreign Policy*, 167.
12. See Stephen Clarkson, *Canada and the Reagan Challenge*, 2nd ed. (Toronto: James Lorimer, 1985).

13. See Nossal, *The Politics of Canadian Foreign Policy*, 167–69.
14. See G. Bruce Doern and Brian W. Tomlin, *Faith and Fear: The Free Trade Story* (Toronto: Stoddart, 1991), ch. 9.
15. See Tucker, *Canadian Foreign Policy*, ch. 1.
16. See Doern and Tomlin, *Faith and Fear: The Free Trade Story*, ch. 2.
17. Ibid., ch. 7.
18. See Stephen Clarkson, "The Canada–United States Trade Commission and the Institutional Basis of the FTA," in Duncan Cameron, ed., *The Free Trade Deal* (Toronto: James Lorimer, 1988), 26–43.
19. See Jock Findlayson, "Canada, Congress, and U.S. Foreign Economic Policy," in D. Stairs and G. Winham, eds., *The Politics of Canada's Economic Relationships with the United States* (Toronto: University of Toronto Press, 1985), 127–78.
20. See Nossal, *The Politics of Canadian Foreign Policy*, 172–84.
21. See G. Bruce Doern and Brian W. Tomlin, "The Free Trade Sequel: Canada–U.S. Subsidy Negotiations," in Frances Abele, ed., *How Ottawa Spends 1991-92* (Ottawa: Carleton University Press, 1991), ch. 6.
22. See G. Bruce Doern, "Regulations and Incentives: The NOx–VOCs Case," in G. Bruce Doern, ed., *Getting It Green* (Toronto: C. D. Howe Institute, 1990), 89–110.
23. See G. Bruce Doern, Allan Maslove, and Michael Prince, *Budgeting in Canada* (Ottawa: Carleton University Press, 1988), ch. 9.

C H A P T E R 15

Macroeconomic and Industrial Policy

Macroeconomic and industrial policies are two entwined policy fields that have undergone a remarkable transformation in both thought and action. Macroeconomic policy refers to fiscal and monetary actions intended to secure noninflationary economic growth and the competitiveness and productivity of the Canadian economy.[1] Industrial policy, after two or three decades of being defined as almost any action affecting the many micro sectors of the economy, is now defined more concretely as actions targeted at specific firms or consortia of firms in order to enhance Canada's international competitiveness.[2]

The transformation has been significant in two overall senses and reflects yet another example of the profound influence of international factors on domestic policy fields and agendas. First, macro policy in the sense of Keynesian demand management, the dominant paradigm of the 1960s and 1970s, has been partially abandoned. Governments are less willing and less confident of their abilities to manage the economy through the manipulation of aggregate spending and taxing decisions, in concert with monetary policy. As we will see, this change has been the product of changes in ideas, economic research and experience, and structural pressure that is worldwide in nature. Second, micro policy in the sense of numerous ad hoc initiatives to benefit sectors such as manufacturing, agriculture, and energy has been replaced, in thought if not always in action, by preferences for stable "framework" oriented policies. Thus, for each of the main factors of production in a modern economy, the preference is for general long-term and stable policies in fields such as taxation, research and development, labour markets and training, trade, and regulatory systems, rather than those that "intervene" to favour particular sectors, regions, and interests as such. In the jargon of the times these framework policies—in some sense, the "new" macroeconomics—have often been referred to as ones that "get the incentives right."

These two changes still leave room for what is more narrowly, indeed much more narrowly, the terrain of industrial policy. Industrial policy does imply intervention in very specific ways (for example, to help leading firms such as Bombardier or Northern Telecom), but is replete with dispute as to whether Canada possesses the technical, political, and structural capacity to carry out such policies successfully and without succumbing to the seemingly inevitable pressure to distribute scarce public investment dollars in a regional porkbarrel fashion.

The transformation sketched above has largely been the scenario of the Mulroney era and hence will be a focal point for analysis in the chapter as a whole. But the journey has not been nearly as orderly as the sketch implies, and it requires a broader look at earlier developments in the evolution of macroeconomic and microeconomic policy. The structures and processes of macro and industrial policy rarely cooperate willingly or fully with the preferred ideas that drive these fields in different historical periods. In particular, both industrial and macro policy, but especially the former, have always had to grapple with regionalism, regional policy, and regional interests, while trying to keep the overall macro and micro economies on a noninflationary growth path.

Macro Ideas: From Keynesian to Framework-Oriented Policy

At its core, overall policy has been associated historically in liberal democracy with the idea of efficiency and economic growth and productivity. The private market economy was the engine of growth and progress.[3] It would shape and mobilize the major factors of production—land, capital, and labour—to yield the highest return. National wealth would be maximized in this way. The job of government was to allow this to happen. It was believed by some that there was a natural self-correcting equilibrium to the market with which governments should not, and ultimately could not, interfere. The idea of efficiency was also linked to the idea of private property and individual freedom. Thus, this view of economic policy was simultaneously a social view as well.

The second dominant idea in economic policy is that of stability of income over time. At its root is Keynesian economics, or what some called in the Canadian context the Second National Policy.[4] In the midst of the depression of the 1930s, Keynes articulated a powerful theoretical case against the claimed self-correcting capabilities of the market. Economic policy at the macro level would have as its overall purpose the stabilization of economic activity. By manipulating taxes and spending, the government could "manage" the economy, stimulate demand and, therefore, investment and employment. Keynes supplied a paradigm that provided an acceptable justification for marginal intervention in a capitalist economy.

It must be stressed as well, however, that the *idea* of stability of income over time has an importance that vastly exceeds the Keynesian notion of stabilization. In many respects stability is the opposite of efficiency. The latter implies unpredictability and change, especially for those elements of capital, labour, and land that are being "mobilized" by someone else. Those who oppose such change are inherently expressing a higher preference for stability and predictability in their own lives. Thus, economic policy is always a struggle between efficiency and change on the one hand, and stability and predictability on the other. Over the decades, Canada has assembled policies that are intended to support both of these ideas simultaneously. This is because *both* are desirable and valued.

While influenced by these broad ideas, economic policy in the period since World War II has been more conventionally debated in relation to its success or failure in meeting the four primary objectives that have accompanied the Keynesian view.[5] The four objectives are:

- economic growth;
- full employment;
- reasonable price stability; and
- balance in international payments.

Governments have nominally adopted these objectives, but their degree of commitment to any one has been in dispute since the dawn of the Keynesian era. Moreover, resolving the contradictions among them necessitates a constant ranking of these objectives, a task that governments for many good reasons often do not like to perform.

Each objective is a source of dispute because each economic purpose has a social dimension. Economic growth has been embroiled in a dual debate. First, there are those who are dissatisfied with the concept of national economic growth and who look for the regional distribution within it. The power of regional forces in Canada makes economic growth per se an insufficiently clear and acceptable objective.[6] A second attack on the concept of economic growth received renewed emphasis in the early 1990s. Under the banner of "sustainable development," environmentalists and others concerned about the nature of growth and the need to conserve resources gained influence.

The commitment to, and meaning of, full employment has similarly been in dispute.[7] The political left has charged with some accuracy that there has never been a policy commitment to full employment. The left tends to argue that this is because government, supported by employers, needs a reasonable amount of unemployment to "discipline" labour and to make sure that the economy has flexibility, that is, "efficiency." Others argue that it is simply difficult to come up with a working definition of what a proper level of unemployment or employment is. We saw this in Chapter 13 when we noted the debate about data on unemployment. The definition of acceptable unemployment does seem to have changed, but not the underlying intensity of the debate. For example, the growing employment participation rate of women in the 1970s and 1980s was accompanied by dispute over whether this was a social frill occasioned by the emergence of the women's movement or an economic necessity.

There were, of course, other challenges to the sanctity of the main objectives. In addition to regional disparities there were other distributional challenges. The inevitable concern about the redistribution of income to low-income Canadians was reflected in several of the disputes over objectives, especially employment, growth, and price stability. As Chapter 16 shows, studies began to appear as early as the late 1960s indicating that, despite the arsenal of social programs, significant redistribution had not been achieved. The gap between the rich and the poor remained about the same or was in fact worsening. By the end of the 1980s the gap had widened further.

While, as we can see, there was always criticism of Keynesian policy, the dominance of the Keynesian idea was not seriously challenged until the heady prosperity of the 1950s and early 1960s came to an end. In particular, it became especially difficult to explain the concurrent existence and increasing persistence of both high unemployment and high rates of inflation, which had heretofore been generally assumed by many to have an inverse relationship to each other. If unemployment rose, it was expected that the rate of price increases would decline. In addition, refinements of Keynesian strategy made it necessary to develop in the 1960s certain policies on the "supply" side of the economy (especially the supply of labour) to remove rigidities and bottlenecks in the flow of different factors of production. This was sometimes called the "new economics" and was reflected in the development of employment policies and some related social policies that, almost by definition, could not operate on the same short-run time frame as had the early demand-management Keynesian strategies.[8] These so-called supply policies were also often directed toward secondary or redistributive goals that, in Canada in particular, meant both an attempt to secure a more equitable distribution of income in general, and the removal, or at least the lessening, of regional economic disparities.

As the economic malaise became more intractable in the 1970s, those seeking to produce both alternative explanations for the worsening economic condition as well as grand prescriptions for its cure tended to group themselves under two other grand paradigms of economic policy, the monetarist paradigm and a more general corporatist view.

Monetarists, under Milton Friedman's leadership, tended in general to attribute the economic decline to the failure of governments both to understand the central signals that money represents in economic transactions and in future price expectations, and to manage the supply of money in such a way as to allow "normal" market forces to operate. Monetarist prescriptions are centred on less government discretion and intervention, the control and reduction of government spending and borrowing, and the proper management of the money supply.[9]

While monetarist and related noninterventionist views were clearly in the ascendancy in the late 1970s, they were by no means the only alternatives. Corporatist views were also available and being practised in the Western world.[10] Corporatist models involved a form of shared decision-making and consensus formation between the state, business, and labour as to how to ensure growth and how to divide up the aggregate pie among the three big institutional bases of power. To work in the West German or Swedish versions, corporatism required functioning and legitimate "peak" associations to arrange such deals.

In Canada, corporatism as such has never existed, but snippets of quasi-corporatism have been tried. Neither business nor labour possessed the peak associations with which a government could deal, and the state itself was fragmented, partly because of federalism, and partly because of divisions among the central agencies of government.[11] In addition, central components of business, labour, and government simply opposed corporatist views on the grounds that they were antithetical to broadly based parliamentary democracy.

Nonetheless, quasi-corporatist experiments (albeit without much real consultation) were attempted during the Trudeau Liberal years. They came in the form of attempted voluntary wage and price control efforts in the early 1970s, a compulsory wage and price program between 1975 and 1978, and the "6 and 5" public sector wage restraint program in 1982–83. Unabashed interventionist experiments also occurred under the Liberals, including the National Energy Program of 1980 and the planned but abortive economic development strategy of November 1981 in which the Liberals hoped to use a series of resource megaprojects as an engine of growth.[12]

During the latter half of the 1970s and the early 1980s Canada's central economic policies and processes reflected an eclectic selection from the above ideas and objectives, both those from the Keynesian point of view and from the "new" contenders.[13] In 1976 a policy of monetary gradualism developed in response to the monetarist critique. For the most part, however, monetary policy was not supported by equivalent fiscal policy restraint, which monetarists would argue is a necessary policy companion.

When the Mulroney government came to power in 1984, its macroeconomic policy ideas were the product both of its ideological critique of state intervention and of Trudeau centralism, but also of the less well known transformation of the replacement ideas for the Keynesian paradigm. These latter ideas were linked to monetarism, but also to a more specific line of economic research and theory that included the debunking of the Phillips curve's alleged trade-off between unemployment and inflation and the development of the concept of the "non-accelerating-inflation rate of unemployment" (NAIRU).[14]

Developed by William Phillips in the late 1950s, the Phillips curve stated that low unemployment was correlated with high inflation and vice versa. This led to an alleged inflation-unemployment trade-off in which governments were told by economists that attempting to achieve price stability would ultimately mean putting more people on the unemployment lines. But the Phillips curve was a statistical observation and not a theory.

In the late 1960s, the Phillips curve came under theoretical attack from economists such as Milton Friedman and Edmund Phelps. Looking at the microeconomic underpinnings, they asked why workers, as the Phillips curve implied, would be continuously mistaken about what was happening to their real wages and why they would keep asking for higher money wages. Friedman and others concluded that workers could not rationally be expected to keep making the same mistake. In short, the notion of a trade-off was unstable in the short run and nonexistent in the long run. Governments, therefore, could not trade off inflation for unemployment. The "stagflation" of the 1970s essentially proved them right. This work led in turn to research that focused on the role of expectations. In short, consideration had to be given to the fact that the inflationary effects of expansionary policy would be anticipated. Workers would demand pay increases to keep their real wages constant. As a result, this would prevent any increase in the demand for labour.

It was a fairly short step from this basic notion that people learn from their mistakes to the development of NAIRU. The concept of NAIRU argues that every economy has a rate of unemployment that is consistent with stable inflation. For Canada in the mid-1980s, it was estimated to be around 7.5 percent unemployment. The NAIRU for the United States was 6.5 percent, and for Japan a startling 2 percent. This so-called natural rate of unemployment is a product of the basic structural features of the economy, especially the degree of rigidity of labour markets. It cannot be changed ultimately by short-term (annual) bursts of demand management. It could only be changed by having solid framework-oriented structural policies that maximize and encourage the continuous adaptability of the economy for each of the main factors of production, labour, capital, land, and knowledge.

By 1983–84, the NAIRU concept was being picked up by bodies such as the Macdonald Royal Commission and by senior Department of Finance economists, as well as by international bodies such as the Organization for Economic Cooperation and Development (OECD). By the end of the 1980s, the central aspects of NAIRU were largely accepted by mainstream economists, but political acceptance and understanding were slower in developing and were inevitably seen through ideologically coloured glasses. The NAIRU concept was certainly criticized by social interest groups who stressed that there was nothing natural about various countries' capacity to pursue full employment. By the time the Mulroney Conservatives came to power in 1984, many of the policies inherent in the "monetarist, expectations theory, NAIRU, noninterventionist" arsenal of ideas were already being tried out by ardent "new right" governments in the United Kingdom and United States, headed respectively by Margaret Thatcher and Ronald Reagan.[15] While "new right" was an appropriate label for some of these ideas, other ideas such as the expectations theory and even NAIRU were in fact not derived from ideology as such, but rather reflected a newly evolving but now congealing macroeconomic paradigm.

The Mulroney Macroeconomic Agenda

While some aspects of the new macroeconomic ideas were already evident in the last two years of the Trudeau government's budget speeches, it was the Mulroney Conservatives who most adopted them as their own. Successive budget speeches set out a fairly consistent line of approach, albeit pockmarked with the usual zigzags of political footwork.

The Conservatives' agenda enunciated by Finance Minister Michael Wilson spoke of achieving goals, in order of priority, such as price stability, enhanced productivity growth, and sustainable growth. It described its macro policies as having two complementary thrusts. One was characterized as structural or framework oriented and was intended to reduce distortions and impediments to growth.[16] The other was cast in the language of getting the macroeconomic environment right. It included getting the federal deficit down, putting inflation on a downward track, and reducing the federal government's demands on the economy's scarce resources.[17]

By the early 1990s, the Conservatives could reasonably argue that they had acted on key parts of both the framework-oriented and macroeconomic-environment aspects of their agenda. Their framework or structural actions included: major tax reform initiatives that included reductions in marginal tax rates and a shift to consumption taxes via the Goods and Services Tax (GST); the Canada–U.S. Free Trade Agreement; significant deregulation of the transportation and energy sectors; and a privatization program. The government was, as we see in Chapter 16, much less forthright in changing labour market policies, one of the keys in lowering the NAIRU for Canada. It also made only halting progress in realizing the internal common market through the reduction of interprovincial trade barriers.

As for inflation reductions, the Conservatives can point to considerable success in the overall period since the inflation rate was cut in half from 8.3 percent during the early Liberal years of the 1980s to about 4.4 percent in the 1985 to 1990 period.[18] After inflation went up in 1991, the Conservatives announced an even more specific set of intermediate inflation targets, which included a commitment to reduce inflation gradually to 2 percent by 1995.[19]

On the debt and fiscal policy side, the Mulroney Conservatives can point to some progress, but of a much more difficult and begrudging kind. As shown in Chapter 7, the level of total government expenditure outlays as a percentage of GDP has been reduced somewhat. This reflects a significant reduction in discretionary program expenditures, but the small amount of the reduction ultimately indicates the persistent growth of interest charges on the national debt and on the extremely large annual deficit. The debt-to-GDP ratio crept up and as the 1990s began was rising faster than the incomes of Canadians and government revenues.[20] This was the case despite the fact that revenue yields had been increased from their deep trough in the late 1970s to the average levels, as a percentage of GDP, of the 1960s. A growing problem was also arising because a higher than normal percentage of overall Canadian debt was being financed by foreigners.

The final aspect of traditional macroeconomic policy, exchange rates, also underwent change. At one level, a market-oriented approach suggests that an exchange rate policy is an oxymoron. Exchange rates, according to this view, reflect the underlying state of the economy as judged by markets. One cannot have a policy as such. Earlier instances where countries, including Canada, depreciated their currencies would be anathema. Exchange rates should be allowed to fluctuate.

In this regard, however, the key is that they not fluctuate too much lest they create instability for investment decisions. Approaches to exchange rates by the Mulroney Conservatives, and more importantly by the Bank of Canada, have tended to be based on a market approach, but with two anomalies or built-in paradoxes. The first is that the revolution in capital and financial markets, which sees money whizzing about the world in unprecedented volume and speed, has raised concerns about the need to "manage" such rates at least within some band of stability. The development of G-7 international meetings of Ministers of Finance has sought to deal with this. The second is that in the late 1980s the Canadian dollar increased in value quite markedly vis-à-vis the American dollar, thus reducing some of the immediate short-term opportunities from the free trade agreement. Some of this increase in the value of the Canadian dollar came from the government's own high interest rate policies. Ordinarily, it would be argued that interest rates merely reflect underlying economic realities as well and cannot be manipulated. During this period, however, the spread between Canadian and U.S. interest rates was unusually high.

It was argued by some that such differentials were part of a side deal related to the free trade agreement in which Canada allegedly undertook to edge up the value of the Canadian dollar. Several members of the U.S. Congress and Senate had been pressing for such a change as a quid pro quo for the free trade agreement. There is no firm evidence that this in fact happened, but the interest rate differential is not easily explained by pure market forces. Regardless of this possible mystery, the fact remained that a high Canadian dollar was adversely affecting the adjustment of the Canadian economy into its post–free trade agreement stance.

An understanding of how some of the above Conservative macro agenda and ideas were sidetracked must await our discussion below of structure and process. In the meantime, the fate of industrial policy ideas under the Conservatives must be briefly examined.

The Idea of an Industrial Policy: In Retreat or in Hibernation?

A good place to begin an appreciation of the industrial policy debate in the 1980s is with a sense of the internal deliberations of the Macdonald Royal Commission.[21] One of the commission studies that received the most discussion by the commissioners was by Richard Harris, an economist from Queen's University.[22] The Harris study supported the concept of free trade, but also argued that there was a good case in economic theory for the practice of an industrial policy and that such an industrial policy was especially necessary for small, open-trading nations such as Canada. The argument is basically as follows.

The standard theory of international trade is based on the concept of comparative advantage. This theory assumes that all countries have access to identical technologies. Moreover, it assumes that factors of production are immobile internationally, but mobile domestically between sectors within an economy. However, as Harris pointed out, other research showed that countries do not possess identical technologies and that therefore differences in the diffusion of technologies are a significant determinant of trade patterns. Technologies are in this sense public goods, and therefore there is a good rationale for governments to help "shape comparative advantage."

Thus far, this was an argument only for broad framework policies. The economic case for firm or sector specific policies—in other words, real industrial policy—resided in the notion that some product development cycles were characterized by both increasing returns to scale and imperfect competition. In theory, a case exists for governments pursuing these even greater gains from trade or practising policies to prevent a country from losing out entirely. In short, there may be both offensive and defensive reasons for practising such an industrial policy. Federal policy in Canada could promote national welfare by seeking a share of these increasing returns.

The Harris pro-industrial policy case was essentially rejected by a majority of the Macdonald Commission members on several grounds. First, other commission research studies by economists pointed out that the distribution of these gains among countries was problematical at best. This was because many countries would practise similar policies and the potential competition would cancel any possible gains. The research was also extremely sceptical about the technical capacity of government, and its slow politicized speed of response, actually to fashion the right mix of policy instruments and to deliver them on time.

In contrast to the economic research for the commission, which advised, in essence, to stick to good framework economic policies and avoid industrial policy-making, the research by the commission's political scientists tended implicitly to be more supportive of industrial policies.[23] This support was not couched in some active "here's how to do it" sense, but rather in the form of saying that industrial policy of some kind is politically inevitable and that the past array of policies was not all that wasteful if one took into account the complex interplay of interests, a wider range of political values than just economic efficiency, and Canada's regional makeup. The research on the politics of industrial policy also tolerated a much wider definition of industrial policy. It could at times include just about anything that government did that influenced sectors or key firms. Indeed, in the 1960s and 1970s that seemed to be the way industrial policy was defined.[24] During the early 1970s, in particular, Ottawa sought to devise industrial strategies of various kinds, including abortive efforts to involve all industrial sectors. Bodies such as the Science Council and the Economic Council engaged in a public debate about the value of industrial policies, with the former favouring them and the latter opposed. Industrial policy during these debates intersected and collided with the always murky world of regional policy. The Macdonald Commission's political research also showed that there were some countries that somehow managed to have high growth and technologically progressive economies that did not practise only a free-market approach. Thus, the Macdonald Commission's prescriptions on industrial policy did not flow from the full body of its research. No commission's work ever does. The Macdonald Commission was itself a smaller reflection of the larger political economic world around it. Moreover, it was writing its report knowing that it would be received, embraced, or rejected by a new Conservative Mulroney government. What then were the new government's views and actions in industrial policy as the Macdonald Commission took pen to hand?

Tory Industrial Policy: Grants Out, Knowledge In?

Over its first few years in office, it became clear that the Mulroney government was sympathetic, by dint of both experience and ideology, to the adage that no industrial policy was the best economic policy. The evidence came gradually but unmistakably in a series of actions and statements. The fall 1984 Wilson statement on economic renewal set the pro-market tone. Prime Minister Mulroney's speeches declaring that Canada was open for business and the conversion of FIRA into Investment Canada with its reduced screening role marked a 180-degree change from previous Liberal policy. The Nielsen Task Force studies on industrial incentives, combined with the Macdonald Commission critique, were among the reasons for the Conservative decision gradually to reduce the use of grants and to move toward a more knowledge- and service-oriented approach to assisting business, especially in the Department of Regional Industrial Expansion (DRIE). The severe federal deficit also made it easier to conclude that the grants or spending approach was increasingly a nonstarter in Tory Ottawa.

In the midst of the free trade negotiations further steps were taken that gave more overall coherence to the Tory approach. First, regional granting decisions were hived off from DRIE and assigned to three separate agencies, the Atlantic Canada Opportunities Agency (ACOA), the Western Development Department (WDD), and an agency for northern Ontario.[25] These agencies were to be located in their respective regions and possessed a great amount of decentralized decision-making power compared to the old DRIE arrangement.

Rising from the ashes of the old DRIE was a new department: Industry, Science and Technology Canada (ISTC).[26] In regional terms, it was the department for Ontario and Quebec, but at the core of ISTC was a new mandate. ISTC was first and foremost to foster scientific excellence and internationally competitive industry. Involving a marriage of the nonregional elements of DRIE with the former Ministry of State for Science and Technology (MOSST), the new department hoped to become unambiguously Ottawa's department of the micro economy. It was here that grant programs would be phased out and a knowledge- and service-oriented approach would prevail. Keeping in mind the concerns about possible U.S. countervail, the financial resources of the department would focus not on the production phase of commercial activity, but on the early "pre-competition" technology development phase and on market development. Programs would be geared to fostering strategic alliances and networks with and among firms on key problems such as the use of strategic materials and process technologies. ISTC would perforce become more of a knowledge and networking department rather than a grant-giving department.

In many ways ISTC was being given a mandate similar to that of the original Department of Industry in 1965, except that the technology role was far more central. ISTC would have a role in fostering excellence in science (a policy for science role), but its core role would be fostering the most rapid use of modern production and process technologies in Canadian industry and in encouraging internationally competitive firms, especially those with high-technology products. All of this was to put institutional flesh to the earlier bare bones of Conservative promises to double Canadian research and development spending as a percentage of GNP. Prime Minister Mulroney's own inflated rhetoric on this subject had initially got the government into difficulty because several early budget-cutting measures had in fact reduced R&D spending by the federal government. Later, however, Mulroney himself took a personal interest in the kind of industry and technology mandate being devised for ISTC early in 1987.

During this time it was by no means certain that a free trade agreement would be successfully concluded. Thus, it must be said that the new ISTC mandate was not itself the product of the free trade deal. Rather, it represented both a practical learning curve for the Tories and an item of ideological belief that later complemented free trade. In terms of the cumulative professional and political critique of past Canadian industrial, regional, and science policies, the Tory approach can be seen as being quite sensible. To the extent that it seeks to be grounded in getting the broad framework policies right and in moving toward a more serious embrace of technology policies, it deserves praise.

In terms of the concerns raised in this chapter, one might say that the Mulroney Conservatives, directionally at least, seem to have got it about 70 to 75 percent right. But it is the remaining 25 to 30 percent (if one can loosely express it in percentages) that constitutes the real industrial policy puzzle. Is this the zone (some will attach a higher or lower percentage figure than we have) where the Harris thesis should operate, either for offensive or defensive reasons? Is this the manoeuvring room for the practice of industrial policy defined as actions coordinated and targeted at specific firms or sectors and that is the vital complement to the larger array of framework policies? Is this the terrain that a small, open-trading nation must be very good at if it is to "shape" comparative advantage?

Structure: The Fall and Rise of the Department of Finance

Macroeconomic and industrial policy structures have both affected and been changed by the changing agenda of the 1960s and 1970s versus the 1980s and early 1990s. Within the Canadian government we look primarily at the Department of Finance, the Bank of Canada, and the Department of Industry, Science and Technology. In terms of nongovernmental structures, we comment briefly on the key role played by the Business Council on National Issues (BCNI) and the problems of forging an interest structure for industrial policy.

The Department of Finance anchors the macroeconomic policy role in Ottawa and hence has always been among the top two or three departments in the federal pecking order. While the Department of Finance has always been powerful in tax and other fiscal policy matters, history suggests that in the late 1960s and during the 1970s the department suffered a partial loss of influence. The evidence for this mild decline comes from the evident loss of control of public expenditure growth, especially in the first half of the 1970s, and from the establishment of several new economic departments during this overall period.[27] The inherent belief or assumption during the heyday of Trudeau largesse that money and resources were plentiful translated into more contending structures for ecomonic policy formation. Perhaps the ultimate evidence of the decline of Finance was seen in the fact that, from 1978 to 1983, there were virtually two budget speeches or the equivalent per year, a real one and a mini budget statement to respond to the latest crisis. Finance was also in some disarray intellectually, precisely because, as noted above, the Keynesian paradigm was being dismantled, but there was no clear agreement as to what should replace it.

All of this changed during the Mulroney years. The Department of Finance became the undoubted home base of the Mulroney macroeconomic policy agenda. Aided greatly by the ministerial stability and longevity of Michael Wilson, Finance reasserted its dominance. The focus on deficit control, the tax reform agenda, and even the free trade agenda depended greatly on Finance and Wilson not losing their nerve while those around them were. This is not to argue that they got their way in all cases. Finance's preferred strategy for deficit reduction was to cut spending rather than increase taxes, but other centres of influence—including the prime minister himself, but also other spending departments—exerted sufficient pressure to ensure that revenue-raising bore its fair share of the deficit reduction burden.

But if Finance supplied the backbone of the Mulroney macro agenda, then it in turn was properly stiffened by the pressure of the business lobby. The 1980s probably brought with it the greatest degree of agreement among the main business interest groups as to what the macro agenda ought to be. Another key difference between the 1980s and the 1970s was that by 1984 the Business Council on National Issues was the undoubted leader of the business lobby.[28] Led by its president, Thomas d'Aquino, it continuously handed the already sympathetic Mulroney ministers and advisers its various macroeconomic blueprint documents. There is little doubt that the free trade initiative would not have proceeded without BCNI pressure, although here the role of the Canadian Manufacturers Association (CMA) was also pivotal.

While business interest group pressure was vital, it is important not to lose sight of the fact that Finance, the business lobby, and the Mulroney entourage in general were all in turn looking over their shoulders at even larger stark realities and pressures. One was the evident fact and memory of both the devasting recession of 1982–83 and the high inflation and unemployment of the late 1970s. Another was that numerous international bodies, from the OECD to the IMF and World Bank, were all both debating and eventually contributing to the articulation and consolidation of a new post-Keynesian approach. It was in this sense that a macroeconomic policy community of views was being forged. In Canada, a particular additional catalyst for this homogenizing experience was the Macdonald Royal Commission.

Also a part of this vital international and domestic network of expert economic opinion and action was the Bank of Canada. The Bank of Canada is an independent institution for monetary policy and is the lender of last resort to the Canadian banking system. The Governor of the Bank of Canada exerts tremendous influence, primarily because if the governor ever resigned on a matter of policy dispute with the Minister of Finance the consequences for the government would be enormous. Financial markets and business interests in general want an independent monetary authority because they do not trust politicians with the money supply. While some of this mystique is misplaced, it is undoubtedly powerful and compelling. Thus, the Bank of Canada is a powerful player in the overall macro posture of the government. The Bank, too, arguably lost some influence in the early 1970s when spending got out of hand. This was not its responsibility, but it could not help but be tarred by the same overall brush of economic mismanagement.[29] When monetarist theory reached new levels of political respectability in the mid and late 1970s, the Bank's influence in turn seemed to be restored. Monetary gradualism was practised and inflation rates abated.

While the early experiment with monetarist policy faltered, the 1982–83 recession also renewed the determination of the Bank to wrestle inflation to the ground. The Bank pressed the Department of Finance and the government hard to keep its eye on the inflationary ball. As inflation was cut in half from over 8 percent to around 4 percent, it demonstrated it was still more determined than ever. The fixing of inflation targets of 2 percent and even musings about zero inflation as a feasible goal indicate that the Bank's role is likely to be unrelenting in the 1990s and thus a significant factor in the overall macroeconomic equation.[30]

Industrial Policy Structures: The Missing Link?

As described previously, the Mulroney government's new flagship for the micro economy was the Department of Industry, Science and Technology Canada, established in 1987. The Conservatives, however, did not see ISTC as a vehicle for industrial policy as defined above. Instead, it was seen as another element of basic framework-oriented policy to be kept somehow separate from regional policy. Before proceeding further, a brief historical account is needed to appreciate how industrial policy structures have evolved in recent decades.

In the 1950s, industrial policy structures centred on the Department of Trade and Commerce, especially in the heyday of C. D. Howe, Canada's one and only industrial policy czar. But industrial policy in those days meant basically an encouragement for foreign investment, and the further building of the infrastructure of the Canadian economy such as the TransCanada Pipeline and the St. Lawrence Seaway.[31]

In the 1960s, and extending into the 1970s, industrial policy structures became much more multidepartmental in nature, and their conceptual nature became extremely fragmented and ad hoc. Thus, new departments such as those for industry, regional economic expansion, science and technology, and consumer and corporate affairs all claimed some part of the action, as did the traditional resource departments such as agriculture, fisheries, and energy. Bodies such as the Science Council of Canada also advocated industrial policies. Despite several abortive efforts to forge industrial strategies, one could not speak of an industrial policy as such, either as defined in the C. D. Howe era or as defined earlier in this chapter.

The only tendency, structural and conceptual, that seemed to be in the ascendancy in the 1970s and early 1980s, was a faith in regional policy, or at least in the political right to spend money in the name of regional policy.[32] The regional presence shifted structurally, first as a separate department, then as a Department of Regional Industrial Expansion where it was hoped that regional and national policy would be integrated, and then separated again with the previously described Mulroney regional agencies, ACOA and the Western Development Department.

Canadian industrial-regional policy structures revealed a perverse "damned if you do, damned if you don't" characteristic. If regional and industrial policy are combined within one department, it leads to conceptual policy chaos. Conversely, if regional policy is separated or ghettoized, then a strong array of regionally based ministers in Cabinet complain of not being in on the distributive politics involved. The Conservatives' ISTC appears to address some of these problems, in part by saying that it is getting out of the granting business and by focusing more clearly on the issue of international competitiveness. But regional issues cannot be that easily segregated from the internal structures of government. Moreover, the ISTC role still begs the question of whether a 1990s-style industrial policy, targeted on key firms or consortia, or even sectors, is needed and can be operationalized successfully.

This issue, in turn, requires a look at a second key element of structure, namely whether an interest group structure can be mobilized in the micro sphere with the same coherence that has occurred in traditional macroeconomic and fiscal policy. The work of Atkinson and Coleman shows that industrial policy is unlikely to occur unless government can draw on "sectoral and regional affiliates of peak (interest group) associations that negotiate the cooperation of individual firms."[33] In short, industrial policy assumes "a set of political institutions capable of engineering the necessary degree of consensus."[34] Since, at best, industrial policies can only produce change at the margins, to be effective they must be "steady and cumulative."[35] This would also apply to what we have referred to in this chapter as framework policies. It cannot be said that Canadian governments have spent much time thinking systematically about how these interest networks for industrial policy should be constructed, let alone maintained. Past episodic consultative exercises have been tried, but in the late 1970s and in the 1980s these were overwhelmed by the larger political realities of regional policy.

But future capacity goes well beyond the issues of interest group intermediation. Consider for example the simple fact that, between 1982 and 1990, DRIE and ISTC had no fewer than seven ministers, seven ministers of state, five deputy ministers, and five associate deputy ministers. Future governments must ensure that the minister and deputy minister of the micro economy are not the minister and deputy minister of musical chairs. Just as Michael Wilson brought some political and economic continuity to the Department of Finance, so must a future federal government invest ISTC with an equivalent base of political and bureaucratic power and continuity. Such a minister would have to become, in the best political-economic sense of the word, a student of the Canadian micro political economy. Like the macro minister, the micro minister would have to have the sustained support of the prime minister over several years.

At the level of information and knowledge, industrial policy capacity also has structural imperatives to meet. As the comprehensive Ontario Premier's Council Report stressed, there are four essential analytical elements of the industrial policy process.[36] The first is the need for detailed competitive analysis of the industry concerned based on good analysis of the international competitive situation facing that industry. Second, policy should be based on longer-term objectives reached after "thorough study and industrial consultation." Third, policy should focus where Canada has real competitive leverage. Fourth, policy has to be based on an understanding of the linkages between other micro policies and macro and micro policies.

In Canada's postwar history, industrial policy, defined loosely, has been extraordinarily ad hoc, reactive, and defensive in nature, and several giant steps removed from the idealized notions of industrial policy hinted at in this chapter. The majority of economic opinion by economists counsels against having an industrial policy for the reasons set out above. The argument that governments ought to stick to developing good framework policies is quite persuasive, and accordingly we have argued that recent federal policy is, directionally at least, correct.

The remaining room for possible but critical industrial policy manoeuvring is still important for two reasons. First, political imperatives are likely to require defensive industrial policies in the area of foreign takeovers. The majority of professional economic opinion suggests that ownership does not matter, but in politics, and in marginal economic ways, ownership does matter. Second, offensive or anticipatory industrial policy, while easy to be sceptical about, especially given the imperatives of regional pressures and bureaucratic and analytical musical chairs, should not be dismissed out of hand. There is a sense in which one can say that it has never truly been tried in Canada. No federal government can be said to have given the issue concerted political thought.

The great paradox of the free trade agreement may ultimately be that, while it was forged as a substitute for industrial policy and based on a rejection of such policies, Canadians now have to think about industrial policy capacity carefully and concretely, in part because there is no choice but to do so and precisely because the agreement is in place. The provisions of the free trade agreement do not all constrain such future capacity. Some policy doors are closed, but others may be given new emphasis. However, even if these are thought through more carefully and acted on more cogently, they will not produce the "economic millennium." Good framework and macroeconomic policies are even more essential. So are good social and labour market policies.

Macro and Industrial Policy Processes

How have the processes of macroeconomic and industrial policy changed, and how have they in turn changed policy and influenced policy outcomes? To deal with these questions we must revisit some of the dynamics of the tax and expenditure process. As mentioned in earlier chapters, these instrument-based processes to some extent lead lives of their own. They have in their own way been influenced by the demise of the Keynesian paradigm, but at the same time cause the outcomes of the new thinking to be diverted and deflected.

Consider first the tax process. Though characterized by some modest consultation in the 1960s and 1970s, the pre-budget decision process—the process that leads to the annual political expression of macroeconomic policy—was basically quite secretive and confined to a small number of players. Successive tax breaks over the 1970s, many given by Finance in the name of sensible short-term demand management or structural policy, had made the tax system a quagmire. Moreover, it had resulted in severe losses of revenue and made the system more regressive as well. Efforts to reform it "on the run," as occurred under Allan MacEachen in 1981, proved to be hopelessly inadequate. Tax decision-making was grinding down under its own weight. Moreover, as mentioned previously, there were in fact virtually two budgets per year from 1978 to 1983.

To change policy, both macroeconomic and structural policy, the process had to be changed. Process changes were not in themselves a sufficient cause for change, but they were a part of the steps needed. Thus, the two phases of tax reform, the 1987 general reforms and the

1990–91 GST, were preceded by quite elaborate consultative processes and by the release of tax reform papers. At the same time, these processes would not have resulted in actual change unless there was a fierce determination by the Mulroney government to stay the course, despite strong public criticism, and to stick to a more or less consistent line of priorities. In this important sense, the Mulroney government's overall priority-setting processes allowed it to do so, something not nearly as evident on the economic front in the Trudeau years.

At the same time, the tax reform process was greatly aided, perhaps even ultimately caused, by the fact that the Americans had undergone a major tax reform in 1986. Thus, international influences were also changing the tax and structural economic decision process in ways that were not evident in earlier periods. U.S. influences have always been important in that Canada's tax system cannot get too far out of line with the larger economy, but here the influence was stark. Canada still has room for action, however. After all, the GST was implemented and has no American federal parallel.

Now that tax reform has occurred, it is interesting to speculate on how tax processes might alter future tax policy. On the one hand, the tax process is still an annual event, and there are still plenty of interests that line up annually asking for a new round of tax breaks. Thus, perhaps by the year 2000, yet another clearing of the tax-break decks will have to occur. On the other hand, there may be strong counter-pressures to prevent or limit this eventuality. For example, the pressure to harmonize continental tax policy may well grow as free trade advances, or deficit reduction pressures may simply be so strong that revenue-raising needs will supersede the desire to give out new tax breaks. The logic of recent tax and macro reform is to keep the tax system as a good framework aspect of the macroeconomic environment, but process may not let this happen to the extent desired by those in the policy chair.[37]

If one looks on the expenditure process side of the equation, it is not hard to see the dynamics and rhythms that have led to less than desired deficit reduction outcomes and to the ad hoc nature of regional-industrial policy. Though the Mulroney government, led by Finance, has adopted new formal processes to control and cut spending and has succeeded in certain respects, the underlying expenditure dynamics have blunted this considerably. Unlike the tax process, the expenditure process is a multidepartmental, multiminister game. Even when engaging in cuts, the expenditure process and public money is still the essential grease for the Cabinet wheel. Thus, the process allows numerous avenues for ministers and departments to fight back. This is true whether one views the engine for these dynamics in terms of a classic battle of spenders versus guardians, or whether one sees it as a clash of regional ministers in a regionally driven political culture.[38]

Taxation and expenditure processes are, of course, not the only ones that weave their way through the macroeconomic and industrial policy terrain. Regulatory processes also affect outcomes. Changes in the Mulroney era that resulted in the deregulation of vertical sectors such as oil and gas and transportation may reinforce the framework-oriented thrust of economic policy, but these may be counteracted or altered by the demands for expanded environmental regulation.

At the symbolic level of debate, there are also differences and constraints. For example, macroeconomic policy, even with the decline of Keynesian generalities, is undoubtedly easier to debate in general public discourse than is industrial policy. The latter's boundaries are scarcely understood in normal media-driven public debate. Thus, those who think industrial policies are a necessary complement to free trade and to the new macro concensus will have to work much harder to communicate the essence of what such policies are and how they might be successfully implemented.

Conclusions

The nature of macroeconomic and industrial policy has undergone a significant transformation. As conducted and debated in the 1990s, it is a significantly different field than its 1970s and early 1980s counterpart. The Keynesian paradigm has been replaced by a more pressing concern for inflation and for getting the framework and structural aspects of the macro economy right. The very notion of the legitimacy of having an industrial policy has been undermined. Some of this transformation is the product of "new right" ideologies, but much of it is more accurately the outcome of cumulative and adverse experience and of changes in economic knowledge. At the same time, the new agenda inherently generates its own limits and counter-pressures, revealed through, and partly caused by, changes in structure and process.

For Canada, it has always been difficult, if not impossible, to separate regional policy from both macro and industrial policy concerns. Moreover, as a small country trading in a larger continental and world market, it would appear that there will be a need for some kind of industrial policy to complement free trade. However, such an industrial policy capacity would involve major structural change in the industrial and economic policy machinery and in the structure of the policy communities involved.

Notes

1. See Michael Parkin and Robin Bade, *Modern Macroeconomics*, 2nd ed. (Scarborough, Ont.: Prentice-Hall, 1986).
2. See Richard Lipsey and Wendy Dobson, eds., *Shaping Comparative Advantage* (Toronto: C. D. Howe Institute, 1987).
3. See Charles Lindblom, *Politics and Markets* (New York: Basic Books, 1977).
4. See Richard W. Phidd and G. Bruce Doern, *The Politics and Management of Canadian Economic Policy* (Toronto: Macmillan, 1978), chs. 7 and 8.
5. Ibid, ch. 2.
6. See Donald Savoie, *Regional Economic Development: Canada's Search for Solutions* (Toronto: University of Toronto Press, 1986).
7. See David Wolfe, "The State and Economic Policy in Canada, 1968–1975," in Leo Panitch, ed., *The Canadian State* (Toronto: University of Toronto Press, 1977), 251–88.
8. See Phidd and Doern, *The Politics and Management of Canadian Economic Policy*, ch. 10.
9. See Milton Friedman, *The Optimum Money Supply and Other Essays* (London: Macmillan, 1969), and John T. Woolley, *Monetary Politics* (London: Cambridge University Press, 1986).
10. See Leo Panitch, "Trade Unions and the Capitalist State: Corporatism and Its Contradictions," *New Left Review* 125 (January–February 1981), 21–44, and Keith Banting, ed., *The State and Economic Interests* (Toronto: University of Toronto Press, 1986).
11. See William Coleman, *Business and Politics* (Montreal: McGill-Queen's University Press, 1988).
12. G. Bruce Doern and Richard W. Phidd, *Canadian Public Policy: Ideas, Structure, Process*, 1st ed. (Toronto: Nelson, 1983), ch. 15.
13. See Canada, *The Way Ahead* (Ottawa: Minister of Supply and Services, 1976).
14. See Canada, Royal Commission on the Economic Union and Development Prospects for Canada, *Final Report* (Ottawa: Minister of Supply and Services, 1985), vol. II, part III, ch. 10.
15. See Desmond King, *The New Right* (London: Macmillan, 1987).
16. For a review, see Canada, *The Budget* (Ottawa: Minister of Supply and Services, February 26, 1991), ch. 5.
17. Ibid., 118–19.
18. Ibid., 112.
19. Ibid., 14.
20. Ibid., 128. For critical reviews of the Tory record, see Maureen Farrow and William Robson, "The Long Road Back to Balance," *Fiscal Policy Monitor* (Toronto: C. D. Howe Institute, 1989).
21. See Royal Commission on the Economic Union and Development Prospects for Canada, *Final Report*.

22. See Richard Harris, *Trade, Industrial Policy and International Competition* (Toronto: University of Toronto Press, 1985).
23. See André Blais, ed., *Industrial Policy* (Toronto: University of Toronto Press, 1986), and G. Bruce Doern, ed., *The Politics of Economic Policy* (Toronto: University of Toronto Press, 1986), ch. 1.
24. Doern and Phidd, *Canadian Public Policy*, 1st ed., ch. 15.
25. See Donald Savoie, "ACOA, Something Old, Something New, Something Borrowed, Something Blue," in Katherine Graham, ed., *How Ottawa Spends 1989-90* (Ottawa: Carleton University Press, 1989), 107-30.
26. See G. Bruce Doern, ed., "The Department of Industry, Science and Technology: Is There Industrial Policy After Free Trade?" in Katherine Graham, ed., *How Ottawa Spends 1990-91* (Ottawa: Carleton University Press, 1990), 49-72.
27. See Phidd and Doern, *The Politics and Management of Canadian Economic Policy.*
28. See Coleman, *Business and Politics*, ch. 5. See also G. Bruce Doern and Brian W. Tomlin, *Faith and Fear: The Free Trade Story* (Toronto: Stoddart, 1991), chs. 2 and 3.
29. See Thomas K. Rymes, "Does the Bank of Canada Matter?" in Michael J. Prince, ed., *How Ottawa Spends 1986-87* (Toronto: Methuen, 1986), 179-207.
30. See Richard Lipsey, ed., *Zero Inflation: The Goal of Price Stability* (Toronto: C. D. Howe Institute, 1990).
31. See Phidd and Doern, *The Politics and Management of Canadian Economic Policy*, ch. 11.
32. See Donald McFetridge, ed., *Canadian Industrial Policy in Action* (Toronto: University of Toronto Press, 1985).
33. See Michael Atkinson and William Coleman, *The State, Business and Industrial Change* (Toronto: University of Toronto Press, 1989), 27.
34. Ibid., 25.
35. Ibid., 25.
36. See Ontario Premier's Council, *Report* (Toronto: Queen's Printer, 1988).
37. See Allan Maslove, "The Goods and Services Tax: Lessons from Tax Reform," in Graham, ed., *How Ottawa Spends 1990-91*, 27-48, and Allan Maslove, *Tax Reform in Canada: The Process and Impact* (Halifax: Institute for Research on Public Policy, 1989).
38. See Donald Savoie, *The Politics of Public Spending in Canada* (Toronto: University of Toronto Press, 1990), and G. Bruce Doern, Allan Maslove, and Michael Prince, *Budgeting in Canada* (Ottawa: Carleton University Press, 1988), ch. 4.

CHAPTER *16*

Social and Labour Market Policy

Of the three overarching policies examined in this analysis, social and labour market policy is without doubt the broadest and most unwieldy. The social half of the equation itself consists of two broad groups of policy activity, one centred on welfare and income security and the other dealing with issues that some refer to broadly as the quality of life.[1] The labour market side usually refers to a set of ideas and actions designed to enable the supply of labour to adjust more rapidly to changing demands.[2]

More specifically, the social welfare state embraces actions to deal with old age security, pensions, social assistance, and unemployment insurance. It also involves the delivery of services in areas such as health, housing, day care, and personal services such as family counselling. The quality of life aspects are often seen to embrace issues such as cultural policy, broadcasting, abortion, multiculturalism, human rights, justice and corrections, law enforcement, and other concerns linked to a person's sense of symbolic and real belonging to a community. The labour market aspects in turn deal with a host of actions on both the demand and supply side of labour markets, including education and training, mobility assistance, immigration, placement and information services.

Lest the above be considered too encompassing, even it is not adequate to capture how this field can be and is often viewed and defined. Thus, social policy is often characterized in terms of clientele groups of varying definitional scope. Policies for children, single mothers with children, youth, the aged, people with disabilities, the working poor, ethnic minorities, and visible minorities are only the starting point for such clientele-defined definitions.

Obviously, no single chapter can do justice to this range of activity, but it is essential within this confine to develop an appreciation of how these two elements—traditional social policy, especially income security, and labour market activity—have been joined in policy debate. They have always been linked in the real world, but not always in a central way in policy debate. At the same time, even these vitally linked issues do not have the field to themselves. In the background of this debate is the clamour for more rights and for the state to reflect symbolically the aspirations of various groups and individuals in what it does in the name of social and labour market policy. Much of the latter climate can be attributed to the influence of the Charter of Rights, though it is also rooted in the changing ethnic and social composition of Canada.

Thus, at the outset current social policy controversies and agendas must be placed in the context of earlier historical phases. Social policy in Canada has evolved in four major phases. In the pre–World War II period, it was basically characterized by efforts at the margin to assist the weak and disadvantaged who were not taken care of by the family and by private charity. The period after World War II to the mid-1960s brought the full flowering of the modern welfare state, including key universal programs such as pensions, medicare, and family allowances. The 1970s brought an initial effort to define even more comprehensive social welfare and preventative health-care measures, but these efforts were quickly displaced by stagflation, oil crises, and the resurgence of the political right. Finally, the 1980s brought both severe fiscal restraint and the need to respond to globalization, but also the aforementioned rise of a rights-oriented set of political demands. The 1980s also brought the jarring reality of both conspicuous wealth and the homeless sleeping in the streets and lining up at food banks.

As we review the postwar evolution of social and labour market policy, and changes in the Trudeau and Mulroney eras, particular focus will be given to the issue of whether a new consensus is emerging under the generic title of "adjustment" policy. This is a concept that implies more generous levels of human investment focused on labour and communities so as to enable the Canadian economy to be more continuously adaptive to international imperatives.[3] Much of the promise and controversy of this debate emerged in the work of the Macdonald Royal Commission in the mid-1980s. It was also central to the free trade issue, but was ultimately buried by the sheer emotion of the free trade battle. It is linked to industrial policy and the deficit and hence deals with all three overarching policy fields.

Ideas: Social Policy as Residual Outcome or Primary Determinant

A central issue of particular importance in understanding the evolving ideas of social and labour market policy is that of determining whether social policy is, and should be seen and/or explained as, a residual outcome of capitalist economies or as a primary determinant of future prosperity. As Wilensky and Lebeaux point out, "the first holds that social welfare institutions should come into play only when the normal structures of supply, the family and the market, break down. The second, in contrast, sees the welfare services as normal 'first line' functions of modern industrial society."[4]

As could be expected, the various policy analysis models examined in Chapter 1 evaluate this residual versus nonresidual question differently. A class analysis approach views social policies as a residual series of "legitimating" adjustments needed to sustain the basic power of capitalism. This view asserts that social policy *ought* to be primary, but could only be so if a capitalist state was replaced by a socialist one. In contrast, a public choice, self-interest, or market model would at best support the residual notion. In extreme form it would argue that the market is itself a social forum because it is supposedly based on noncoercive or free exchange. An incremental liberal and/or pluralist view might regard the two fields as evenly balanced, with existing social welfare programs being evidence of progressive change.

The redistribution of income and power is certainly a major idea in social policy, but it has not been the central concept. In this sense social policy has been residual. Both the original "welfare" assistance programs of the pre–welfare state era and the most recent income supplementation programs such as the Guaranteed Income Supplement (GIS) and the child tax credit can be said to be redistributive. But the vast array of larger programs established between these periods have not been created for redistributive reasons. As we will see, other ideas have been present.

One of the ideas that served to counteract the redistributive idea was the notion of equity, often reflected in concepts such as equality and equalization. One notion of equity implies treating people in like circumstances equally. In public finance this is known as horizontal equity. The idea can, in principle, be applied to taxpayers and to governments. The strength of the idea of regionalism, reinforced and embodied by federalism, has elevated this kind of equity to a high plateau. It was initially reflected in the equalization arrangements of federal–provincial fiscal relations, whereby provincial revenues were equalized to some agreed-upon level to allow public services to be offered to Canadians without unduly burdensome tax levels. This notion of regional equity easily melded into the larger idea of national unity.

The use of the term "equalization" to describe what we would otherwise define as being closer to the idea of equity shows the importance of the rhetorical language of debate and the labelling of policies. Equalization payments to provinces and thus indirectly to taxpayers are not the same as paying redistributive benefits to low-income Canadians, most of whom pay no taxes. They may be helped in a general way by the extra revenue given to their provincial government, but they are not necessarily the prime beneficiary of such "equalization" policies.[5]

The latter appeal to remove other "regional disparities" is a further reflection of the equity idea. It is also a manifestation of a spatial-geographic definition of policy, one that only partially coincides with redistribution by income class. As noted in Chapter 8, the Diefenbaker government epitomized this sense of regional injustice and launched a series of programs that would later be consolidated under the Liberals' Department of Regional Economic Expansion (DREE). By the 1980s, however, it could be shown that "little if any improvement in the reduction of regional disparities"[6] had occurred. Moreover, any limited reductions in the income gaps could virtually all be attributable to transfer payments such as unemployment insurance payments. This evidence did not in itself destroy the *idea* or strength of regionalism or equity. It only questioned the results of policies intended to help solve these problems. It can easily be seen how ideas such as regionalism and equity combine to form a stout defence of the idea of stability. If incomes cannot be redistributed, regionally or otherwise, then they can at least be stabilized and made more predictable and therefore socially humane.

Also melding with the above ideas was the debate over universality versus the stigma of means tests. Universality implied that programs were a right and a condition of Canadian citizenship, not welfare handouts.[7] At a practical political level this could also be interpreted to mean that some social programs had to be offered to everyone so that the middle class would politically support welfare for the poor. At the same time, however, this greatly increased the costs of social expenditures, and by the late 1970s governments were looking for and finding ways of targeting programs to particular lower-income groups without directly and openly attacking the universality idea. The universality idea had to be approached by stealth rather than by "rational" debate. This was evident in the emergence of programs such as the GIS and the child tax credit noted above.

Even this survey does not by any means exhaust the ideas inherent in social policy. For example, unemployment insurance has had to face a backlash linked to support for the idea of the work ethic.[8] As such, it involves a political tussle between the idea of insurance against bad times and welfare. In the early and mid-1970s changes to this policy field brought it into significant partisan dispute among political parties as to its appropriate "welfare," "insurance," and "work ethic" components. Critics charged that it was harming the "efficiency" of Canada's labour markets as well.

Ideas collide in the effort to bundle several social policies under the catch-all concept of improving the "quality of life." This was present not only in the social regulation fields identified in Chapters 7 and 12, but also in health care. For example, in the early 1970s the Department of National Health and Welfare launched an effort to gain support for a preventative lifestyle approach to health care as opposed to the curative doctor-dominated system now in place. It got nowhere, but reflected an idea that had the support of a modest political constituency.[9] This constituency grew in the 1980s.

A major social policy event of the early 1980s was, of course, the entrenchment of the Charter of Rights in the Canadian constitution. These rights included the rights of women, people with disabilities, Canada's native peoples, and the aged. While these represent an assertion of the idea of individual liberty and dignity, this idea was not entrenched in an absolute way. Room for manoeuvre was left in the "override" provisions whereby legislatures could temporarily infringe on some of these rights, a concession to parliamentary sovereignty and to a collective view of the common will. Nonetheless, the Charter has undoubtedly changed social policy in many important ways as citizens, through the courts and through direct political action, seek redress of their rights.

One could go on and on in the realm of social ideas—consumer free choice in the realm of radio and television versus Canadian content; language policy, education, and minority rights; multiculturalism versus a bicultural view of Canada; law and order policing versus citizen rights and the rights of criminals. The point to be stressed is that many ideas merge and separate and rise and fall as policies evolve and society changes.

During the Trudeau period as a whole, however, Canadian social and labour market policy was characterized by four major initiatives, all cast under the Trudeauesque label of "the Just Society." This phrase was intended to evoke movement away from the traditional welfare state, which had been largely put in place by the mid-1960s, and toward a looser mélange of initiatives linked to the quality of life. In the late 1960s and early 1970s there was also an ingrained sense that all or most such measures were affordable. As already mentioned, the Charter became the centrepiece of Trudeau's social policy. Although not achieved until the early 1980s, it was advocated very early by Prime Minister Trudeau.[10]

Another important initiative, albeit an abortive one, was the Lalonde Orange Paper exercise. Led by Health Minister Marc Lalonde, the initiative involved an elaborate federal–provincial consultative exercise in the 1970s to totally revamp the income security system.[11] While it did not advocate a guaranteed annual income approach, and eventually failed due to provincial opposition and fiscal pressures, it nonetheless provided an early example of the intense political difficulties involved in attempting potentially radical social policy reform. This was to be repeated in some respects by the later Macdonald Commission process described below in the Mulroney era.

After a long and indirect process, the Lalonde exercise did contribute to the adoption in the late 1970s of the child tax credit. The child tax credit was in fact part of an effort to cancel or reduce family allowance payments as deficit pressures rose in the late 1970s. But it also reflected concerns about redistribution, including the need to target money toward single women with children, an increasing aspect of poverty in the 1970s. The child tax credit would subsequently be enriched several times in the 1980s.

On the labour market side, the main Trudeau initiative was to change the unemployment insurance system in the early 1970s. These changes, occurring at a time when federal coffers were flush, or at least believed to be so, added social and regional dimensions to what had hitherto been basically an insurance-based program.[12] Once in place, these quasi-welfare elements became entrenched and contributed to what later critics referred to as a dependency syndrome, especially in poorer provinces such as Newfoundland and in Atlantic Canada in general. It was the noninsurance parts of the program that the Macdonald Commission later advocated should be rolled back and replaced with an integrated income and training system as set out below.

The Adjustment Idea and Labour Market Policy in the Mulroney Era

Once again, a useful place to begin an understanding of the 1980s social and labour market policy debate, and the emergence of the adjustment idea in the 1980s, is with the work of the Macdonald Royal Commission. While the commission is best known for its free trade recommendation and for its disavowal of previous industrial policy, these recommendations were accompanied by a complementary look at social and labour market policy. Unlike popular rhetorical debates about social policy, which tended to keep these realms separate, the Macdonald Commission linked them closely.[13]

The adjustment policy idea is a concept long advocated by those critical of the ad hoc industrial interventionism of the 1960s and 1970s. It is basically a set of actions by government whose central purpose is to facilitate change in the movement and use of the factors of production—capital, land, labour, and knowledge—in a way that follows market forces and decisions rather than leads them and that enables structural change to occur in a more positive way. At this level, adjustment policy is synonymous with our discussion in Chapter 15 of the need for basic, steady framework-oriented economic policy.

Adjustment policy is to be directed particularly at facilitating the exit of factors of production from declining industries. However, for the majority of adjustment policy advocates, this means that ideally policies should be targeted at labour and at adversely affected communities—in short, at human capital—rather than at firms (where most of the earlier protectionist measures and bail-out funds had gone). This is because labour is the least mobile of the factors of production. In comparison, capital and even knowledge are more nimble and adaptable. By implication, adjustment policy funds should go directly to workers and their families, rather than to corporations.

But what kinds of funds or programs would be so targeted in the new reformed world of merged social adjustment policy? The central recommendation of the Macdonald Commission concerning adjustment was the establishment of a Transitional Adjustment Assistance Program (TAAP). It would provide adjustment assistance for Canadians who had exhausted their unemployment benefits. The aid would go "to those for whom no immediate job opportunities can be identified provided that they are willing to move to accept employment or to undertake retraining."[14] The nature of the assistance would be both flexible and wide-ranging, including compensation for losses in assets such as housing as a result of the decline of communities.[15]

The commission explicitly linked this adjustment concept with a major reform of the income security system. By eliminating a series of existing social welfare expenditure and tax programs, the commission argued that a single replacement Universal Income Security Program (UISP) could be instituted that would "pay a basic income supplement to all Canadians, with the supplement progressively reduced as incomes rose."[16] It argued that the UISP would remove some of the traps and disincentives, in short, the inefficiencies, in the current welfare state and would be more generous to low-income Canadians. Above all, it would be an inducement, in concert with the adjustment package in TAAP, for the employable unemployed person to take the risks of change.

A logical corollary of the Macdonald package was that the unemployment insurance system would be restored to an insurance program and the resulting savings of several billions would form the basis of the TAAP program. The implication of the TAAP program was that it would be generous and flexible to meet the diverse personal circumstances of Canadians facing dislocation. The implication also was that "people would go to jobs" rather than "jobs to people," a credo not shared by advocates of traditional regional job-creation programs in Canada. The implication of the UISP was that the principle of universality in social programs would be *preserved* since all Canadians would be entitled to it, but that benefits would be taxed back for higher-income Canadians.

The overall messsage of the Macdonald Commission was that a combined adjustment and social guaranteed income component—a reformed generous welfare state writ large—was a necessary precondition to make Canada more competitive and adaptive in the face of the new global economy. The Macdonald Commission stressed that such a social adjustment package was necessary not just as the logical complement to the pressures unleashed by free trade, but also to face the even larger pressures from the newly industrialized countries that were already impacting upon Canadians, regardless of a Canada–U.S. free trade deal.

The Macdonald Commission examined and proposed these measures in the mid-1980s in the context of the data it marshalled on Canada–U.S. comparative social policy expenditures. Overall, Canada did spend a higher percentage of its GNP on social spending than the United States, but not by much.[17] Canada was much closer to the United States than it was to Western European countries. Canada's health-care expenditures were lower than total U.S. spending, but were socially more generous because all Canadians were covered by universal medicare. The United States spent more on pensions, but was more niggling on unemployment insurance and union laws. On the other hand, U.S. unemployment rates were two or three percentage points lower than Canadian rates. While this difference reflected in part different statistical ways of counting the unemployed, the lower U.S. rate was nonetheless in itself a partially successful social policy indicator.

In drawing out the essence of the Macdonald Commission logic in this way, we do not mean to indicate that it did not have its immediate critics. Rather, the point being stressed is that the commission's work became one of the first junctures where an integrated social adjustment policy debate was beginning to form out of the shell shock of the 1982 recession and out of the comfortable assumptions of the post–World War II social welfare concensus.

None of this kind of "new" social adjustment policy argument had crystallized during the period of the free trade debate, however, and for good reasons. First, it was not, and is not, an argument that can easily be conveyed in modern media-compressed debates. Second, many groups simply did not trust the messenger. The Macdonald Commission was seen as the free trade, pro-market commission, but its quite radical and interventionist social adjustment policy proposals were partly ignored and partly mistrusted because of the content of its free trade sections. Third, and most important, there were few takers for the social policy half of the free trade equation because the Mulroney government's social policy agenda was both erratic and deeply mistrusted by anti–free trade forces.[18]

Tory Social Adjustment Policy: Adopting the Macdonald Agenda by Stealth?

There is little doubt that the heated social policy concerns that arose during the free trade debate from 1986 to 1988 were as much the product of criticism of the larger evolving set of Mulroney social policy decisions as they were of the Canada-U.S. Free Trade Agreement (FTA). Three elements of Conservative policy deserve attention in this regard—the universality debate, unemployment insurance and training, and adjustment policy related to free trade—all of them overshadowed by the looming presence of the huge federal deficit. The deficit in turn raises issues about whether it itself is influencing choices or whether right-wing ideologues are using it to pursue an anti–social policy agenda. The deficit, according to the latter argument, becomes a stalking horse for an agenda of social policy retrenchment that would not be supported by Canadians if these policies were presented on their own merits. At the same time, the possibility exists that the Mulroney Tories, if they succeed in coming to terms with the deficit, may well be adopting by stealth the essential features of the Macdonald Commission social agenda.

With respect to the universality principle of Canadian social policy, the Mulroney government's decisions indicate practised ambivalence. The principle of universality—that social policy benefits in programs such as family allowances and old age security are a matter of a right of citizenship, regardless of income—has been central to the social policy community. When the Conservatives attempted to limit the indexation of old age pension benefits in 1985 and were forced to backtrack, they earned the animosity of both the social policy community, which saw universality as being under attack, and the business community, which argued that social programs need not go to upper-income Canadians and that social spending should be restrained to solve the deficit problem. Similar reactions occurred in the social policy community when the Conservatives included a tax "clawback" of family allowance benefits and old age security payments in the 1989 budget speech. The technical formula used meant that a 100 percent taxback would occur above a certain income level. The social policy community immediately argued that this was the death of universality because the recipients of such programs would no longer end up with some meaningful benefit as a matter of entitlement.[19]

On the other hand, in both phases of the Conservatives' tax reform initiatives the Mulroney government greatly expanded the use of social tax credits, first through an enriched child tax credit and later through a sales tax credit. Several social policy commentators have argued that this sets the scene for the eventual full-scale adoption of a guaranteed annual income concept universally available to all Canadians in principle, but taxed back progressively. Technically speaking, such a program would be paid to recipients during the year and hence would be received by them but then taxed back, up to 100 percent, once their annual income is known and income taxes are paid. This could still be regarded as a universal program. Thus, different component parts of Tory decisions point in different directions along the universality criteria.

In the general realm of unemployment insurance and training, the Tory record seems sympathetic to the Macdonald Commission ideas in theory, but not fully in practice. Thus, first through the Forget Commission on unemployment insurance and later in 1988 through restrictions on unemployment insurance benefits, the Mulroney Tories have sought to move unemployment insurance toward a purer insurance system. They have also sought to link unemployment insurance benefits to compulsory training programs. The corollary to this, a Macdonald-styled human capital adjustment fund with *increased* resources devoted to it, has not materialized. Conservative spending on training has, in fact, been reduced in real dollar terms since the mid-1980s. Undoubtedly much of this failure to commit resources is caused by the deficit, but certainly not all of it. The reluctance is also caused by forces in the Tory caucus and in business and bureaucratic circles who oppose putting more money into public sector training institutions when evaluations have increasingly shown that public sector delivery of such skills has been dubious in many areas and contrary to the way such skills are delivered in virtually all other Western countries.[20]

Accordingly, in several areas, the Mulroney government pursued a market-oriented approach to labour market issues. Its Canadian Jobs Strategy announced in 1985 gave a market emphasis to what Prince and Rice have called "supply-side social policy."[21] Suspicious of any direct job creation programs, the modest 1985 program ensured that the limited funds in place would be allocated to reflect new Conservative principles. They would be "decentralized in decision making, more privatized in delivery, and retrenched in program funding."[22]

Similarly, its main training initiative, the 1989 Labour Force Development Strategy, sought to go part way toward the Macdonald Commission concept.[23] It did want to help workers adjust, and hence it took unemployment insurance funds and linked them to training. The training would be efficiency oriented in that it would focus on skill shortages and upgrading rather than on the employment disadvantaged. Unlike the Macdonald plan, however, it involved no net new resources, so the level of human resource investment was simply inadequate. Moreover, as Mahon points out, the program is likely to "exacerbate the already visible polarization of the economy into good and bad jobs."[24]

The link between these aspects of evolving Tory decisions and the issue of specific FTA-related adjustment support is on the one hand direct, but on the other complicated by practical realities. During the free trade battle from 1986 to 1988, there was consistent pressure by the Liberals and the NDP on the government to announce an adjustment support program for those adversely affected by the FTA. At one point, Prime Minister Mulroney promised such a program only to be contradicted the next day by Finance Minister Michael Wilson, who indicated that existing programs were adequate for this task. This confusion, along with other pressures, led to the establishment of the Advisory Council on Adjustment headed by Jean de Grandpré, the chairman of Bell Canada Enterprises.

The de Grandpré Report was tabled after the 1988 election and basically rejected the notion of any specific FTA-related adjustment program.[25] The report stressed that "a fundamental obstacle in this regard is the problem of distinguishing between the effects of the FTA and those of the larger global economy."[26] This position was essentially correct on practical grounds and would have led to unfairness in how some persons were treated depending on the source or cause of their economic dislocation. Instead, the report focused on ways to "promote the swift reintegration into the work force of all workers displaced by economic change of any kind."[27] It sought to portray its understanding of the links between social policy and adjustment by referring to a "trampoline" instead of the conventional imagery of the social policy "safety net."

The trampoline metaphor, while accurate in some respects, was hardly a reassuring or humane-sounding image. It evoked a social-athletic capacity and a degree of body and soul control by displaced workers that was as threatening to them as the larger free trade initiative. On the other hand, who could possibly be against "adjusting" to make the economy better? The very word exudes a confidence in the virtues of orderly change. One does not have to pick winners as in the discredited industrial policy route. Rather, one can go with the flow of the market, with governments gently nudging Canadians along with appropriate packages of carrots and sticks.

At one level, it is possible to understand the vital need for this conceptual approach and how it may be superior to the hodgepodge of things done in the name of industrial policy and multiprogram "safety net" social policy. It suggests, initially at least, a more generic "hands off" role for government regarding business and capital (no industrial policy, no subsidies), but considerable interventionism and social investment regarding labour and threatened communities. But all of these aspects of the possible new world of social adjustment policy imply a generosity in the investment in human capital and a reform of many institutions and practices for it to be believable in the eyes of its alleged beneficiaries. It is here that the enormous federal deficit raises its ugly head. There are simply not sufficient funds in the short to medium term to give real meaning to the underlying notion of social adjustment. Clearly, there are some elements of the Mulroney government and caucus that would like to give more complete meaning to the promise of the social adjustment concept, but equally there are strong elements of the "new right" who see the deficit as a way to put into practice a far less generous concept of modern social policy.

Even the above brief discussion of the social adjustment concept and of the Tory message and messenger does not do justice to the full social policy agenda of the Mulroney era. Issues such as regional policy, day care, gender policies, and the possible privatization of some social services also influenced the social and labour market agenda.[28] Moreover, in 1990, the Conservatives announced an elaborate environmental Green Plan. Centred in the concept of "sustainable development" and backed by a $3-billion fund, the initiative, together with the undoubted public pressures to increase social regulation, has the potential to redefine by the late 1990s all economic and social policy in quite radical ways.[29]

Structure in the Trudeau Years

Several departments and agencies have traditionally constituted the main structures of social and labour market policy. These include National Health and Welfare, Employment and Immigration, Labour, Justice, the Solicitor General, Correctional Services, the Secretary of State, the Canadian Broadcasting Corporation, the RCMP, and Indian Affairs and Northern Development.

In the 1980 to 1984 period, the organizational focal point for social policy was the Cabinet Committee on Social Development and its agency, the Ministry of State for Social Development (MSSD).[30] The dynamics of this organization varied according to changes in both people and circumstances. The first Minister of Social Development, Jean Chrétien, was concurrently Minister of Justice. During much of his tenure he was preoccupied with constitutional negotiations. These led to the entrenched Charter of Rights, arguably the most significant social policy initiative of the early 1980s, but forged with virtually no involvement by MSSD or the Cabinet committee. The first deputy in MSSD was Bruce Rawson, a former deputy minister of Health and Welfare, whose interests were primarily in the income maintenance field. He knew little of other social policy domains then lumped in the envelope. Their successors were Senator Jack Austin as minister and Gordon Smith as deputy, the former an unelected politician with previous experience as the prime minister's principal secretary and the latter a longtime central agency PCO official. As with the Lalonde social security review referred to earlier, developments here showed the increased influence of the central agencies in social policy formulation. This was undoubtedly a reflection of the evolving cost-consciousness and fiscal restraint in the late

1970s and early 1980s, as social policy expenditures were projected to decline relative to other fields.

In earlier periods the focus of coordination for social programs did not reside in the central agencies to the same degree. The Department of National Health and Welfare was the focal point of social policy defined in social welfare and social service terms. The Department of Finance has always had a strong say in such matters, especially when the statutory fiscal arrangements were scheduled for renegotiation. In the mid-1960s, in the Pearson era, a special planning secretariat in the PCO also sought, without much success, to impose some kind of order on Canada's then styled "war on poverty." Prior to the envelope system, a Cabinet committee on social programs existed, but it suffered from the same problems as did all the committees then, namely the separation of policy approval from resource approval.

By the end of the 1970s, the structures of labour market policy were decidedly complex and unwieldy. Early attempts to devise a more integrative approach between "manpower" and "employment" concepts were reflected in the establishment of the Department of Manpower and Immigration in the mid-1960s. This was restructured as the Department of Employment and Immigration a decade later.[31] The restructuring also involved a more catholic name for the old Unemployment Insurance Commission, which became the Canada Employment and Immigration Commission and retained its tripartite business, labour, and government representation on the commission. The Department of Labour continued to operate, but it was joined in the overall labour market policy structures by the Treasury Board, with its major collective bargaining role, and by temporary bodies such as the Prices and Incomes Commission, and later the Anti-Inflation Board.

It is essential to stress that the Department of Labour could have been strengthened in influence and power had it been given the original "manpower" mandate forged in 1966. But structurally the Labour department was left to preside over its traditional referee-like role in the labour–management relations process. In part, this was done to weaken the focal point for labour representation, but it also reflected a divergence of professional views between traditional labour relations specialists, who were often lawyers, and the then newer breed of labour economists. To a considerable extent this difference of views exists to this day, not only in government, but in university education as well.

Somewhat less conspicuous in an Ottawa setting, but of major structural import in the broad scheme of things, were the burgeoning white-collar education bureaucracies at both the university and community college levels and the often beleaguered Canada Manpower offices located in the regions. By the end of the 1970s, the former had acquired an enormous vested interest in "labour market" funds and had enjoyed years of generally heady expansion. The two sectors respectively continued to personify differences in the "education" versus "training" dichotomy. For Canada Manpower offices, problems were clearly traceable to the earliest days of the debate about the efficacy of the then existing placement offices.[32] In theory, these offices were to be the linchpin between the demand and supply sides of the labour market. In practice, however, they show how "implementation," as a marriage of private and public behaviour, affects policy development. The net effect of the virtual parade of new labour market initiatives in the 1960s and 1970s was to convert regional and local employment offices into veritable supermarkets of labour market services. They became loaded with such a panoply of tasks, from information services to placement counselling to direct job-creation grants, that they could scarcely cope in the face of "yet another" initiative from Ottawa.

The above array of concerns about public policy and decision-making structures, and thus about the organization of power, resulted in a larger debate about structural reform, especially in the last half of the 1970s. In the midst of the wage and price controls debate about tripartism and corporatism, the Canadian Labour Congress advocated the establishment of a powerful tripartite "labour market board" that would have a full range of decision-making, investment, and regulatory powers over the policy levers that impact on labour markets. The government rejected this idea of shared power by arguing it would violate the idea of responsible cabinet-parliamentary government and ministerial accountability. When the Liberals returned to office in 1980, the Minister of Employment and Immigration, Lloyd Axworthy, considered briefly the idea of broadening the representative basis of the Employment and Immigration Commission, possibly to incorporate representation from women's groups and small business. In the final analysis, no restructuring occurred. This was partly due to the fact that Axworthy was being asked to consider another structural reform package as well. This one emerged as a rare joint proposal from the Canadian Labour Congress and the Business Council on National Issues (BCNI). The BCNI-CLC proposal was for a new labour market institute. It would be incorporated and given a bipartite business–labour board, but would be funded primarily by federal and provincial governments.[33] Its purpose would be a limited one focused on improving labour market supply-demand information. The BCNI-CLC proposal was thus premised on two issues of policy and decision-making structure: the need to foster and actually experience greater business–labour trust and cooperation through a practial joint endeavour, and the need to overcome the perceived weakness of bureaucratic approaches to providing labour market information. On the latter point, the two organizations believed that through their first-hand knowledge of member companies and union locals, and with an appropriate committee structure, they could do a better job than the governmental bureaucracies in providing the critical advance knowledge and intelligence about demand and supply.

Structure in the Mulroney Era

The structures of social and labour market policy changed in four major ways in the Mulroney era, some of them intended and others unintended. These changes are: the emergence of the Department of Finance as the main de facto social policy-maker, pushing the Department of Health and Welfare further into the background; the role of inherent federal–provincial agency and program structures as a break on even further social expenditure cuts; the concerted effort to devise business–labour structures to make and deliver labour market policy; and the growing role of the courts, Charter-based rights groups, and free trade–related and mass-based social policy coalitions.

While the Department of Finance has always had an important role in social policy, if for no other reason than that social expenditures are the largest single element of the budget, its role grew markedly in the Mulroney period. It was Finance, through its tax reform and expenditure control measures, that most changed social policy in the 1980s. Tax changes brought the greater use of tax credits, which in general are redistributive. But reform also brought the lifetime capital gains initiative, numerous increases in sin taxes, and the Goods and Services Tax (GST). Meanwhile, the traditional lead agency, Health and Welfare, was left with the much smaller, even symbolic social initiatives such as support for AIDS research, help for hemophiliacs, and other low-budget gestures of concern.

While most commentators agree that redistribution was not enhanced, indeed was worsened, in the 1980s, the effects of efforts to cut spending were in fact blunted by the inherent density and staying power of the underlying structure of federal, provincial, and joint programs.[34] In other words, the same complex bureaucracy that is properly the despair of those who see the inefficiencies and welfare traps of the social welfare system was a significant defence when it came to keeping down the level of aggregate cuts. It is important to remember in this regard that the structure of programs and hence of bureaucracies in the social policy field is quite different than in industrial policy. Industrial policy consists of numerous small grant-based programs that can be more readily changed on an annual basis.

Social and labour market spending, in contrast, consists to a far greater extent of a small number of very large transfer programs, both to individuals and to provinces.[35] Thus, large demogrant programs (e.g., family allowance and old age security), insurance programs, social assistance programs, and income supplementation programs quickly affect vast numbers of people and large organizations. Moreover, they are interdependent programs. Changes in one can automatically imply changes in others. Though it is clear that the Mulroney government wanted to make further changes and cuts, it was prevented from doing so by the inherent density of the program structure itself.

In labour market policy per se, the most significant development of the Mulroney period was the effort to devise new business–labour structures both for policy and delivery. The previously mentioned BCNI-CLC initiative for a labour market institute did reach fruition in the establishment of the Canadian Labour Market Productivity Centre (CLMPC). As Mahon points out, for several years the centre "languished in benign neglect,"[36] mainly because poor economic conditions sapped business interest in any further experimentation. However, by the latter half of the 1980s, some of the same fear of international competitive exclusion that led to the free trade initiative began to have its effects on business and labour in labour market issues. Moreover, the provinces were increasingly looking for new approaches. Accordingly, in 1989 the Mulroney government, through the CLMPC, organized seven task forces whose very titles evoked the complex kinds of structures and relationships inherent in labour markets. Task forces worked on issues of human resource planning, unemployment insurance recipients, apprenticeship, entry-level training, social assistance benefits, older workers, and cooperative education.[37]

While progress was made in some areas, there remained sharp divisions between business and labour regarding delivery, financing, and regulatory mechanisms. For example, business interests opposed the notion of a training tax, opting instead for a voluntary approach.[38] Both business and labour favoured bipartite delivery mechanisms, but the business preference was that this too had to be on a voluntary basis. For its part, labour favoured more compulsory measures and mechanisms and the use of public institutions, especially since its concerns extended more readily to issues of labour market equity and other social goals. While structurally the new labour market era was to be more bipartite in nature, the key government agencies were no mere bystanders. They still would determine how much money would go into programs and whether tax measures for training would be adopted at all.

If the labour market initiatives were supposed to advance in an intended way the cause of structural decentralization, then the last of the structural changes of the Mulroney era can be considered to be a form of unintended or uncontrollable decentralization. This centred on the continued unfolding of the Charter of Rights and the role it gave to the courts and to litigants heretofore shut out of the social policy process. In the 1990s, there are hundreds of Charter cases wending their way through the courts. As Courchene suggests, there are three areas where the courts and citizens are likely to influence social policy: in age requirements, the definition of family status, and the definition of income.[39] The equality provision of the Charter (section 15) and the prohibition of age discrimination have, in Courchene's view, "the potential for undermining the entire social policy framework."[40] There is particular fiscal danger if the courts, as in the *Schacter* case, resolve discrimination by "levelling up" to the most generous existing provisions. Under these situations the budgetary costs in large programs such as unemployment insurance could be enormous.

Much depends on the pattern of final cases that receive Supreme Court judgment and on the activeness of judicial decision-making. It is clear, however, that the courts and Canadian litigants are already a part of the structure of social policy-making in ways that few would have predicted in the 1960s or 1970s. These effects are not confined to social spending. The social regulatory state is also influenced in areas such as abortion policy, policing practices, and environmental assessment processes.[41]

The emergence of rights-oriented litigation can also be linked to the larger emergence of a significantly more integrated political coalition of interest groups supportive of past and new social policy initiatives. This coalition seemed to be quite cohesive during the free trade debate, but its staying power in the 1990s is more problematic. During the battle over free trade, the Pro-Canada Network (PCN) was formed to serve as a counterweight to what it saw as the BCNI-led Mulroney agenda. Composed of social policy groups, women's groups, labour unions, and church and environmental groups, the PCN claimed to speak for over ten million Canadians.[42] It saw the free trade agreement as being a frontal assault on Canada's social policy in two senses. First, it claimed that some provisions of the agreement would threaten medicare. While this was a dubious claim, its larger attack won considerable sympathy among Canadians. This attack was based on the overall belief that gradually market-oriented views would undermine public support for the values that underpin the social welfare state.

It is unlikely that the PCN as a structure will be able to sustain its current form once the free trade battle becomes distanced in political memory. The PCN was strong in the free trade battle, in part because the Liberals and the NDP were evenly matched as opposition forces. If the Liberal Party can once again muster support, many of the component groups that formed the coalition will probably revert to their pre–free trade style of political operation. These prior positions ranged from labour's official support for the NDP to stances of partisan and electoral neutrality by many of the other groups. Nonetheless, there has probably been a new sense of solidarity and awareness permanently created by the free trade experience. Organized initially for defensive purposes in the late 1980s, these component groups may take a more aggressive form to help forge social policy as the 1990s evolve.

Process: The Primacy of Deficit Control Dynamics

There is little doubt that the dominant feature of social and labour market policy processes has been the dynamics of the deficit control process. In other words, for most of the 1980s and early 1990s, there has been no approach to social policy that began as an explicit democratically open approach that set out to reform social and labour market policy to meet the needs of the rest of the century. Instead, social policy as a whole has been the resultant outcome of related processes, most of which were, directly or indirectly, deficit related.

Thus, as previously stated, tax reform, carried out for other reasons, led to social policy change. The annual dynamics of the spending process, in which there was a constant need to find more program expenditures to cut, meant that social programs had to be hit since they were the largest single expenditure component. Labour market spending was also constantly affected in this way. Thus, even though new directions were promised for labour market policy, including bipartite processes for delivery, the shortfall of money always served to question the seriousness of the Mulroney government's good labour market intentions.

A normally unseen part of the budgetary process also influenced the nature of social and labour market outcomes. This part deals with the fact that public sector accounting conventions do not, as do private sector practices, distinguish between capital and operating expenditures. Thus, expenditures and tax measures that might in fact be best treated as genuine investments are treated the same way as, say, spending on paper clips.[43] Not all aspects of labour market and educational spending are investment oriented, but a significant part is. To the extent that there is no recognition of the difference, there is a serious distortion of the content and outcomes of social policy.

How has the regulatory process changed, or been affected by, social and labour market policies? The answers here are not as clear as for social policy expressed through spending and taxation. The first element to emphasize is the international trade regulatory process. Paradoxically, in one sense free trade may strengthen the case for social and adjustment policies. In the debate about subsidies and what constitutes a subsidy, the pattern of developments suggests that eventually international rules will confirm that generally available programs will not be subject to countervail actions, while those that are targeted and firm-specific will be countervailable.

A second element of the regulatory process concerns the regular internal Cabinet processes for assessing regulatory decisions. As shown in Chapter 12, changes made in the Mulroney era now apply to all kinds of regulations. Previously, there was a bias in the earlier assessment process against social regulation because, until the mid-1980s, only social regulatory statutes were subject to central vetting. Now, at least nominally, the system treats all proposed regulations on an equal footing. In short, the bias of the system is no longer, as it arguably once was, to slow down the pace of social regulation only. This can be considered only a nominal improvement at this point since the proof depends upon how actual assessments occur, and this is a process not yet well researched.

The third element of the regulatory process, begun late in the Mulroney second term and hence more difficult to gauge, is the new requirement that all federal policies and projects be subject to environmental assessment.[44] This is social regulation writ large and has the potential to be a radical change. In the past, only projects were subject to environmental assessment, but under the aegis of growing political support for the concept of sustainable development, the Mulroney Conservatives committed themselves, on a nonstatutory basis, to a process by which every Cabinet policy and decision would undergo a prior environmental assessment.

All of the above regulatory changes are more problematic than the ongoing processes of deficit reduction. However, looming even larger as a part of both the process and content of social policy is the inherent nature of underlying changes in the demographics of the Canadian population.[45] The aging of the population, the changing patterns of family formation, the probable shrinking of the middle class, and changes in the ethnic composition of Canada are but a few of the changes that will ensure that the social and labour market policies and processes of the 1990s will not be like those of the 1960s or of the overall post–World War II heyday of the social welfare state.

Conclusions

Social and labour market policies have always been connected in the real world, but only recently have they been seriously linked in Canadian public policy debate. Much of this linkage has come in the form of discussion about adjustment policy, which sees social and labour market policy as a vital aspect of a competitive economy. Social and labour market policy does not involve a simple trade-off between efficiency and equality. The ideas of social policy are more elaborate and complex, embracing notions of universality, citizenship, stability, equity, and regional disparities. Though some argue that a crisis of social policy has characterized the Mulroney years, the evidence suggests a more complex picture. A "new right" ideology has been articulated, and social redistribution has been arrested. However, the Canadian version has been much milder than its Reaganite or Thatcherite counterparts. Some of the edge of social policy retrenchment has been blunted by the structure of social policy, in short, by the inherent programmatic and federal–provincial density of the Canadian welfare state. Moreover, the very nature of social policy agendas has been changed because of the Charter of Rights and the formation of a more rights-oriented populace.

Notes

1. See Michael Hill and Glen Bramley, *Analysing Social Policy* (London: Blackwell, 1986), and Hugh Heclo, "Toward a New Welfare State," in Peter Flora and H. J. Heidenheimer, eds., *The Development of Welfare States in Europe and America* (London: Transaction Books, 1984), 383–406.
2. See Richard W. Phidd and G. Bruce Doern, *The Politics and Management of Canadian Economic Policy* (Toronto: Macmillan, 1978), ch. 10.
3. See Michael Trebilcock, M. A. Chandler, and Robert Howse, *Trade and Transition: A Comparative Analysis of Adjustment Policies* (London: Routledge, 1990).

4. See Harold Wilensky and Charles Lebeaux, *Industrial Society and Social Welfare* (New York: Free Press, 1968), 138.
5. See Thomas J. Courchene, *Social Policy in the 1990s: Agenda for Reform* (Toronto: C. D. Howe Institute, 1987).
6. See Harvey Lithwick, "Regional Policy: The Embodiment of Contradictions," in G. Bruce Doern, ed., *How Ottawa Spends Your Tax Dollars 1982* (Toronto: James Lorimer, 1982), 135.
7. See Keith Banting, "Universality and the Development of the Welfare State," in Alan Green and Nancy Olewiler, eds., *Report of the Forum on Universality and Social Policies in the 1990s* (Kingston: Queen's University Press, 1985).
8. See Reuben Hasson, "The Cruel War: Social Security Abuse in Canada," *Canadian Taxation* 3, no. 3 (Fall 1981), 114–47.
9. See Betty Muggah, "A New Perspective: The Making of a New Paradigm for Health Policy," *Macdonald Essays* (Ottawa: School of Public Administration, Carleton University, 1982).
10. See Michael Mandel, *The Charter of Rights and the Legalization of Politics in Canada* (Toronto: Thompson, 1991).
11. See Richard Van Loon, "Reforming Welfare in Canada," *Public Policy* 27, no. 4 (Fall 1979), 469–504.
12. See Dennis Guest, *The Emergence of Social Security in Canada* (Vancouver: University of British Columbia Press, 1980), and Leslie A. Pal, "Revision and Retreat: Canadian Unemployment Insurance, 1971–1981," in J. S. Ismael, ed., *Canadian Social Welfare Policy: Federal and Provincial Dimensions* (Kingston: Queen's University Press, 1985), 75–104.
13. See Canada, Royal Commission on the Economic Union and Development Prospects for Canada, *Final Report*, vol. II (Ottawa: Minister of Supply and Services, 1985).
14. Ibid., 541.
15. Ibid., 542.
16. Ibid., 541.
17. Ibid., ch. 14.
18. See James J. Rice, "Restitching the Safety Net: Altering the National Social Security System," in Michael J. Prince, ed., *How Ottawa Spends 1986–87* (Toronto: Methuen, 1986), 211–36.
19. See National Council of Welfare, *The 1989 Budget and Social Policy* (Ottawa: Minister of Supply and Services, 1989), 2–3.
20. See Economic Council of Canada, *Good Jobs, Bad Jobs: Employment in the Service Economy* (Ottawa: Minister of Supply and Services, 1990).
21. See Michael J. Prince and James J. Rice, "The Canadian Job Strategy: Supply Side Social Policy," in Katherine Graham, ed., *How Ottawa Spends 1989–90* (Ottawa: Carleton University Press, 1989), 247–88.
22. Ibid., 273.
23. See Rianne Mahon, "Adjusting to Win? The New Training Initiative," in Katherine Graham, ed., *How Ottawa Spends 1990–91* (Ottawa: Carleton University Press, 1990), 73–112.

24. Ibid., 75.
25. Advisory Council on Adjustment, *Adjusting To Win: Report of the Advisory Council on Adjustment* (Ottawa: Supply and Services, 1989).
26. Ibid., xvii.
27. Ibid., xvii.
28. See Susan D. Phillips, "Rock-a-Bye Brian: The National Strategy on Child Care," in Graham, ed., *How Ottawa Spends 1989–90*, 165–208.
29. See G. Bruce Doern, "Shades of Green: Gauging Canada's Green Plan" (C. D. Howe Institute, Commentary, Toronto, 1991).
30. See G. Bruce Doern, Allan Maslove, and Michael Prince, *Budgeting in Canada* (Ottawa: Carleton University Press, 1988), ch. 8.
31. Phidd and Doern, *The Politics and Management of Canadian Economic Policy*, ch. 10.
32. See Employment and Immigration Canada, *Labour Market Development in the 1980s* (Ottawa: Minister of Supply and Services, 1981).
33. See "A Proposal by the Business Council on National Issues and the Canadian Labour Congress for the Establishment of a National Manpower Board," Ottawa, January 17, 1980.
34. See Keith Banting, *The Welfare State and Canadian Federalism*, 2nd ed. (Montreal: McGill-Queen's University Press, 1987).
35. Doern, Maslove, and Prince, *Budgeting in Canada*, ch. 11.
36. Mahon, "Adjusting to Win?" in Graham, ed., *How Ottawa Spends 1990–91*, 89.
37. Ibid., 97–100.
38. Ibid., 90–93.
39. Thomas Courchene, "Toward the Reintegration of Social and Economic Policy," in G. Bruce Doern and Bryne Purchase, eds., *Canada at Risk: Canadian Public Policy in the 1990s* (Toronto: C. D. Howe Institute, 1990), 139–42.
40. Ibid., 139.
41. See Leslie A. Pal, "How Ottawa Dithers: The Conservatives and Abortion Policy," in Frances Abele, ed., *How Ottawa Spends 1991–92* (Ottawa: Carleton University Press, 1991), 269–306.
42. See G. Bruce Doern and Brian W. Tomlin, *Faith and Fear: The Free Trade Story* (Toronto: Stoddart, 1991), chs. 9 and 10.
43. See Douglas Auld, *Budget Reform: Should There Be a Capital Budget for the Public Sector?* (Toronto: C. D. Howe Institute, 1985).
44. See G. Bruce Doern, "Canadian Environmental Policy: Why Process is Almost Everything" (C. D. Howe Institute, Commentary, 1990).
45. See David K. Foot, "Demographics: The Human Landscape of Public Policy," in Doern and Purchase, eds., *Canada at Risk*, 25–45.

CHAPTER 17

Conclusions:
Toward 2000

Using an approach that explores the interplay among the ideas, structures, and processes of Canadian public policy, we have looked at policy dynamics in four settings. First, we examined the context in which policy is studied and practised. This involved a brief look at contending approaches used in the study and practice of policy formation. It also involved an appreciation of the basic features of the Canadian political economy and of the key institutions of the Canadian political system. Second, we examined what the basic elements of the framework used in this book—ideas, structure, and process—involve. This approach to understanding public policy required that each component be examined in some detail. Thus, in the realm of ideas, it is essential to probe for the wide array of ideas at different levels, from ideologies and dominant ideas to paradigms and specific goals and objectives. Public policy is a purposeful activity, and hence to ignore ideas is to ignore a large part of policy reality.

In a similar vein, the role of structure must be understood to include not only the main organizations of the state, interest groups, and policy communities, but also the complex and important array of statutes and programs. Similarly, the process of policy formulation, the regular rhythms and cycles of policy- and decision-making activity, must be seen in terms of the overall priority-setting and Cabinet approval process, but also in terms of processes driven by the competing requisites of the main instruments of governing. Thus, we have shown the functioning of the tax, expenditure, and regulatory processes as dynamics with lives of their own.

These first two tasks were essential preparation for understanding the remaining two parts of the book. By examining in greater detail the dynamics of resource allocation in Part III and how three overarching policy fields have evolved in Part IV, it is possible to see policy formation as it is. The analysis as a whole shows the continuous need to appreciate that there is indeed a central and regular rhythm to the policy process and that, to this extent, the ship of state is steered and guided according to some broad, democratic impulse. But policymaking also involves numerous interrelated structures and subprocesses whose decisions are driven by the pressure of interests, the characteristics of different policy instruments, and the continuous clash over ideas and priorities. In this sense, the image of a small boat tossed in an unwelcoming sea may be the more appropriate metaphor.

The analysis of resource allocation and of the three key policy fields also suggests the importance of six major issues that deserve concluding attention. As Canadians move toward the year 2000 and the beginning of a new century, they must deal with and understand: the gradual realignment rather than reduction in the role of the state; the federal deficit as the main immobilizer of Ottawa; the need to reform executive government; the growing role of international influences on domestic policy formation; the changed relationship between social and economic ideas and policy writ large; and the need to narrow the gap between policy rhetoric and reality.

The Role of the State: Reduction versus Realignment

At one level, what happened to the policy process and to politics in the 1980s seems clear. There was a reduction in the role of the state, and the evidence for it came in the form of policies such as free trade, privatization, and deregulation. But beneath this overlay of reduction and restraint were a series of other actions. On balance, these actions suggest that what really took place was more a realignment of the role of the state. Thus, environmental policy demands imply significant new roles for government, as do adjustment interventions, and perhaps new narrowly defined but vitally important forms of firm-specific industrial policy. Such a realignment is not occurring clearly or simply. Complex societies almost never learn uniformly how their institutions change and evolve over time. Moreover, as we have seen, the policy process is not just a single undifferentiated process. There are many arenas in which to secure policies whose net effects, intended and unintended, must be determined empirically rather than rhetorically.

The realignment thesis does not mean that things remain static. The rate of growth of public spending was arrested in the 1980s. Social programs were squeezed. The subsidization of industry was constrained. Bureaucracies and public service salaries were pinched. Public attitudes about government and politicians became decidedly less complimentary and supportive. In many cases, the restraining of the state flowed from genuine problems and proper criticism. In numerous other instances, the pattern of criticism led to self-fulfilling prophecies. Thus, the more one said that government was weak or incompetent, the more that the proper role of government was weakened. But with all this, the net size of the state did not contract. Taxes increased, new regulations took hold, and a Charter of Rights enabled individuals to use the state to advance their rights.

The Mulroney Conservatives can be said to have had a good idea of what kind of government they did not want, but not the kind of state they did want. This was best illustrated in the free trade and Meech Lake episodes. Both policies were intended to reduce the role of the federal government, the former in favour of markets and the latter in favour of the provinces. But there is little evidence that the two initiatives were ever considered jointly in terms of what their effects would be on the kinds of governmental powers and capacity needed for the year 2000 and beyond. In part, this was because the two initiatives followed different policy tracks, but it is also simply the case that big policy initiatives such as these are always partly acts of faith. For example, it could equally be said that the Trudeau Liberals did not consider what the integrated effects of a Charter of Rights would be on the future governing capacities of the federal government.

If a realignment of the role of the state has occurred, will it move in the 1990s to a point where it can be seen to be guided by a more consistent set of ideas, even a public philosophy? The concept of a social market is a current issue in Western European political debate. Intended to capture the new marriage between a market economy and supportive social policy, the social market approach is indicative of a new direction, but hardly one that is clear to everyone. Moreover, the North American political culture has always been somewhat more suspicious of such labels. Nonetheless, some of the contours of the new realignment are emerging. On the economic front, they suggest that the proper role of government is broadly to keep to basic framework-oriented policy and to eschew intervening in particular industrial sectors. On the social front, they suggest that government's role will be vital in general redistribution, in adjustment investment, and in environmental framework laws. They also suggest that the federal government will have to be more engaged in ensuring that sufficient domestic concensus occurs to negotiate Canada's place and prosperity in the new institutions of the international political economy. This, in turn, is dependent upon the next two issues to be discussed.

The Deficit and the Immobilization of Ottawa

Our account of the Mulroney era, of the dynamics of resource allocation, and of the relationships between the taxing and spending processes shows that the huge federal deficit has been a key reason for the immobilization of Ottawa and for the difficulties any federal government will face in the 1990s. As a neoconservative regime, with its political base in Quebec and the West, the Mulroney Conservatives certainly sought to reduce the role of Ottawa and of government in Canadian affairs. To do this, the Mulroney Cabinet acted decisively on big issues such as free trade, the Meech Lake Accord, and tax reform. It also acted quite significantly on several areas of privatization and deregulation. On the deficit, however, it basically played a containment game.

Despite some success in reducing levels of program spending, the fact remains that the deficit is huge and cannot help but continue to immobilize Ottawa. By immobilization, we mean the reduction in the inherent leadership and governing capacity of the federal government. Any national government, even one committed to restraining the role of government, needs flexible resources to back new initiatives, including unforeseen ones, to meet the needs of the 1990s. These future national projects, from day care to adjustment programs, and from economic infrastructure investment to education, are already queuing up.

In such a situation the imperatives of the deficit could cut both ways. On the one hand, it could mean that there are so few resources that future federal governments will resort to symbolic spending and tax decisions only. That is, they will be forced to spend little symbolic dribbles on many small initiatives to keep interests at bay, but with no initiative capable of actually beginning to solve problems. Or, on the other hand, the severity of restraint may force debate to focus on a more serious effort to set realistic priorities and to debate both the costs and benefits of programs. It is clear, however, that on an overall basis Ottawa's inherent policy capacity in the 1990s is partially tied to whether or not the deficit can be politically and economically managed in a steady downward direction. Without this, there will be little room for real manoeuvre by the federal government.

Executive Government versus Mobilized Policy Communities

If such realignments of the role of the state and of a re-energized Ottawa are to contribute to a revitalized respect for the policy process, then there is little doubt that the structures of policy formation will have to change and be made more effective and legitimate in the eyes of Canadians. At the centre of this structural relationship is the place of the Cabinet itself and that of the increasingly complex network of interests and policy communities. Almost by definition, then, the roles of Canada's political parties and Parliament are also at issue. The more that international imperatives press on Canada's policy process, the more it will be critical for Canada's representative political structures to be in better working order.

It is increasingly clear that a federal Cabinet of forty ministers, although understandable in the context of regional representation, is simply too unwieldy in terms of giving ministers the time and wherewithal to discuss and devise policy in a careful and considered way. However, if a much smaller Cabinet and more cohesive executive is to be put in place in the name of more considered executive decision-making, then it follows that the arenas of representation must be strengthened elsewhere. Inevitably this involves measures to strengthen Parliament, a regionally based elected Senate, and ways to build in even more consultation with relevant policy communities. It also requires the building of a new respect for Canada's political parties.

All of these latter concerns about access and legitimacy are important under any democratic circumstances, but they are even more crucial when one is faced with the international policy imperatives of the 1990s, including the positive opportunities that they will also offer. The world will not casually wait while Canada gets its policy ideas, structures, and processes in better working order.

The urgency of this situation is apparent in the Mulroney government's constitutional proposals of September 1991. Going well beyond the usual patchwork of change, the constitutional package envisions radical changes, including a distinct society provision for Quebec, an elected Senate, greater provincial powers, expanded federal control over the economic union, and a new Council of the Federation with intergovernmental coordinative powers. But even these kinds of change may prove ineffective unless they are accompanied by changes that greatly trim the size of the federal Cabinet, give it greater policy coherence, and force political parties to become more intelligent policy engines rather than just election machines.

The Growing Internationalization of Policy Formation

Canadian public policy has always been influenced by international and foreign policy imperatives, but there is little doubt that the internationalization of policy formation has reached a new and permanent importance. It means that few policies can be crafted or implemented without taking into account international factors and the direct role of multilateral and bilateral international institutions. While this development is symbolized most by the Canada–U.S. Free Trade Agreement, which greatly institutionalizes the Canada–U.S. bilateral relationship, it goes much further than this. It embraces, in fact, a host of developments and policy fields. These include the need to contemplate policy in terms of the world's apparent division into three overall trading blocs: the European Community, North America, and the Japan–Pacific Rim. These blocs may increasingly negotiate with each other as distinct entities on major economic and trade matters. Not all policy will be forged in this way, but key areas are likely to be.

A further impetus for the enhanced role of international factors is also likely to come from the reactions that set in during the 1990s to the pro-market deregulation and privatization of the 1980s. Just as a burst of international institution-building occurred in the immediate post–World War II era, so is there now pressure for a new generation of institution-building among states to deal with the excesses of international capitalism. These are already beginning to form in areas such as financial markets, the environment, and in minimum social policy charters affecting labour and employment.

There is little doubt, then, that the role of the nation-state will itself be further changed, with some policy tasks devolved to the provinces, others shared with international institutions, and still others reshaped to become the new national projects of the 1990s and beyond.

The Social Policy–Economic Policy Relationship

We have drawn particular attention to the role of ideas in public policy. At the centre of the available cluster of ideas, those concerned with efficiency and equality often deserve the most attention. Put simply, they are the surrogates for the evolving debate about economic versus social policy, or more broadly for the continuous need to remain economically competitive in international terms while at the same time building a sense of community and fairness in the division of the economic pie and in other changes that modern life offers.

Public policy developments in recent years could easily lead to the conclusion that social policy has been abandoned, or is in deep crisis. It could lead to a view that confirms the residualist notions of social policy referred to in Chapter 16. This view holds that social policy writ large is a residual outcome that flows from economic prosperity rather than contributing significantly to such prosperity. In the 1980s, this residualist view in some respects gained strength. First, there was a purely ideological attack against the social welfare state that reached its most strident form in the Thatcherite and Reagan eras and that was joined, in milder form, by the Mulroney Conservatives as well. This attack was strong and rooted in often extreme views of the importance of individual liberty. Moreover, it was advocated often despite what the evidence suggested about the benefits of the welfare state.

But there were other less ideological and far more valid criticisms of social policy and unthinking government intervention that also emerged. These were often more empirically based and showed the ways in which many persons were in fact entrapped by the welfare state. The debate over adjustment policy, which sought to marry social welfare measures with labour market policy, was a major part of this more thoughtful debate. It was not, and is not, a debate that can be easily communicated in television politics. Gradually, however, a new form of literacy about the social policy–economic policy relationship seems to be emerging. The 1990s already bear witness to the fact that social and labour market policies are less likely to be viewed as a mere residual. Instead, there is likely to be an increased salience to the view that such policies are a precondition or co-condition for economic prosperity.

Moreover, the notion of what the "socialness" of policy contains in the 1990s is likely to go beyond even the breadth of this emerging social welfare–labour market axis of activities. It will contain a mixture of notions ranging from diverse individual and group rights under the continuing influence of the Charter of Rights, but also concepts of environmental rights and sustainable development. In addition, as the population ages the difficult issues of intergenerational equity will grow in importance. So too will the issues of investing in basic public goods such as education and public works infrastructures, areas allowed to deteriorate in the 1980s.

Narrowing the Gap Between Policy Rhetoric and Reality

To some extent, rhetorical policy debate and symbolic discourse is always necessary in political life. The need arises first because broad coalitions of political opinion and action, from political parties to populist movements, need broad ideological expressions and shorthand codes to keep alliances together. Second, it arises because of the continuing democratic need to have and express hopes about a better future. It also arises in the context of televised politics where the exigencies of the one-minute news byte or the five-minute interview force the use of often perverse symbolic language to sum up what are usually complex issues.

Nonetheless, despite the need for basic symbolic discourse, there is a need to narrow the gap between policy rhetoric and reality so that change occurs to meet new challenges, but also so that such change is actually brought to fruition. For example, in the free trade debate, the symbolic discourse, centred on the idea of sovereignty, was several steps removed from underlying reality. This does not mean that concerns about sovereignty had no place in the debate, but rather that they were used too often as if the word was itself a substitute for debate about actual policy issues. There was too little focus on what might be referred to as "policy capacity." By policy capacity we mean an assemblage of characteristics. These characteristics include the actual possession of policy levers or instruments; the knowledge of how and when to use them in pursuit of goals; and the capacity to mobilize interests in support of policy ideas and action. By definition a debate on policy capacity would require a closer and more serious public discussion of both ends and means.

The social policy debate of the recent past also often exhibited this kind of gap between rhetoric and reality. Too many changes were couched in the symbolism of the universality principle, when in fact the social policy agenda was undergoing bewilderingly complex change that defied such labels. In any event, attributes of universality, through the evolution toward a guaranteed annual income, may have in fact been gaining strength just as the concept of universality was being buried by many social policy commentators.

Although the gap between rhetoric and reality must be reduced, there is no guarantee that this will occur in the 1990s. More solid and continuous public debate and information are always prerequisites, but there are also many pressures that may make the gap grow rather than lessen. In short, the need to understand and reform the ideas, structures, and processes of Canadian policy formation is a permanent democratic obligation.

Selected Bibliography

Advisory Council on Adjustment. *Adjusting To Win: Report of the Advisory Council on Adjustment*. Ottawa: Minister of Supply and Services, 1989.

Allison, Graham. *Essence of Decision*. Boston: Little, Brown, 1971.

Atkinson, Michael, and Marsha Chandler, eds. *The Politics of Canadian Public Policy*. Toronto: University of Toronto Press, 1983.

Atkinson, Michael, and William Coleman. *The State, Business and Industrial Change in Canada*. Toronto: University of Toronto Press, 1989.

Aucoin, Peter. "Organizational Change in the Machinery of Canadian Government: From Rational Management to Brokerage Politics." *Canadian Journal of Political Science* 19, no. 1 (1986), 3–27.

Aucoin, Peter, and Richard French. *Knowledge, Power and Public Policy*. Ottawa: Science Council of Canada, 1974.

Bakvis, Herman. "Regional Ministers, National Policy and the Administrative State in Canada." *Canadian Journal of Political Science* 21, no. 2 (1988), 539–67.

Banting, Keith. *The Welfare State and Canadian Federalism*, 2nd ed. Montreal: McGill-Queen's University Press, 1987.

Banting, Keith. "Universality and the Development of the Welfare State." In Alan Green and Nancy Olewiler, eds. *Report of the Forum on Universality and Social Policies in the 1990s*. Kingston: Queen's University Press, 1985.

Blais, André, ed. *Industrial Policy*. Toronto: University of Toronto Press, 1986.

Brander, James A. *Government Policy Towards Business*. Toronto: Butterworths, 1988.

Braybrooke, David, and Charles E. Lindblom. *A Strategy of Decision*. New York: Free Press, 1963.

Brooks, Stephen. *Public Policy in Canada: An Introduction*. Toronto: McCelland and Stewart, 1989.

Campbell, Colin. "Mulroney's Brokerage Politics: The Ultimate in Politicized Incompetence." In Andrew B. Gollner and Daniel Salee, eds. *Canada Under Mulroney*. Montreal: Véhicule Press, 1988, 309–34.

Canada. Royal Commission on the Economic Union and Development Prospects for Canada. *Final Report*. Volumes I, II, and III. Ottawa: Minister of Supply and Services, 1985.

Clarkson, Stephen. "The Canada–United States Trade Commission and the Institutional Basis of the FTA." In Duncan Cameron, ed. *The Free Trade Deal*. Toronto: James Lorimer, 1988, 26–43.

Clarkson, Stephen. *Canada and the Reagan Challenge*, 2nd ed. Toronto: James Lorimer, 1985.

Coleman, William. *Business and Politics*. Montreal: McGill-Queen's University Press, 1988.

Coleman, William, and Grace Skogstad, eds., *Policy Communities and Public Policy in Canada*. Toronto: Copp Clark Pitman, 1990.

Courchene, Thomas. "Toward the Reintegration of Social and Economic Policy." In G. Bruce Doern and Bryne Purchase, eds. *Canada at Risk: Canadian Public Policy in the 1990s*. Toronto: C. D. Howe Institute, 1990, 125–48.

Courchene, Thomas. "Global Financial Developments: Implications for Canada." In James McRae and M. Desbois, eds. *Traded and Non-Traded Services*. Halifax: Institute for Research on Public Policy, 1988, 243–54.

Courchene, Thomas. *Social Policy in the 1990s: Agenda for Reform*. Toronto: C. D. Howe Institute, 1987.

Doern, G. Bruce. "Tax Expenditures and Tory Times: More or Less Policy Discretion?" In Katherine Graham, ed. *How Ottawa Spends 1989–90*. Ottawa: Carleton University Press, 1989, 75–106.

Doern, G. Bruce, ed. *The Regulatory Process in Canada*. Toronto: Macmillan, 1978.

Doern, G. Bruce, and Peter Aucoin, eds. *Public Policy in Canada*. Toronto: Macmillan, 1979.

Doern, G. Bruce, Allan Maslove, and Michael Prince. *Budgeting in Canada*. Ottawa: Carleton University Press, 1988.

Doern, G. Bruce, and Bryne Purchase, eds. *Canada at Risk: Canadian Public Policy in the 1990s*. Toronto: C. D. Howe Institute, 1990.

Doern, G. Bruce, and Brian W. Tomlin. *Faith and Fear: The Free Trade Story*. Toronto: Stoddart, 1991.

Doern, G. Bruce, and V. Seymour Wilson, eds. *Issues in Canadian Public Policy*. Toronto: Macmillan, 1974.

Doerr, Audrey. *The Machinery of Government in Canada*. Toronto: Methuen, 1981.

Dunleavy, Patrick. *Democracy, Bureaucracy and Public Choice*. London: Harvester Wheatsheaf, 1991.

Economic Council of Canada. *Responsible Regulation*. Ottawa: Minister of Supply and Services, 1979.

Foot, David. "Demographics: The Human Landscape of Public Policy." In G. Bruce Doern and Bryne Purchase, eds. *Canada at Risk: Canadian Public Policy in the 1990s*. Toronto: C. D. Howe Institute, 1990, 25–45.

Gollner, Andrew B., and Daniel Salee, eds. *Canada Under Mulroney*. Montreal: Véhicule Press, 1988.

Goodin, R. E. *Political Theory and Public Policy*. Chicago: University of Chicago Press, 1982.

Graham, Katherine, ed. *How Ottawa Spends 1990–91.* Ottawa: Carleton University Press, 1990.

Graham, Katherine, ed. *How Ottawa Spends 1989–90.* Ottawa: Carleton University Press, 1989.

Ham, C., and M. Hill. *The Policy Process in the Modern Capitalist State.* London: Wheatsheaf, 1986.

Harris, Richard. *Trade, Industrial Policy and International Competition.* Toronto: University of Toronto Press, 1985.

Hartle, Douglas. *Public Policy, Decision Making and Regulation.* Montreal: Institute for Research on Public Policy, 1979.

Heclo, Hugh. *Modern Social Politics in Britain and Sweden.* New Haven: Yale University Press, 1974.

Heidenheimer, A. J., Hugh Heclo, and Carol Teich Adams, eds. *Comparative Public Policy*, 3rd ed. New York: St. Martin's Press, 1990.

Hill, Michael, and Glen Bramley. *Analysing Social Policy.* London: Blackwell, 1986.

Hogwood, B., and L. A. Gunn. *Policy Analysis for the Real World.* London: Macmillan, 1984.

Jenkins, William. *Policy Analysis.* London: Martin Robertson, 1978.

Johnson, Richard. *Public Opinion and Public Policy in Canada.* Toronto: University of Toronto Press, 1986.

Jones, Catherine. *Patterns of Social Policy.* London: Tavistock, 1985.

King, Desmond. *The New Right.* London: Macmillan, 1987.

Lipsey, Richard. *Zero Inflation: The Goal of Price Stability.* Toronto: C. D. Howe Institute, 1990.

Lipsey, Richard, and Wendy Dobson, eds. *Shaping Comparative Advantage.* Toronto: C. D. Howe Institute, 1987.

Mahon, Rianne. "Adjusting to Win? The New Training Initiative." In Katherine Graham, ed. *How Ottawa Spends 1990–91.* Ottawa: Carleton University Press, 1990, 73–112.

Mandel, Michael. *The Charter of Rights and the Legalization of Politics in Canada.* Toronto: Thompson, 1991.

Manzer, Ronald. "Social Policy and Political Paradigms." *Canadian Public Administration* 24, no. 4 (Winter 1981), 641–48.

Maslove, Allan. *Tax Reform in Canada: The Process and Impact.* Halifax: Institute for Research on Public Policy, 1989.

McFetridge, Donald, ed. *Canadian Industrial Policy in Action.* Toronto: University of Toronto Press, 1985.

Nossal, Kim Richard. *The Politics of Canadian Foreign Policy*, 2nd ed. Scarborough: Prentice-Hall, 1989.

Organization for Economic Cooperation and Development. *The Public Sector: Issues for the 1990s.* Paris: OECD, 1991.

Osbaldeston, Gordon. *Keeping Deputy Ministers Accountable.* London: National Centre for Management Research and Development, 1988.

Pal, Leslie A. *Public Policy Analysis*, 2nd ed. Toronto: Nelson, 1992.

Pal, Leslie A., and David Taras, eds. *Prime Ministers and Premiers.* Scarborough: Prentice-Hall, 1989.

Panitch, Leo, ed. *The Canadian State.* Toronto: University of Toronto Press, 1977.

Parkin, Michael, and Robin Bade. *Modern Macroeconomics*, 2nd ed. Scarborough: Prentice-Hall, 1986.

Phidd, Richard, and G. Bruce Doern. *The Politics and Management of Canadian Economic Policy.* Toronto: Macmillan, 1978.

Phillips, Susan. "Rock-a-Bye Brian: The National Strategy on Child Care." In Katherine Graham, ed. *How Ottawa Spends 1989-90.* Ottawa: Carleton University Press, 1989, 165-208.

Prince, Michael J., ed. *How Ottawa Spends 1986-87.* Toronto: Methuen, 1986.

Prince, Michael J., and James Rice. "The Canadian Job Strategy: Supply-side Social Policy." In Katherine Graham, ed. *How Ottawa Spends 1989-90.* Ottawa: Carleton University Press, 1989, 247-88.

Pross, A. Paul. *Group Politics and Public Policy*, Toronto: University of Toronto Press, 1986.

Rice, James J. "Restitching the Safety Net: Altering the National Social Security System." In Michael J. Prince, ed. *How Ottawa Spends 1987-88.* Toronto: Methuen, 1987, 211-36.

Savoie, Donald. *The Politics of Public Spending in Canada.* Toronto: University of Toronto Press, 1990.

Savoie, Donald. *Regional Economic Development: Canada's Search for Solutions.* Toronto: University of Toronto Press, 1986.

Schultz, Richard. "Regulating Conservatively: The Mulroney Record: 1984-1988." In Andrew B. Gollner and Daniel Salee, eds. *Canada Under Mulroney.* Montreal: Véhicule Press, 1988, 186-205.

Simeon, Richard. "Globalization and the Canadian Nation State." In G. Bruce Doern and Bryne Purchase, eds. *Canada at Risk: Canadian Public Policy in the 1990s.* Toronto: C. D. Howe Institute, 1990, 46-58.

Simeon, Richard. "Studying Public Policy." *Canadian Journal of Political Science* 9 (December 1976), 547-80.

Skogstad, Grace. *The Politics of Agricultural Policy-Making in Canada.* Toronto: University of Toronto Press, 1987.

Stanbury, William T. "Privatization and the Mulroney Government: 1984-1988." In Andrew B. Gollner and Daniel Salee, eds. *Canada Under Mulroney.* Montreal: Véhicule Press, 1988, 119-57.

Stanbury, William T., and Fred Thompson. *Regulatory Reform in Canada.* Montreal: Institute for Research on Public Policy, 1982.

Strick, John C. *The Economics of Government Regulation: Theory and Canadian Practice.* Toronto: Thompson, 1991.

Sutherland, Sharon L. "Responsible Government and Ministerial Responsibility: Every Reform Is Its Own Problem." *Canadian Journal of Political Science* 24 (March 1991), 91–120.

Sutherland, Sharon L., and G. Bruce Doern. *Bureaucracy in Canada: Control and Reform.* Toronto: University of Toronto Press, 1986.

Trebilcock, Michael, Marsha Chandler, and Robert Howse. *Trade and Transition: A Comparative Analysis of Adjustment Policies.* London: Routledge, 1990.

Trebilcock, Michael, R. Prichard, D. Hartle, and D. Dewees. *The Choice of Governing Instruments.* Ottawa: Minister of Supply and Services, 1982.

Tupper, Allan, and G. Bruce Doern, eds. *Privatization, Public Corporations and Public Policy in Canada.* Halifax: Institute for Research on Public Policy, 1988.

Van Loon, Richard. "Reforming Welfare in Canada." *Public Policy* 27, no. 4 (Fall 1979), 469–504.

Vickers, Sir Geoffrey. *The Art of Judgement.* New York: Basic Books, 1965.

Vogel, David. *National Styles of Regulation.* Ithica: Cornell University Press, 1986.

Wildavsky, Aaron. *Budgeting: A Comparative Theory of Budgetary Processes*, rev. ed. New York: Transaction Books, 1986.

Wilson, V. Seymour. *Canadian Public Policy: Theory and Environment.* Toronto: McGraw-Hill Ryerson, 1981.

Zussman, David. "Walking the Tightrope: The Mulroney Government and the Public Service." In Michael J. Prince, ed. *How Ottawa Spends 1986–87.* Toronto: Methuen, 1986, 250–82.

Index